MICHIGAN
IN THE NOVEL
1816–1996

GREAT LAKES BOOKS

*A complete listing of the books in this series
can be found at the back of this volume.*

Philip P. Mason, Editor
Department of History, Wayne State University

Dr. Charles K. Hyde, Associate Editor
Department of History, Wayne State University

MICHIGAN
IN THE NOVEL
1816–1996

AN ANNOTATED BIBLIOGRAPHY

COMPILED BY

ROBERT BEASECKER

WAYNE STATE UNIVERSITY PRESS   Detroit

Library of Congress Cataloging-in-Publication Data

Beasecker, Robert, 1946–

    Michigan in the novel, 1816–1996 : an annotated bibliography / compiled by Robert Beasecker.

      p.   cm. — (Great Lakes books)

    Includes bibliographical references and indexes.

    ISBN 0-8143-2712-5 (alk. paper)

    1. American fiction—Michigan—Bibliography.   2. Michigan—In literature—Bibliography.

I. Title. II. Series.

Z1297.B43   1998

[PS283.M5]

016.813008'032774—dc21   97-32194

For Ryan

Hic est filius meus dilectus,
inquo mihi complacui

Contents

Acknowledgments

Without the help and advice from a great many people the completion of this bibliography would not have been possible, and I am pleased to be able to acknowledge that assistance. Errors of exclusion, inclusion, citation, or any others are mine alone.

In the course of identifying the books to be included, literally thousands had to be examined first hand. To that end, the indefatigable efforts of Laurel Balkema, Interlibrary Loan Librarian at Grand Valley State University Library, and her staff need to be mentioned first, as do those of her predecessor, Pamela Grudzien. Thanks also are due to countless interloan librarians, from the Library of Congress to the more modest village public libraries, for their willingness to share materials from their institutions.

A number of librarians kindly examined fragile, rare, or unique copies of books in their repositories that could not be loaned and described them to me or provided photocopies. Some brought to my attention special items in their collections, the existence of which I was not aware. Others offered suggestions and encouragement. Among those who were thus helpful include the following: Sharon Book, Popular Culture Library, Bowling Green State University; Patrick Coleman, Minnesota Historical Society; Alice Dalligan and staff, Burton Historical Collection, Detroit Public Library; Mary Dalzell, Flint Public Library, Flint, Michigan; Judith Dow, Library of Michigan; Marla Ehlers, Grand Rapids Public Library; Clark Evans, Library of Congress; Chad Flake, Special Collections, Brigham Young University Library; Mary Fleischer, Eugene C. Barker Texas History Center, University of Texas at Austin; Elizabeth Glynn, Marshall Public Library, Marshall, Michigan; Pamela Grudzien, Central Michigan University Library; Richard Hathaway, Library of Michigan; Bill Hill, Grand Rapids Public Library; Elaine Hoag, National Library of Canada; Evelyn Leasher, Clarke Historical Library, Central Michigan University; Brenda McCallum, Popular Culture Library, Bowling Green State University; Robert McCown, Special Collections, University of Iowa Libraries; Kathleen E. Marten, Department of

Special Collections, Kent State University Libraries; Jay Martin, Institute for Great Lakes Research, Bowling Green State University; Karen Mason, Bentley Historical Library, University of Michigan; Sandra Naiman, Northern Illinois University Libraries; Phoebe B. Peacock, Library of Congress; Mary Jo Pugh, Bentley Historical Library, University of Michigan; M. Reed, Howell Carnegie Library, Howell, Michigan; Alison Scott, Popular Culture Library, Bowling Green State University; Katheryn Seestedt, Marine City Public Library, Marine City, Michigan; Wilma Slaight, Wellesley College Library; Carmen Königsreuther Socknat, Victoria University Library, Toronto; Theresa Spence, Archives and Copper Country Historical Collections, Michigan Technological University Library; Anne Tracy, Special Collections, Michigan State University Library; Max Yela, Special Collections, University of Delaware Library; and Julia Young, Bentley Historical Library, University of Michigan.

Antiquarian bookmen, secondhand booksellers, and bookstore owners are often underappreciated for their specialized expertise and wide-ranging knowledge of books and their contents. Those providing valuable assistance in identifying and locating obscure Michigan titles as well as offering valuable advice include the following: James Babcock, Harsens Island; Tom Nicely of Leaves of Grass Books, Ann Arbor; Don Teets, formerly of Don's Book Store, Grand Rapids; Ray Walsh of Curious Book Shop, East Lansing; Guy Wood of Peninsula Books, Traverse City; and Patricia Vinge, formerly of Call Me Ishmael Books, Saugatuck and ultimately Kalamazoo.

Many authors themselves graciously replied to my queries by mail or personal interview concerning suspected Michigan locales used in their novels. These include Doug Allyn, Lilian Jackson Braun, Dorothy Salisbury Davis, Jack Driscoll, Philip Freund, Tom Kakonis, Rob Kantner, Mildred Lawrence, Elizabeth Howard Mizner, T. R. Peters, Willo Davis Roberts, Hilda Stahl, Jane Toombs, and Josephine Wunsch.

Because of the bibliographic difficulties inherent with the romance genre, the assistance given by a number of romance novelists also proved invaluable. They provided specific titles and suggested other authors to examine. Special thanks go to Jill Culby, Carol Katz, Terry Lawrence, Diane Richter, Maris Soule, Laure Sparrow, Carol Wagner, and Donna Winters.

Words of appreciation also go to a variety of people, mostly researchers and academics, who unselfishly shared the results of their investigations and their accumulated knowledge in a number of literary areas. For general background on Michigan proletarian novels of the 1920s and 1930s, as well as for identifying "James Steele" as Robert Cruden, I am indebted to David D. Anderson of Michigan State University. Clarence Andrews of the University of Iowa gave numerous titles of obscure publications that would prove useful to this bibliography. Victoria Brehm of Grand Valley State University shared much of her specialized knowledge of Great Lakes literature and offered many helpful editorial and publication suggestions. For biographical information on "Fanny Woodville" and her real identity as Frances Traver, I am grateful to Phyllis Burnham, Regional History Collections, Western Michigan University; Lynn Smith Houghton, Kalamazoo Public Museum; and Florence Schweiss, Ladies' Library Association, Kalamazoo. Myrtle Elie of the Pioneer Memorial Association of Fenton and Mundy Townships, Fenton, Michigan, provided biographical details on Cynthia Gorton, the "Blind Bard of Michigan." For supplying biographical information for a number of authors who happened to be University of Michigan alumni, I wish to thank Lauralee Ensign and her staff, of that institution's Alumni Records Office. Father Karl Hubble, pastor of St. Mary's Catholic Church, St. Clair, Michigan, related the circumstances of the gift of Mary Frances Doner's personal library and its present location. Allen J. Hubin generously shared on numerous occasions his preliminary indexes of locales from his bibliography of crime fiction and its supplements. Jeremy Kilar of Delta College, University Center, Michigan, answered questions about Beaumont de la Bonninière's 1835 novel. For his encyclopedic knowledge of all things dealing with Michigan's history and literary heritage, Larry B. Massie of Allegan rates special mention and much thanks. Mary DeJong Obuchowski of Central Michigan University kindly shared not only her knowledge of Ann Arbor literature, but that of Gene Stratton Porter as well.

I would also like to acknowledge the continual assistance of Harvey E. Lemmen of Grand Rapids, who not only graciously allowed me access to his personal collection of Michigan novels, but also brought to my attention a great many previously unknown books that ultimately were added to this bibliography.

For financial support of this project through the years, I am grateful to Grand Valley State University and its Research and Development Center. A sabbatical leave, interloan fees, travel and research costs were just some of the items generously supported by the University.

Finally, I would like to thank my present and former colleagues at Grand Valley State University Library not previously mentioned for their interest, support, assistance, and suggestions. These include Alice Baker, Stephen Ford, Carol Garey, Myrtle Goff, Lisa Ham, Judith D. King, Lee Lebbin, Frank Mols, Debbie Morrow, Diane Murray, Kim Ranger, Elizabeth Sloan Smith, Nancy Terry, Sharon Van Der Laan, Rita Vandermeer, Donna Westley, and Linda K. Woods.

Robert Beasecker
Grand Valley State University

Introduction

The purpose of this enumerative bibliography is to record those novels that have been published from 1816 through 1996 and are set wholly or partially within the geographical boundaries of the present state of Michigan. "Novel" is defined here as a separately published work of narrative fiction bound as a unit regardless of length. There were no requirements imposed concerning the place of birth or the residence of the author. Foreign works, whether in English or another language, also have been added to this bibliography.

In addition to mainstream fiction, mystery and romance novels, juveniles, religious tracts and dime novels, and other so-called marginal or "popular" genre literature have been included. To be included, a novel must have at least ten pages with a Michigan locale. Types of literature omitted (and left for future bibliographers) are short stories; poetry; dramas, screenplays, and pageants; and serially published novels that appeared in newspapers or magazines but have had no subsequent separate publication.

The basic rule of entry has been to record only the first edition of a particular work irrespective of its place of publication. In the case of foreign language novels, a note is added to the entry describing any English translation.

This bibliography, listing 1,744 items, is reasonably complete, to the extent that any bibliography can be so considered. I am only too aware that there are probably many more Michigan novels that have eluded my net. In the field of general fiction, along with mysteries, juveniles, and science fiction, I estimate that I have identified the majority of them. However, I feel less confident about the romance genre. The vast numbers of this type of novel published without the benefit of announcements, publicity, or reviews make locating and examining each of them a difficult and intimidating task. Of this category, I may have identified only a small percentage of the total that have Michigan locales. Consequently, I welcome and encourage users of this bibliography to alert me to items that I may have overlooked.

I have not attempted to write a literary history of Michigan although one is sorely needed. David Anderson's *Michigan: A State Anthology* and Clarence Andrews's *Michigan in Literature* are two relatively recent surveys of the literary heritage of Michigan. They both are useful starting points: the former intends to illuminate generally the high spots, but the latter, which attempts to be thorough, falls short. Other good studies exist, but are either limited in scope or are out of date, or both. See the Sources Consulted section of this bibliography for other titles.

Michigan novels are by definition a regional literature, with all of the strengths and weaknesses that accompany this type of writing. In this respect, they are no different from what was being written elsewhere in the Midwest, or indeed in the rest of the country. However, these novels with Michigan settings use and develop certain recurring themes and subjects that are a direct result of the distinctive history, culture, geography, and industry of this state.

The history of the indigenous peoples of the Great Lakes region and their relations with the white explorers, soldiers, settlers, and eventually with modern society have some unique links to Michigan. The European struggle for control over North America during the French and Indian War, the Revolutionary War, the 1763 threat from the Ottawa leader Pontiac, and the War of 1812 resulted in considerable activity in the then strategic Michigan area.

From the beginning, Michigan's location in the heart of the Great Lakes made it a natural route for exploration and the fur trade, and later those waters became an important artery for shipping and commerce. The four large bodies of fresh water that touch the state, as well as the thousands of inland lakes, continue to provide an area for fishing, recreation, and adventure.

The favorable reports from geological and geographic expeditions brought to the Upper Peninsula miners who searched out and extracted copper and iron in prodigious quantities. Lumbermen and loggers virtually clear-cut thousands of square miles of the two peninsulas, not only altering the landscape but also finally bringing the realization that natural resources are finite.

The origins of the industrialization of the state are to be found with the Michigan lumbermills, which supplied wood for building, furniture, and carriages. The fortuitous combination of ready money, handy raw materials, and local inventor-tinkerers, such as Ford and Olds, gave a great impetus for the nascent automobile industry to take firm hold in Michigan. The influence that this one industry has had on the economy, politics, structure, and the society of the state is inestimable.

The people of Michigan, too, give a special voice to its literature. The clans and tribes of the Ojibwas and Potawatomis; the French, the English, and the later immigrants from the Netherlands, Finland, Hungary, Italy, Germany, and Cornwall; those who labored in the mines, the forests, the factories, and on farms all have their own stories and their unique points of view. As with any regional and national literature, the people portrayed therein run the gamut of characters and characterization: successes and failures, heroes and villains, sacred and profane. They all portray the varieties of the human experience that have contributed to the development of Michigan.

This bibliography is meant to serve as a map by which students, teachers, scholars, and readers may explore Michigan's vast, varied, and rich literary landscape. Annotations generally have been written to describe to the user what the novel is about, not to ascribe literary value. Fads and fashions in literary taste come and go, both with authors and with the books themselves, but what is paramount here is that the books have content relative to Michigan locales.

Mechanics of Compilation

This bibliography had its genesis in the early 1970s while I was researching biographical and bibliographical data on the Michigan author Della Thompson Lutes. I came across Albert Black's *Michigan Novels: An Annotated Bibliography* (1963) and noticed that only two of six novels by Lutes containing Michigan settings were listed. Black, in his introduction, claimed that his "list is reasonably complete, though juveniles and out-of-print items are not entirely covered." With two-thirds of Lutes's output missing, I wondered what other gaps might exist. Twenty-plus years later and after reading literally thousands of novels, the result is this bibliography.

I began with Black's bibliography and rechecked each of his authors, assuming that if a particular individual wrote one Michigan novel then it was entirely possible that he or she wrote others as well. This proved true in a surprisingly large number of cases. Each book in his bibliography was reexamined as well, and more than a tenth were found to be either short stories, nonfiction, or set outside Michigan.

Many serial publications were carefully consulted. An examination of each year's cumulative volume of *Book Review Digest* from 1905 early in the life of this project added to the list of novels to examine firsthand, as did most of the references listed in the Sources Consulted section of this bibliography. The periodical *Michigan in Books,* issued by the Michigan State Library (later Library of Michigan) from 1958 through 1984, contained much useful information about Michigan books—fiction as well as nonfiction—in that library's collection. Older state library periodicals, such as *Michigan Library Bulletin* and *Michigan School Librarian,* often had notices of Michigan novels and information on Michigan authors. Most useful for recently published books have been the announcements and reviews in *Publishers Weekly* and *Booklist.* The use of bibliographies, reference works, and other sources invariably lead the researcher to more of the above, and many individuals also gave suggestions for further reading.

Over the course of compiling this bibliography many Michigan libraries were visited and their collections examined. It should come as no surprise that the most comprehensive collection of Michigan literature, including novels, poetry, short fiction and drama, written by both Michigan-born authors and others, is held at the Library of Michigan in Lansing. It is apparent that over the years conscious efforts have been made to seek out and acquire this type of material.

A significant portion of the Michigan novels in the Library of Michigan have come from the Flint Public Library, whose director in the 1920s and 1930s was William Webb. Webb wrote personal letters to authors of Michigan novels requesting autographed copies of their books for his library. Some of these letters and the authors' replies to them have been placed in the books themselves and give interesting details about the novels and writers.

One of the hazards facing bibliographers is that they can become collectors of the books they intend to list. Over seven hundred Michigan novels that I accumulated in the process of compiling this book now reside in the Regional Historical Collections of Grand Valley State University Library. Other libraries with substantial collections of Michigan novels include the Clarke Historical Library at Central Michigan University, Grand Rapids Public Library, the Burton Historical Collection at the Detroit Public Library, and Traverse Area District Library in Traverse City.

System of Arrangement

Entries Books are arranged alphabetically by author when known. Names beginning with "Mac" and "Mc" are interfiled, following the Library of Congress convention. Names appearing within square brackets indicate that the author's name did not appear on the title page in that form, or at all. Pseudonymous works are listed under the author's actual name and a cross reference made from the pseudonym. In the case of novels written by more than one person, the first name given on the title page is chosen as the main entry, with additional cross references made from the other authors. Books that have no acknowledged author or for which one cannot be ascertained are entered under their titles.

Titles Complete titles and any subtitles from the title page of the book are given. Half titles and binding titles are also added in the notes section, along with any subsequent title under which the book was also published. Authors' names follow the titles in instances where the name differs from the entry, usually as a pseudonym.

Imprints Place of publication and publisher are given when known. Contrary to Library of Congress practice, places that are distinctly in Michigan even though they may exist in other states as well, e.g., Grand Rapids or Mount Pleasant, are not followed by the abbreviation "Mich." Imprint information supplied in square brackets has been obtained from other sources, and material followed by a "?" indicates that this information constitutes an educated guess.

Dates Dates of publication are given without indication of whether they are taken from the title page or copyright page. Educated guesses are indicated by a "?" or "ca." (circa). Dates supplied through other sources are put within square brackets.

Pagination Numbered pages of text are stated in arabic numerals.

Series Publishers' series are noted within parentheses, for example, (Beadle's Pocket Novels, no. 181) and (Harlequin Superromance, no. 426).

Annotations and Notes Notes on each of the entries are for the most part self-explanatory. A brief one- or two-sentence summary of the book is given in each case where the book has been located and examined, or could be gleaned from other sources. If the novel is set in a fictitious city or other location, that name appears in quotation marks along with its real-world equivalent within parentheses, if it can be identified; for example, "New Zebedee" (Marshall) and "Goodhaven" (Fairport?).

The phrase "copy not seen" indicates that I have not had the occasion to examine the book and that the summary given relies upon other sources.

Later changes in titles are noted, as is author information when pertinent.

Novel genres and types are given when the book is a dime novel, juvenile, mystery, romance, science fiction, or graphic novel, the latter also known as a trade comic.

References to "Black," "Streeter," or the three volumes of "Wright" indicate that the entry in question is also cited in these sources. For complete bibliographical information on these three, see their particular entries in the Sources Consulted section of this bibliography.

Locations of first edition copies are given for various libraries using the symbols listed in *Symbols of American Libraries,* 14th ed. (Washington, D.C.: Library of Congress, 1992), with minor refinements. Those used in this bibliography are identified in the section Symbols of Libraries. In most cases, only those books that are difficult to find for one reason or another are given limited locations. Michigan locations are always listed first, and in instances where the book is not owned in-state, out-of-state holdings are noted. Locations have been verified by using the various compilations of the *National Union Catalogue,* the OCLC database, or personal visits to the actual libraries themselves. The note "copy not located" means that although no library reports having that particular book as part of its collection, the existence of the book is not in question.

The user of this bibliography is reminded that the relative scarcity of a novel in its first edition may be misleading in that it may in fact be fairly common in subsequent printings, cheap reprints, or in paperback format.

Holdings of books available in microform are not given. Thankfully, a substantial number of nineteenth- and early twentieth-century American novels have been preserved in this manner, as has much of the dime-novel literature. Larger university and research libraries are most likely to own one or more of these microform series.

Sources Consulted

In the compilation of this bibliography, many hundreds of reference works, including checklists, biographies, bibliographies, encyclopedias, and critical essays were consulted. The most important and most helpful of these are listed below.

Anderson, David D. "The Fiction of the Great Lakes." *Northwest Ohio Quarterly* 34 (winter 1961–62): 18–28.

————, ed. *Michigan: A State Anthology. Writings About the Great Lake State, 1641–1981, Selected from Diaries, Journals, Histories, Fiction, and Verse.* Detroit: Gale Research Co., 1983.

Possibly the best anthology of Michigan writings, this book places the state in its rightful literary niche. The essays and critical notes are indispensable.

————. "Michigan Proletarian Writers and the Great Depression." In *Michigan in the Great Depression; Symposium Proceedings,* 118–41. East Lansing: Michigan State University, 1980.

Andrews, Clarence A. "A Bibliography of Fiction and Drama by Women from Iowa and Michigan." *Great Lakes Review* 6 (summer 1979): 56–68.

A briefly annotated list of 241 items. The rather curious juxtaposition of Iowa and Michigan is explained by the fact that the author has lived and worked in both states.

————. "A Bibliography of the Literature and Lore, Together with Historical Materials, of the Upper Peninsula of Michigan." *Great Lakes Review* 3 (summer 1976): 37–65.

A fairly inclusive list of 623 Upper Peninsula items dealing with novels, short fiction, poetry, folklore, and history. Some entries are annotated.

————. *Michigan in Literature.* Detroit: Wayne State University Press, 1992.

Despite numerous inaccuracies, this is a basic survey of Michigan authors, settings, and themes as they have appeared in novels, drama, short fiction, and poetry.

Archer, Marion Fuller, ed. *The Upper Midwest.* (Reading for Young People). Chicago: American Library Association, 1981.

The Upper Midwest is defined here as Minnesota, Wisconsin and Michigan. Contains 278 well-annotated citations, of which twenty-six are Michigan novels.

Ash, Edith. *A Literary History of Mackinac Island.* (Michigan Literary Landmarks: Monograph One). N.p.: Michigan Council of Teachers of English, 1973.

————. *Wafting Winds of the Revolution in Michigan Literature.* Grand Marais, Mich.: Voyager Press, 1976.

Barnett, Le Roy, comp. *Shipping Literature of the Great Lakes; a Catalog of Company Publications, 1852–1990.* East Lansing: Michigan State University Press, 1992.

Bedford-Jones, H. "The Fiction Field of Michigan History." *Michigan History* 12 (July 1928): 450–53.

Bernard, Harry. *Le Roman Régionaliste aux États-Unis, 1913–1940.* Montréal: Fides, 1949.

The discussion of Michigan literature appears on pages 188–93.

Black, Albert G. "Michigan Novels: A Checklist of Novels with Michigan Background." Ann Arbor: Department of English, University of Michigan, 1956.

A six-page typed list of 208 items, not all of which find their way into his 1963 bibliography (see below).

————. *Michigan Novels: An Annotated Bibliography.* Ann Arbor: Michigan Council of Teachers of English, 1963.

An annotated list of 303 novels with Michigan settings. This should be used with caution because more than 10 percent of the entries either do not have Michigan locales or are not novels. In addition, a number of the annotations are misleading and spelling errors abound.

————. "The Pontiac Conspiracy in the Novel, 1833–1954." *Michigan History* 43 (March 1959): 115–19.

Boys, Richard C. "The American College in Fiction." *College English* 7 (1946): 379–87.

Brehm, Victoria. "A Romance en Route: The Advertising Fiction of the Detroit & Cleveland Steam Navigation Company." *American Neptune* 52 (summer 1992): 149–54.

Bullock, Penelope L. *Michigan Bibliographies and Indexes.* Ypsilanti: Eastern Michigan University, 1960.

Clark, Dan Elbert. "The Appeal of the Middle West to the Literary Historian." *The Midland* 2 (February 1916): 33–38.

Collins, Sara Dobie. "A Check List of Non-Official Michigan Imprints for the Years 1859 and 1860 with a Historical Introduction." Master's dissertation, Catholic University of America, 1966.

Cowden, Roy W. "Creative Writers in the Making: The Record of Michigan's Hopwood Prize Program." *Michigan Alumnus Quarterly Review* 54 (July 1948): 293–300.

Dailey, Sheila. "Little Bear and Other Stories: A Look at the Life and Works of Michigan Children's Author Frances Margaret Fox." *Great Lakes Review* 8 (spring 1982): 25–30.

Dance, James C. "Michigan in Fiction." *Among Friends* (Detroit Public Library), no. 71 (summer 1978): 2–12.

DeMarr, Mary Jean, and Jane S. Bakerman. *The Adolescent in the American Novel Since 1960.* New York: Ungar, 1986.

For coverage of the years 1920–1960, see Witham, below.

DePuy, E. Cora. "List of Authors and Poets of Michigan." Detroit: n.p., 1918.

Detroit Public Library. *Michigan in Books.* Detroit: Detroit Public Library, 1956.

Includes 123 briefly annotated citations to adult and juvenile Michigan novels.

———. *Michigan Readings; Discover More About Your State.* Detroit: Detroit Public Library, 1987.

Dickason, David H. "Chief Simon Pokagon: 'The Indian Longfellow.' " *Indiana Magazine of History* 57 (1961): 127–40.

Dunbar, Willis Frederick. "Literature." In *Michigan through the Centuries.* Vol. 2, 393–406. New York: Lewis Historical Pub. Co., 1955.

"The Editor's Corner." *Michigan Alumnus Quarterly Review* 59 (1953): 173–74.

Part of these editorial musings includes a list of books of fiction that use Ann Arbor and the University of Michigan as locales.

Ellison, Elizabeth Love. "The Literature of the Upper Peninsula." *Michigan History* 30 (July–September 1946): 508–17.

Flanagan, John T. "American Literary Bibliography in the Twentieth Century." *Library Trends* 15 (January 1967): 550–72.

———. "A Half-Century of Middlewestern Fiction." *Critique* 2 (winter 1959): 16–34.

———. "The Middle Western Historical Novel." *Journal of the Illinois State Historical Society* 37 (March 1944): 7–47.

Foster, Bernice M. *Michigan Novelists.* Ann Arbor: George Wahr, 1928.

Lists novelists who were born or have resided in Michigan along with titles of their books.

Fuller, George N. "Literature." In *Michigan: A Centennial History of the State and Its People.* Vol. 2, 561–83. Chicago: Lewis Pub. Co., 1939.

Gillard, Kathleen Isabel. *Our Michigan Heritage.* New York: Pageant Press, 1955.

A useful survey of Michigan writing, both nonfiction and fiction.

Goldstein, Laurence. "The Image of Detroit in Twentieth Century Literature." *Michigan Quarterly Review* 25 (spring 1986): 269–91.

Goodrich, Madge Knevels. *A Bibliography of Michigan Authors.* Richmond, Va.: Richmond Press, 1928.

An extensive list of Michigan authors, their works, and references to biographical sources.

Hanna, Archibald. *Mirror for the Nation: An Annotated Bibliography of American Social Fiction, 1901–1950.* New York: Garland Publishing, 1985.

Based on Hanna's personal collection. Unfortunately for many of the Michigan entries, he has uncritically accepted Black's entries and annotations. See Black, above.

Harkness, David James. "The Great Lakes States and Alaska and Hawaii in Literature; a Manual for Schools and Clubs." *University of Tennessee News Letter* 38 (December 1959): 24–30.

The author describes a number of Michigan novels in a critical essay.

Hartman, Donald K., and Jerome Drost, comps. *Themes and Settings in Fiction: A Bibliography of Bibliographies.* Westport, Conn.: Greenwood Press, 1988.

Hilbert, Rachel M. *Michigan Authors.* Ann Arbor: Michigan Association of School Librarians, 1960.

Biographical and bibliographical sketches of selected Michigan authors, past and present. Additional names are listed in the supplement, below.

For the second and third editions, see Michigan Association for Media in Education and Smallwood respectively, below.

————, ed. *Michigan Poets, with Supplement to Michigan Authors 1960.* Ann Arbor: Michigan Association of School Librarians, 1964.

Hotchkiss, Jeanette. *American Historical Fiction and Biography for Children and Young People.* Metuchen, N.J.: Scarecrow Press, 1973.

Hubin, Allen J. *Crime Fiction II: A Comprehensive Bibliography, 1749–1990.* Rev. and updated ed. 2 vols. New York: Garland Publishing, 1994.

The ultimate bibliography of detective and mystery literature. Includes a comprehensive settings index.

Jager, Joanne, comp. *Michigan in Fiction.* Lansing: State Library Services, Michigan Department of Education, 1976.

Arranged by region, eighty-three Michigan novels have lengthy annotations. For an earlier edition, see Michigan Department of Education, Library Division, below.

Johannsen, Albert. *The House of Beadle and Adams and Its Dime and Nickel Novels; the Story of a Vanished Literature.* 3 vols. Norman: University of Oklahoma Press, 1950–62.

A thorough discussion of this publisher and an exhaustive bibliography of its publications. Includes author biographies, alternate titles, and annotations.

Johnson, Deidre, comp. *Stratemeyer Pseudonyms and Series Books. An Annotated Checklist of Stratemeyer and Stratemeyer Syndicate Publications.* Westport, Conn.: Greenwood Press, 1982.

Kramer, John E., Jr. *The American College Novel: An Annotated Bibliography.* New York: Garland Publishing, 1981.

Kramer, John E., Jr., and John E. Kramer, III. *College Mystery Novels: An Annotated Bibliography, Including a Guide to Professorial Series-Character Sleuths.* New York: Garland Publishing, 1983.

Lachman, Marvin. "The American Regional Mystery: Part IX—The Middle West." *Mystery Reader's Newsletter* 6 (July 1973): 1–13.

Literary Michigan: A Sense of Place, A Sense of Time. Lansing: Michigan Council for the Humanities, 1988.

> A collection of ten essays and bibliographies by a variety of authors concerning Michigan's literary output in fiction, poetry, and screenwriting.

Logasa, Hannah. *Regional United States: A Subject List.* Boston: F. W. Faxon, 1942.

Los Angeles City College. *A Guide to Contemporary American Fiction; Arranged Regionally and Topically.* Los Angeles: Los Angeles City College, 1939.

Lyons, John O. *The College Novel in America.* Carbondale: Southern Illinois University Press, 1962.

———. "The College Novel in America, 1962–1974." *Critique: Studies in Modern Fiction* 16 (1974): 121–28.

McGarry, Daniel D., and Sarah H. White. *World Historical Fiction Guide.* 2d ed. Metuchen, N.J.: Scarecrow Press, 1973.

Massie, Larry. *From Frontier Folk to Factory Smoke: Michigan's First Century of Historical Fiction.* AuTrain, Mich.: Avery Color Studios, 1987.

> Excerpts from fifteen Michigan novels with historical and critical discussions of each.

———. "The Literature of Mackinac Country." In *Early Mackinac: A Sketch Historical and Descriptive* by Meade C. Williams, 1–12. AuTrain, Mich.: Avery Color Studios, 1987.

———. "Regional Fiction as a Source of Michigan History." Specialist's thesis, Western Michigan University, 1977.

Mattson, E. Christian, and Thomas B. Davis. *A Collector's Guide to Hardcover Boys' Series Books, or, Tracing the Trail of Henry Hudson.* Newark, Del.: Mad Book Co., 1997.

Maxwell, Donald W. *Literature of the Great Lakes Region: An Annotated Bibliography.* New York: Garland Publishing, 1991.

An odd compilation fraught with errors and omissions. Uncritically accepts Black's entries and annotations. Should be used with extreme caution.

Meyer, Roy W. *The Middle Western Farm Novel in the Twentieth Century.* Lincoln: University of Nebraska Press, 1965.

The classic and so far unsuperseded study of the genre.

Michigan Association for Media in Education. *Michigan Authors.* 2d ed. Ann Arbor: Michigan Association for Media in Education, 1980.

For the first edition, see Hilbert, above; for the third edition see Smallwood, below.

Michigan Department of Education, Library Division. *Michigan in Novels.* Lansing: Michigan Department of Education, 1968.

Fifty-nine Michigan novels are listed by region and have lengthy annotations. For a later edition, see Jager, above.

Michigan Historical Records Survey. *Preliminary Check List of Michigan Imprints, 1796–1850.* Detroit: Michigan Historical Records Survey Project, 1942.

Michigan State Library. *Michigan in Books: A Selected List.* Lansing: Michigan State Library, 1957.

Michigan Writers' Program. "Literature." In *Michigan, a Guide to the Wolverine State,* 145–51. New York: Oxford University Press, 1941.

Monroe County Library System. *Michigan Materials: Books and Other Media on Michigan in the Monroe County Library System.* Monroe, Mich.: Monroe County Library System, 1971.

Mosher, Edith R. and Nella Dietrich Williams. *From Indian Legends to the Modern Book-Shelf, an Anthology of Prose and Verse by Michigan Authors Prepared Especially for the Youth of the State.* Ann Arbor: George Wahr, 1931.

A dated but still useful anthology of writings by Michigan authors.

Mulder, Arnold. "Authors and Wolverines: The Books and Writers of Michigan." *Saturday Review of Literature* 19 (4 March 1939): 3–4, 16.

———. "Michigan as a Field for the Novelist." *Michigan History Magazine* 6 (1922): 142–55.

———. "Michigan's Writing Men." *Michigan History* 35 (September 1951): 257–70.

Mulder's three articles above, giving his observations of the Michigan literary scene from three decades, are literate and opinionated.

Nemanic, Gerald, ed. *A Bibliographical Guide to Midwestern Literature*. Iowa City: University of Iowa Press, 1981.

A scholarly bibliographic survey of the Midwestern literary experience, covering a variety of themes, subjects, and authors. Dated, but an important source.

Nilon, Charles H. *Bibliography of Bibliographies in American Literature*. New York: R. R. Bowker, 1970.

Orians, George Harrison. "Cannon Through the Forest: Novels of the Land Battles of the War of 1812 in the Old Northwest." *Ohio History* 72 (July 1963): 195–219.

———. "Pontiac in Literature." Parts 1 and 2. *Northwest Ohio Quarterly* 35 (autumn 1963): 144–63; 36 (winter 1964): 31–53.

Pearson, Alice L. "The Upper Peninsula in Fictional Literature." *Michigan History* 24 (summer 1940): 329–38.

Prestridge, Virginia. *The Worker in American Fiction: An Annotated Bibliography*. Champaign: Institute of Labor and Industrial Relations, University of Illinois, 1954.

Price, Robert. "Mary Hartwell Catherwood's Literary Record of the Great Lakes and French America." *Michigan History* 30 (October–December 1946): 759–63.

Rogers, Denis R. "A Publication Pattern: Being a Study of the Porter & Coates/ Henry T. Coates/John C. Winston Editions of Juvenile Fiction by Edward S. Ellis Issued Between 1883 and 1930." Parts 1 and 2. *Roundup* 41 (September 1972): 80–90; 41 (October 1972): 96–106.

Ruddon, Elaine Marie. "A Preliminary Checklist of Non-Official Imprints for the State of Michigan, 1851–55, with a Historical Introduction." Masters dissertation, Catholic University of America, 1951.

Sammons, Vivian Ovelton. "A Check List of Michigan Imprints for the Years 1856–1858, with a Historical Introduction." Masters dissertation, Catholic University of America, 1966.

Scannell, Francis X. "Michigan Fiction of the Fifties." *Michigan in Books* 3 (summer 1960): 146–47.

———. "The Novelist and Michigan." *Detroit Historical Society Bulletin* 21 (fall 1964): 4–12.

Silberman, Eve. "Michigan in Fiction." *Michigan Today* 20 (December 1988): 1–5.

The title refers to the University of Michigan. Subsequent letters to the editor over the next two years mentioned and described many more University of Michigan novels.

Simony, Maggy, ed. "Michigan." In *Traveler's Reading Guides: Background Books, Novels, Travel Literature and Articles.* Vol. 2, 108–10. Bayport, N.Y.: Free Lance Publications, 1982.

Smallwood, Carol, ed. *Michigan Authors.* 3d ed. Hillsdale, Mich.: Hillsdale Educational Publishers, 1993.

A highly selective list of approximately eight hundred living and deceased Michigan authors of nonfiction and fiction. For the first and second editions, see Hilbert and Michigan Association for Media in Education respectively, above.

Stace, Frances, Sister. "Michigan's Contribution to Literature." *Michigan History* 14 (spring 1930): 226–32.

Stevens, Wystan. "Ann Arbor in Fiction." Ann Arbor: Ann Arbor Public Library, 1974.

Streeter, Floyd Benjamin. *Michigan Bibliography; a Partial Catalogue of Books, Maps, Manuscripts and Miscellaneous Materials Relating to the Resources, Development and History of Michigan from Earliest Times to July 1, 1917. . . .* 2 vols. Lansing: Michigan Historical Commission, 1921.

Incomplete, long out of date, and based only on a few large library collections, this bibliography nonetheless is an important list of Michigania.

Taylor, Donna, ed. *The Great Lakes Region in Children's Books; a Selected Annotated Bibliography.* Brighton, Mich.: Green Oaks Press, 1980.

Includes fiction and nonfiction titles about Michigan, Illinois, Indiana, Minnesota, Ohio, Wisconsin, and Ontario. A total of 226 entries concern Michigan.

U.S. Library of Congress, Division of Bibliography. *List of Michigan Authors and Their Works.* Washington: Library of Congress, 1915.

VanDerhoof, Jack. *A Bibliography of Novels Related to American Frontier and Colonial History.* Troy, N.Y.: Whitson Pub. Co., 1971.

An impressive list of 6,390 novels, arranged by author. Its use is limited, however, by the lack of a title or subject index.

Webb, William, comp. *Fiction with Michigan Background: A Partial List.* Flint: Flint Public Library, 1934.

This six-page list contains author, title, and date entries for novels and short stories arranged by Michigan counties.

————. "Some Novels About Life in Michigan." In *Michigan Today; Its Human and Physical Resources as They Affect Education,* 280–83. Lansing: Michigan Department of Public Instruction (Michigan Department of Public Instruction Bulletin, no. 307): 1937.

West Bloomfield Township Public Library. *Michigan Books & Authors.* West Bloomfield, Mich.: West Bloomfield Township Public Library, 1986.

Witham, W. Tasker. *The Adolescent in the American Novel, 1920–1960.* New York: Frederick Ungar, 1964.

For coverage of the subject since 1960, see DeMarr, above.

Wright, Lyle H. *American Fiction, 1774–1850: A Contribution Toward a Bibliography.* 2d rev. ed. San Marino, Calif.: Huntington Library, 1969.

————. *American Fiction, 1851–1875: A Contribution Toward a Bibliography.* San Marino, Calif.: Huntington Library, 1957.

————. *American Fiction, 1876–1900: A Contribution Toward a Bibliography.* San Marino, Calif.: Huntington Library, 1966.

These three volumes by Wright list nearly twelve thousand books written by Americans and published in the United States between 1774 and 1900. The accompanying annotations sometimes provide information on the book's setting.

Symbols of Libraries

Symbols of libraries are listed alphabetically by symbol, except for Michigan, which is placed first.

Michigan

Mi	Library of Michigan, Lansing
MiA	Alma Public Library
MiAC	Alma College
MiAdC	Adrian College
MiAdS	Siena Heights College
MiAlbC	Albion College
MiAllG	Grand Valley State University
MiAlle	Allegan Public Library
MiAlp	Alpena County Library
MiAlpC	Alpena Community College
MiBar	Barryton Public Library
MiBatK	Kellogg Community College
MiBatW	Willard Library, Battle Creek
MiBeld	Alvah N. Belding Library, Belding
MiBir	Baldwin Public Library, Birmingham
MiBlo	Bloomfield Township Public Library
MiBoy	Boyne City Public Library
MiBrF	Ferris State University
MiBsA	Andrews University
MiCad	Cadillac-Wexford Public Library, Cadillac
MiCenl	Central Lake Township Library, Central Lake
MiChe	Cheboygan Area Public Library
MiChv	Charlevoix Public Library
MiCor	Shiawassee County Library, Corunna

MiD	Detroit Public Library
MiDU	University of Detroit, Mercy
MiDW	Wayne State University
MiDo	Dorr Township Library, Dorr
MiEM	Michigan State University
MiEaj	Jordan Valley District Library, East Jordan
MiElk	Elk Rapids District Library
MiEmp	Glen Lake Community Library, Empire
MiFli	Flint Public Library
MiFliL	Genesee District Library, Flint
MiFra	Benzie Shores District Library, Frankfort
MiGay	Otsego County Library, Gaylord
MiGr	Grand Rapids Public Library
MiGr-L	Personal Collection of Harvey E. Lemmen, Grand Rapids
MiGrA	Aquinas College
MiGrB	Cornerstone College
MiGrC	Calvin College
MiHM	Michigan Technological University
MiHanS	Suomi College
MiHas	Hastings Public Library
MiHilC	Hillsdale College
MiHly	Holly Township Library, Holly
MiHolH	Hope College
MiInr	Indian River Area Library
MiIrwG	Gogebic Community College
MiJac	Jackson District Library
MiK	Kalamazoo Public Library
MiKC	Kalamazoo College
MiKW	Western Michigan University
MiL	Clarence H. Rosa Public Library, Lansing
MiLC	Lansing Community College
MiLac	Missaukee District Library, Lake City
MiLapC	Lapeer County Library
MiLe	Leland Township Public Library, Leland
MiLivS	Schoolcraft College
MiMack	Mackinaw Area Public Library, Mackinaw City
MiMani	Manistee County Library
MiMarl	Marlette District Library, Marlette
MiMarq	Peter White Public Library, Marquette
MiMarqN	Northern Michigan University
MiMio	Oscoda County Library, Mio

MiMo	Monroe County Library System
MiMtcM	Mt. Clemens District Library
MiMtp	Veterans Memorial Library, Mt. Pleasant
MiMtpT	Central Michigan University
MiMtpT-C	Clarke Historical Library, Central Michigan University
MiMu	Hackley Public Library, Muskegon
MiMuC	Muskegon Community College
MiNb	New Buffalo Public Library
MiNhL	Lenox Township Library, New Haven
MiNi	Niles Community Library
MiNop	Leelanau Township Public Library, Northport
MiOC	Olivet College
MiOt	Otsego District Public Library
MiOw	Shiawassee District Library, Owosso
MiPet	Petoskey Public Library
MiPetN	North Central Michigan College
MiPh	St. Clair County Library System, Port Huron
MiPhS	St. Clair County Community College
MiRic	Richmond Public Library
MiRoch	Rochester Hills Public Library
MiRochOU	Oakland University
MiRog	Presque Isle District Library, Rogers City
MiRos	Roseville Public Library
MiSaS	Spring Arbor College
MiSc	Mason County District Library, Scottville
MiSf	Southfield Public Library
MiSsB	Bayliss Public Library, Sault Ste. Marie
MiSsL	Lake Superior State University
MiStc	St. Clair Shores Public Library
MiSte	Lincoln Township Public Library, Stevensville
MiStep	Menominee County Library, Stephenson
MiSth	Sterling Heights Public Library
MiStjo	Bement Public Library, St. Johns
MiT	Traverse Area District Library
MiTN	Northwestern Michigan College
MiTop	Topinabee Public Library
MiTr	Troy Public Library
MiU	University of Michigan
MiWalv	Walkerville Public School Library
MiWar	Warren Public Library
MiWol	Wolverine Community Library, Wolverine

MiYEM   Eastern Michigan University

Alabama

AAP   Auburn University
AB   Birmingham Public and Jefferson County Free Library
ABAU   University of Alabama, Birmingham

Arkansas

ArNlr   William F. Laman Public Library, North Little Rock
ArSsJ   John Brown University
ArU   University of Arkansas

Arizona

AzF   Flagstaff City-Coconino County Public Library
AzG   Glendale Public Library
AzPh   Phoenix Public Library
AzPr   Prescott Public Library
AzSaf   Safford City-Graham County, Safford
AzTeS   Arizona State University
AzU   University of Arizona

California

CEs   El Segundo Public Library
CFP   Fresno Pacific College
CFlS   California State University, Fullerton
CHu   Huntington Beach Public Library
CL   Los Angeles Public Library
CLO   Occidental College
CLS   California State University
CLU   University of California, Los Angeles
CMerC   Merced County Library, Merced
COPL   Oakland Public Library
COc   Oceanside Public Library
CRdb   Redondo Beach Public Library
CSbC   California State University, San Bernardino
CSd   San Diego Public Library
CSdS   San Diego State University

CSf	San Francisco Public Library
CSj	San Jose Public Library
CSjU	San Jose State University
CSmH	Huntington Library, San Marino
CSt	Stanford University
CStclU	Santa Clara University
CSto	Stockton-San Joaquin County Public Library
CU	University of California, Berkeley
CU-Riv	University of California, Riverside
CU-S	University of California, San Diego
CValA	California Institute of the Arts, Valencia

Canada

CaOONL	National Library of Canada, Ottawa

Colorado

CoD	Denver Public Library
CoU	University of Colorado

Connecticut

CtHT	Trinity College
CtS	Stamford Public Library
CtY	Yale University

District of Columbia

DGC	Gallaudet College
DLC	Library of Congress

Delaware

DeU	University of Delaware

Florida

FDb	Volusia County Public Library System, Daytona Beach
FJ	Jacksonville Public Libraries
FMU	University of Miami

FOFT   Florida Technological University
FTS   University of South Florida
FTU   University of Tampa
FTaSU   Florida State University
FWpR   Rollins College

Georgia

GA   Atlanta-Fulton Public Library
GAuA   Augusta College
GEU   Emory University
GEU-T   Candler School of Theology, Emory University
GSA   Armstrong State College
GVaS   Valdosta State University

Illinois

IArlh   Arlington Heights Memorial Library
IC   Chicago Public Library
ICL   Loyola University
ICMB   Moody Bible Institute
ICN   Newberry Library, Chicago
ICNE   Northeastern Illinois University
ICRMC   Robert Morris College
ICSU   Chicago State University
ICU   University of Chicago
ICarbS   Southern Illinois University
IChamL   Lincoln Trail Libraries System, Champaign
ICharE   Eastern Illinois University
IDeKN   Northern Illinois University
IDec   Decatur Public Library
IEN   Northwestern University
IGenD   DuPage Library System, Geneva
IHi   Illinois State Historical Library, Springfield
IMonC   Monmouth College
INS   Illinois State University
IQ   Quincy Public Library
IRivfR   Rosary College
ISL   Lincoln Library, Springfield
ISS   University of Illinois, Springfield
IWW   Wheaton College

Iowa

IaAS	Iowa State University
IaCfT	University of Northern Iowa
IaDL	Luther College
IaDa	Davenport Public Library
IaDm	Public Library of Des Moines
IaDuL	Loras College
IaOcN	Northwestern College
IaPeC	Central College
IaU	University of Iowa

Indiana

In	Indiana State Library
InAnd	Anderson City, Anderson, Stony Creek & Union Townships Public Library
InBer	Berne Public Library
InBlo	Monroe County Public Library, Bloomington
InE	Evansville-Vanderburgh County Public Library
InFrf	Frankfort Community Public Library
InFw	Allen County Public Library, Fort Wayne
InFwB	Taylor University, Fort Wayne
InG	Gary Public Library
InGar	Garrett Public Library
InGrD	DePauw University
InHam	Hammond Public Library
InI	Indianapolis-Marion County Public Library
InL	Tippecanoe County Public Library, Lafayette
InLP	Purdue University
InLap	La Porte County Public Library
InMar	Marion Public Library
InMarC	Indiana Wesleyan University
InMit	Mitchell Community Public Library
InMu	Carnegie Library, Muncie
InNd	University of Notre Dame
InSMW	St. Mary of the Woods College
InTI	Indiana State University
InU	Indiana University
InWinG	Grace College and Theological Seminary, Winona Lake

Kansas

KAS	Benedictine College, North Campus
KEmU	Emporia State University
KHayF	Fort Hays State University
KHu	Hutchinson Public Library System
KKc	Kansas City Kansas Public Library
KMK	Kansas State University
KWi	Wichita Public Library
KWiU	Wichita State University

Kentucky

KyFSC	Kentucky State University
KyHhN	Northern Kentucky University
KyLnC	Sue Bennett College, London
KyLo	Louisville Free Public Library
KyLoU	University of Louisville
KyOw	Daviess County Public Library, Owensboro
KyRE	Eastern Kentucky University
KyU	University of Kentucky

Louisiana

LNT	Tulane University
LNX	Xavier University
LNaN	Northwestern State University of Louisiana
LU	Louisiana State University

Massachusetts

MB	Boston Public Library
MBAt	Boston Athenaeum
MBU	Boston University
MH	Harvard University
MW	Worcester Public Library
MWA	American Antiquarian Society
MWC	Clark University
MWalB	Brandeis University
MWelC	Wellesley College

Maryland

MdBE   Enoch Pratt Free Library, Baltimore
MdBJ   Johns Hopkins University

Maine

MeU   University of Maine

Minnesota

MnBemS   Bemidji State University
MnHi   Minnesota Historical Society, St. Paul
MnM   Minneapolis Public Library
MnManS   Mankato State University
MnManTD   Traverse des Sioux Library System, Mankato
MnMohC   Concordia College
MnSP   Saint Paul Public Library
MnU   University of Minnesota
MnVA   Arrowhead Library System, Virginia
MnVM   Mesabi Community College

Missouri

MoCgS   Southeast Missouri State University
MoIM   Mid-Continent Public Library Service, Independence
MoK   Kansas City Public Library
MoSW   Washington University
MoSpA   Assemblies of God Graduate School, Springfield
MoSpE   Evangel College
MoU   University of Missouri

Mississippi

MsCleD   Delta State College
MsCliM   Mississippi College
MsHaU   University of Southern Mississippi
MsJ   Jackson-Hinds Library System

New York

N   New York State Library, Albany

NAlU	State University of New York, Albany
NBuBE	Buffalo and Erie County Public Library System
NBuU	State University of New York, Buffalo
NIC	Cornell University
NN	New York Public Library
NNC	Columbia University
NOneoU	State University of New York, Oneonta
NR	Rochester Public Library
NRU	University of Rochester
NSyU	Syracuse University

Nebraska

NbLL	Lincoln City Libraries
NbLU	Union College
NbPerS	Peru State College
NbU	University of Nebraska

North Carolina

NcD	Duke University
NcGU	University of North Carolina at Greensboro
NcR	Wake County Public Library System, Raleigh
NcU	University of North Carolina

New Hampshire

NhD	Dartmouth College
NhU	University of New Hampshire

New Jersey

NjMD	Drew University
NjMlA	Atlantic County Library, Mays Landing
NjNetS	Sussex County Library System, Newton
NjTS	Trenton State College
NjUpM	Montclair State University
NjWhiM	Morris County Free Library, Whippany

Ohio

O	State Library of Ohio

OAU	Ohio University
OAlM	Mount Union College
OBgU	Bowling Green State University
OC	Public Library of Cincinnati and Hamilton County
OCU	University of Cincinnati
OCl	Cleveland Public Library
OClW	Case Western Reserve University
OCo	Columbus Metropolitan Library
OCoO	Ohioana Library, Columbus
ODaTS	United Theological Seminary, Dayton
ODaWU	Wright State University
OKentU	Kent State Univesity
OLor	Lorain Public Library
OMC	Marietta College
OO	Oberlin College
OOxM	Miami University
OSW	Wittenberg University
OSteC	Franciscan University of Steubenville
OT	Toledo-Lucas County Public Library
OTU	University of Toledo
OU	Ohio State University
OXe	Greene County Public Library, Xenia
OYU	Youngstown State University

Oklahoma

OkT	Tulsa City-County Library
OkTU	University of Tulsa

Oregon

OrCS	Oregon State University
OrRoD	Douglas County Library System, Roseburg
OrU	University of Oregon

Pennsylvania

PA	B. F. Jones Memorial Library, Aliquippa
PBa	Academy of the New Church, Bryn Athyn
PGC	Gettysburg College
PLhS	Lock Haven University

PMA	Allegheny College
PNo	Montgomery County-Norristown Public Library, Norristown
PPG	German Society of Pennsylvania, Philadelphia
PPL	Library Company of Philadelphia
PPiU	University of Pittsburgh
PRA	Albright College
PSt	Pennsylvania State University
PU	University of Pennsylvania
PWcS	West Chester University

Rhode Island

RP	Providence Public Library
RPB	Brown University
RPaw	Pawtucket Public Library
RUn	University of Rhode Island
RWe	Westerly Public Library

South Carolina

ScCF	Charleston County Library, Charleston
ScCleU	Clemson University
ScCoR	Richland County Public Library, Columbia
ScPT	Tri-County Technical College
ScSp	Spartanburg County Public Library, Spartanburg
ScSuM	Morris College
ScU	University of South Carolina

South Dakota

SdAbA	Alexander Mitchell Library, Aberdeen
SdBro	Brookings Public Library
SdSifA	Augustana College

Tennessee

T	Tennessee State Library and Archives
TC	Chattanooga-Hamilton County Bicentennial Library
TN	Public Library of Nashville and Davidson County
TNJ	Vanderbilt University
TU	University of Tennessee

Texas

TxAlpS	Sul Ross State University
TxAm	Amarillo Public Library
TxAu	Austin Public Library
TxCM	Texas A & M University
TxCc	Corpus Christi Public Libraries
TxDaM	Southern Methodist University
TxFTC	Texas Christian University
TxH	Houston Public Library
TxHuT	Sam Houston State University
TxSa	Central Library System, San Antonio
TxU	University of Texas
TxU-Hu	Humanities Research Center, University of Texas
TxWB	Baylor University

Utah

UCS	Southern Utah University
UM	Salt Lake County Library System
USl	Salt Lake City Public Library
UU	University of Utah

Virginia

ViBlbV	Virginia Polytechnic Institute and State University
ViBluC	Bluefield College
ViFGM	George Mason University
ViLC	Lynchburg College
ViN	Norfolk Public Library
ViR	Richmond Public Library
ViU	University of Virginia
ViVbR	Regent University
ViW	College of William and Mary

Vermont

VtU	University of Vermont

Wisconsin

WAL	Lawrence University

WAPL	Appleton Public Library
WEU	University of Wisconsin, Eau Claire
WGr	Brown County Library, Green Bay
WGrU	University of Wisconsin, Green Bay
WKen	Kenosha Public Library
WLac	La Crosse Public Library
WLacU	University of Wisconsin, La Crosse
WM	Milwaukee Public Library
WMUW	University of Wisconsin, Milwaukee
WMani	Manitowoc Public Library
WOsh	Oshkosh Public Library
WOshU	University of Wisconsin, Oshkosh
WPlaU	University of Wisconsin, Platteville
WRac	Racine Public Library
WS	Superior Public Library
WSpU	University of Wisconsin, Stevens Point
WU	University of Wisconsin, Madison
WWau	Waukesha Public Library
WWhiwU	University of Wisconsin, Whitewater

Washington

WaO	Timberland Regional Library, Olympia
WaS	Seattle Public Library
WaSpCo	Spokane County Library District
WaT	Tacoma Public Library
WaU	University of Washington

West Virginia

WvBeC	Bethany College

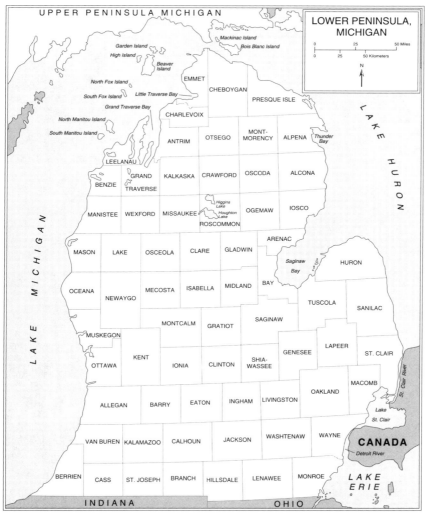

UPPER PENINSULA MICHIGAN

LOWER PENINSULA,
MICHIGAN

0   25   50 Miles

0   25   50 Kilometers

N

LAKE HURON

Mackinaw
City
Cheboygan
Cross
Village
Harbor Springs
Rogers City
Petoskey
Charlevoix
Suttons
Bay
Leland
Gaylord
Atlanta
Alpena
Glen Haven
Bellaire
Elk Rapids
Traverse
City
Kalkaska
Grayling
Mio
Harrisville
Beulah
Interlochen
South
Boardman
Greenbush
Frankfort
Bear
Lake
Roscommon
Higgins Lake
Higgins
Lake
West
Branch
Tawas City
Manistee
Cadillac
Lake City
Houghton
Lake
Houghton Lake
Harrison
Au Gres
Standish
Port Hope
Ludington
Baldwin
Reed City
Gladwin
Bad Axe
Clare
Pinconning
Pentwater
Hart
Big Rapids
Mt. Pleasant
Midland
Bay City
Caro
Montague
White Cloud
Fremont
Alma
Saginaw
Sandusky
Stanton
Ithaca
Frankenmuth
Muskegon
Greenville
Grand Haven
Grand
Rapids
Ionia
Lyons
Ovid
St. Johns
Owosso
Corunna
Flint
Lapeer
Port Huron
Byron
Center
Fenton
St. Clair
Holland
Marine City
Algonac
Saugatuck
Hastings
Grand Ledge
East Lansing
Lansing
Howell
Pontiac
Mt.
Clemens
Allegan
Nashville
Charlotte
Mason
Bloomfield Hills
Birmingham
Plainwell
Eaton Rapids
Pinckney
Farmington
South Haven
Kalamazoo
Marshall
Jackson
Ann Arbor
Livonia
Dearborn
Detroit
Battle
Creek
Albion
Ypsilanti
Belleville
Benton Harbor
St. Joseph
Paw Paw
Horton
CANADA
Dowagiac
Union City
Jonesville
Niles
Cassopolis
Three Rivers
Centreville
Coldwater
Hillsdale
Adrian
Monroe
Luna Pier
LAKE
ERIE
Constantine

LAKE MICHIGAN

INDIANA

OHIO

CARTO-GRAPHICS, Eau Claire, Wisconsin

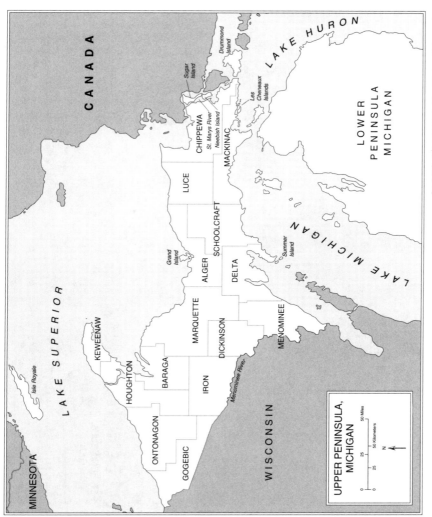

UPPER PENINSULA, MICHIGAN

CARTO-GRAPHICS, Eau Claire, Wisconsin

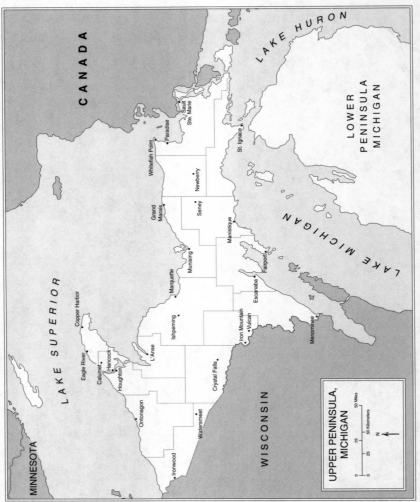

UPPER PENINSULA, MICHIGAN

CARTO-GRAPHICS, Eau Claire, Wisconsin

A

1 Acland, Eric
Adventure Westward. Camden, N.J.: Thomas Nelson & Sons, 1967. 263 p.

Narrated by a young Swiss army officer, the story is based on the 1767 copper-hunting expedition of Alexander Henry (1739–1824) to the Upper Peninsula and Mackinac Island.

Juvenile.

Mi   MiD   MiMtp   MiStc   MiWar

2 Adams, Roy William 1883–
Peg Leg, a Tale of Pioneer Adventure in the Grand River Valley. Eaton Rapids, Mich.: Sherman Printing Co., 1950. 215 p.

A seventeen-year-old with a wooden leg sets out on his own from New York to Michigan and travels along the Grand River from Jackson to Grand Rapids in 1835.

Black, 2.

Mi   MiAlbC   MiAllG   MiD   MiMtpT

3 ———.
When This Cruel War Is Over. New York: Vantage Press, 1970. 117 p.

Two Michigan brothers have a number of adventures when they join the Union army and volunteer to act as spies. Twenty pages are set in south-central Michigan in 1863.

Mi   MiAllG   MiFli   ArNlr

4 [Adams, William Taylor] 1822–1897
Out West; or, Roughing It on the Great Lakes. By Oliver Optic [pseud.]. Boston: Lee and Shepard; New York: Charles T. Dillingham, 1877. 361 p.

(Great Western Series, no. 2)

A young man seeking his fortune encounters a poor farmer, a cruel ship captain, and a mysterious Englishman. Set in "Montomercy" (Mt. Clemens), the "Glinten River" (Clinton River), Lake Huron, and the Saginaw area.

Juvenile.

Mi   MiDW   IaDuL   OBgU   ViU

5 [———].
Lake Breezes; or, The Cruise of the Sylvania. By Oliver Optic [pseud.]. Boston: Lee and Shepard Publishers, 1878. 325 p.

(Great Western Series, no. 3)

A group of young men are involved in stolen bonds and a yacht chase from Lake St. Clair to Lake Superior. Set in "Montomercy" (Mt. Clemens) and on the "Glinten River" (Clinton River).

Sequel to *Out West.*

Juvenile.

OBgU   OKentU   MnU   RPB   ViU

6 [———].
Going South; or, Yachting on the Atlantic Coast. By Oliver Optic [pseud.]. Boston: Lee and Shepard Publishers; New York: Charles T. Dillingham, 1879. 333 p.

(Great Western Series, no. 4)

A young man and his yacht are hired to take a few men on a sailing expedition to Florida. Partially set in Detroit, "Montomercy" (Mt. Clemens), and on the "Glinten River" (Clinton River).

Sequel to *Lake Breezes.*

Juvenile.

MiDW   MH   OBgU   OKentU   ViU

Aikman, Henry G., pseud. *see* Armstrong, Harold Hunter

Aimard, Gustave, joint author *see* Auriac, Jules Berlioz d'

7 Allen, Elizabeth 1914–1984
Margie. New York: E. P. Dutton & Co., 1969. 125 p.

An unhappy young woman half-heartedly attends graduate school where her father teaches. Set at the University of Michigan in Ann Arbor in the mid-1930s.

Juvenile.

Mi MiBatW MiMtp MiRog MiStjo

8 Allen, Emory Adams 1853–1933
A Jolly Trip: Or, Where We Went and What We Saw Last Summer by E. A. Adams. Cincinnati: Central Publishing House, 1891. 264 p.

A family spends a summer travelling across the United States and visits a variety of locales. Partially set in Detroit, on Mackinac Island, and in Sault Ste. Marie.

OCl

9 Allen, Merritt Parmelee 1892–1954
Black Rain. New York: Longmans, Green, 1939. 213 p.

A young man—allegedly the brother of Major Henry Gladwin (1729–1791), who was the commander of Fort Detroit—is among the garrison during Pontiac's siege in 1763.

Juvenile.

Mi MiAllG MiDW InFw ViBlbV

10 ———.
The Wilderness Way. New York: David McKay Co., 1954. 246 p.

A fictionalized account of the travels of Sieur de La Salle (1643–1687) in New France. Fifteen pages are set at Michilimackinac and the St. Joseph River area in the 1680s.

MiFliL IChamL InE InG WWhiwU

10A Allison, David P.
Welded Links. Grand Rapids: Wm. B. Eerdmans Publishing Co., 1939. 196 p.

A Scotsman and his wife join his brother in a lumbermill town where he soon finds work, and with his Christian beliefs, aids many people. Set mostly in "Kelso" in northern Michigan around 1900.

MiGr-L OU

Allison, Penny, pseud. *see* Katz, Carol

11 Allyn, Douglas L. 1942–
The Cheerio Killings. New York: St. Martin's Press, 1989. 252 p.

Detective Sergeant Lupe Garcia leads Detroit police in the search for a serial killer and seems to have found the prime suspect—a musician who is an ex-convict.

Mystery.

12 ———.
Motown Underground. New York: St. Martin's Press, 1993. 233 p.

Detective Sergeant Garcia is a suspect in the murder of his Detroit nightclub-owner friend and two other persons while he searches for the actual perpetrator.

Mystery.

13 ———.
Icewater Mansions. New York: St. Martin's Press, 1995. 247 p.

A professional diver, Michelle Mitchell, returns home to "Huron Harbor" (Alpena?) on Lake Huron to look into her father's death and to run his tavern.

Mystery.

14 ———.

Black Water. New York: St. Martin's Press, 1996. 217 p.

Michelle Mitchell reluctantly takes a diving job to locate a sunken car and its drowned occupant, and becomes involved in a mystery. Set in "Huron Harbor" (Alpena?).

Mystery.

15 **Alter, Judith MacBain** 1938–
Libbie by Judy Alter. New York: Bantam Books, 1994. 404 p.

The fictionalized life of Elizabeth Bacon Custer (1842–1933) and her romance with, marriage to, and life with George Armstrong Custer. Partially set in Monroe.

Romance.

Alter, Judy *see* Alter, Judith MacBain

16 **Altrocchi, Julia Cooley** 1893–1972
Wolves Against the Moon. New York: Macmillan Co., 1940. 572 p.

The fictionalized family chronicle and adventures of Joseph Bailly (1774–1835), a French fur-trader in the Great Lakes region. Partially set in Frenchtown, L'Arbre Croche, and Detroit, and on Mackinac Island.

Black, 3.

Mi MiAllG MiD MiMtpT-C MiU

17 **Altsheler, Joseph Alexander** 1862–1919

The Border Watch; a Story of the Great Chief's Last Stand. New York: D. Appleton and Co., 1912. 370 p.

(Young Trailers, no. 8)

In 1779 a captive Kentuckian is taken to Detroit where he ultimately escapes to join George Rogers Clark's expedition to Vincennes. Set partially in Detroit.

Juvenile.

MiD MiDW MiFliL MiGr MiLapC

18 **Ambers, Henry J.**
The Unfinished Building. Massapequa Park, N.Y.: Edelweiss Press, 1974. 400 p.

The story, probably a fictionalized autobiography, of a young man and his experiences growing up between 1916 and the 1930s. Partially set in Detroit.

MiMtpT-C KMK NcD OU

19 **[Anderson, Olive Santa Louise]** 1842–1886
An American Girl and Her Four Years in a Boy's College. By Sola [pseud.]. New York: D. Appleton and Co., 1878. 269 p.

Most of the academic adventures of a female college student and her social life as described here are autobiographical. Set at the University of Michigan in Ann Arbor in the 1870s.

Wright III, 111.

MiEM MiU MoU OKentU ViU

20 **Anderson, Willard C.** 1900–
Of Life's Essence. New York: Pageant Press, 1952. 385 p.

This story of a man's life is a mixture of homespun philosophy and medicine.

Set in an unnamed southern Michigan city, probably Lansing, in the 1940s.

Mi   MiAllG

Anderson, William H., joint author *see* Stowers, Walter H.

21 Andrews, Barbara
Emerald Fire. New York: Dell Publishing Co., 1983. 285 p.

(Candlelight Ecstasy Supreme, no. 2)

A jewelry store owner and a rich customer begin a relationship when they are suddenly kidnapped together at gunpoint. Partially set in Ann Arbor and Grosse Pointe.

Romance.

MiAllG   MiGr   AzSaf   OBgU   PNo

22 Antona, Annetta Halliday
Captives of Cupid: A Story of Old Detroit. Detroit: J. F. Eby and Co., 1896. 122 p.

The daughter of a French trader and Potawatomi woman rescues an American captive while Detroit is under British occupation during the War of 1812.

Romance.

Black, 4. Wright III, 124.

MiD   MiU   OBgU

23 Apple, Max 1942–
Zip: A Novel of the Left and the Right. New York: Viking Press, 1978. 183 p.

A young Jewish man in the scrap business tries to energize his life by managing a Puerto Rican boxer and becoming involved in the radical underground. Set in Detroit.

24 ———.
Roommates; My Grandfather's Story. New York: Warner Books, 1994. 211 p.

The fictionalized reminiscences of the author's life and experiences with his grandfather. Set in Grand Rapids and Ann Arbor, mostly in the 1960s.

25 Armer, Alberta Roller 1904–
Screwball. Cleveland: William Collins/World Publishing Co., 1963. 202 p.

A young boy stricken with polio gains confidence by building a racing car and competing in the national Soap Box Derby. Set in Detroit.

Juvenile.

26 Armstrong, Charlotte 1905–1969
The Case of the Weird Sisters. New York: Coward-McCann, 1943. 279 p.

(Gargoyle Mystery)

A young bride, meeting her new in-laws for the first time, suspects them of murderous intentions. Set in the failing Upper Peninsula mining town of "Ogaunee."

Subtitle on cover: *A MacDougal Duff Story.*

Mystery.

MiAllG   AAP   NhU   OC   WU

27 [———**].**
The Trouble in Thor by Jo Valentine [pseud.]. New York: Coward-McCann, 1953. 251 p.

The story of a mine disaster and how it affects members of the local community. Set in the Upper Peninsula iron-mining town of "Thor" (Vulcan).

Also published as *And Sometimes*

Death (New York: Pocket Books, 1955).

Black, 8.

28 [Armstrong, Harold Hunter] 1884–1979

The Groper, by Henry G. Aikman [pseud.]. New York: Boni and Liveright, 1919. 282 p.

A young man goes to the big city to seek his fortune and becomes involved in the automobile industry and the real estate business. Set in Detroit from 1907 to 1915.

Black, 5.

Mi MiAllG MiD MnU OU

29 [———].

Zell, by Henry G. Aikman [pseud.]. New York: Alfred A. Knopf, 1921. 326 p.

A young man inextricably caught in an unhappy marriage tries to make the best of his domestic, social, and business lives. Set in Detroit.

Black, 7.

Mi MiD MiEM MiHM MiKC

30 ———.

The Red-Blood. New York: Harper and Brothers, 1923. 479 p.

The story of the rise and decline of an overly ambitious man searching for power and fame. In the process he serves a term as mayor of Detroit.

Black, 6.

Mi MiAllG MiD MiDW OCl

Arnold, Birch, pseud. *see* Bartlett, Alice Elinor Bowen

31 Arnold, Elliott 1912–1980

White Falcon. New York: Alfred A. Knopf, 1955. 246 p.

A Kentucky boy who is kidnapped by a group of Ottawas in the 1770s has many adventures and tribulations during his captivity. Twenty pages are set in Michigan.

Juvenile.

32 Arnow, Harriette Louisa Simpson 1908–1986

The Dollmaker. New York: Macmillan, 1954. 549 p.

A rural Kentucky family arrives in Detroit during World War II to find work in the armaments industry, only to find cold indifference and personal tragedy.

Black, 9.

33 ———.

The Weedkiller's Daughter. New York: Alfred A. Knopf, 1970. 371 p.

A fifteen-year-old girl rejects the values of her well-to-do and overbearing parents and escapes into her own private world. Set in "Eden Hills" (Barton Hills?).

34 Arundel, Louis

Motor Boat Boys on the Great Lakes; or, Exploring the Mystic Isle of Mackinac. Chicago: M. A. Donohue & Co., 1912. 227 p.

(Motor Boat Boys, no. 3)

Six plucky lads have a number of adventures on the Great Lakes while encountering storms and villains. Half of the book is set in Michigan and on Mackinac Island.

Juvenile.

Streeter, 158.

Mi MiAllG MiD MiEM MiMtpT-C

35 **Assiniwi, Bernard** 1935–
L'Odawa Pontiac: L'Amour et la Guerre. Montréal: XYZ Editeur, 1994. 197 p.

(Les Grandes Figures, no. 2)

A fictional treatment of the life of the great Ottawa chief, including his efforts to organize various tribes against the English in 1763. Partially set in Detroit.

In French.

MiAllG CaOONL

36 **Atkinson, Eleanor Stackhouse** 1863–1942
Hearts Undaunted; a Romance of Four Frontiers. New York: Harper and Brothers, 1917. 348 p.

A fictionalized account of the life of the Chicago fur-trader John Kinzie (1763–1828). Partially set in Detroit and the St. Joseph River area from the 1780s to 1813.

Black, 10.

Mi MiD IC InFw OCl

Atwood, Dascomb, pseud. *see* White, Georgia Atwood

37 **Augustine, Robertson M.**
Kau-Bau-Gwas-Shee; a Flat River Story. Greenville, Mich.: Robertson M. Augustine, 1973. 207 p.

A fictionalized chronicle of pioneer days and adventures along the Flat River and in the Greenville area from 1780 to 1850 that centers on an Ojibwa trapper.

Mi MiAllG MiD MiEM MiMtpT-C

38 **Auriac, Jules Berlioz d'** 1820–
Les Forestiers du Michigan par J.-B. d'Auriac et Gustave Aimard. Paris: P. Brunet, 1867. 230 p.

In French.

Copy not seen.

NN

39 **Avery, Burniece** 1908–
Walk Quietly through the Night and Cry Softly. Detroit: Balamp Publishing, 1977. 193 p.

The story of the progress of and changing values of an African-American community in the northern suburbs of Detroit from 1918 to 1967.

40 **Avery, Joan**
Angel of Passage. New York: Harper-Paperbacks, 1993. 339 p.

(Harper Monogram)

An idealistic young woman becomes involved with the abolitionist movement and the Underground Railroad. Set in Detroit and Windsor in the 1850s.

Romance.

Mi MiAllG MiBlo MiD MiFliL

B

41 **Babcock, Elinor Gage** 1881–1967
Absalom. New York: Greenwich Book Publishers, 1955. 115 p.

A bitter man enters into a loveless marriage but has a son whom he cherishes. Set on a Huron River homestead, probably in Livingston County, in the 1840s.

Mi MiA MiAC MiAllG MiTop

42 **[Badger, Joseph Edward]** 1848–1909

The Indian Scout; or, Crazy Slack, the Whiskey Trader, by Harry Hazard [pseud.]. New York: Frank Starr & Co., 1871. 97 p.

(Frank Starr's American Novels, no. 68)

A story concerning the illegal liquor trade among the Ottawas and Hurons in New France in the 1690s. Set in western Michigan and on Lake Michigan.

Also published as *Crafty Crazy Slack; or, The French Fugitive* (New York: Beadle and Adams, 1889 [Beadle's Boy's Library, no. 253; octavo edition]).

Dime novel.

Black, 13.

Copy not located.

43 ————.

The Border Renegade; or, The Lily of the Silver Lake. New York: Beadle and Adams, 1872. 102 p.

(Beadle's Dime Novels, no. 250)

A homesteader and his daughter are saved from marauding Delawares by a hunter who turns out to be the notorious renegade George Girty. Set in the Lake St. Clair area in 1812.

Dime novel.

Black, 11.

Mi

44 ————.

Caribou Zip; or, The Forest Brothers. A Tale of the Fall of Michilmackinack. New York: Beadle and Adams, 1874. 99 p.

(Beadle's Dime Novels, no. 306)

The adventures and escapes of an American forest scout during the period of Pontiac's Conspiracy and the Ojibwa capture of Fort Michilimackinac in 1763.

Dime novel.

Black, 12.

Mi MiL

Baldwin, Faith *see* Cuthrell, Faith Baldwin

45 **Balmer, Edwin** 1883–1959
Resurrection Rock. Boston: Little, Brown, 1920. 383 p.

A young man orphaned as an infant tries to unravel the mystery of his origins. Mostly set in "St. Florentin" on Lake Huron in the Upper Peninsula.

Black, 14.

MiAllG MiFli MiPet MiWar OBgU

46 ————.
Dangerous Business. New York: Dodd, Mead & Co., 1927. 279 p.

A young Chicago man marries the wrong sort of girl but perseveres and saves the family business. Twenty-five pages are set in Emmet County at the Straits of Mackinac.

Mi MiU OBgU OCl OU

47 ————.
When Worlds Collide by Edwin Balmer and Philip Wylie. New York: Frederick A. Stokes Co., 1933. 344 p.

A wandering planet on a collision course with Earth spells doom for mankind, but scientists and engineers build a spaceship in the Upper Peninsula for the escape of a select few.

Science fiction.

MiBatW InFw InU KyLo OU

————, joint author, *see* MacHarg, William Briggs

48 Banér, Skulda Vanadis 1897–1964
Latchstring Out. Boston: Houghton Mifflin Co., 1944. 277 p.

Swedish family life in an Upper Peninsula mining town in 1900 is described through the relationship between a father and daughter. Set in "Iron Valley" (Iron Mountain).

Black, 15.

49 Banks, Florence E. Stovel 1914–
The House Coveted. Swartz Creek, Mich.: Broadblade Press, 1996. 292 p.

A farmer, giving in to his wife's desire for a fine house, builds her one, but, over the years, her pride and greed bring tragedy. Set in Sault Ste. Marie from 1910 to 1937.

MiAllG MiFli

50 Bannon, Laura 1894–1963
Billy and the Bear. Boston: Houghton Mifflin Co., 1949. 48 p.

The story of a small boy's efforts to prevent the local sheriff from shooting a tame bear. Set in "Cedarville," which here is not the Upper Peninsula town.

Juvenile picture book.

MiDW MiMack IC MnU OCo

51 ———.
Who Walks the Attic? Chicago: Albert Whitman & Co., 1962. 126 p.

Strange sounds coming from an upper floor in an old house provide a mystery for three siblings to solve. Set in Acme, on Grand Traverse Bay.

Juvenile.

52 Banta, Mykal Mayfield
No Ceiling But Heaven. New York: St. Martin's Press, 1987. 196 p.

A family chronicle supposedly narrated by the retarded son of a Chrysler worker whose unique point of view gives the story special poignancy. Set in an unnamed Detroit neighborhood.

53 Barleau, Hazel
The Moon for Sara. New York: Julian Messner, 1938. 280 p.

An heiress and a gentlemanly ex-convict become romantically involved despite her suspicions of his motives. Set in Detroit and its northeastern suburbs.

Romance.

Mi MiAllG OU

54 ———.
Philomena Leigh. Boston: Christopher Publishing House, 1941. 428 p.

A reticent middle-aged woman takes up with the local Methodist minister in a farming community. Set in "Mylo" (Ada) and Grand Rapids.

Mi MiAlbC MiAllG MiGr

55 Barlow, Ruth C. 1898–
Lisbeth Holly. New York: Dodd, Mead & Co., 1947. 209 p.

A young girl and her family take a summer vacation in southwestern Michigan on Lake Michigan where they have a variety of adventures and experiences.

Juvenile.

Mi MiBatW MiKW MiMtp MiYEM

56 Barnaby, Horace Thomas 1870–1952
The Decade; a Story of Political and Municipal Corruption. Grand Rapids: Wolverine Book Publishing Co., 1908. 325 p.

A man is wrongfully accused of being implicated in the notorious Grand

Rapids "Water Scandal." Set in "Industrial City" (Grand Rapids) and "Wayfield" (Wayland) at the turn of the century.

Also published as *The Water Scandal; a Story of Political and Municipal Graft and Corruption* (Grand Rapids: Shaw Publishing Co., 1910).

Black, 16 and 17.

Mi MiAllG MiGr MiKW OU

57 **Barr, Nevada**
A Superior Death. New York: G. P. Putnam's Sons, 1994. 303 p.

A female park ranger investigates the connection between the suspicious drowning of a diver and a shipwreck. Set on Isle Royale and its surrounding waters.

Mystery.

58 **Barr, Robert** 1850–1912
The Victors; a Romance of Yesterday Morning & This Afternoon. New York: F. A. Stokes Co., 1901. 567 p.

The adventures, progress, and setbacks of three young men setting out in the world of business. The first 130 pages are set in rural Ann Arbor.

Black, 18.

Mi IaCfT InLP OCl OU

Barrow, Adam, pseud. *see* Kakonis, Thomas E.

Barry, Joe, pseud. *see* Lake, Joe Barry

Barry, Mike, pseud. *see* Malzberg, Barry Nathaniel

59 **[Barthel-Winkler, Lisa]** 1893–
Pontiac, von F. L. Barwin [pseud.]. Heidenau bei Dresden: B. Langer & Co., 1943. 360 p.

A story of the great Ottawa chief and his efforts to drive the British out of tribal lands. Set in Detroit and on Mackinac Island in 1763.

In German.

MiD CU

60 [————.]
Der Verrat von Detroit, von F. L. Barwin [pseud.]. Heidenau bei Dresden: B. Langer & Co., 1944. 364 p.

Life on the Great Lakes frontier is described through the adventures of a British magistrate. Partially set in Detroit in the 1760s.

In German.

MiD CU MH PU TNJ

Bartlett, Alice Elinor Bowen *see* Detroit & Cleveland Navigation Co.

Barwin, F. L., pseud., *see* Barthel-Winkler, Lisa

60A **Bassett, John M.** 1914–
The Couriers for General Brock. Toronto: Thomas Allen & Son, 1967. 128 p.

A Canadian boy and his Shawnee friend serve as couriers for the British General Brock during the War of 1812. Partially set at Fort Detroit.

Juvenile.

MiGr-L

61 **Bateman, Doris I.**
The Secret of Allenby Acres. Philadelphia: Westminster Press, 1946. 224 p.

Four siblings solve a mystery on their farm to help a local boy recover his missing legacy. Set in southwestern Michigan near "Willowbridge."

Juvenile.

Mi ICSU IaOcN ViR

62 [Baum. Lyman Frank] 1856–1919
Tamawaca Folks; a Summer Comedy,
by John Estes Cooke [pseud.]. N.p.:
Tamawaca Press, 1907. 186 p.

A fictionalized account of how a summer cottage association wrests control
from two unscrupulous businessmen.
Set at "Tamawaca" (Lake Macatawa)
and in the Holland area.

Allegedly limited to ninety-nine
copies.

Mi MiGr MiHolH MiKW MiMtpT-C

63 Baxter, Betty
Daughter of the Coast Guard. Chicago:
Goldsmith Publishing Co., 1938. 252
p.

Two high school girls researching a
newspaper story become involved with
fur smugglers on Lake Michigan. Set in
"Lake Haven" (Grand Haven).

Juvenile.

Mi MiAllG MiEM FTS IEN

64 Baxter, Charles 1947–
First Light. New York: Viking Press,
1987. 286 p.

The story of the relationship between a
brother and sister from the 1950s to the
1980s. Half of the novel takes place in
"Five Oaks" (Pinconning?).

65 ———.
Shadow Play. New York: W. W. Norton
& Co., 1993. 399 p.

A city manager must balance the pos-
itive and negative aspects of bringing
a questionable industry to his econom-
ically depressed town of "Five Oaks"
(Pinconning?).

66 [Bean. Wiley E.] 1935–
The Morning of the Fourth Day by
Myron "Bud" Wheeler [pseud.]. N.p.:
Wiley E. Bean, 1992. 389 p.

A story of murder, justice, retribution,
and the social and moral implications
of the death penalty. Partially set in
Marquette and Lansing.

Limited to five hundred copies.

A revised edition was published in
1995.

Mystery.

MiL

67 Beans, Florence Amstutz 1908–
Canaan Tomorrow. Jackson, Mich.:
Ray Printing Co., 1995. 274 p.

Based on the author's family, the book
traces a young Mennonite farm couple's move from drought-stricken Iowa
to Michigan in the early 1900s. Set
partially in Rhodes in Gladwin County.

MiAllG MiJac

68 Beatty, Robert Alan
Journey of the Tern. Landenberg, Pa.:
Ecopress, 1994. 205 p.

A General Motors executive investigating his brother's shooting becomes
involved with an environmental society. Set in Detroit, "Choker Ridge"
(Grayling?), and on "Eagle Island" in
Lake Huron.

Mi MiAllG MiBir MiLapC OU

69 ———.
Sapo. Corvallis, Oreg.: Ecopress,
1996. 285 p.

A computer programmer unwittingly
becomes involved with a ruthless phar-
maceutical company when he witnesses an assault on one of its couriers.
Partially set in Detroit.

Mystery.

MiAllG CoD NBuBE WM

70 Beaumont de la Bonninière, Gustave August de 1802–1866

Marie; ou, l'Esclavage aux États-Unis, Tableau de Moeurs Américaines. Paris: C. Gosselin, 1835. 2 vols.

A tale of ill-fated love between a Frenchman and a racially mixed woman set mostly in Saginaw and Detroit. Much of the description in the novel is based on the author's visit to Michigan with Alexis de Tocqueville in 1831.

In French.

English translation by Barbara Chapman published as *Marie; or, Slavery in the United States: A Novel of Jacksonian America* (Stanford, Calif.: Stanford University Press, 1958).

Black, 19.

MiD ICU LU MnU OOxM

71 Beebe, Ralph

Who Fought and Bled. New York: Coward-McCann, 1941. 329 p.

An Ohio man joins the Detroit garrison under General Hull during the War of 1812 and witnesses the fort's disgraceful surrender to the British.

Black, 24.

Mi MiAllG MiD MiU OCl

72 Beek, James R.

Bradford's Trials. New York: Carlton Press, 1969. 405 p.

A defense lawyer represents a wealthy industrialist accused of soliciting the murder of a judge. Set in a large unnamed Michigan city.

Mystery.

Mi MiAC MiAllG MiD MiYEM

73 Bellairs, John 1938–1991

The House with a Clock in Its Walls. New York: Dial Press, 1973. 179 p.

Ten-year-old Lewis Barnavelt and his magician uncle become involved with a dead wizard and his plan for the end of the world. Set in "New Zebedee" (Marshall) in 1948 and 1949.

Juvenile.

74 ———.

The Figure in the Shadows; Sequel to the House with a Clock in Its Walls. New York: Dial Press, 1975. 155 p.

Lewis finds an old magic amulet that gives him frightening powers and ultimately summons an evil ghost. Set in "New Zebedee" (Marshall) in 1949.

Sequel to *The House with a Clock in Its Walls.*

Juvenile.

75 ———.

The Letter, the Witch, and the Ring. New York: Dial Press, 1976. 188 p.

Lewis, Rose Rita, and Mrs. Zimmermann, a kindly witch, contend with the terrifying powers of a magic ring. Set in "New Zebedee" (Marshall) and the Upper Peninsula in 1950.

Sequel to *The Figure in the Shadows.*

Juvenile.

76 ———.

The Ghost in the Mirror by John Bellairs; completed by Brad Strickland. New York: Dial Books for Young Readers, 1993. 169 p.

Rose Rita and Mrs. Zimmermann mysteriously find themselves in 1828 Pennsylvania. The first fifteen pages are set in "New Zebedee" (Marshall) in 1951.

Juvenile.

77 ⸺.

The Doom of the Haunted Opera by John Bellairs; completed by Brad Strickland. New York: Dial Books for Young Readers, 1995. 153 p.

Lewis and Rose Rita explore an abandoned theater where they discover a musical manuscript that holds the power to awaken the dead. Set in "New Zebedee" (Marshall).

Juvenile.

78 **Bendle, Susan C.**
Cricket by S. C. Bendle. New York: Vantage Press, 1979. 91 p.

A thirteen-year-old girl tries to come to terms with her father's death and, at the same time, helps her family with their adjustment. Set in Grand Rapids.

Juvenile.

MiAllG MiGr IaAS InFw WAPL

79 **[Benson, Mildred Augustine Wirt]**
1905–
The Secret of the Sundial by Ann Wirt [pseud.]. Chicago: Goldsmith Publishing Co., 1932. 123 p.

(Madge Sterling Series, no. 3)

The strange appearance of a figure digging on the grounds of an old abandoned house has a group of girls investigating the mystery. Set in "Claymore."

Juvenile.

MiAllG MiEM MiWar InNd OBgU

80 **Berg, Melody Gay Dantuma**
Round by the Point. Dorr, Mich.: Lake Superior Publishing, 1989. 98 p.

A young woman rescues a disfigured man from Lake Superior during a storm and is attracted to his "inner self." Set in Whitefish Point.

MiAllG

81 ⸺.

A Safe Harbor. Dorr, Mich.: Lake Superior Publishing, 1990. 139 p.

The captain of a Great Lakes freighter falls in love with a young woman whose small craft he sank in a collision. Set mostly in Whitefish Point.

MiAllG

Berliss, J. Richie, ed. *see* Cochon, Jon Poe, pseud.

82 **Bertsch, Lory**
Willy Visits Tulip Time. Smithtown, N.Y.: Exposition Press, 1983. 40 p.

A young boy visits the Holland Tulip Festival and describes all of the picturesque events, from the street cleaning to the exhibits.

Juvenile picture book.

MiGr

83 **Bessie, Alvah Cecil** 1904–1985
Dwell in the Wilderness. New York: Covici, Friede, 1935. 468 p.

A mismatched marriage between a merchant and his puritanical wife causes family discord through three generations. Set in "Paulsville" from 1876 to 1925.

Black, 26.

MiAllG MiDW MiEM MiU MiYEM

84 **Bird, Dorothy Maywood** 1899–
Granite Harbor. New York: Macmillan Co., 1944. 211 p.

A teenage girl reluctantly moves to "Granite Harbor" from Texas with her parents and ultimately adapts to her new home. Set in the Marquette area on Lake Superior.

Juvenile.

Mi MiAllG MiD MiGay MiMarqN

85 ——.

Mystery at Laughing Water. New York: Macmillan Co., 1946. 203 p.

While at an Upper Peninsula summer camp, a girl discovers information about the disappearance of some ancestors in the 1820s. Set near "Copper Bay" (Copper Harbor).

Juvenile.

Mi MiAlbC MiD MiGay MiMarqN

86 ——.

The Black Opal. New York: Macmillan Co., 1949. 202 p.

A college student becomes involved in a mystery based on the notorious Walker Tavern murder. Set at "Colbert College" near Cambridge Junction.

Juvenile.

Mi MiD MiGay MiMarqN MiWar

87 **Bischoff, Julia Bristol** 1909–1970

Great-Great Uncle Henry's Cats. New York: Young Scott Books, 1965. 62 p.

A farm family has a number of adventures with the many felines that reside in a relative's home and barn. Set in rural Michigan in the 1800s.

Juvenile.

88 ——.

A Dog for David. New York: William R. Scott, 1966. 111 p.

A young farm boy and his family begin the involved process of finding the right sort of pet. Set in the Michigan Thumb area in 1905.

Juvenile.

89 ——.

Paddy's Preposterous Promises. New York: Young Scott Books, 1968. 160 p.

A newly hired and fast-talking farm hand bamboozles the farmer's five children into doing his chores. Set in Lapeer County in 1903.

Juvenile.

90 **Bissell, Irving J.**

A Sow's Ear. New York: Julian Messner, 1937. 250 p.

The story of a philandering husband who ultimately destroys his marriage and social standing in the community. Set in Grand Rapids and the Baldwin area.

Black, 27.

Mi MiGr AzU OU

Blacklock, Alaska, pseud. *see* Lewis, George Edward

91 **Blaine, Laurence**

Black Muscle. Los Angeles: Holloway House Publishing Co., 1976. 224 p.

An African American, who is a former boxer and now a troubleshooter for a UAW local, becomes involved in escalating automobile union violence. Set in Detroit.

Mystery.

Mi MdBE MoK NBuBE OAU

92 ——.

Sweet Street Blues. Los Angeles: Holloway House Publishing Co., 1978. 220 p.

An African-American jazz saxophonist falsely convicted on drug charges searches for his betrayer and attempts to rebuild his life. Set in Detroit.

Mystery.

Mi MiAllG CU OT

Blake, Eleanor, pseud. *see* Pratt, Eleanor
Blake Atkinson

93 Blakemore, Howard 1900–
Special Detail. Philadelphia: Dorrance, 1944. 367 p.

The story of three members of the
U.S. Immigration and Border Patrol
and their investigation of smuggling
activities along the St. Clair River. Set
in Marine City.

Black, 28.

MiAllG MiD MiPh InU OC

94 Blanchard, Amy Ella 1856–1926
Bonny Lesley of the Border. Boston: W.
A. Wilde Co., 1904. 331 p.

(Pioneer Series, no. 2)

From 1836 to 1838, a young woman
finds a home with her grandfather in
the Michigan frontier settlement of
"Woodstock," located north of Detroit.

Also one of the books in the publisher's
"American Girls Series."

Juvenile.

MiAllG MH NAIU NcGU

Blind Bard of Michigan, The *see* Gorton,
Cynthia M. Roberts

95 Blish, James 1921–1975
VOR. New York: Avon Publications,
1958. 159 p.

An alien spacecraft lands in the northern part of the Lower Peninsula and, although imparting information of other
worlds, presents a grave danger to
earth.

Science fiction.

MiAllG InU OBgU OU ViU

96 Bliss, May Cummisky
Dr. Joy, with Illustrations from Life.
Saginaw: F. R. Ganschow & Son, Print-
ers, 1899. 299 p.

An episodic account of a doctor's life
and practice in Saginaw in the late
1800s. The book is evidently a tribute
to the real-life "Dr. Joy" (Dr. Bliss)
written by his wife.

Black, 29.

Mi MiMtpT-C OU

97 Blos, Joan Winsor 1928–
*Brothers of the Heart; a Story of the
Old Northwest, 1837–1838.* New York:
Charles Scribner's Sons, 1985. 162 p.

In 1837, a fourteen-year-old boy runs
away from home to join a trading expedition in the Michigan wilderness. Set
in Detroit, "Millville," and the Manistee River area.

Juvenile.

98 Boatman, Alan
Summer's Lie. New York: Harper &
Row, 1970. 259 p.

A college student has a summer job
checking power poles that sends him
to Greenville, Ann Arbor, Saginaw,
Owosso, Fenton, Durand, Muskegon,
and Grand Haven.

99 Bodenheim, Maxwell 1893–1954
A Virtuous Girl. New York: Horace
Liveright, 1930. 260 p.

A rebellious young girl sneers at the
hypocritical social conventions of her
native Chicago. Partially set in South
Haven and Kalamazoo in 1900.

MiGr-L IC IaU InTI OU

100 Bond, Larry
The Enemy Within. New York: Warner
Books, 1996. 483 p.

An international group of terrorists led by an Iranian mastermind begin an all-out campaign against the United States. Twenty pages are set in Detroit.

Mystery.

Bonner, Margerie *see* Lowry, Margerie Bonner

Boris, Robert, joint author *see* Hannibal, Edward

101 Borisch, Sarah Allan
The Protocol. New York: Simon and Schuster, 1981. 448 p.

Issues regarding medical treatment of cancer, patient dignity, and family wishes are dramatized in a large city hospital. Set in "Brandenburg" (Grand Rapids).

101A Bosch, Linda 1951–
Life in a New Land. Grand Rapids: CRC Publications, 1991. 72 p.

The father of a large poor family in the Netherlands is persuaded by his brother to emigrate to America and live with him. Partially set in Muskegon from 1916 to 1920.

MiGr-L IArlh InI MoIM ScSp

102 Bouldrey, Brian
The Genius of Desire. New York: Ballantine Books, 1993. 274 p.

The story of a young gay man's coming of age and growing self-awareness in an eccentric Catholic family. Partially set in "Monsalvat" (Frankenmuth).

103 Bowman, James Cloyd 1880–1961
Mystery Mountain. Chicago: Albert Whitman & Co., 1940. 293 p.

While visiting her relatives in the Upper Peninsula, a young Chicago girl solves the mystery of an apparently haunted hotel. Set in Marquette.

Juvenile.

Mi MiYEM IC InFw ViR

104 Boyd, Thomas Alexander 1898–1935
Shadow of the Long Knives. New York: Charles Scribner's Sons, 1928. 354 p.

The adventures of a frontier scout and advocate for Native Americans on the Ohio frontier. Partially set at Fort Detroit between 1774 and 1794.

Black, 32.

MiU IC InFw OCl OU

Boyer, Brian, joint author *see* Weisman, John

105 Boylan, Malcolm Stuart 1897–
Tin Sword. Boston: Little, Brown and Co., 1950. 312 p.

A young man with proclivities towards military life has a number of picaresque and humorous adventures. Partially set in Battle Creek between 1910 and 1916.

Black, 33.

Mi MiAllG MiD MiGr MiWar

106 Boyle, T. Coraghessan 1948–
The Road to Wellville. New York: Viking, 1993. 476 p.

A humorous account of J. H. Kellogg's (1852–1943) famous health sanitarium and its wealthy clientele undergoing intense and sometimes painful treatments. Set in Battle Creek in 1907.

107 Bradbury, Osgood
Pontiac; or, The Last Battle of the Ottawa Chief. A Tale of the West. Boston: F. Gleason, 1848. 100 p.

A fanciful version of Pontiac's attack on Fort Detroit in 1763, in which the Ottawa chief is portrayed as the "Noble Savage" and the British as treacherous villains.

Wright I, 396.

MBAt NN

108 ———.
Manita of the Pictured Rocks; or, The Copper Speculator. A Tale of Lake Superior. Boston: F. Gleason, 1848. 100 p.

The adventures of a young mineral explorer in the Upper Peninsula and the beginnings of a copper- and silver-mining operation in the Ontonagon region in the 1840s.

Wright I, 387.

MnHi RPB

109 **[Braden, Jenness Mae]** 1880–
Uncle Sam's Star Route; a Romance of a Rural Mail Route and the New Parcel Post, of Michigan's "Iron Country" and Its Southern Sand Hills, of the Glorious Farm Lands to the South and West of Lake Michigan, and of Love, Politics and Personal Efficiency Everywhere. By Betsey Ross [pseud.]. Chicago: Twentieth Century Publishing Co., 1913. 228 p.

An epistolary novel covering the subjects and locales described in the title.

Mi MiD MiHM MiMtpT-C MiU

110 **Bramhall, Marion**
Murder Is Contagious. Garden City, N.Y.: Doubleday & Co., 1949. 188 p.

(Crime Club)

A young couple living in married housing at an unnamed school (Michigan State University) tries to solve a pair of murders in the midst of a measles epidemic.

Mystery.

MiAllG MBAt OBgU OU TxCM

111 **Brashler, William** 1947–
The Chosen Prey. New York: Harper & Row, 1982. 297 p.

A former Chicago police officer hoping for a quieter life as a small-town sheriff is faced with a series of murders in "Beach Haven" (South Haven) in 1952.

Mystery.

———. *see* Evers, Crabbe, pseud.

112 **Bratton, Helen** 1899–
Only in Time. New York: David McKay Co., 1967. 186 p.

A teenage girl learns to cope with her disfiguring scar and makes new friends while attending the National Music Camp at Interlochen.

Juvenile.

MiCad MiFra MiMtp IChamL OCl

113 **Braun, Lilian Jackson** 1916?–
The Cat Who Could Read Backwards. New York: E. P. Dutton & Co., 1966. 191 p.

Jim Qwilleran, a crime reporter turned feature writer, solves a series of murders with the help of Koko, a Siamese cat that belonged to one of the victims. Set in Detroit, which is unnamed.

Mystery.

114 ———.
The Cat Who Ate Danish Modern. New York: E. P. Dutton & Co., 1967. 192 p.

Koko and Qwilleran, first introduced in *The Cat Who Could Read Backwards,* are involved in a series of robberies and murder concerning the interior decorating business. Set in Detroit.

Mystery.

115 ———.

The Cat Who Turned On and Off. New York: E. P. Dutton & Co., 1968. 186 p.

Koko, Qwilleran, and another Siamese cat, Yum Yum, prove that the death of an antique dealer was no accident. Set in Detroit.

Mystery.

116 ———.

The Cat Who Saw Red. New York: Berkley Publishing Group, 1986. 183 p.

The cats and Qwilleran puzzle over a suicide that turns out to be a murder as well as strange doings in an old mansion. Set in Detroit.

Mystery.

117 ———.

The Cat Who Played Brahms. New York: Berkley Publishing Group, 1987. 185 p.

The cats and Qwilleran vacation in "Pickax City, Moose County," which is "four hundred miles north of everywhere," where they become involved in murder. Set in the Upper Peninsula.

Mystery.

118 ———.

The Cat Who Played Post Office. New York: Berkley Publishing Group, 1987. 186 p.

The cats and Qwilleran inherit millions from his aunt and begin to enjoy their new social status until murder inter-
rupts. Set in "Pickax City" in the Upper Peninsula.

Mystery.

119 ———.

The Cat Who Knew Shakespeare. New York: Jove Books, 1988. 201 p.

The cats and Qwilleran attempt to solve the baffling murder of the local newspaper publisher. Set in "Pickax City" in the Upper Peninsula.

Mystery.

120 ———.

The Cat Who Sniffed Glue. New York: G. P. Putnam's Sons, 1988. 207 p.

The cats and Qwilleran search for a motive and clues to the murders of a newlywed couple. Set in "Pickax City" in the Upper Peninsula.

Mystery.

121 ———.

The Cat Who Went Underground. New York: G. P. Putnam's Sons, 1989. 223 p.

The cats and Qwilleran become involved in the apparent serial murders of local carpenters. Set in "Mooseville" in the Upper Peninsula.

Mystery.

122 ———.

The Cat Who Lived High. New York: G. P. Putnam's Sons, 1990. 239 p.

Back in Detroit for a brief visit, the cats and Qwilleran find murder connected with the efforts to save a historic apartment building.

Mystery.

123 ———.

The Cat Who Talked to Ghosts. New York: G. P. Putnam's Sons, 1990. 239 p.

The cats and Qwilleran become immersed in a mystery involving death, the supernatural, and a sinister secret society. Set in "Moose County" in the Upper Peninsula.

Mystery.

124 ———.
The Cat Who Knew a Cardinal. New York: G. P. Putnam's Sons, 1991. 240 p.

The cats and Qwilleran investigate the murder of the obnoxious local high school principal. Set in "Pickax City" in the Upper Peninsula.

Mystery.

125 ———.
The Cat Who Moved a Mountain. New York: G. P. Putnam's Sons, 1992. 239 p.

Vacationing in what is probably North Carolina, the cats and Qwilleran clear an innocent man of murder. Twelve pages are set in "Pickax City" in the Upper Peninsula.

Mystery.

126 ———.
The Cat Who Wasn't There. New York: G. P. Putnam's Sons, 1992. 238 p.

The cats and Qwilleran investigate the mysterious death of a local resident and search for suspects. Set in "Pickax City" in the Upper Peninsula.

Mystery.

127 ———.
The Cat Who Went Into the Closet. New York: G. P. Putnam's Sons, 1993. 235 p.

The cats and Qwilleran question why an apparently happy and healthy elderly woman would commit suicide. Set in "Pickax City" in the Upper Peninsula.

Mystery.

128 ———.
The Cat Who Came to Breakfast. New York: G. P. Putnam's Sons, 1994. 240 p.

The cats and Qwilleran investigate a series of strange accidents occurring at a new island resort. Set in "Moose County" in the Upper Peninsula.

Mystery.

129 ———.
The Cat Who Blew the Whistle. New York: G. P. Putnam's Sons, 1995. 240 p.

The cats and Qwilleran become involved with financial misdeeds and embezzlement at a local credit union. Set in "Pickax City" and "Moose County" in the Upper Peninsula.

Mystery.

130 ———.
The Cat Who Said Cheese. New York: G. P. Putnam's Sons, 1996. 245 p.

The cats and Qwilleran investigate a bombing that destroys a hotel, kills a woman, and disrupts a gourmet food extravaganza. Set in "Moose County" in the Upper Peninsula.

Mystery.

Breitenbach, Louise M. *see* Clancy, Louise Marks Breitenbach

Bremer, Joanne, joint author *see* Carroll, Joellyn

131 **Brennan, Alice**
The Brooding House. New York: Lancer Books, 1965. 254 p.

A young nurse hired to give home-care to a dying cancer patient encounters terror and menace within the house. Set in Port Hope on Lake Huron.

Mystery.

MiAllG PNo

132 ———.

Fear No Evil. New York: Prestige Books, 1970. 256 p.

A young woman returns to an isolated Upper Peninsula resort to find answers to disturbing childhood memories. Set on the Lake Superior shore.

Mystery.

MiAllG OBgU PNo

133 ———.

Never to Die. New York: Prestige Books, 1971. 255 p.

An impressionable newlywed suspects her husband has a secret past and endeavors to find out the truth. Set near "Calcaska" (Kalkaska).

Mystery.

MiAllG OBgU

134 ———.

Thirty Days Hath July. New York: Avon Books, 1975. 160 p.

A woman has blackouts and sinister dreams, and is ultimately possessed by the spirit of a drowning victim. Set on "Handson Island" in Lake Superior.

Mystery.

MiAllG

134A **Briggs-Bunting, Jane**

Whoop for Joy: A Christmas Wish. Oxford, Mich.: Black River Trading Co., 1995. 25 p.

An eleven-year-old Ohio girl is unhappy to be moving to rural Michigan but is delighted when she discovers a retired race horse resides next door.

Juvenile.

MiMtcM MiRochOU AzTeS FJ MoIM

135 **Brill, Ethel Claire** 1877–

When Lighthouses Are Dark; a Story of a Lake Superior Island. New York: Henry Holt and Co., 1921. 292 p.

Four teenagers in a small boat become lost in a Lake Superior fog, are marooned on Isle Royale, and have many adventures before being rescued.

Juvenile.

Mi MiAllG MiD CL MnHi

136 ———.

The Island of Yellow Sands. Philadelphia: Macrae Smith Co., 1925. 308 p.

An Ojibwa and two boys travel the Lake Superior country in search of a secret island reportedly rich in treasure. Partially set on Isle Royale in the 1790s.

Juvenile.

Mi FTS MnHi MnSP SdSifA

137 ———.

The Secret Cache. Philadelphia: Macrae Smith Co., 1926. 304 p.

Two boys search the Lake Superior region for a valuable cache of furs hidden by their deceased father. Partially set on Isle Royale in the 1770s.

Juvenile.

MiAllG MnHi MnSp

138 ———.

White Brother: A Story of the Pontiac Uprising; Told by Alan Davidson, Called Nekah by the Ojibwas. New York: Henry Holt and Co., 1932. 250 p.

The adventures of a half-Ojibwa, half-white boy on Mackinac Island during the time of Pontiac's Conspiracy and the attack on Fort Michilimackinac from 1761 to 1763.

Juvenile.

Mi MiAlbC MiGr CtY MnHi

139 ———.
Copper Country Adventure. New York: Whittlesey House, 1949. 213 p.

In 1846, a sixteen-year-old boy has many adventures among copper miners and thieves on the Keweenaw Peninsula and elsewhere in the Upper Peninsula.

Juvenile.

Mi MiAllG MiD MiKW MiMarqN

140 Briskin, Jacqueline 1927–
The Onyx. New York: Delacorte Press, 1982. 504 p.

The story of the founder of an automobile empire, patterned after Henry Ford, from his beginnings as a mechanic to his death. Set in Detroit from 1894 to 1947.

141 Britton, Frederic H. 1870–
Teddie; a Simple, Little Out-of-Door Story About a Child, in the Telling of Which a Promise to a Friend Is Redeemed. Detroit: F. B. Dickerson Co., 1910. 315 p.

A tongue-in-cheek parody of dime-novel adventures and their stereotypical characters. Set in Lansing and its environs mostly in 1848.

Black, 34.

Mi MiEM MiKW

Broad Churchman, A *see* Warriner, Edward Augustus

142 Brock, Emma Lillian 1886–1974
Heedless Susan Who Sometimes Forgot to Remember. New York: Alfred A. Knopf, 1939. 169 p.

A young girl spends the summer with her grandmother and has a number of adventures. Set in an unnamed village near Rochester and Detroit in the 1890s.

Juvenile.

MiDW MiFliL MiLap MiYEM OCl

Brodie, Alma Routsong *see* Routsong, Alma

143 Brody, Catharine
Nobody Starves. New York: Longmans, Green and Co., 1932. 281 p.

The Depression makes life very difficult for a young factory worker and his wife. Set in Detroit and Flint.

Black, 36.

Mi MiD MiDW MiEM MiU

144 ———.
Cash Item. New York: Longmans, Green and Co., 1933. 303 p.

A young woman hopes to go to New York and become a dancer, but becomes involved with a bank teller and embezzler. Set in "Micmac" (Flint?) in 1930 and 1931.

Black, 35.

MiAllG ICarbS InU MnU OCl

145 Broner, Esther Masserman 1930–
Her Mothers. New York: Holt, Rinehart and Winston, 1975. 245 p.

A successful writer reflects upon her life and its effect on her writing. Partially set in Detroit.

146 Brown, Elizabeth Louise 1924–
Candle of the Wicked. Grand Rapids: Zondervan Publishing House, 1972. 192 p.

A Baptist minister is wrongly accused of murder, and he attempts to prove his innocence. Set in Anchorville and Anchor Bay on Lake St. Clair.

Mystery.

MiGr-L IC ICMB NBuBE TxH

147 [Brown, Forman George] 1901–
Better Angel by Richard Meeker [pseud.]. New York: Greenberg: Publisher, 1933. 284 p.

The story of a young gay man's coming of age in his hometown of "Barton" and at the University of Michigan, and his ultimate success as a composer in New York.

Also published as *Torment* (New York: Universal Publishing and Distributing Corp. [1950?]).

MiEM

148 Brown, Gita 1958–
Be I Whole. Aspen, Colo.: MacMurray & Beck, 1995. 267 p.

An elderly woman relates the story of the marriage and lives of an urban bar owner and a rural herbal healer. Partially set in Detroit in the 1950s.

149 Brown, Katherine Holland 1876–1931
Philippa at Halcyon. New York: Charles Scribner's Sons, 1910. 422 p.

The story of a young woman's social and academic life during her first two years at college. Set in Ann Arbor and at "College Hill" (University of Michigan).

MiU IQ MnU OCl OOxM

150 Brown, Vera 1896?–1976
Tarnished Fame. New York: Grosset & Dunlap Publishers, 1934. 306 p.

A young woman aviator loses her pilot friend to a rich society woman when he becomes famous after breaking a speed record. Ten pages are set in northern Michigan.

Originally published as a serial under the title *Sally of Sky Alley.*

Romance.

MiGr-L OU

151 ——.
Wings of Love; the Love Story of a Girl Aviator. New York: Grosset & Dunlap Publishers, 1934. 310 p.

The experiences of a young female pilot and her romantic involvements. The first fourteen pages take place in Detroit.

Romance.

OU

152 Brucker, Margaretta 1883–1958
Poison Party. New York: Phoenix Press, 1938. 256 p.

A fatal poisoning for which there are many suspects takes place at an exclusive northern Lake Michigan resort. Set in "Little Harbor" (Harbor Springs).

Mystery.

Mi MH

153 ——.
Lover's Choice. New York: Gramercy Publishing Co., 1939. 251 p.

A young woman begins to date the handsome acquaintance of her roommate's boyfriend despite some misgivings. Set in Detroit and "Little Harbor" (Harbor Springs).

Romance.

OBgU OU

154 ———.
There Goes the Bride. New York: Gramercy Publishing Co., 1940. 256 p.

An impoverished young woman is given money to deliver some documents to a person in New York and meets a wealthy man on the train. The first twenty pages are set in Detroit.

Romance.

DLC

155 ———.
The Country Girl. New York: Gramercy Publishing Co., 1942. 254 p.

A young postal worker meets a handsome summer resort visitor and falls in love, despite her better judgment. Set in "Little Harbor" (Harbor Springs).

Romance.

OU

156 ———.
A Rich Girl. New York: Gramercy Publishing Co., 1942. 250 p.

A wealthy young woman falls in love with a poor lawyer, and their differing social classes pose obstacles to their romance. Set in Detroit.

Romance.

PNo

157 ———.
Summer Date. New York: Ariel Books, 1953. 192 p.

A sixteen-year-old girl must decide between a local farm helper and a rich summer resort resident. Set in "Little Harbor" (Harbor Springs) and "Bayport" (Bay View).

Juvenile.

GA IC InE InFw ScSp

158 ———.
Big, Brave and Handsome. New York: Farrar, Straus and Cudahy, 1956. 184 p.

A seventeen-year-old girl frets about losing her sports-minded boyfriend to an attractive rival. Set in "Little Harbor" (Harbor Springs).

Juvenile.

MiAlle InFw InG MnManTD OCo

159 ———.
Three Boys and a Girl. New York: Farrar, Straus and Cudahy, 1957. 192 p.

A seventeen-year-old girl must deal with the humiliation of her thwarted elopement the previous year. Set in "Little Harbor" (Harbor Springs).

Juvenile.

MiDW MiNhL InFw TxAm

Bryant, Dorthea A. *see* Curwood, James Oliver

160 Buehrig, Gordon M. 1904–
A Savior in the White House. New York: Vantage Press, 1976. 213 p.

A young Michigan lawyer becomes an unlikely third-party candidate for President of the United States in the 1976 election. Partially set in Gaylord.

MiGr-L

161 Bunce, William Harvey 1903–
War Belts of Pontiac. New York: E. P. Dutton and Co., 1943. 214 p.

A young man helps defend Fort Detroit during Pontiac's siege in 1763 and acts as messenger between the Ottawa chief and the British.

Juvenile.

Mi MiStc IC OCl OT

162 Bunn, Thomas 1944–
Worse Than Death. New York: Henry Holt and Co., 1989. 278 p.

(Jack Bodine Mystery)

A desperate couple hires a private investigator when their newly adopted baby, illegally obtained from a baby broker, is kidnapped. Set in Lansing and East Lansing.

Mystery.

163 Burgess, Barbara Hood 1926–
Oren Bell. New York: Delacorte Press, 1991. 182 p.

A story about a pair of African-American siblings and their concern about the evil goings-on in the abandoned house next door. Set in Detroit.

Juvenile.

164 ———.
The Fred Field. New York: Delacorte Press, 1994. 180 p.

A young African-American boy decides to have the empty lot next door dedicated to his murdered friend and enlists the aid of his family and friends. Set in Detroit.

Sequel to *Oren Bell.*

Juvenile.

165 Burke, Dorothy Preisler 1913–
Thanks to Letty. Chicago: The Junior Literary Guild and Rand McNally & Co., 1952. 271 p.

A sixteen-year-old girl tries to run the family farm after her father's death and overcomes a variety of obstacles. Set in the Lansing and Charlotte area.

Juvenile.

MiMarl MiSW MiWol OBgU OCo

166 Burnham, Lila Mae 1883–
The White Lilac Tree. New York: Pageant Press, 1952. 182 p.

Every-day village life from 1890 to 1899 is observed and described by a lilac tree. Set in "Cobbs Corners" (Byron Center) and "Valley City" (Grand Rapids).

Black, 37.

MiGr InFw

166A Burns, Virginia Law 1925–
William Beaumont, Frontier Doctor. Bath, Mich.: Enterprise Press, 1978. 159 p.

The fictionalized biography of Dr. William Beaumont (1785–1853), including his famous observations of and experiments with human digestion. Set partially on Mackinac Island.

Juvenile.

Mi MiD MiGrA MiMarqN MiMtpT-C

167 ———.
Lewis Cass, Frontier Soldier. Bath, Mich.: Enterprise Press, 1980. 176 p.

The fictionalized biography of Lewis Cass (1782–1866) from his boyhood, to his work as Governor of the Michigan Territory, and to his role as U.S. Senator. Partially set in Detroit.

Juvenile.

167A ———.
Tall Annie. Laingsburg, Mich.: Enterprise Press, 1987. 108 p.

The fictionalized biography of Ana Klobuchar Clemenc (1888–1956), daughter of Slovenian immigrants, who worked for Socialist causes and was an important figure in the 1913 Camulet copper miners' strike in the Upper Peninsula.

Juvenile.

Mi MiAllG MiD MiMtpT-C MiU

168 Burton, Frederick Russell 1861–1909

Redcloud of the Lakes. New York: G. W. Dillingham Co., 1909. 374 p.

The chronicle of three generations of an Ojibwa clan and the effect of the coming of the white man has on them. Set in the Lake Huron and Lake Superior areas.

Black, 38.

Mi MiMtpT-C NNC OU ViU

169 Busch, Niven 1903–1991
The Hate Merchant. New York: Simon and Schuster, 1953. 338 p.

A bogus radio evangelist preaching a gospel of hate comes to Detroit in 1943 where his message is partly responsible for the riot that year. Partially set in Detroit.

Black, 39.

170 Bushnell, William H. 1823–1909?
The Beautiful Scout; or, The Indian Maiden's Sacrifice. A Tale of the Lake Country. Boston: Elliott, Thomes & Talbot, 1868. 97 p.

Set in Detroit and on Mackinac Island.

Copy not seen.

IaU

171 Buten, Howard
Burt. New York: Holt, Rinehart and Winston, 1981. 156 p.

The story of an eight-year-old boy whose psychiatric misdiagnosis leads to his institutionalization. Set in northwestern Detroit in the late 1950s.

MiAllG MiD MiFliL MiMtpT-C MiWar

172 Butler, Beverly Kathleen 1932–
The Lion and the Otter. New York: Dodd, Mead & Co., 1957. 275 p.

A young French woman who falls in love with one of the British soldiers at Fort Detroit helps the garrison during Pontiac's siege in 1763.

Juvenile.

Mi MiCad MiD MiDW OCl

173 Buzzelli, Elizabeth Kane 1937–
Gift of Evil. New York: Bantam Books, 1983. 301 p.

When an unassuming Detroit woman begins to have dreams in which she sees murder victims, she becomes a celebrity, but death begins to stalk her friends and family.

Mystery.

MiGr CSj IC TxAu UM

174 Byfield, Barbara Ninde 1930–
Forever Wilt Thou Die. Garden City, N.Y.: Doubleday & Co., 1976. 174 p.

(Crime Club)

The wife of a Cleveland sausage magnate is murdered at a reunion party. Set in the Upper Peninsula town of "Goodhaven" (Fairport?).

Mystery.

C

175 Cadwell, Clara Gertrude
De Barr's Friends, or Number Seventeen. Trip to Lake Superior with a Romance. Founded Upon Facts. Cleveland: The Ohio Farmer, 1881. 142 p.

On route to Duluth aboard an excursion ship, a young man falls in love with a farm girl who has a past. Twelve pages are set in Detroit, Sault Ste. Marie, Marquette, and Houghton.

MiMtpT-C MnHi OBgU OCl OOxM

176 Caesar, Eugene Lee 1927–
Mark of the Hunter by Gene Caesar. New York: Sloane, 1953. 250 p.

A young ex-Marine quits the University of Michigan and takes a job as caretaker at a lodge. Set in and near "Vurden's Mill" in northern Michigan in the late 1940s.

Black, 40.

Mi MiA MiAlp MiBatK MiMtpT-C

177 [————].
King of the Harem Heaven. The Amazing True Story of a Daring Charlatan Who Ran A Virgin Love Cult in America by Anthony Sterling [pseud.]. Derby, Conn.: Monarch Books, 1960. 159 p.

(Monarch Americana Books, MA300)

The fictionalized and sensationalized story of Benjamin Purnell (1861–1927), the founder of the House of David, a religious sect. Set partially in Benton Harbor.

Mi MiD MiKW NN

178 [————].
Harem Island. The Astounding True Story of a Self-Proclaimed Saint Who Made Religion a Business and Turned Sin Into a Virtue by Anthony Sterling [pseud.]. Derby, Conn.: Monarch Books, 1961. 140 p.

(Monarch Americana Books, MA310)

The fictionalized and sensationalized story of James Jesse Strang (1813–1856) and his founding of a Mormon kingdom on Beaver Island in the 1840s.

MiD MiKW

179 Calvert, Patricia 1931–
Picking up the Pieces. New York: Charles Scribner's Sons, 1993. 166 p.

Confined to a wheelchair after an accident, a teenage girl learns to cope with disability. Set on "Frenchman's Island" in the Upper Peninsula.

Juvenile.

180 Cameron, Donald Clough 1906–1954
White for a Shroud. New York: Published for Mystery House by S. Curl, 1947. 224 p.

A newspaper reporter becomes involved in the murder of the owner of a financially insecure paper mill. Set in "Red Rock" in the Upper Peninsula.

Mystery.

MiGr-L CLO IC OC ScCF

181 Campbell, Scott 1945–
Touched. New York: Bantam Books, 1996. 313 p.

A twelve-year-old boy tells his parents that a neighbor man has been sexually molesting him; the story is then told by four of the persons involved. Set in Jackson.

182 Cannon, Bettie Waddell 1922–
A Bellsong for Sarah Raines. New York: Charles Scribner's Sons, 1987. 184 p.

A fourteen-year-old girl's alcoholic father commits suicide, and her family then moves back to Kentucky. The first twenty pages are set in Depression-era Detroit.

Juvenile.

183 Caputo, Philip 1941–
Indian Country. New York: Bantam Books, 1987. 419 p.

A psychologically disturbed Vietnam veteran tries to put his life back together in the Upper Peninsula. Set in and around "Vieux Desert," near Marquette.

184 Card, Orson Scott 1951–
Red Prophet. New York: Tom Doherty Associates, 1988. 311 p.

(Tales of Alvin Maker, book 2)

In an America with an alternate history, a young man possesses occult powers of magic and healing. Set partially along "Lake Mizogan" (Lake Michigan) and in Detroit in the 1810s.

Sequel to *Seventh Son.*

Science fiction.

Carey, Elisabeth *see* Magoon, Carey, pseud.

185 Carmichael, Jack B.
A New Slain Knight; a Short Novel. Mason, Mich.: Dynamics Press, n.d. 91 p.

A retired African-American army officer and CIA operative passes along coded messages in the guise of erotic poetry before being murdered. Set in Grand Ledge.

Mystery.

MiGr-L

186 ———.
Black Knight; the Second Short Novel. Mason, Mich.: Dynamics Press, 1991. 89 p.

Friends and relations of a murdered CIA agent try to discover the reasons behind his death. Set partially in Midland and Grand Ledge.

Sequel to *A New Slain Knight.*

Mystery.

MiGr-L

187 ———.
Tales of the Cousin. Mason, Mich.: Dynamics Press, 1992. 77 p.

The nephew of a slain CIA agent continues the search for his uncle's murderer and the reason for the killing. Partially set in Midland and Grand Ledge.

Sequel to *Black Knight.*

Mystery.

MiGr-L

188 ———.
Memoirs of the Great Gorgeous. Mason, Mich.: Dynamics Press, 1992. 49 p.

The mystery of a murdered African-American CIA agent is solved, with secrets and relationships revealed. Partially set in Midland and Grand Ledge.

Sequel to *Tales of the Cousin.*

Mystery.

MiGr-L

189 Carr, Annie Roe, pseud.
Nan Sherwood at Pine Camp; or, The Old Lumberman's Secret. New York: George Sully & Co., 1916. 246 p.

(Nan Sherwood, no. 1)

While staying with her lumberman uncle, teenage Nan Sherwood helps him settle a boundary dispute with a conniving villain. Mostly set in "Hobart Forks" in Marquette County.

"Annie Roe Carr" is a Stratemeyer Syndicate pseudonym.

Juvenile.

MiAllG MoU ViR

190 ———.
Nan Sherwood at Lakeview Hall; or, The Mystery of the Haunted

Boathouse. New York: George Sully &
Co., 1916. 243 p.

(Nan Sherwood, no. 2)

Nan and her chum Bess attend a girls'
boarding school in "Freeling" on Lake
Huron and have many adventures involving an arrogant classmate and a
destitute orphan.

Juvenile.

MiAllG

191 ———.
*Nan Sherwood's Winter Holidays; or,
Rescuing the Runaways.* New York:
George Sully & Co., 1916. 248 p.

(Nan Sherwood, no. 3)

While taking the train home from
Lakeview Hall in "Freeling," Nan and
her chum Bess become stranded in a
blizzard and help locate two runaway
girls. Partially set in Michigan.

Juvenile.

MiAllG ViR

192 Carr, Harriett Helen 1899–
Where the Turnpike Starts. New York:
Macmillan Co., 1955. 216 p.

A fifteen-year-old girl arriving from
New York State with her family adjusts
to her new life on the Michigan frontier.
Set mostly in Jonesville in 1835.

Juvenile.

Mi MiAllG MiD MiMtpT-C MiOC

193 ———.
The Mystery of Ghost Valley. New
York: Macmillan Co., 1962. 149 p.

An eleven-year-old boy visiting his
Pennsylvania relatives becomes interested in a mystery concerning an old
house. Twenty pages are set in Detroit.

Juvenile.

MiD MiEaj MiNhL MiWar OBgU

Carra, Emma, pseud. *see* Spenser, Avis S.

194 Carroll, Joellyn, pseud.
A Flight of Splendor. New York: Dell
Publishing Co., 1983. 187 p.

(Candlelight Ecstasy Romance, no.
159)

A young socialite whose inheritance is
controlled by her grandmother works
as an assistant to a handsome ornitholo-
gist. Set in Paradise in the Upper Peninsula.

"Joellyn Carroll" is the joint pseudonym of Joanne Bremer and Carol I.
Wagner.

Romance.

MiAllG MiInr OBgU ViN

195 Carroll, Marisa, pseud.
Gathering Place. Toronto: Harlequin
Books, 1988. 299 p.

(Harlequin Superromance, no. 318)

A nurse misses the child her family
forced her to put up for adoption years
earlier, and falls in love with a man with
a son. Partially set on Mackinac Island.

"Marisa Carroll" is the joint pseudonym of Marian F. Scharf and Carol I.
Wagner.

Romance.

MiAllG MiGr MoK OBgU WAPL

196 ———.
Ties That Bind. Toronto: Harlequin
Books, 1989. 250 p.

(Harlequin American Romance, no.
286)

A man unable to face life and looking
for solitude rents a cabin from an at-

tractive conservation officer. Set in the Marquette area in the Upper Peninsula.

Romance.

MiAllG InG MoK NjMlA OBgU

197 ———.
Refuge from Today. Toronto: Harlequin Books, 1990. 301 p.

(Harlequin Superromance, no. 426)

A Vietnam veteran tries to cope with the memories of the war by devoting himself to the study of endangered birds. Set in the Munising area in the Upper Peninsula.

Book 2 of the author's trilogy, *Saigon Legacy.*

Romance.

MiAllG MiGr MiWar OXe USl

198 ———.
The Man Who Saved Christmas. Toronto: Harlequin Books, 1996. 298 p.

(Harlequin Superromance, no. 718)

An Ohio policeman comes to the aid of a pregnant woman and her two children when a fire destroys their home and possessions. Set in "North Star" in the Upper Peninsula.

Romance.

MiAllG IArlh InE OXe WM

199 Carse, Robert 1903–1971
The Beckoning Waters. New York: Scribner, 1953. 438 p.

The story of the rise of an Irish sailor, from a hand on a schooner to a Great Lakes shipping tycoon, between 1876 and 1932. Set in a variety of Michigan ports.

Black, 41.

Mi MiAllG MiD MiEM MiMtpT-C

200 Carter, Herbert
The Boy Scouts on Sturgeon Island; or, Marooned Among the Game-Fish Poachers. New York: A. L. Burt Co., 1914. 250 p.

(Boy Scout Series, no. 7)

A group of Boy Scouts on a camping expedition discover an illegal fishing enterprise on "Sturgeon Island" in Lake Superior.

St. George Rathborne has been suggested as the author.

Juvenile.

Mi MiEM NcD OU OYU

Carthew, Annick Hivert *see* Hivert-Carthew, Annick

201 Caslow, Winfield H. d.1969
The Sob-Squad. Grand Rapids: Grand Rapids Calendar Co., 1928. 307 p.

The economic ruin of local storekeepers looms when the townspeople begin buying through mail-order catalogs. Set in the village of "Pomoroy" near Grand Rapids.

Mi MiAllG MiGr MiMtpT-C MiU

202 Catherwood, Mary Hartwell 1847–1902
The White Islander. New York: Century Co., 1893. 164 p.

During the massacre of the English garrison at Fort Michilimackinac in 1763, an Ojibwa chief helps a French resident conceal Alexander Henry (1739–1824), an English fur-trader.

Black, 42. Streeter, 621. Wright III, 952.

Mi MiD MiEM MiKW MiMtpT-C

203 Catton, Bruce 1899–1978
Banners at Shenandoah: A Story of Sheridan's Fighting Cavalry. Garden City, N.Y.: Doubleday & Co., 1955. 254 p.

A seventeen-year-old boy joins the 2nd Michigan Cavalry and becomes General Philip Sheridan's (1831–1888) orderly. Partially set in "Pine Bay" (Benzonia) and Grand Rapids.

Juvenile.

204 Cauffman, Josef Gardner 1900–
Half a Day's Journey. N.p.: Living Arts Publishing, n.d. 67 p.

The fictionalized memoirs of the boyhood and early manhood of the author, which describe small-town life in Dowagiac from 1905 to 1920.

MiBatW MiEM

205 Caval, Patrice
Girls in Bondage. N.p.?: Publishers Export, 1967.

Supposedly set in Detroit, this novel is listed in Allen Hubin's *Crime Fiction II: A Comprehensive Bibliography, 1749–1990* (New York: Garland, 1994).

Mystery.

Copy not seen; copy not located.

206 Caylor, Edward Hamilton
The Late Dr. Sedgwick and the Spirit Medium (Based Upon Facts). A Fascinating Narrative Revealing in a Story a Comprehensive and Concise Outline of Spirit Philosophy and the Methods Employed by Mediums to Foist It Upon a Credulous Public Together with a Chapter on Psychic Law (Glossary Appended). By Rev. E. H. Caylor. Dayton, Ohio: United Brethren Publishing House, 1900. 100 p.

The lengthy title summarizes the subject and purpose of the novel. Set in Detroit and the nearby town of "B———."

MiGr-L GEU-T ODaTS WU

207 Céline, Louis-Ferdinand 1894–1961
Voyage au Bout de la Nuit. Paris: Denoël et Steele, 1932. 623 p.

The adventures of a disaffected and cynical Frenchman, primarily based on the author's own life. Fourteen pages are set in the Detroit automobile factories of the late 1920s.

In French.

English translation by John H. P. Marks published as *Journey to the End of the Night* (Boston: Little, Brown, 1934).

CU ICU InGrD MnU RPB

208 Chafets, Ze'ev 1947–
The Bookmakers by Zev Chafets. New York: Random House, 1995. 261 p.

A young author suffering from writer's block after his acclaimed first novel is the target of a conspiracy. Partially set in the Detroit suburb of "Oriole."

209 ———.
Hang Time by Zev Chafets. New York: Warner Books, 1996. 305 p.

While touring Israel, two Detroit basketball stars are kidnapped by terrorists; a brother of one of the abductees organizes a rescue mission. Partially set in Detroit.

Mystery.

210 Chambers, Pamela Quint
Family Recipe. New York: Jove Books, 1995. 294 p.

(Homespun Romance)

The local gossips pity a young woman who has lost her family wealth until she meets a widower logger with two children whom she marries. Set in mid-Michigan in the 1880s.

Romance.

MiD MiGr InE OCo WM

———, ed. *see* Winters, Donna M.

211 Chaperon, John
Cry Fear, Cry Anger. New York: Vantage Press, 1988. 270 p.

A gritty story of the police, the criminal element, corruption, revenge, and the limitations of the legal system. Set mostly in Detroit.

Mystery.

Mi MiMtpT-C OU

212 Chapman, Allen, pseud.
The Darewell Chums on a Cruise; or, Fenn Masterson's Odd Discovery. New York: Cupples & Leon, 1909. 248 p.

(Darewell Chums, no. 4)

Four boys on board a Great Lakes freighter discover a group of men smuggling Chinese from Canada. Partially set in Sault Ste. Marie and on the south shore of Lake Superior.

Also published as *Fenn Masterson's Discovery; or, The Darewell Chums on a Cruise.*

"Allen Chapman" is a Stratemeyer Syndicate pseudonym.

Juvenile.

CtY FTS OBgU ViR

213 Chappel, Bernice M. Klein 1910–
In the Palm of the Mitten; a Memory Book of the Early 1900's. Brighton, Mich.: Great Lakes Books, 1981. 271 p.

A fictionalized autobiography and chronicle of the Klein and Avery families in rural Michigan. Set in Livingston County from 1915 to 1923.

Mi MiAllG MiD MiEM MiMtpT-C

214 ———.
Bittersweet Trail; an American Saga of the 1800's. Brighton, Mich.: Great Lakes Books, 1984. 471 p.

A fictionalized historical narrative and chronicle of the Atkins and Avery families between 1836 and 1895. Set in southern and central Michigan.

Mi MiAllG MiBatW MiD MiMtpT

215 ———.
Reap the Whirlwind; a Documentary of Early Michigan. Fowlerville, Mich.: Wilderness Adventure Books, 1987. 412 p.

The history of Michigan as seen through the eyes of members of the fictitious Parker family from 1795 to 1866. Set mostly in Adrian and Owosso.

Mi MiAllG MiBatW MiD MiMtpT-C

216 Chase, Leah May Howland 1891?–
The Song of the Maples. New York: Exposition Press, 1958. 87 p.

A young man from Chicago and a Michigan farm girl fall in love despite a number of hardships and misunderstandings. Set in "Riverdale" near the Raisin River.

Mi MiAllG MiGr MiMtpT-C MiPetN

217 Cheley, Frank Hobart 1889–1941
The Three Rivers Kids, by F. H. Cheley. Cincinnati: Jennings and Graham; New York: Eaton and Mains, 1914. 255 p.

Three young boys experience camp life, have a variety of adventures, and meet new friends while staying at Camp Eberhart near Three Rivers one summer.

Juvenile.

Mi OCl

218 **Childs, Walter C.**
Crisis Corporation. New York: Vantage Press, 1972. 130 p.

A story of corporate politics, incompetent management, and general inefficiency in the Detroit automobile industry where action seems only to be the result of crises.

MiMtpT-C CSdS PBa PWcS

219 **Chipman, William Pendleton** 1854–1937
Roy Gilbert's Search. A Tale of the Great Lakes. New York: A. L. Burt, 1889. 277 p.

While trying to locate missing relatives, two sixteen-year-old boys have many adventures on the Great Lakes. Partially set in Detroit, Sault Ste. Marie, Marquette, and Houghton.

Juvenile.

MiAllG MiDW MiEM MiMtpT OBgU

220 **[Cicala, Theresa]**
If Nothing Happens in the Sky by T. Stellini [pseud.]. West Bloomfield, Mich.: Cielo Publishing, 1996. 369 p.

A middle-aged woman growing apart from her husband and dissatisfied with her life takes an opportunity to travel to Italy. Partially set in Union Lake.

Romance.

MiAllG

220A [————.]
A Full Moon on Christmas Eve by Terry Stellini [pseud.]. West Bloomfield, Mich: Cielo Publishing, 1996. 85 p.

Walking alone early on Christmas day, a middle-aged female journalist meets a mysterious man, and they begin a relationship via fax when she is assigned to Italy. Partially set in West Bloomfield.

Romance.

MiAllG

Clair, Ames, pseud. *see* Codrescu, Andrei

221 **[Clancy, Louise Marks Breitenbach]** 1876–1963
Eleanor of the Houseboat, by Louise M. Breitenbach. Boston: The Page Co., 1916. 300 p.

A fourteen-year-old girl and her family spend a summer on a houseboat where she learns to be less selfish. Set in the Upper Peninsula on "Lake Windermere."

Juvenile.

ViU

222 ————.
Christine of the Young Heart. Boston: Small, Maynard & Co., 1920. 341 p.

Through various experiences, a spoiled young woman finally learns the meaning of love and friendship. Set in Detroit and "Merrivale."

CLU ICarbS MH OU

223 ————.
You're Young But Once. Boston: L. C. Page & Co., 1926. 322 p.

A silk-mill heiress unhappy with her family's wealth and her growing responsibilities assumes a false identity and runs away to Detroit.

Mi MiD MB WU

224 [———].
Love Isn't Important; the Experiences of Gay Elwell, by Louise Jerrold [pseud.]. Boston: Issued for the St. Botolph Society by L. C. Page & Co., 1932. 318 p.

A young hatcheck girl at a posh nightclub plans to move up in society by marrying a rich man, but ultimately marries a poor inventor. Set in Detroit.

Romance.

DLC NN

225 [———].
I'll Marry Tomorrow, by Louise Jerrold [pseud.]. New York: Greenberg, Publisher, 1936. 256 p.

A self-sacrificing young woman caters to her overbearing mother and beautiful selfish sister, and endures many heartaches before finding happiness. Set in Detroit.

Romance.

DLC

226 [———].
Till You Find Love, by Louise Jerrold [pseud.]. New York: Greenberg, Publisher, 1937. 252 p.

Set in Detroit and its northern suburbs.

Copy not seen.

Romance.

DLC

227 Clark, A. Arnold 1861–1891
Beneath the Dome; a Posthumous Novel. Chicago: Schulte Publishing Co., 1894. 361 p.

A young man obtains a clerkship in the State Department of Labor and studies law before being disillusioned by politics. Set in "Capitol City" (Lansing).

Wright III, 1049.

Mi MiAlbC MiAllG MiU

Clark, Ada R. E., joint author *see* E.L.T. Club

Clark, Al C., pseud. *see* Goines, Donald

228 [Clark, Charles Dunning] 1843–1892
Red Lightning; or, The Black League. A Tale of the Trading-Posts in 1760. By W. J. Hamilton [pseud.]. New York: Beadle and Adams, 1872. 96 p.

(Beadle's Dime Novels, no. 248)

In 1763, an English scout at Fort Detroit deals with treacherous Frenchmen and their conspiracies, rescues his fiancée, and survives Pontiac's siege.

Reprinted in 1881 under the same title in Beadle's Pocket Novels series, no. 181.

Dime novel.

Black, 44.

MiU IaU DLC

229 Clark, David
Goodbye, Yesterday. New York: Vantage Press, 1988. 287 p.

Cited in a now-lost source, this novel supposedly has eighteen pages set in Grand Rapids.

Copy not located.

230 Clark, Geoffrey D. 1940–
Jackdog Summer. Davis, Calif.: Hi Jinx Press, 1996. 224 p.

A student tries to decide on the course of his life while home during the summer of 1959 with his family and friends. Set in "Ermine Falls" in Kalkaska County and at "Central State University" (Central Michigan University) in "Mt. Haven" (Mt. Pleasant).

MiAllG IC

231 Clark, Jacob Wendell 1878–
In the Sight of God. Chicago: Covici-McGee Co., 1924. 369 p.

Stigmatized by her illegitimacy, a woman overcomes societal conventions to become a leading expert in eugenics. Set in Calumet in the Upper Peninsula.

Black, 45.

Mi MiHM ICarbS KyLoU OU

232 ———.
White Wind. New York: J. H. Sears & Co., 1927. 338 p.

The story of a miner's son who leaves Calumet for college, World War I, and ultimately Paris before returning to marry the girl he loves.

Black, 46.

MiHM AAP KyLoU OU ViR

Clavers, Mary, pseud. *see* Kirkland, Caroline Matilda Stansbury

233 Clawson, Troy E.
Mrs. McBane's Wolf and the Dutchman's Goat. Grand Rapids: Patterson Printing Co., 1920. 161 p.

The story of a teenage farm boy and his progress through the rural school at "Poverty Huddle" (Monterey Center) in Allegan County between 1909 and 1912.

MiAllG

Cleveland, Clifford S., pseud. *see* Goldsmith, David

234 Cline, Leonard Lanson 1893–1929
God Head. New York: Viking Press, 1925. 221 p.

An unscrupulous labor agitator finds refuge in a Lake Superior Finnish settlement where, after hearing local folktales, he sets himself up as a demigod.

Black, 48.

Mi MiD MiEM MiHM MiU

235 Cloutier, Helen H. 1909–
Isle Royale Calling. New York: Dodd, Mead, 1957. 215 p.

An Isle Royale forest ranger and his three sons use a ham radio to stay in touch with the mainland, as well as to aid a ship in distress and trap a moose.

Juvenile.

Mi MiD MiDW MiMarqN MiMtpT-C

236 ———.
Murder, Absolutely Murder. Chicago: Chicago Paperback House, 1962. 191 p.

A red-haired beautician makes trouble for a man and his fiancée by involving them in blackmail and eventually murder. Set in Escanaba.

Mystery.

MiAllG CSbC CU-S

237 Coatsworth, Elizabeth Jane 1893–1986
The Last Fort; a Story of the French Voyageurs. Philadelphia: John C. Winston Co., 1952. 250 p.

(Land of the Free)

In 1762 a young man travels with an expedition from Quebec to locate territory not controlled by the British.

Twelve pages are set at Michilimackinac.

Juvenile.

237A Cochon, Jon Poe, pseud.
Heard on an Autumn's Saturday. Edited
by J. Richie Berliss. Ann Arbor: Sarah
Jennings Press, 1987. 111 p.

Allegedly written by a University of
Michigan professor, this satire takes
aim at the football program, coaches,
players, and fans at "Upper Midwest
University" in "Ehsquare" (Ann Arbor).

Subtitle on half-title page: *Football in
Ehsquare, U.S.A.*

MiFli

238 [Codrescu, Andrei] 1946–
The Repentance of Lorraine by Ames
Clair [pseud.]. New York: Pocket
Books, 1976. 207 p.

A young writer, a professor's wife, and
a secretary engaged in a ménage à trois
search for an ancient erotic artifact.
Set in Ann Arbor at the University of
Michigan.

CU-S LNT

Coffin, Peter, pseud. *see* Latimer, Jonathan
Wyatt

239 Cogan, Priscilla 1947–
*Winona's Web: A Novel of Discov-
ery.* Mount Horeb, Wis.: Face to Face
Books, 1996. 280 p.

A psychologist attempts to change the
mind of an elderly Sioux woman who
predicts and welcomes her own imminent death. Set in Suttons Bay on the
Leelanau Peninsula.

MiAllG

Cole, Lois Dwight *see* Dwight, Allan,
pseud.

240 Condon, Helen Browne 1900–
State College. Philadelphia: Penn Publishing Co., 1938. 316 p.

The story of a young woman's freshman year at "State" (University of
Michigan) in "Huron" (Ann Arbor),
particularly her academic progress and
her social life.

Juvenile.

Mi MiEM MiKW IC

241 ———.
Two Career Girls. Philadelphia: Penn
Publishing Co., 1940. 303 p.

Two girls earn money for college by
running a tourist resort in the summer
and have a number of experiences. Set
in "Arrowhead" (Elk Rapids?).

Juvenile.

Mi MiEM IC ViR

242 ———.
Cowbells for Forget-Me-Not. New
York: Thomas Nelson and Sons, 1942.
72 p.

A story of the generally pleasant but
strenuous life of Swiss immigrants
who operate a northern Michigan farm
and the special care they show their
livestock.

Juvenile.

AB CoD IC

243 Conrad, Lawrence Henry 1898–
Temper. New York: Dodd, Mead and
Co., 1924. 305 p.

An Italian immigrant worker experiences noise, dirt, and dehumanizing
labor in a factory and dreams of his
advancement. Set in Detroit.

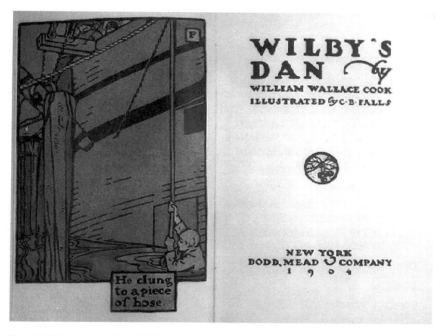

Special Collections, Grand Valley State University Library

Black, 49.

Mi MiAllG MiEM MiYEM MiU

244 Conroy, Jack 1899–1990
The Disinherited. New York: Covici, Friede, 1933. 310 p.

A young man from Missouri travels around the Midwest looking for work during the Depression. Partially set in some Detroit automobile plants.

MiEM MiYEM ICU InLP OU

245 Cook, William Wallace 1867–1933
Wilby's Dan. New York: Dodd, Mead and Co., 1904. 325 p.

A twelve-year-old boy, the son of an es-

caped convict, becomes involved with a gang of confidence men and is falsely accused of murder. Partially set in southwest Michigan.

Mi MiAllG CL

Cooke, John Estes, pseud. *see* Baum, Lyman Frank

246 Coomes, Oliver 1845–1921
The Giant Rifleman; or, Wild Life in the Lumber Regions by Oll Coomes. New York: Beadle and Adams, 1880. 27 p.

(Beadle's Dime Library, no. 99)

A gang of counterfeiters, lumbermen, and mysterious mail carriers are some of the characters in this story, which takes place on the Black River and in South Haven.

Dime novel.

Black, 50.

Mi CU IaU NRU

247 ———.
Long Beard, the Giant Spy; or, Happy Harry, the Wild Boy of the Woods by Oll Coomes. New York: Beadle and Adams, 1881. 27 p.

(Beadle's Dime Library, no. 137)

The adventures and predicaments of the forest scout Long Beard against the British and Hurons during the War of 1812. Set in the Lake St. Clair area.

Dime novel.

Black, 52.

Copy not located.

248 ———.
One-Armed Alf, the Giant Hunter of the Great Lakes; or, The Maid of Michigan. A Romance of the War of 1812 by Oll Coomes. New York: Beadle and Adams, 1881. 21 p.

(Beadle's Dime Library, no. 148)

A frontier scout escapes from the British during the War of 1812. Set at "Point Michigan" in the Muskegon area and on Lake Michigan.

Dime novel.

Black, 53.

IaU NRU

Coomes, Oll *see* Coomes, Oliver

249 **Cooper, Charles Arthur** 1906–1972
We Pass This Way. New York: Exposition Press, 1950. 183 p.

The author fictionalizes some of his experiences as a physician, as well as village life, in the copper and iron mining areas of the Upper Peninsula.

Black, 54.

Mi MiD MiEM MiGr MiWar

250 **Cooper, Gerald Jay**
Safari Home. N.p., 1992. 285 p.

After a world financial crisis strands a man and his son in Africa, they make their way home through chaos and adventures. Partially set on Beaver Island.

Limited to one hundred copies.

MiGr-L

251 ———.
Fox Island. N.p., 1993. 323 p.

A pendant with magical powers and an intergalactic traveller are critical elements in an effort to locate missing "Little Fox Island" in Lake Michigan.

Limited to one hundred copies.

Science fiction.

MiGr-L

252 ———.
Fox Island 2187. N.p., 1994. 201 p.

The means of time travel are discovered in a mysterious station built by aliens on "Little Fox Island" and used to return to the world of 1000 B.C.

Sequel to *Fox Island.*

Limited to one hundred copies.

Science fiction.

MiGr-L

253 ———.
Santa Visits the Cooper Lodge. N.p., 1996. 9 p.

While on a November practice run, Santa becomes lost in a fog and ends up stuck in a swamp where a man and his sons come to his aid. Set in Missaukee County.

Juvenile picture book.

MiGr-L

254 **Cooper, James Fenimore** 1789–1851

The Bee-Hunter; or, The Oak Openings. London: Richard Bentley, 1848. 3 vols.

A woodsman finds himself in the middle of the War of 1812 and a Potawatomi attack with a British spy and an American army messenger. Set in southwestern Michigan.

First American edition published under the title *The Oak Openings; or, The Bee Hunter* (New York: Burgess, Stringer & Co., 1848. 2 vols.)

Black, 55. Streeter, 829. Wright I, 654.

CU CU-S DeU MH ViU

255 **Cooper, Sylvia** 1903–

Thunder Stone. New York: Simon and Schuster, 1955. 243 p.

A Detroit-area ophthalmologist must weigh the medical, moral, and ethical questions of whether to operate on a child without parental consent.

Mi MiD MiLapC MiStc MiU

256 ———.

The Self-Made Man. New York: Random House, 1960. 246 p.

A sixty-year-old man reflects on his life and the circumstances that led to his successful rise in the trucking business. Set in Detroit.

Black, 56.

Mi MiAllG MiD MiStc MiWar

257 **Copeland, Lori** 1941–

Fool Me Once. New York: Dell Publishing, 1990. 387 p.

A Philadelphia debutante comes to Michigan to sell the lumber company she inherited but suffers amnesia in a train accident. Set in "Watersweet" (Watersmeet?) in the 1870s.

Romance.

MiAllG MiD MiFli MiGr MiPh

258 **Corbett, Sidney** 1891–1961

The Cruise of the Gull-Flight. New York: Longmans, Green and Co., 1937. 367 p.

Five cousins taking a summer sailing cruise to Georgian Bay on a schooner via the Detroit River run afoul of smugglers. Partially set on Grosse Ile.

Juvenile.

Mi MiAllG MiD MiEM MiStc

259 ———.

The Gull-Flight Sails Again. New York: Longmans, Green and Co., 1939. 328 p.

The same five cousins introduced in the preceding book take another adventurous cruise on the schooner, this time to the West Indies. Ten pages are set on Grosse Ile and in Detroit.

Sequel to *The Cruise of the Gull-Flight*.

Juvenile.

Mi MiAlbC MiD MiDW OCl

260 **Corcoran, Charles**

Blackrobe. Milwaukee: Bruce Publishing Co., 1937. 377 p.

The fictionalized life and explorations of the Jesuit missionary Jacques Marquette (1637–1675). Partially set at St. Ignace and Sault Ste. Marie.

Mi MiAlbC MiGr-L InFw MnU

Corey, Gayle, pseud. *see* Hauptman,
Elaine

261 Corkey, Alexander 1871–1914
*The Vision of Joy; or, When "Billy"
Sunday Came to Town. A Sequel to
"The Victory of Allan Rutledge."* New
York: H. K. Fly Co., 1913. 319 p.

When the famous evangelist Billy Sunday (1863–1935) visits a small town,
he influences a number of its inhabitants. Set in Bronson in Branch County.

Sequel to *The Victory of Allan Rutledge,* which is set in Iowa.

ArU InWinG MWC OU WPlaU

262 [Coryell, John Russell] 1852?–
1924
*Nick Carter's Battle Against Odds; or,
The Mystery of the Detroit Pawnbroker*
by the Author of "Nicholas Carter."
New York: Street & Smith, 1903. 30 p.

(New Nick Carter Weekly, no. 348)

Detective Nick Carter investigates the
murder of a pawnbroker, which leads
him through a cross section of society.
Set in Detroit.

Dime novel.

MiEM MiMtpT-C MnU

Couch, Sir Arthur Thomas Quiller *see*
Quiller-Couch, Sir Arthur Thomas

263 Coughlin, Joseph Welter 1919–
Jack Dawn and the Vanishing Horses.
Chicago: Van Kampen Press, 1946.
175 p.

A young man solves a mystery involving horses while at an Upper Peninsula camp. Set on the northern shore
of Lake Huron in the Les Cheneaux
Islands area.

Juvenile.

MiEM IWW MoSpA

263A Coughlin, William Jeremiah
1929–1992
The Destruction Committee. London:
Harrap, 1971. 278 p.

Six Vietnam veterans form an organization to murder those they judge to be
dangerous to society and that the legal
system is unable to stop, including the
vice-president elect. Set in Detroit and
other Michigan locales.

Mystery.

Copy not located.

264 ———.
The Stalking Man. New York: Delacorte Press, 1979. 277 p.

A maniacal murderer of women hunts
his victims in a variety of cities and
then turns on the police officer pursuing him. Partially set in Niles, Grand
Rapids, and Detroit.

Mystery.

265 ———.
Day of Wrath. New York: Delacorte
Press, 1980. 346 p.

A group of municipal criminal court
employees are taken hostage by a gang
of urban terrorists. Set in a number of
Michigan locales.

Mystery.

266 ———.
No More Dreams. New York: A & W
Publishers, 1982. 299 p.

The death of one of the U.S. Supreme
Court Justices leads to the investigation
of his possible successor, the dean of
the law school at Michigan State University.

Mystery.

267 ———.

In the Presence of Enemies. London: Sidgwick & Jackson, 1989. 426 p.

A probate attorney is involved with a case contesting a billionaire banker's will. Set in Detroit and the northern Michigan town of "Gladding."

Mystery.

268 ———.

Shadow of a Doubt. New York: St. Martin's Press, 1991. 390 p.

Charley Sloan, attorney and recovering alcoholic, defends a heiress accused of murdering her father. Set in the St. Clair River town of "Pickerel Point" and Detroit.

Mystery.

269 ———.

Death Penalty. New York: Harper-Collins, 1992. 353 p.

Charley Sloan represents a doctor accused of murdering wealthy patients for the benefit of their heirs. Set in "Pickerel Point," Detroit, and "Broken Axe" (Bad Axe).

Mystery.

270 Covert, William Chalmers 1864–1942

Glory of the Pines; a Tale of the Ontonagon. Philadelphia: Westminster Press, 1914. 245 p.

The story, based on the author's personal experiences, of a minister assigned to a vast parish in the Ontonagon area inhabited mostly by lumbermen.

Black, 57.

Mi MiAllG MiHM MiMtpT-C OBgU

271 Cowles, Inez

Ball Four by Inez and Loys Cowles. New York: Pageant Press, 1953. 218 p.

A humorous story about a Detroit couple that buys a cabin and the misadventures that follow. Set in the Upper Peninsula on the Lake Superior shore in the 1930s.

Mi MiAllG MiFli MiMtpT-C InE

Cowles, Loys, joint author *see* Cowles, Inez

272 Cragin, Isabella Sophronia

Saint Peter and Tom; or, Two Unlikely Heroes. Boston and Chicago: Congregational Sunday-School and Publishing Society, 1888. 196 p.

A Sunday-school tract concerning two boys who journey through Michigan to the Upper Peninsula copper mines and the temptations they meet along the way.

Juvenile.

DLC MB PPL

273 Crawford, Christina 1939–

Black Widow. New York: William Morrow & Co., 1982. 239 p.

A beautiful controlling woman is challenged by her twenty-year-old stepdaughter. Partially set in the Upper Peninsula at a hunting lodge.

274 Crawford, James Edward

Officer in Trouble: The Detroit Cop Who Refused To Play the Games. Orlando, Fla.: T.A.T. Publications, 1992. 204 p.

The fictionalized autobiography of a Detroit policeman who tried to stay honest despite pressure from his corrupt fellow officers to take bribes and payoffs.

MiU FWpR

275 Crawford, Linda 1938–
Something To Make Us Happy. New York: Simon and Schuster, 1978. 256 p.

A family chronicle of Scots immigrants and their assimilation into American society from 1908 to 1932. Half of the novel is set in Detroit.

276 Creeth, Edmund Homer 1928–
Deerlover by E. H. Creeth. Woodstock, Vt.: Foul Play Press/Countryman Press, 1987. 290 p.

An animal rights activist stalks and kills hunters during deer season. Set in Au Gres and the Leelanau Peninsula.

Mystery.

Mi MiAllG MiBatW MiMtpT-C
MiStc

277 Crofoot, Frederic S.
Detroit Unveiled. A Graphic and Startling Revelation of the Mysteries of Michigan's Metropolis. Detroit: Sunday World Print, 1887. 86 p.

A loosely connected narrative describing the dark side of Detroit, emphasizing everything from prostitution to abortion. This piece of sensational literature was written by a former editor of the *Detroit Sunday Sun.*

Streeter, 863. Wright III, 1305.

MiD DLC

278 Cross, Genevieve 1910–
The Engine That Lost Its Whistle. New York: Cross Publications, 1945. 28 p.

A story, based on an actual event, of the Fruit Belt Train, which ran from South Haven to Kalamazoo in the 1890s carrying produce to city markets.

Juvenile picture book.

MiKW IC InU ViR WM

279 ——.
Tommy and the Indians. New York: Cross Publications, 1950. 35 p.

The young son of pioneer settlers encounters and befriends a group of Potawatomis. Set in the Paw Paw area around 1840.

Juvenile.

Mi MiMack MiWar IC InG

280 Cross, Melinda
The Call of Home. London: Mills & Boon, 1986. 186 p.

A troubled wildlife painter from California finds refuge at her father's cabin near the Upper Peninsula town of "Potter" and soon finds a love interest.

Romance.

IArlh InFrf MW

281 Crowley, Mary Catherine 1869–1920
A Daughter of New France; with Some Account of the Gallant Sieur Cadillac and His Colony on the Detroit. Boston: Little, Brown, and Co., 1901. 409 p.

The brother-in-law of Antoine de la Mothe Cadillac (1656–1730) recounts the latter's appointment to Michilimackinac and the founding of Detroit in 1701.

Black, 58. Streeter, 869.

Mi MiAllG MiD MiMtpT-C MiU

282 ——.
The Heroine of the Strait; a Romance of Detroit in the Time of Pontiac. Boston: Little, Brown, and Co., 1902. 373 p.

The story of Pontiac's (d. 1769) attempt to capture Detroit in 1763 and a French family's effort to warn the British garrison of the Ottawa chief's plan.

Black, 59. Streeter, 870.

Mi MiAllG MiD MiMtpT-C MiU

283 ———.

Love Thrives in War; a Romance of the Frontier in 1812. Boston: Little, Brown, and Co., 1903. 340 p.

The story of General Hull's surrender of Detroit to the British in the War of 1812, as well as of a young woman who faces many perils to save the man she loves.

Black, 60. Streeter, 871.

Mi MiAllG MiD MiFli MiStc

284 [Cruden, Robert Lunan] 1910–

Conveyor by James Steele [pseud.]. New York: International Publishers, 1935. 222 p.

A young man endures the brutal exploitation of workers in the Detroit automobile factories and ultimately finds solidarity in the union during the Depression.

Black, 252.

MiAllG MiDW MiEM MiFli OBgU

285 [Culby, Jill] 1948–

Kisses from Heaven by Jeanne Grant [pseud.]. New York: Berkley Publishing Group, 1984. 182 p.

(Second Chance at Love, no. 167)

A woman who is a whirlwind of efficiency at the office lives a chaotic life at home until a persistent handyman insinuates himself into her life. Set in Detroit.

Romance.

Mi MiAllG MiInr IChamL OBgU

286 [———**].**

Sunburst by Jeanne Grant [pseud.]. New York: Berkley Publishing Group, 1984. 183 p.

(To Have and To Hold, no. 14)

A concerned couple try to save their failing marriage through a variety of ways. Partially set in the Upper Peninsula on the Lake Superior shore.

Romance.

Mi OBgU

287 [———**].**

Wintergreen by Jeanne Grant [pseud.]. New York: Berkley Publishing Group, 1984. 183 p. (Second Chance at Love, no. 184)

A woman whose dead husband had accused her of infidelity falls in love with her brother-in-law, who does not believe her version of the past. Set in Ann Arbor.

Romance.

Mi MiAllG MiInr IGenD OBgU

288 [———**].**

Silver and Spice by Jeanne Grant [pseud.]. New York: Berkley Publishing Group, 1984. 184 p. (Second Chance at Love, no. 220)

A roguish man with a penchant for volatile financial investments pursues an attractive, conservative woman banker. Partially set in Grosse Pointe.

Romance.

MiAllG IGenD OBgU TxAu

289 [———**].**

Cupid's Confederates by Jeanne Grant [pseud.]. New York: Berkley Publishing Group, 1984. 181 p.

(To Have and To Hold, no. 41)

A widow moves in with her daughter and son-in-law on their southwestern Michigan farm and proceeds to upset their lives. Set in "Silver Oaks" near Lake Michigan.

Romance.

MiAllG OBgU

290 [———].
Minx by Jennifer Greene [pseud.]. New York: Silhouette Books, 1987. 189 p.

(Silhouette Desire, no. 366)

A divorced woman inherits a mink farm from her uncle and, not wanting it, decides to set the animals free. Set in the Upper Peninsula town of "Silverwater."

Romance.

MiAllG AzG MoK NRU OBgU

291 [———].
Lady of the Island by Jennifer Greene [pseud.]. New York: Silhouette Books, 1988. 189 p. (Silhouette Desire, no. 463)

A woman—who is wanted by the police and sought by a violent ex-husband—and her young son find refuge on an isolated island in the middle of "Clover Lake."

Romance.

MiAllG MiGr InG OBgU PNo

292 [———].
Devil's Night by Jennifer Greene [pseud.]. New York: Silhouette Books, 1989. 251 p. (Silhouette Intimate Moments, no. 305)

A firefighter investigates a series of suspicious fires and becomes involved with a psychologist who is threatened by a pyromaniac. Set in Detroit.

Romance.

MiAllG MiGr IChamL MoK OBgU

293 [———].
Slow Dance by Jennifer Greene [pseud.]. New York: Silhouette Books, 1990. 187 p. (Silhouette Desire, no. 600)

A fruit farmer comes upon an expectant mother on a back road and helps deliver her premature baby. Set on a peach farm in southwestern Michigan.

Romance.

MiAllG IChamL OBgU OCo NRU

294 [———].
A Groom for Red Riding Hood by Jennifer Greene [pseud.]. New York: Silhouette Books, 1994. 185 p.

(Silhouette Desire, no. 893)

Her marriage plans ruined, a young woman flees to an isolated town to work in a bar but meets a handsome wolf researcher. Set in "Eagle Falls" in the Upper Peninsula.

Publisher's subseries: *Jilted!*

Romance.

MiAllG IChamL InMu OXe WM

295 Cuomo, George Michael 1929–
Family Honor; an American Life. Garden City, N.Y.: Doubleday & Co., 1983. 591 p.

The story of the rise of a man involved in the American labor movement from 1911 to 1937. Partially set in Flint during the 1936 General Motors strike.

296 Curtis, Christopher Paul
The Watsons Go to Birmingham—1963. New York: Delacorte Press, 1995. 211 p.

A ten-year-old African-American boy tells amusing stories about his family, their life in Flint, and the terror of racism they encounter when they visit his grandmother in Alabama in 1963.

Juvenile.

297 Curtis, Rebecca S.

Charlotte Avery on Isle Royale. Mount Horeb, Wis.: Midwest Traditions, 1995. 191 p.

In 1872, a young girl accompanies her family to Isle Royale, where her father works for a mining company, and hears the lore of the island from many of the inhabitants.

Juvenile.

MiAllG MiFli MiHM MiKW MiMtpT-C

298 Curwood, James Oliver 1878–1927

The Courage of Captain Plum. Indianapolis: Bobbs-Merrill Co., 1908. 319 p.

The captain of a Great Lakes sloop stops at Beaver Island in 1856 and rescues two women from James Strang (1813–1856) and his Mormon colony.

Black, 62.

Mi MiAllG MiFli MiMtpT-C MiStc

299 ———.

Green Timber. Completed by Dorthea A. Bryant. Garden City, N.Y.: Doubleday, Doran and Co., 1930. 299 p.

A Detroit gangster marked for death by the Mob is saved through the good offices of the Michigan northern woods and the love of a young woman. Set in Detroit and Roscommon.

Black, 63.

Mi MiChv MiEM MiMtpT-C MiStc

300 Curzon, Daniel 1938–

Something You Do in the Dark. New York: Putnam, 1971. 351 p.

The grim story of a mentally disturbed gay man who is persecuted by a particularly vindictive vice squad officer. Set in Detroit.

A revised edition was published under the same title by Ashley Books (Port Washington, N.Y.) in 1979.

Mi MiD MiKW MiSsL MiU

301 Cushman, Dan 1909–

The Grand and the Glorious. New York: McGraw-Hill, 1963. 214 p.

A variety of episodes during the 1916 Fourth of July celebration are recounted by the teenage son of the local pickle-packer. Set in "Red Wing" in western Michigan.

302 Cuthrell, Faith Baldwin 1893–1978

Love's a Puzzle by Faith Baldwin. New York: Farrar & Rinehart, 1933. 300 p.

A young man whose father's stockbrokerage business failed in the 1929 crash goes to work in his grandfather's Detroit auto plant.

Romance.

Black, 64.

MiGr-L KAS OC NR

303 Cutler, Hal L. 1873–

Ne-Bo-Shone (At the Bend in the River). In Which Is Incorporated an Indian Lullaby "Ne-bo-shone" Composed by Lexie Woodruff Abbott. Chicago: Reilly & Britton Co., 1917. 315 p.

The fact-based chronicle of a settler's life and the establishment of a sportsman's camp at a bend in the Pine River from 1872 to 1912. Set in Manistee and Lake Counties.

Black, 61.

Mi MiAllG MiEM MiGr MiMtpT-C

D

304 Dailey, Janet 1944–
Enemy in Camp. London: Mills & Boon, 1980. 187 p.

A young woman tries to protect her father from a ruthless journalist but becomes romantically involved with him. Set in Detroit and on Mackinac Island.

Romance.

MiInr MW TxH

305 Dalm, P. A.
Een Immigrant (Naar het Engelsch). Kalamazoo: Dalm Printing Co., n.d. 277 p.

An English immigrant finds work as a journalist and becomes involved in a labor dispute at his newspaper. Set in "Bronson" (Kalamazoo) in the 1910s and 1920s.

In Dutch.

Mi MiGrC MiMtpT-C

Dalton, Jackie, pseud. *see* Troutman, Jacqueline D.

306 Daly, Edwin 1936–
Some Must Watch. New York: Charles Scribner's Sons, 1956. 306 p.

The story of a young man's rapid maturity resulting from an affair with a married woman and his father's suicide. Partially set at the "Macaboo Inn," a summer resort in Holland.

MiAdS MiD MiDW MiEM MiU

307 ———.
A Legacy of Love. New York: Charles Scribner's Sons, 1958. 310 p.

Romantic entanglements involve numerous people one summer. Set in "Sheffield" on Lake Michigan (probably located between Muskegon and Ludington).

MiBatW MiPh MiRos InG OCl

308 D'Amato, Barbara Steketee 1938–
Hard Tack: A Cat Marsala Mystery. New York: Charles Scribner's Sons, 1991. 229 p.

A female reporter, Cat Marsala, investigates a murder aboard a luxury sailboat in the Michigan waters of southern Lake Michigan. The last ten pages are set in Holland.

309 ———.
Hard Christmas: A Cat Marsala Mystery. New York: Scribner, 1995. 282 p.

Invited to spend Thanksgiving at a Christmas tree farm, Cat Marsala investigates a mysterious death apparently caused by a crop-dusting aircraft. Set in the Holland area.

Mystery.

310 Damrell, Joseph
Gift: A Novel of the Upper Peninsula. St. Cloud, Minn.: North Star Press of St. Cloud, 1992. 120 p.

An old trapper who shot at snowmobilers who strayed onto his traplines is pursued by the state police. Set in Ewen and its environs in the Upper Peninsula.

Mi MiAllG MiHM MiKW MiMtpT-C

Daring, Hope, pseud. *see* Johnson, Anna

311 Daudert, Charles
In the Wake of the Northern Lights.
Chicago: Hansa-Hewlett Publishing
Co., 1988. 360 p.

A young Austrian immigrant working
as a fisherman rescues the crew of a
freighter during a fierce Lake Michigan storm. Partially set in "Southport"
(South Haven) in 1940.

MiCad MBU

d'Auriac, Jules Berlioz *see* Auriac, Jules
Berlioz d'

312 [Davenport, Willard Goss] 1843–
1919
*The Isle of the Lake, an "Outing" Story
for Boys* by Willard Goss [pseud.].
Elgin, Ill.: David C. Cook Publishing
Co., 1903. 95 p.

A dozen boys from a Lake Huron town
are shipwrecked on a Lake Superior
island while en route to the 1893 Chicago World's fair in a schooner. Twelve
pages are set in Michigan.

Juvenile.

Mi KHayF OBgU PWcS UCS

313 Davis, Barbara J.
In the Way: A Novel of Love and Loss.
New Brighton, Minn.: Finnish Ameri-
cana, 1993. 320 p.

A seven-year-old is terrorized by her
new stepmother. Set in the Finnish
settlement of Kaleva in northwestern
Michigan from 1910 to 1920.

Mi MiAllG MiBatW MiMu MiT

314 Davis, Dorothy Salisbury 1916–
The Judas Cat. New York: Charles
Scribner's Sons, 1949. 227 p.

The apparently senseless murder of
an old man exposes old feelings of
hate in a small town. Set in "Hillside"
and "Riverdale" (Hillsdale) in southern
Michigan.

Mystery.

MiGr-L IC InG OCl WSpU

315 ———.
A Town of Masks. New York: Charles
Scribner's Sons, 1952. 190 p.

The murder of a prominent middle-
aged woman affects her childhood acquaintance and the rest of the town in
different ways. Set in the Lake Michigan town of "Campbell's Cove."

Mystery.

Mi MiAllG MiEM MiFli OBgU

316 Davis, Leila E. 1936–
Lover Boy. New York: Avon Books,
1989. 168 p.

(Avon Flare)

An eleventh grader finds his exagger-
ated reputation is an obstacle when
he is attracted to a proper girl. Set in
"Lockwood."

Juvenile.

317 Davis, Verne Theodore 1889–1973
The Time of the Wolves. New York:
William Morrow & Co., 1962. 127 p.

Two Michigan farm boys try a variety
of methods to protect their herd of cattle from wolves. Set in rural Michigan
during one severe winter in the 1870s.

Juvenile.

318 ———.
The Runaway Cattle. New York:
William Morrow & Co., 1965. 128 p.

Two farm boys search the woods and
adjacent lands for their missing cattle,

which seem to have wandered off. Set in western Michigan in the 1890s.

Juvenile.

319 Dean, Frederic Alva 1859–1936
The Heroines of Petosega. New York: Hawthorne Publishing Co., 1889. 283 p.

The story of a lost civilization in northern Michigan and its destruction by a floating mountain. Set in "Petosega" (Petoskey) and "Effelda" (Mackinac Island) around 1000 B.C.

Wright III, 1452.

MiGr MiU CSmH OU PU

Deane, Susan Bendle *see* Bendle, Susan C.

320 Deaner, Janice
Where Blue Begins. New York: Dutton, 1993. 423 p.

A ten-year-old girl tells her family's story of love and deception. The first twenty-one pages are set in Detroit and the remainder in upstate New York.

321 De Angeli, Marguerite Lofft 1889–1987
Copper-Toed Boots. New York: Doubleday, Doran & Co., 1938. 92 p.

The adventures of a ten-year-old boy and his friend, as well as the former's hopes for a dog and special boots. Set in Lapeer in the 1870s.

Juvenile.

Dearborn, Andrew, pseud. *see* Gardner, Lewis J.

DeGroot, John H. *see* Keuning, J.

322 De Jong, David Cornel 1905–1967
Belly Fulla Straw. New York: Alfred A. Knopf, 1934. 321 p.

A family chronicle of Dutch immigrants in which the two sons are soon acclimated to life in the United States, but the father ultimately returns to Holland. Set in Grand Rapids from 1914 to the 1930s.

Black, 66.

Mi MiAllG MiEM MiGr MiMtpT-C

323 ———.
Two Sofas in the Parlor. Garden City, N.Y.: Doubleday, 1952. 253 p.

The story of newly arrived Dutch immigrants and their adjustment to school, employment, their neighborhood, and family life in America. Set in Grand Rapids in 1913.

Black, 67.

Mi MiAllG MiD MiEM MiHolH

324 Delbanco, Nicholas Franklin 1942–

In the Name of Mercy. New York: Warner Books, 1995. 310 p.

A young physician who assisted his wife's suicide becomes the director of a hospice but falls under suspicion when his patients begin dying quickly. Set in "Bellehaven."

Mystery.

325 Dempsey, Vincent
Cabin Boy. New York: Coward-McCann, 1956. 256 p.

The adventures of a young cabin boy on a Great Lakes vessel. Twenty pages are set on the Michigan coast of Lake Superior and in Sault Ste. Marie.

Juvenile.

Mi MiFra MiLapC InFw OCl

326 [Dent, Lester] 1905–1959

The Monsters; a Doc Savage Adventure by Kenneth Robeson [pseud.]. New York: Bantam Books, 1965. 138 p.

(Doc Savage, no. 7)

Doc Savage, possessor of superhuman strength and genius, investigates the breeding of evil giants in the Upper Peninsula. Set partially in "Trapper Lake."

First published in *Doc Savage Magazine* in April 1934.

Mystery.

Mi MiAllG CSbC OBgU PNo

327 Dereske, Jo
Savage Cut. New York: Dell Publishing, 1996. 322 p.

(Ruby Crane Mystery)

A woman returns to her parent's cabin with her teenage daughter and gets caught up in town gossip and murder. Set in "Waters County" in northwestern Michigan.

Mystery.

MiAllG InE MnM OCl USl

328 Derleth, August William 1909–1971
Bright Journey. New York: Charles Scribner's Sons, 1940. 424 p.

(Sac Prairie Saga)

The fictionalized biography of furtrader Hercules Dousman (1800–1868) in the Old Northwest. Partially set on Mackinac Island from 1812 to 1815.

329 ———.
The Captive Island. New York: Duell, Sloan and Pearce, 1952. 189 p.

Two sixteen-year-old boys secretly assist the American forces in the War of 1812. Set on Mackinac Island and in Detroit from 1812 to 1815.

Juvenile.

MiAllG MiMtpT-C MiOC MiSth MiWar

330 ———.
Land of Sky-Blue Waters. New York: Aladdin Books, 1955. 214 p.

The fictionalized biography, adventures, and explorations of Henry Rowe Schoolcraft (1793–1864) as he searches for the source of the Mississippi. Set mostly in Michigan in the 1820s.

Juvenile.

Mi MiAllG MiAlp MiDW MiMarqN

331 ———.
Sweet Land of Michigan. New York: Duell, Sloan and Pearce, 1962. 149 p.

A seventeen-year-old boy volunteers for the Toledo War, becomes a spy, and ultimately joins a surveying expedition. Set in numerous Michigan locales in the 1830s.

Juvenile.

Destouches, Louis-Ferdinand *see* Céline, Louis-Ferdinand

332 [Des Voignes, Jules Verne] 1886–1911
The Novelty Circus Company by Oliver Olney [pseud.]. Philadelphia: George W. Jacobs & Co., 1907. 374 p.

A group of boys whose cleverly produced entertainments earn money for local civic improvement must compete with a real circus for audiences. Set in "Quarry" (Cassopolis) in "LaGrand County" (Cass County), "East Haven," "Trenton," "Deer Rapids," "Corey," and "Prescott" in southwestern Michigan.

Juvenile.

MiU DLC

333 Detroit and Cleveland Navigation Co.

A Hero of Manila; a Summer Trip via Detroit & Cleveland Navigation Company, the Coast Line to Mackinac. Detroit: John Bornman & Son, Printers, 1899. 76 p.

To recover his health, a young Spanish-American War veteran takes a lake cruise from Toledo to Mackinac Island with his aunt and uncle aboard a D&C steamship. The novel is a travelogue and advertising pamphlet.

Streeter, 1396.

Mi MiD MiMtpT-C OBgU

334 ———.

The Spirit of the Inland Seas. A Story of a Summer Tour on the Great Lakes. Detroit: John Bornman & Son, Printers, 1901. 79 p.

A group of seven friends spend their summer holiday on a D&C steamship going from Cleveland to Mackinac Island and enjoy the scenery and accommodations.

Alice Elinor Bowen Bartlett ("Birch Arnold") has been suggested as the author.

MiD NBuBE OO

335 ———.

The Mystery of the Monogram. Story of a Summer Tour on the Great Lakes via the Detroit & Cleveland Navigation Co. Detroit: John Bornman & Son, Printers, 1904. 55 p.

A Scotland Yard detective tries to solve a mystery concerning a missing heir with the D&C steamship line and its voyage to Mackinac Island serving as background.

Alice Elinor Bowen Bartlett ("Birch Arnold") has been suggested as the author.

Mystery.

MiU

336 Detroit and Cleveland Steam Navigation Co.

Col. Clayton's Lake Tour. Detroit: John Bornman & Son, Printers, 1897. 123 p.

A Kentucky colonel, his niece, and nephew travel from Toledo to Mackinac Island aboard a D&C steamship, all the while extolling the magnificent scenery and the virtues of the D&C line.

MiGr DLC

———. *see also* Ingram, Helen K.

337 Detzer, Clarice Nissley 1895–1982

The Island Mail. New York: Harcourt, Brace and Co., 1926. 198 p.

Two girls in a sailboat attempt to deliver mail from the mainland to "Four Wind Island" (probably located in the Beaver Island group).

Juvenile.

Mi OBgU MnU

338 Detzer, Karl William 1891–1988

The Marked Man, a Romance of the Great Lakes. Indianapolis: Bobbs-Merrill, 1927. 322 p.

A young man enters the lighthouse service to overcome his fears and the label of coward. Set in "Madrid Bay," a fishing village on northern Lake Michigan.

Black, 68.

Mi MiAllG MiGr MiKW MiMtpT-C

339 ———.

Pirate of the Pine Lands: Being the Adventures of Young Tom Lansing Afloat and Ashore on the Michigan Frontier in the Years 1852 to 1854, and Particularly His Part in the Historic Matter of King James Strang, the Notorious Great Lakes Pirate, Told Here by Himself from Memory. Indianapolis: Bobbs-Merrill, 1929. 302 p.

The story, set partially on Beaver Island, is summarized in the subtitle.

Juvenile.

Black, 69

MiGr InFw OBgU OSW TNJ

340 DeVries, Peter 1910–1993
Slouching Towards Kalamazoo. Boston: Little, Brown and Co., 1983. 241 p.

The humorous story of a sexually precocious eighth grader who gets his teacher in trouble. Partially set in Kalamazoo.

341 Dickinson, Charles 1951–
Waltz in Marathon. New York: Alfred A. Knopf, 1983. 276 p.

The story of a Flint-area loanshark whose life is complicated by romance, which has made him less ruthless toward deadbeats. Set in "Marathon" between 1920 and 1981.

342 Dickinson, Lulu J. 1874–1962
A Table in the Wilderness. Grand Rapids: Wm. B. Eerdmans Publishing Co., 1959. 244 p.

The chronicle of a Michigan pioneer family from 1818 until the turn of

the century. Set mostly in Iosco, now known as Parkers Corners, in Livingston County.

Mi MiAllG MiDW MiGr MiMtpT-C

343 Dixon, Franklin W., pseud.
The Lone Eagle of the Border; or, Ted Scott and the Diamond Smugglers. New York: Grosset & Dunlap, 1929. 214 p.

(Ted Scott Flying Stories, no. 8)

An intrepid young man foils a gang smuggling diamonds between Canada and the United States and brings them to justice. Set partially in Detroit.

"Franklin W. Dixon" is a Stratemeyer Syndicate pseudonym.

Juvenile.

Mi MiAllG MiD OBgU WU

344 Dobyns, Stephen 1941–
The House on Alexandrine. Detroit: Wayne State University Press, 1990. 234 p.

Searching for his runaway sister, a young Canadian man comes to Detroit in 1973 and takes up residence in a boarding house where he meets a variety of characters.

345 Dodge, Ed
Dau: A Novel of Vietnam. New York: Macmillan, 1984. 243 p.

The story of a young man's tour of duty in Vietnam and the post-traumatic stress disorder from which he suffers after he returns. Partially set in Michigan, probably near Lansing.

346 Doner, Mary Frances 1893–1985
The Dancer in the Shadow: A Love Story. New York: Chelsea House, 1930. 247 p.

A young and dedicated dancer must reluctantly leave her baby with an aunt while on tour with her husband. Twenty pages are set in Detroit.

Romance.

Mi MiAllG OU

346A ———.
The Lonely Heart: A Love Story. New York: Chelsea House, 1930. 215 p.

A young man is expected to take over the running of the family salt business, but he marries an heiress instead and leaves for New York. Partially set in "Barryton" near Port Huron.

Romance.

MiU

347 ———.
Fool's Heaven. A Love Story. New York: Chelsea House, 1932. 249 p.

A young woman passes herself off as the niece of a wealthy old man and falls in love with a rich bachelor. Set in "Castleton" on Lake Huron.

Romance.

Mi MiPh

348 ———.
Forever More; a Love Story. New York: Chelsea House, 1934. 247 p.

A young woman finds herself married to a farmer whom she does not love. Set in "Port Clair," probably a combination of St. Clair and Port Huron.

Romance.

MiAllG MiPet OU

349 ———.
Gallant Traitor. Philadelphia: Penn Publishing Co., 1938. 322 p.

Young lovers, members of two feuding families, overcome obstacles on their

way to happiness. Set in "St. Gabriel" (St. Clair) on a dairy farm.

Romance.

Black, 73.

Mi MiMtpT-C MiPh MnM OC

350 ———.
Some Fell Among Thorns. Philadelphia: Penn Publishing Co., 1939. 377 p.

The daughter of a small-town physician married to a Great Lakes ship captain wishes for an exciting life. Set in "Riverbend" (St. Clair?).

Romance.

Mi MiAllG MiGr MiPh OBgU

351 ———.
Chalice. Philadelphia: Penn Publishing Co., 1940. 448 p.

The story of a woman's life, including her struggle as an artist, her unhappy marriage, and her search for true love. Set mostly in Detroit and "Riverbend" (St. Clair?) from 1898 on.

Romance.

Black, 71.

Mi MiAllG MiD MiPet MiPh

352 ———.
The Doctor's Party. Philadelphia: Penn Publishing Co., 1940. 162 p.

A small-town doctor holds a dinner party and helps six young people with their problems. Set in "Pine Harbor" in southeastern Michigan.

Mi MiAllG MiMack MiMtpT-C MiPh

353 ———.
Not by Bread Alone. Garden City, N.Y.: Doubleday, Doran and Co., 1941. 322 p.

A chronicle of three generations of women in a Great Lakes shipping family and the sacrifices they must make. Set in "St. Gabriel" (St. Clair).

Black, 75.

Mi MiAllG MiD MiMtpT-C OBgU

354 ———.
Glass Mountain. Garden City, N.Y.: Doubleday, Doran and Co., 1942. 299 p.

A man and woman pursue their respective dreams of succeeding in the Great Lakes shipping industry and on the Chautauqua circuit. Set mostly in "St. Gabriel" (St. Clair).

Black, 74.

Mi MiAllG MiD MiMtpT-C MiStc

355 ———.
O Distant Star! Garden City, N.Y.: Doubleday, Doran and Co., 1944. 301 p.

A woman marries the wrong man but stays with him as he pursues a career in the iron ore industry. Set partially in Marquette and "St. Gabriel" (St. Clair) in the 1870s.

Black, 76.

Mi MiAllG MiD MiMtpT-C MiPet

356 ———.
Blue River. Garden City, N.Y.: Doubleday and Co., 1946. 274 p.

A talented musician marries an automobile company magnate, but life is made difficult by her nasty sister-in-law. Set partially in "Anchor Shores" and "New Dundee" on "Blue River" (St. Clair River).

Black, 70.

Mi MiAllG MiD MiMtpT-C MiStc

357 ———.
Ravenswood. Garden City, N.Y.: Doubleday and Co., 1948. 254 p.

A chonicle about the St. George family and the ups and downs of their salt refining business. Set in "Ravenswood" on "Blue River" (St. Clair River).

Black, 77.

Mi MiAllG MiEM MiMtpT-C MiStc

358 ———.
Cloud of Arrows. Garden City, N.Y.: Doubleday & Co., 1950. 252 p.

A young aspiring magazine artist finds her inspiration in "Straitsmouth" (Port Huron?) and in the Michigan sugar beet industry.

Black, 72.

Mi MiAllG MiD MiMtpT-C MiStc

359 ———.
While the River Flows—a Story of Life Along the Great Lakes Waterways, of the Sailors and Their Loves. New York: Avalon Books, 1962. 224 p.

A man returns to town after a fifteen-year absence and uses a young woman in his plan for revenge for the way the town treated him earlier. Set in "Marineville" (Marine City?) on "Blue River" (St. Clair River).

Romance.

MiPh IChamL MnManTD OC WAPL

360 ———.
The Wind and the Fog. New York: Avalon Books, 1963. 192 p.

The story of a Great Lakes ship captain and the two women who love him. Set in "St. Gabriel" (St. Clair) on "Blue River" (St. Clair River) in 1910.

Romance.

Mi MiFli MiJac MiMack MiPh

361 ———.

Cleavenger vs. Castle; a Case of Breach of Promise and Seduction. Philadelphia: Dorrance & Co., 1968. 246 p.

The fictionalized account of a notorious lawsuit in which a wealthy realtor ends a ten-year engagement by marrying another woman. Set in Detroit in 1929.

Mi MiCad MiPh NBuBE WM

362 ———.

Return a Stranger. New York: Avalon Books, 1970. 190 p.

A young widow returns to her hometown to deal with many unhappy memories before she can begin a new life of happiness. Set in "Riverbend" (St. Clair?).

Romance.

MiAllG MiGr MiPh MiRic MiRog

363 ———.

Thine Is the Power. New York: Avalon Books, 1972. 176 p.

An artist and an engineer for a pumped storage project are at odds philosophically before falling in love. Set in "Channel City" (Ludington) on "Lake Mohican" (Lake Michigan).

Romance.

MiA MiAllG MiCad MiPh MiRog

364 ———.

Not by Appointment. New York: Avalon Books, 1972. 190 p.

A young man tries to end the unhealthy infatuation a young woman has with a suave opportunist. Thirty pages are set in "Port Marquette" (Ludington).

Romance.

MiA MiChe MiPh MiRog InAnd

365 ———.

The Darker Star. New York: Avalon Books, 1974. 189 p.

A self-effacing waitress falls in love and begins a relationship with a wealthy and seemingly arrogant man. Set in "Windemere-on-the-Lake" (Ludington).

Romance.

MiPh MiRog MiSsB MiWar InAnd

———, ed. *see* Hawley, Rose Damaris

366 **Dos Passos, John Roderigo** 1896–1970

The 42nd Parallel. New York: Harper and Bros., 1930. 426 p.

(*U.S.A.* trilogy, vol. 1)

A sweeping panoramic narrative of American life, experience, and societal changes between 1917 and 1927. Fifteen pages are set near Saginaw and in Gaylord.

367 ———.

The Big Money. New York: Harcourt, Brace and Co., 1936. 561 p.

(*U.S.A.* trilogy, vol. 3)

A continuation of Don Passo's panoramic narrative of the American experience between 1919 and the 1930s. Thirty-five pages are set in the Detroit and Flint auto plants.

368 **Douglas, Amanda Minnie** 1837–1916

A Little Girl in Old Detroit. New York: Dodd, Mead & Co., 1902. 362 p.

A story of Detroit as seen through the eyes of a young French girl from its inclusion in United States in 1796 until the destructive fire of 1805.

Juvenile.

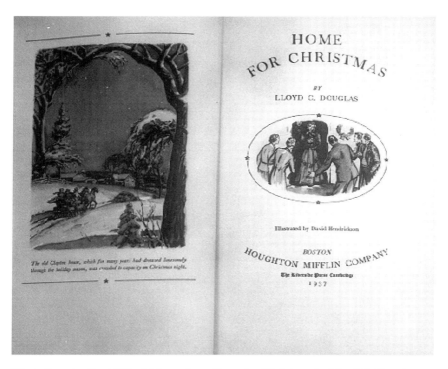

The old Clayton home, which for many years had drowsed lonesomely through the holiday season, was crowded to capacity on Christmas night.

HOME
FOR CHRISTMAS

BY
LLOYD C. DOUGLAS

Illustrated by David Hendrickson

BOSTON
HOUGHTON MIFFLIN COMPANY
The Riverside Press Cambridge
1937

Illustrations by David Hendrickson from *Home for Christmas* by Lloyd C. Douglas. Copyright 1935 and 1937, Lloyd C. Douglas. Copyright © renewed 1965 by Betty Douglas Herman and Virginia Douglas Dawson. Reprinted by permission of Houghton Mifflin Company. All rights reserved.

Black, 78. Streeter, 1538.

Mi MiAllG MiD MiMtpT-C MiSsL

369 Douglas, Lloyd Cassel 1877–1951
Magnificent Obsession. Chicago: Willett, Clark & Colby, 1929. 330 p.

A brain surgeon employs idealistic Christian healing philosophies advocated by his predecessor, Dr. Hudson, as he ministers to his patients. Set in

Detroit.

Black, 81.

370 ———.
Home for Christmas. Boston: Houghton Mifflin, 1937. 118 p.

Five middle-aged siblings agree to meet for an old-fashioned Christmas at the family farm. Set near "Wimple" in southeastern Michigan.

371 ———.
Disputed Passage. Boston: Houghton Mifflin, 1939. 432 p.

A young medical student tries to work efficiently with an arrogant neurologist. Set at the medical school at "State University" (University of Michigan).

Black, 79.

372 ———.
Doctor Hudson's Secret Journal. Boston: Houghton Mifflin, 1939. 295 p.

The 1913–1921 diary of a fictional Dr. Hudson, in which he elaborately sets forth his own special Christian philosophy of healing, is reproduced. Set in Detroit.

Sequel to *Magnificent Obsession*.

Black, 80.

373 **Drago, Harry Sinclair** 1888–1979
Where the Loon Calls. New York: Macaulay Co., 1928. 317 p.

Among the old French settler families, a girl is the love object of two different men. Set in the marsh country south of Monroe in the late 1800s.

Black, 82.

Mi MiAllG MiD MiKW OC

374 **Drapkin, Frita Roth** 1913–
Papa's Golden Land. New York: Comet Press Books, 1960. 182 p.

The fictionalized memoirs of a Czechoslovakian family of immigrants and their attempt to find a home among strangers. Set in Detroit between 1923 and 1932.

MiAllG MiD MiDW MiSf N

375 **Dreyer, Myrta M.**
Beckoning Hands. The Story of a Fearful Crime and Its Final Strange Solution. Detroit: Herold Publishing Co., 1930. 340 p.

Four murders take place among a group of society people at a snow-bound lodge in northern Michigan. Set on "Lake Eden" near Oscoda and in Detroit.

Mystery.

Black, 83.

Mi MiAllG MiD MiMack MiMo

376 **Driscoll, Jack** 1946–
Skylight. New York: Orchard Books, 1991. 180 p.

A young man and woman from different social backgrounds fall in love and have some difficulties. Partially set in northwestern Michigan.

Juvenile.

377 **Drogas, John** 1929–
Closing Doors Behind Me. Emmett, Mich.: Great Lakes Press, 1988. 292 p.

The story of a Vietnam veteran unhappily married to a socialite who tries to prove his worth despite many setbacks. Mostly set in Detroit and Grosse Pointe.

MiAllG MiD MiL MiPh MiStc

378 **DuBay, Sandra** 1954–
Wilder Shores of Love. New York: Leisure Books, 1988. 439 p.

A young New York heiress becomes involved with a handsome recluse while resisting the advances of a cad. Partially set on Mackinac and the Beaver Islands in 1890.

Romance.

MiAllG MiGr CSf IChamL IaDa

379 ——.

By Love Betrayed. New York: Leisure Books, 1993. 427 p.

Hoping to avenge her husband's death at the hands of American troops, a woman agrees to become a spy for the British. Partially set on Mackinac Island during the War of 1812.

Romance.

MiAllG MiBatW IChamL OCl WM

380 **Ducey, Jean Sparks** 1915–
Out of This Nettle. Grand Rapids: Baker Book House, 1983. 148 p.

A twelve-year-old is a delivery boy for an abolitionist newspaper and becomes involved with a local individual who steals slaves. Set in Niles in 1845.

Juvenile.

Mi MiAllG MiFli MiGr MiL

381 ——.

The Bittersweet Time. Grand Rapids: William B. Eerdmans Publishing Co., 1995. 109 p.

When her father loses his job at the beginning of the Depression, a thirteen-year-old girl begins a family diary. Set in Niles in 1929 and 1930.

Juvenile.

MiAllG MiBir MiD MiGrC OCl

382 **Duffield, Alexander** 1906–
Any Smaller Person. New York: Loring & Mussey, 1935. 288 p.

After returning from Paris, an aspiring painter becomes a bank teller and generally wastes his talents while making a failure of his life. Set in Detroit.

Black, 84.

Mi MiD MiDW MiU MiWar

383 **Duncan, Lois** 1934–
Daughters of Eve. Boston: Little, Brown, 1979. 239 p.

A faculty advisor gradually exerts a malignant influence over the ten members of an exclusive high school service sorority. Set in "Modesta."

Juvenile.

384 **Dunne, John Gregory** 1932–
Playland. New York: Random House, 1994. 494 p.

A Hollywood writer discovers a child star who had mysteriously disappeared in the 1940s and pieces together her history. Partially set in Detroit.

385 **DuVal, John Anthony** 1900–
To Whom We Are Born by J. A. DuVal. Cynthiana, Ky.: Hobson Book Press, 1944. 293 p.

A young Finnish woman from L'Anse leaves her home, family, and friends to make a career in Detroit and has a number of adventures before finding success.

Mi DLC

386 **Du Vall, Dean F. V.**
The Big Dream. Secaucus, N.J.: Lyle Stuart, 1979. 231 p.

The rise and fall of a financial wizard who gains enough fame and support to run for the American presidency. Partially set in Michigan between 1940 and 1981.

Mi MiL MiStc IC InHam

387 **Dwight, Allan,** pseud.
Drums in the Forest. New York: Macmillan Co., 1936. 255 p.

The story of a young boy in New France and the numerous adventures in which he becomes involved. Fifteen pages are set at Michilimackinac and Fort St. Joseph in the 1680s.

"Allan Dwight" is the joint pseudonym of Allan Taylor and Lois Dwight Cole.

Juvenile.

Mi MiD MiMtpT-C IC OCo

388 Dyer, Ethelyn
The Victories of a Boy. Chicago: M. A. Donohue & Co., 1912. 184 p.

A ten-year-old orphan boy from the lumber camps prevents a train wreck and is given a home by one of the passengers. Set in "Woodlock" (Boyne City?) and Detroit.

Mi MiAllG MiEM MiPetN

E

389 E.L.T. Club, Albion, Michigan
Was It a Mistake? A Composite Story Written by the Ladies of the E. L. T. Club. Albion, Mich.: n.p., 1896. 47 p.

An episodic and convoluted story of critical letters not received, family secrets, and a lost love regained. Set partially in Homer.

The individual authors of the six chapters are Dedie Hayes-Kilian, Annie Morley Gale, Ada R. E. Clark, Fannie Frost, Metta Gardner, and Belle Throop.

The abbreviation E.L.T. corresponds to the Latin "emitte lucem tuam" ("send forth your light").

MiGr-L

390 Eames, Anne
Two Weddings and a Bride. New York: Silhouette Books, 1996. 185 p.

(Silhouette Desire, no. 996)

At her wedding reception, a young woman discovers her new husband in a compromising situation with a bridesmaid, so she leaves with a handsome guest. Set in Detroit.

Romance.

MiAllG MiFli IChamL OXe WM

391 ———.
You're What?! New York: Silhouette Books, 1996. 185 p.

(Silhouette Desire, no. 1025)

When a divorced woman in her thirties becomes pregnant, she wonders if it was from her visit to a sperm bank or her week-long affair with a doctor. Set partially in Detroit.

Publisher's subseries: *Bachelors & Babies.*

Romance.

MiAllG IChamL OCo OXe WM

Early, Jack, pseud. *see* Scoppettone, Sandra

392 East, Ben 1898–
The Last Eagle: The Story of Khan. New York: Crown Publishers, 1974. 144 p.

The fictionalized life history of the supposedly only surviving bald eagle and his struggle for existence. Set in the Upper Peninsula.

393 Eaton, Geoffrey Dell 1894–1930
Backfurrow. New York: G. P. Putnam's Sons, 1925. 332 p.

A young man finds himself trapped on a farm despite his dreams to make something of himself in the big city. Set in rural central Michigan and Detroit around 1917.

Mi MiAllG MiD MiEM MiU

394 ———.
John Drakin. Milwaukee: Gutenberg Publishing Co., 1937. 440 p.

The story of a young man's growing up in southeastern Michigan between 1905 and 1926 and his attendance at a university. Set in Detroit, Ann Arbor, and Frankfort.

MiAllG CLU WM WWhiwU

395 **Eaton, Seymour** 1859–1916
Dan Black, Editor and Proprietor. Philadelphia: Library Publishing Co., 1904. 54 p.

A gruff and cynical newspaper editor in a northern Michigan lumbertown falls in love with a waitress to his and the town's total surprise and delight.

Black, 91.

Mi MiEM MiMtpT-C MiU OBgU

396 **Eberle, Gary** 1951–
Angel Strings. Minneapolis: Coffee House Press, 1995. 315 p.

Having left his wife, a rock band guitarist sets out on his own and meets a single mother with whom he travels around the country. Partially set in Detroit.

397 **Eckert, Allan W.** 1931–
The Frontiersmen; a Narrative. Boston: Little, Brown & Co., 1967. 626 p.

(Winning of America Series, book 1)

A fictionalized historical narrative of events in the Northwest Territory between 1755 and 1813. Partially set in Detroit.

398 ———.
Wilderness Empire; a Narrative. Boston: Little, Brown & Co., 1969. 653 p.

(Winning of America Series, book 2)

A fictionalized historical narrative of the struggle between the British and the French from 1715 to 1760 for the mastery of North America. Set partially in Detroit and Michilimackinac.

399 ———.
The Conquerors; a Narrative. Boston: Little, Brown & Co., 1970. 720 p.

(Winning of America Series, book 3)

A fictionalized historical narrative of the British occupation of former French land in the Great Lakes area from 1758 to 1765. Set partially in Detroit and Michilimackinac.

400 ———.
Gateway to Empire. Boston: Little, Brown & Co., 1983. 688 p.

(Winning of America Series, book 5)

A fictionalized historical narrative of events in the Old Northwest between 1769 and 1816. Set partially in Detroit and Fort Mackinac.

401 **Edwards, Andrea,** pseud.
Ghost of a Chance. New York: Silhouette Books, 1988. 252 p.

(Silhouette Special Edition, no. 490)

A widow and her young daughter move into an old house in South Bend where they meet a handsome professor who is a tenant. Twelve pages are set in southwestern Michigan.

"Andrea Edwards" is the joint pseudonym for Anne and Ed Kolaczyk.

Romance.

MiAllG MiGr IChamL OBgU OXe

402 ———.
Places in the Heart. New York: Silhouette Books, 1990. 253 p.

(Silhouette Special Edition, no. 591)

After thirteen years, a man returns to the small hometown he longed to escape to discover that the child of an old girlfriend is his. Set in Edwardsburg.

Romance.

MiAllG MiGr MiPh IChamL OBgU

403 ———.
Sweet Knight Times. New York: Silhouette Books, 1992. 251 p.

(Silhouette Special Edition, no. 740)

An accountant with a penchant for local politics has an encounter with a single mother who delivers a pizza to him by mistake. Set in Holland.

Romance.

MiAllG IChamL OBgU TxAu

404 ———.
Father: Unknown. New York: Silhouette Books, 1992. 252 p.

(Silhouette Special Edition, no. 770)

A woman returns, with a fatherless nine-year-old, to the town she fled ten years ago and attracts the attention of a man who wonders about her secret. Set in Niles.

Romance.

MiAllG MiFli IChamL OBgU WM

405 ———.
A Rose and a Wedding Vow. New York: Silhouette Books, 1995. 250 p.

(Silhouette Special Edition, no. 944)

A Chicago policeman comes to town to attend to matters concerning his younger brother's death and finds himself disturbingly attracted to his brother's widow. Set mostly in "Stony Mountain."

Book 2 of the author's trilogy *This Time, Forever.* Neither book 1 (*A Ring and a Promise*) nor book 3 (*A Secret and a Bridal Pledge*) is set in Michigan.

Romance.

MiAllG IChamL OBgU OCo WM

406 **Edwards, Cassie**
Savage Passions. New York: Leisure Books, 1996. 439 p.

(Savage Series, no. 10)

The eighteen-year-old daughter of a frontier preacher becomes attracted to the handsome Ottawa chief of the nearby village. Set on the Grand River in 1840.

Romance.

MiAllG InE OCl OXe WM

407 **Effinger, George Alec** 1947–
Shadow Money. New York: Tom Doherty Associates, 1988. 281 p.

Four men develop an elaborate scheme to extort vast sums of money from Ford, General Motors, and Chrysler. Set in Detroit.

Mystery.

408 **Ellett, Frank Gates** 1860–
A Modern Hamilton. Detroit: Press of Frank H. West, 1912. 217 p.

A political novel in which the protagonist attacks the current colonial policy of the United States. Set in southwestern Michigan.

Mi MiL MiMtpT-C MiSsL OU

409 **[Ellis, Edward Sylvester]** 1840–1916
Pontiac, Chief of the Ottawas; a Tale of the Siege of Detroit by Colonel H. R. Gordon [pseud.]. New York: E. P. Dutton & Co., 1897. 300 p.

Two resourceful forest rangers try to thwart Pontiac and his Ojibwa and Ottawa warriors in their attempt to capture Detroit from the British in 1763.

A later printing states that this book is a part of the publisher's "Boy's Own Favorite Series."

Juvenile.

Black, 85. Streeter, 1594.

Mi MiD MiEM MiFli MiMtpT-C

410 ——.
The Forest Messengers. Philadelphia: John C. Winston Co., 1907. 340 p.

(Paddle Your Own Canoe Series, no. 1)

A fifteen-year-old Canadian boy who is a friend of Pontiac witnesses the attacks on various English forts in 1763. Partially set at Detroit.

Juvenile.

Streeter, 1593.

Mi FTS IDeKN

411 **Ellis, Melvin Richard** 1912–1984
An Eagle to the Wind by Mel Ellis. New York: Holt, Rinehart and Winston, 1978. 141 p.

A fifteen-year-old boy comes of age in the Michigan backwoods. Set in the Upper Peninsula on the Lake Superior shore in 1893.

Juvenile.

412 **Ellison, James Whitfield** 1929–
I'm Owen Harrison Harding. Garden City, N.Y.: Doubleday, 1955. 250 p.

A high school student copes with life with his friends, family, and new girlfriend. Set in "Fleming" (Lansing) in 1944 and 1945.

Mi MiAllG MiGr MiKW MiMtpT-C

412A **Ellsworth, Dorothea Jorgensen** 1923–
No Time To Dream. Edmore, Mich.: Anderson Printing Co., 1987. 200 p.

(Dream Series, no. 1)

Agnes, daughter of Danish immigrants, grows up in the small community of "Pleasant Hill" in Montcalm County during the 1890s and hopes to become a teacher. This book and its sequels are based on the life of the author's aunt.

Mi MiFliL MiGr MiLac MiMtpT-C

412B ——.
Give Me My Dream. Edmore, Mich.: Anderson Printing Co., 1988. 343 p.

(Dream Series, no. 2)

Now a teenager, Agnes has a job doing housework for a family which she thinks will keep her from her dream of becoming a teacher. Set in Entrican in Montcalm County in the early 1900s.

Sequel to *No Time To Dream.*

Mi MiA MiFliL MiGr MiMtpT-C

412C ——.
Dreams Do Come True. Edmore, Mich.: Anderson Printing Co., 1989. 285 p.

(Dream Series, no. 3)

After earning tuition money by working in a silk factory, Agnes eventually attends Ferris Institute, becomes a teacher, and marries. Set in Entrican, Belding, and Big Rapids in the early 1900s.

Sequel to *Give Me My Dream.*

Mi MiA MiFliL MiGr MiMtpT-C

412D ——.
This Dream Is Real. Edmore, Mich.: Anderson Printing Co., 1990. 349 p.

(Dream Series, no. 4)

Agnes and her husband move to a farm, have two boys, endure the First World War, and deal with a variety of family crises. Set in the Entrican area in Montcalm County from 1910 to 1928.

Sequel to *Dreams Do Come True.*

Mi MiFli MiGr MiLac MiMtpT-C

412E ———.
The Long Awaited Dream. Edmore, Mich.: Anderson Printing Co., 1991. 327 p.

(Dream Series, no. 5)

Agnes and her husband provide a home for their niece when Agnes's sister-in-law dies and raise her as the daughter they always wanted. Set in Entrican from 1928 to 1937.

Sequel to *This Dream Is Real.*

Mi MiFliL MiGr MiLac MiMtpT-C

413 Emery, Anne 1907–
A Spy in Old Detroit. Chicago: Rand McNally, 1963. 206 p.

Despite his conflicting feelings of loyalty, a fifteen-year-old French boy becomes a spy for the British during Pontiac's siege of Detroit in 1763.

Juvenile.

414 Enger, L. L., pseud.
Sacrifice; a Gun Pedersen Mystery. New York: Pocket Books, 1993. 245 p.

The discovery of his friend's bones twenty years after the murder has an ex-Detroit Tiger investigating the crime. Set in "Copper Strike" in the Upper Peninsula.

"L. L. Enger" is the joint pseudonym for Leif and Lin Enger.

Mystery.

MiAllG MiBatW MiD MiFliL MiMtpT-C

Enger, Leif *see* Enger, L. L.

Enger, Lin *see* Enger, L. L.

415 Enright, Thomas
The King of Nobody's Island. New York: Gibson Publishing Co., 1909. 202 p.

A man from the Chicago Board of Trade spends a few months in the woods to regain his health and finds love as a bonus. Probably set in Gogebic County.

Black, 88.

Mi LU OU

415A Erdmann, Naomi
Grandpa Remembers; Based on the Reminiscences of Bert Wood. N.p., 1967. 39 p.

The fictionalized biography of an elderly man as he recalls his early life in a small Michigan town. Set mostly in Franklin in Oakland County.

MiD

416 Erlandson, Oscar S.
Alice Cracks the Looking-Glass. New York: Vantage Press, 1951. 157 p.

A story of the rivalry between an upper-class town and a lower-class village. Set in "Avondale" and "Wirtt" on the Looking Glass River.

Mi FTU TxHuT

417 Erni, Bill
Papa's Gift. New York: Citadel Press, 1963. 256 p.

An amiable story about the patriarch of an Italian-American family and the humorous and outrageous schemes he concocts. Set in Detroit in the 1930s.

Mi MiD MiMtp ABAU IEN

418 Erno, Richard B. 1923–
My Old Man. New York: Crown Publishers, 1955. 224 p.

A sixteen-year-old boy resents and is ashamed of his drunken father. Set in the small town of "Barton Corners" in northern Michigan in the late 1930s.

Black, 90.

Mi MiAllG MiD MiEM MiPet

419 ———.
The Hunt. New York: Crown Publishers, 1959. 220 p.

A party of deer hunters is guided by a man still brooding over the accidental shooting death of his friend years before. Set in northern Michigan.

Black, 89.

Mi MiD MiPet MiU MiWar

420 ———.
The Catwalk. New York: Crown Publishers, 1964. 253 p.

A man prepares for a turning point in his life by building a catwalk along the roof of his house. Set in "Walloon Beach" on Walloon Lake.

421 Estleman, Loren D. 1952–
Motor City Blue. Boston: Houghton Mifflin Co., 1980. 219 p.

Private investigator Amos Walker is hired to find a gangster's missing ward and becomes involved in a labor leader's murder. Set in Detroit and Grosse Pointe.

Mystery.

422 ———.
Angel Eyes; an Amos Walker Mystery. Boston: Houghton Mifflin Co., 1981. 203 p.

Amos Walker is hired by a nightclub dancer to prevent her own disappearance and soon is connected with an ex-convict union boss. Set in Detroit and "Huron" (Dexter).

Mystery.

423 ———.
The Midnight Man. Boston: Houghton Mifflin Co., 1982. 230 p.

Amos Walker's client seeks vengeance for her husband's ruined life, and Walker soon finds himself dealing with three murderers and the police. Set in Detroit.

Mystery.

424 ———.
The Glass Highway. Boston: Houghton Mifflin Co., 1983. 179 p.

Amos Walker is hired by a newscaster to search for a son abandoned years before, and the investigation involves Walker with two drug lords. Set in Detroit.

Mystery.

425 ———.
Kill Zone. New York: Mysterious Press, 1984. 237 p.

Retired Mob hitman Peter Macklin is persuaded to assist the FBI when the Boblo Boat, a Detroit River excursion steamer, is hijacked by terrorists. Set in Detroit.

Subtitle on book jacket: *A Macklin Novel.*

Mystery.

426 ———.

Sugartown. Boston: Houghton Mifflin Co., 1984. 220 p.

Amos Walker helps an old Polish woman locate her grandson and becomes involved with an exiled Soviet writer. Set in Detroit and Hamtramck.

Mystery.

427 ———.

Roses Are Dead. New York: Mysterious Press, 1985. 233 p.

Ex-hitman Peter Macklin is stalked by the Mob while trying to dissuade his son from becoming a killer like himself. Set in Detroit.

Subtitle on book jacket: *A Macklin Novel of Suspense.*

Mystery.

428 ———.

Every Brilliant Eye. Boston: Houghton Mifflin Co., 1986. 252 p.

When a newspaper reporter and friend disappears, Amos Walker searches Detroit for him, and the search leads him into the worlds of car theft rings, organized crime, and book publishing.

Mystery.

429 ———.

Any Man's Death. New York: Mysterious Press, 1986. 209 p.

Ex-hitman Peter Macklin is involved in a dispute between rival gangs and desperately tries to keep his headstrong son out of it. Set in Detroit.

Subtitle on book jacket: *A Macklin Novel of Suspense.*

Mystery.

430 ———.

Lady Yesterday. Boston: Houghton Mifflin Co., 1987. 194 p.

Amos Walker finds himself surrounded by crime and drugs when he looks for a woman's father in the Detroit jazz music scene.

Mystery.

431 ———.

Downriver. Boston: Houghton Mifflin Co., 1988. 210 p.

Amos Walker is hired to sort out takeover plots and stock manipulation within a small automobile company. Set in Detroit and its southern riverside suburbs.

Mystery.

432 ———.

Silent Thunder. Boston: Houghton Mifflin Co., 1989. 202 p.

When a large detective agency hires Amos Walker to locate evidence for a murder trial, he stumbles onto illicit arms dealers. Set in Detroit.

Mystery.

433 ———.

Peeper. New York: Bantam Books, 1989. 215 p.

Ralph Poteet, a sleazy, unscrupulous, and obese private investigator, becomes involved in the death of a priest under possibly scandalous circumstances. Set in Detroit.

Mystery.

434 ———.

Sweet Women Lie. Boston: Houghton Mifflin Co., 1990. 193 p.

The reappearance of Amos Walker's ex-wife brings the CIA, government assassins, and general mayhem into his life. Set in Detroit.

Mystery.

435 ——.
Whiskey River. New York: Bantam Books, 1990. 262 p.

(Detroit Series, book 1)

Newspaper reporter Connie Minor investigates the illegal liquor trade's connection with organized crime. Set in Prohibition-era Detroit from 1928 to 1931.

Mystery.

435A ——.
Eight Mile and Dequindre. Eugene, Oreg.: Mystery Scene Press, Pulphouse Publishing, 1991. 45 p.

(Mystery Scene Short Story Hardback, no. 2)

While waiting for a client in a diner, Amos Walker witnesses a murder and while investigating becomes involved with the victim's girlfriend. Set in Detroit.

First published in *Alfred Hitchcock's Mystery Magazine* in 1985.

Limited to one hundred copies.

Mystery.

MiGr-L

436 ——.
Motown. New York: Bantam Books, 1991. 292 p. (Detroit Series, book 2)

An ex-cop working for an automobile manufacturer becomes involved in a war between the Mob and street gangs. Set in Detroit in 1966.

Mystery.

437 ——.
King of the Corner. New York: Bantam Books, 1992. 294 p.

(Detroit Series, book 3)

An ex-major league ballplayer gets a job as a driver for a bail bondsman and soon is caught up in a murder investigation. Set in Detroit in 1990.

Mystery.

438 ——.
Edsel: A Novel of Detroit. New York: Mysterious Press, 1995. 291 p.

(Detroit Series, book 4)

Newspaper reporter Connie Minor is hired by the Ford Motor Company to initiate an advertising campaign for its new model, the Edsel. Set in Detroit in the 1950s.

Mystery.

439 ——.
STRESS. New York: Mysterious Press, 1996. 276 p.

(Detroit Series, book 5)

An African-American police officer is assigned to investigate the shootings of three persons during a robbery by STRESS, the controversial Detroit anticrime unit.

Mystery.

440 Ethridge, Kenneth E. 1950–
Toothpick. New York: Holiday House, 1985. 118 p.

An eleventh-grade boy overcomes the ridicule of his classmates and befriends a new girl at school, only to discover she has a terminal illness. Set in "Glenwood."

Juvenile.

441 ――――.
Viola, Furgy, Bobbi, and Me. New York: Holiday House, 1989. 164 p.

A ninth-grade boy and two friends try to prevent an old woman's daughters from putting her in a nursing home. Set in the Detroit area.

Juvenile.

442 **Etter, Lester Frederick** 1904–
Morning Glory Quarterback. Indianapolis: Bobbs-Merrill Co., 1965. 215 p.

A quarterback and a fullback try to put their mutual animosities aside for the good of the football team. Set at "Midwestern University" (University of Michigan).

Juvenile.

CLS InFw NBuBE TxAm WWhiwU

443 ――――.
Bull Pen Hero. Indianapolis: Bobbs-Merrill Co., 1966. 212 p.

A college pitcher is recruited by a team, and works his way up from their farm club. Partially set at "Midwest University" (University of Michigan) and in Detroit.

Juvenile.

Mi InFw MnManTD OCl WM

444 ――――.
Soccer Goalie. New York: Hastings House, 1969. 127 p.

A former football player joins the soccer team and helps it attain varsity status while playing goalie. Set at "Midwestern University" (University of Michigan).

Juvenile.

MiSsB MiTr IC OCl MnM

445 ――――.
Cool Man on the Court. New York: Hastings House, 1969. 125 p.

Befriended by the "Midwestern University" (University of Michigan) tennis coach, a fifteen-year-old African American quickly becomes a promising player.

Juvenile.

MiRog MiSsB MiTr IC OCl

446 ――――.
Fast Break Forward. New York: Hastings House, 1969. 128 p.

A former high school all-star basketball player has difficulty adjusting to college life at "Midwestern University" (University of Michigan).

Juvenile.

Mi MiBatW MiMtpT-C MiSsB MiTr

447 **Eugenides, Jeffrey** 1960?–
The Virgin Suicides. New York: Farrar Straus Giroux, 1993. 249 p.

The narrator reminisces about his teenage years in Detroit and how he and his friends reacted to a peculiar family who lived in the neighborhood.

448 **Evans, Virginia**
The Cautious Husband. New York: Coward-McCann, 1949. 218 p.

A newly married army veteran and his wife discover that their personalities clash. Set at an unnamed midwestern college that is most likely the University of Michigan.

Black, 92.

GA IC InG OAU OCl

449 **Evers, Crabbe,** pseud.
Tigers Burning; a Duffy House Mystery. New York: William Morrow and Co., 1994. 246 p.

Duffy House, a special investigator for the baseball commissioner, is asked to examine a suspicious fire at Tiger Stadium in Detroit.

"Crabbe Evers" is the joint pseudonym of William Brashler and Reinder Van Til.

Mystery.

450 Ezekiel, Tish O'Dowd 1943–
Floaters. New York: Atheneum, 1984. 248 p.

The story of a Catholic girl's life from the 1940s to the 1960s. Set in "Pinkerink" (Pinckney) in southern Michigan.

F

451 Faasen, Neal 1937–
The Toyfair. New York: Simon and Schuster, 1963. 186 p.

A thirteen-year-old male truant and troublemaker skips school with two girls and runs off to Chicago to locate his father. Partially set in Grand Rapids.

Mi MiAllG MiEM MiGr MiU

452 Farley, Carol J. McDole 1936–
Mystery of the Fog Man. New York: Franklin Watts, 1966. 116 p.

Two thirteen-year-old cousins, Kip and Larry, investigate a connection between the sudden appearance of an old man and money missing from a ship. Set in Ludington.

Juvenile.

453 ———.
Mystery in the Ravine. New York: Franklin Watts, 1967. 114 p.

Kip and Larry become involved with a mysterious man who tells the unlikely story that he is searching for Mohawk artifacts in a ravine. Set in Ludington.

Juvenile.

Mi MiFliL MiLapC MiMtp MiOw

454 ———.
Sergeant Finney's Family. New York: Franklin Watts, 1969. 240 p.

A mother and her four children move to a small Michigan town and await her husband's return from Vietnam. Set in "Creekton" (Ludington?).

Juvenile.

MiAllG MiD MiFliL MiLapC MiOw

455 ———.
The Bunch on McKellahan Street. New York: Franklin Watts, 1971. 246 p.

A group of high-spirited and rambunctious children from a working-class neighborhood have various adventures. Set in "Piney Ridge" (Ludington?) in 1945.

Juvenile.

Mi MiD MiFliL MiLapC MiOw

456 ———.
The Most Important Thing in the World. New York: Franklin Watts, 1974. 133 p.

A rich woman undertakes a trip to consider which of her relatives will inherit her wealth. Partially set in "Marlecrest" (Ludington?) and East Lansing.

Juvenile.

MiAllG MiAlp MiBatW MiD MiWar

457 ———.
The Garden Is Doing Fine. New York: Atheneum, 1975. 185 p.

An adolescent girl learns to deal with and ultimately accept her father's imminent death. Set in "Pointer" (Ludington?) in 1945.

Juvenile.

458 ———.

Loosen Your Ears. New York: Atheneum, 1977. 214 p.

The humorous, homespun, and charming anecdotes and stories of an elderly narrator about his Michigan farm family around 1910.

Juvenile.

459 ———.

Settle Your Fidgets. New York: Atheneum, 1977. 147 p.

The elderly narrator of *Loosen Your Ears* shares more humorous and outrageous stories about the same Michigan farm family and their doings in and around 1910.

Sequel to *Loosen Your Ears.*

Juvenile.

460 ———.

Twilight Waves. New York: Atheneum, 1981. 131 p.

An Illinois boy travels to "Seagulls Point" on Lake Michigan to find information about his father, who is thought to be lost in a shipwreck.

Juvenile.

Mi MiAllG MiD MiLapC MiMtp

461 ———.

The Mystery of the Fiery Message. New York: Avon Books, 1983. 106 p.

Cousins Kip and Larry investigate a series of mysterious fires that seem to be the work of an arsonist, but turn

out to have deeper significance. Set in Ludington.

Juvenile.

Mi MiBlo MiChe MiStep MiSth

462 ———.

The Case of the Vanishing Villain. New York: Avon Books, 1986. 71 p.

Two young sisters, Flee Jay and Clarice, are trapped on a Lake Michigan car ferry with an escaped convict. Partially set in "Grand Channel" (Ludington).

Juvenile.

MiAllG MiBatW MiChe MiFliL MiMtp

463 ———.

The Case of the Lost Lookalike. New York: Avon Books, 1988. 104 p.

Flee Jay and Clarice vacation at their aunt's cottage and get mixed up in a forty-year-old kidnapping mystery. Set at "Magic Lake" in northern Michigan.

Juvenile.

Mi MiAllG MiChe MiFliL MiStjo

464 ———.

Songs in the Night. Cincinnati: Standard Publishing, 1990. 128 p.

A fourteen-year-old spends part of his summer with his uncle and tries to cope with the recent death of his younger brother. Set in northern Michigan on Lake Michigan.

Juvenile.

MiAllG MiMtp InAnd InMar MB

465 ———.

The Case of the Haunted Health Club. New York: Avon Books, 1991. 101 p.

Flee Jay and Clarice become involved in a mysterious death and the attempted poisoning of a local fortune teller. Set in "Grand Channel" (Ludington).

Juvenile.

MiAllG MiChe MiD MiFliL MiSth

Feikema, Feike *see* Manfred, Frederick Feikema

466 **Fenner, Carol Elizabeth** 1929–
Yolonda's Genius. New York: Margaret K. McElderry Books, 1995. 211 p.

An African-American girl who misses Chicago when her mother moves to a safer Michigan town promotes her brother's musical abilities. Partially set in "Grand River."

Juvenile.

467 **Fenton, Julia,** pseud.
Blue Orchids. New York: Jove Books, 1992. 399 p.

Two sisters become successful recording artists but develop a bitter rivalry that leads to their embarking on separate careers. Twenty pages are set in Detroit in 1979.

"Julia Fenton" is the joint pseudonym of Julia Grice and Robert L. Fenton.

MiAllG MiBlo MiFliL MiMtcM MiSth

Fenton, Robert L., joint author *see* Fenton, Julia, pseud.

468 **Fenwick, Elizabeth** 1920–
The Make-Believe Man. New York: Harper & Row, 1963. 183 p.

While staying in her mother's house, a woman and her eleven-year-old son are terrorized by a former roomer. Set in Detroit and Dearborn.

Mystery.

469 **Ferber, Edna** 1887–1968
Come and Get It. Garden City, N.Y.: Doubleday, Doran & Co., 1935. 518 p.

A chronicle of the rise of a lumber baron from his early beginnings as a lumber camp chore boy. Set in Wisconsin and the Upper Peninsula from 1850 to 1929.

470 **Ferjutz, Kelly**
Secret Shores. New York: Berkley Books, 1993. 310 p.

(Stories of Love on the Great Lakes)

The handsome son of a French trader and his Algonquin wife meets the beautiful and outspoken daughter of a shipbuilder. Set on Mackinac Island from 1861 to 1862.

Sequel to *Windsong.*

Romance.

Mi MiBatW InI OCl WM

471 ———.
Windsong. New York: Jove Books, 1994. 313 p.

A French voyageur meets a young Algonquin widow but obligations to her family bring obstacles to their relationship. Partially set on Mackinac Island in 1837.

Prequel to *Secret Shores.*

Romance.

MiGr-L InI OCl OCo OXe

472 **Fernald, Helen Clark** 1888–
The Shadow of the Crooked Tree. New York: D. McKay Co., 1965. 244 p.

A young schoolteacher is assigned to a lonely district and eventually overcomes her dislike for it. Set in the L'Arbre Croche area near Harbor Springs in 1900.

Juvenile.

Mi MiAllG MiD MiMtpT-C MiPet

473 Ferry, Charles 1927–
O Zebron Falls! Boston: Houghton
Mifflin Co., 1977. 213 p.

The story of a sheltered girl's senior
year in high school and the many
changes that she must face. Set in "Zebron Falls" (Rochester?).

Juvenile.

474 ———.
One More Time! Boston: Houghton
Mifflin Co., 1985. 171 p.

A teenage member of a big band orchestra recounts their last tour as World
War II begins. Set in the Midwest with
fourteen pages in Detroit.

Juvenile.

475 ———.
Binge. Rochester, Mich.: Daisy Hill
Press, 1992. 94 p.

An eighteen-year-old drunk driver kills
four teenagers and must face the guilt,
self-loathing, and legal ramifications of
his act. Set in "Bridgton."

Juvenile.

475A ———.
A Fresh Start. Ann Arbor: Proctor Publications, 1996. 81 p.

Four high school seniors in a treatment
and support program for teenage alco-
holics compare their situations and life
stories. Set in "Bridgton" in western
Michigan.

Juvenile.

MiBlo MiFli MiMtcM MiRochOU
MiT

476 Finder, Joseph 1958–
The Moscow Club. New York: Viking
Penguin, 1991. 548 p.

A clever CIA analyst stumbles upon a
sinister plot and saves the world from
a group of ruthless Soviet hardliners.
Eleven pages are set in Michigan.

477 Fischer, Pauline Benedict
Clay Acres. Philadelphia: Penn Publishing Co., 1938. 399 p.

The story of a New York couple that
buys 160 acres of farm land, raises
a family, and generally becomes successful. Set in the Ionia area from 1860
to the 1930s.

Black, 93.

Mi MiAllG MiD MiEM MiGr

478 Fisher, Aileen Lucia 1906–
Timber! (Logging in Michigan). New
York: Aladdin Books, 1955. 191 p.

(American Heritage Series)

In 1884, a fifteen-year-old boy, against
the wishes of his mother, finds employment in his uncle's lumber camp on the
Brule and Menominee Rivers.

Juvenile.

Mi MiAllG MiD MiMarqN
MiMtpT-C

479 Fisher, George P., Jr.
*Out of the Woods; a Romance of Camp
Life.* Chicago: A. C. McClurg, 1896.
270 p.

A group of young people camp out and
have various outdoor adventures. Set
on Round Lake in Delta County and in
the mining town of "Keating."

Wright III, 1872.

Mi CLU IaU OCIW OU

480 **Flanigan, Ron**
Fateful Deception. Lexington, Mich.: Blue Water Press, 1995. 298 p.

A pair of attorneys defend a state senator when the latter is accused of murdering a colleague with ties to the Michigan Militia. Set in Lansing and Port Huron.

Mystery.

MiAllG MiEM

481 **Fleischmann, Albert C.** 1920–
Where the Rivers Meet. New York: Vantage Press, 1959. 93 p.

The day-to-day experiences of a settler on the Michigan frontier. Set at Fort Detroit and environs around 1770.

MiD MiRog

482 **Fleury, Barbara Frances** 1907–
Luckypiece. New York: Macmillan Co., 1936. 146 p.

An eleven-year-old boy runs away from an orphanage and has many experiences while trying to make a new life for himself. Set in Detroit in 1879.

Juvenile.

Mi MiD MiDW InBer InFw

483 ———.
The Runaway Deer. New York: Macmillan Co., 1938. 32 p.

A yearling dissatisfied with the small confines of "Beautiful Isle" (Belle Isle) swims the river to Detroit and has an exciting, though frightening, time.

Juvenile picture book.

MiAllG MiD InE InFw WU

484 ———.
Faith the Root. New York: E. P. Dutton & Co., 1942. 250 p.

The story of an aging parish priest and his influence on the lives of the inhabitants of a small St. Clair River village. Set in "Algonquin" (Algonac?).

Black, 94.

Mi MiAllG MiD MiMtpT-C MiStc

485 **Flower, Elliott** 1863–1920
Delightful Dodd. Boston: L. C. Page & Co., 1904. 295 p.

An elderly cherry farmer adds rustic charm to a romance between two young people. Set in Traverse City and on Old Mission Peninsula.

Black, 95.

Mi MiAllG MiGr MH OU

Foehl, Harold M., joint author *see* Hargreaves, Irene M.

486 **Ford, Bette**
For Always. New York: Pinnacle Books, 1995. 379 p.

(Arabesque Romance)

An African-American high school counselor and a gruff widowed attorney, who are initially at odds about his troubled daughter, are soon attracted to one another. Set in Detroit.

Romance.

MiAllG MiBatW MiD MiFli OBgU

487 ———.
Forever After. New York: Pinnacle Books, 1995. 319 p.

(Arabesque Romance)

An African-American man and woman struggle with their different backgrounds and the mistakes they have made while rebuilding their relationship. Set partially in Detroit.

Romance.

MiAllG MiD MiFli InI OCl

488 Ford, Richard 1944–
The Sportswriter. New York: Vintage
Books, 1986. 375 p.

The self-absorbed narrator reflects on
his decision to become a sportswriter
despite a promising literary career. Partially set in Detroit.

489 Ford, Richard Clyde 1870–1951
*The White Captive; a Tale of the Pon-
tiac War.* Chicago: Rand, McNally &
Co., 1915. 296 p.

Freed from captivity, a young man
helps defend Fort Detroit during Pontiac's siege. Set at Forts St. Joseph,
Michilimackinac, and Detroit from
1760 to 1763.

Also published as *Campfire and Trail
(The White Captive).*

Juvenile.

Black, 96. Streeter, 1727.

Mi MiDU

490 ———.
*Sandy MacDonald's Man, a Tale of the
Mackinaw Fur Trade.* Lansing: Michi-
gan School Service, 1929. 207 p.

A young man embarks on a trading
expedition with his uncle's fur company. Set on Mackinac Island and in
the Upper Peninsula in the 1820s.

Juvenile.

Black, 97.

Mi MiAllG MiD MiEM MiMtpT-C

491 Forman, James D. 1932–
Becca's Story. New York: Charles
Scribner's Sons, 1992. 180 p.

A young girl is wooed by two soldiers
in the same Michigan regiment. Based

on actual diaries and letters, the story
is set in Jonesville between 1860 and
1866.

Juvenile.

Forrester, Dexter J., pseud. *see* Goldfrap,
John Henry

492 Foster, Doris Van Liew 1899–
Honker Visits the Island. New York:
Lothrup, Lee & Shepard Co., 1962.
38 p.

While flying north in the spring, a
Canadian goose stops to rest on an
island in a Michigan lake and decides
to spend the summer there.

Juvenile picture book.

MiAdC MiCad MiDW MiLapC
MiWar

493 Fox, Diana
New Beginnings. New York: Avalon
Books, 1996. 186 p.

A famous concert pianist is annoyed
when she must tend her late grandfather's apple orchard in accordance with
his will. Set in "Willow Junction" near
Kalamazoo.

Romance.

MiAllG IChamL InFw OCl WMani

494 Fox, Frances Margaret 1870–1959
Betty of Old Mackinaw. Boston: L. C.
Page & Co., 1901. 109 p.

(Cosy Corner Series)

Betty and her two brothers have many
adventures one summer when their parents leave them in the care of an aunt.
Set in Mackinaw City.

Juvenile.

Streeter, 1742.

Mi MiAllG MiD MiGr MiMtpT-C

495 ———.

Little Lady Marjorie. Boston: L. C. Page & Co., 1903. 286 p.

(Princess Series)

A baby rescued by three sailors during a storm on Lake Michigan is cared for by a Mackinaw City family until reunited with her mother a few years later.

Juvenile.

MiMtpT-C InU

496 ———.

Brother Billy. Boston: L. C. Page & Co., 1904. 128 p.

(Cosy Corner Series)

The further adventures of the Mackinaw City siblings introduced in *Betty of Old Mackinaw* are related, with this volume mostly concerning Betty's brother Billy.

Sequel to *Betty of Old Mackinaw.*

Juvenile.

Mi MiMtpT-C

497 ———.

The Rainbow Bridge. Boston: W. A. Wilde Co., 1905. 254 p.

The adventures and troubles of a little Michigan girl as she searches for a father figure and a home that will make her happy and secure.

Juvenile.

Mi MiMtpT-C

498 ———.

Ellen Jane. Chicago: Rand McNally & Co., 1924. 104 p.

A twelve-year-old girl leaves her aunt and uncle in Massachusetts to live with her family in an old abandoned lighthouse. Set in Mackinaw City.

Juvenile.

MiEM MiMack MiMtpT-C CoD OBgU

499 ———.

Nancy Davenport. New York: Rand McNally & Co., 1928. 261 p.

A little girl from Virginia travels to the Old Northwest and has many experiences en route. The last one hundred pages are set at Michilimackinac from 1811 to 1812.

Juvenile.

Mi MiMack

500 ———.

Nannette. Joliet, Ill.: P. F. Volland Co., 1929. 80 p.

An eleven-year-old orphan girl unhappily works at a boarding house and is eventually adopted by a loving family. Set in Mackinaw City.

Juvenile.

MiAllG MiMtpT-C IC NRU PNo

501 ———.

The Magic Canoe; a Frontier Story of the American Revolution. Chicago: Laidlaw Bros., 1930. 271 p.

(Young America Series)

The fictional eleven-year-old niece of George Washington is kidnapped and has a variety of adventures. Partially set at Michilimackinac from 1775 to 1779.

Juvenile.

Mi MiAllG MiFra MiMtpT-C MiPet

502 ———.

Little Mossback Amelia. New York: E. P. Dutton and Co., 1939. 86 p.

The story of how a young girl and her pioneer family move from Ohio to the Michigan woods and establish a homestead. Set somewhat south of Petoskey in the 1870s.

Juvenile.

Mi MiAllG MiMtpT MiPet MiYEM

503 Fox, Genevieve May 1888–1959
Army Surgeon. Boston: Little, Brown and Co., 1944. 244 p.

The fictionalized biography of surgeon William Beaumont (1785–1853). Partially set at Fort Mackinac where he made his famous discoveries about digestion.

Juvenile.

Mi MiD MiFliL MiMack MiMu

504 Franks, Owen
Gotcha, Gipper! by Owen Franks and Arnold S. Hirsch. Southfield, Mich.: 4–D Press, 1974. 159 p.

A speculative story about football at Michigan State University and the big showdown with the Notre Dame team. Set in East Lansing in 1977.

Mi MiAllG MiEM OBgU

504A Fraser, Nancy
Courting Trouble. New York: Kensington Publishing Corp., 1996. 159 p.

(Precious Gem Romance, no. 53)

A sophisticated young city woman comes to a small rural town to research recipes for a cookbook she is writing, and she meets the handsome local sheriff who tries to convince her to stay. Set in "Brant Mills."

Romance.

MiGr

505 Frazier, Neta Osborn Lohnes
1890–1990

Little Rhody. New York: Longmans, Green, 1953. 152 p.

A spunky ten-year-old girl moves with her family to a farm where she is involved in numerous humorous escapades. Set in Shiawassee County in 1875.

Juvenile.

Mi MiD MiMtp MiOw MiWar

506 ———.
Somebody Special. New York: Longmans, Green, 1954. 148 p.

Twelve-year-old Rhoda learns that she and others in her family all have a special talent. Set on a Shiawassee County farm in 1876.

Sequel to *Little Rhody.*

Juvenile.

Mi MiD MiGr MiLapC MiWar

507 ———.
Secret Friend. New York: Longmans, Green and Co., 1956. 148 p.

Twelve-year-old Rhoda tries to help her financially troubled father by selling a story to a magazine. Set on a Shiawassee County farm in 1877.

Sequel to *Somebody Special.*

Juvenile.

Mi MiDW MiGr MiLapC MiWar

508 ———.
The Magic Ring. New York: Longmans, Green and Co., 1959. 149 p.

Ten-year-old Becky, the daughter of Rhoda from the previous three books, is given a magic ring and overcomes initial selfishness to help others. Set in Owosso in 1900.

Juvenile.

Mi MiDW MiFliL MiOw MiWar

509 Frederick, John Towner 1893–1975
Green Bush. New York: Alfred A. Knopf, 1925. 304 p.

A young man gives up a college education and a literary career to run his family's small farm and edit the local newspaper. Set in Greenbush on Lake Huron.

Black, 98.

Mi MiAllG MiEM MiMtpT-C OU

510 French, Allen 1870–1946.
The Colonials; Being a Narrative of Events Chiefly Connected with the Siege and Evacuation of the Town of Boston in New England. New York: Doubleday, Page and Co., 1902. 504 p.

A young English girl who is the adopted daughter of a Lake Huron chief has perilous and exciting adventures. Partially set in the Saginaw Bay area and in Detroit in 1772.

Black, 99.

Mi MiU OBgU OCl OU

511 Freund, Philip Herbert 1909–
The Evening Heron. New York: Pilgrim House, 1937. 218 p.

A story of the mystical and philosophical beliefs of—and conversations among—an actress, her cousin, and friend. Set mostly on an island in Van Ettan Lake in Iosco County.

Black, 100.

MiAllG MiD MiFli ICarbS OCl

512 Frey, Hildegard G.
The Camp Fire Girls on Ellen's Isle; or, The Trail of the Seven Cedars. New York: A. L. Burt Co., 1917. 261 p.

(Camp Fire Girls, no. 6)

A group of girls spend the summer on a Lake Huron island that one of their fathers has bought. "Ellen's Isle" is near "St. Pierre" (St. Ignace?).

Juvenile.

MiAllG MB MoU NAlU TxFTC

513 Frost, Eleanor
Elusive Paradise. New York: New American Library, 1984. 184 p.

(Rapture Romance, no. 53)

A stained-glass artisan gets a commission for a large window from the handsome owner of a new inn. Set in Paradise in the Upper Peninsula.

Romance.

MiAllG AzSaf OBgU

Frost, Fannie, joint author *see* E.L.T. Club

514 Fuessle, Newton Augustus 1883–1924
Gold Shod. New York: Boni and Liveright, 1921. 243 p.

The story of a man's rise to the top of an automobile company and his later regret that he did not pursue a career in the arts. Set in Detroit from 1900 to 1919.

Black, 101.

Mi MiD MiEM MnU OU

515 Fuller, Iola 1906–1993
The Loon Feather. New York: Harcourt, Brace and Co., 1940. 419 p.

The far-ranging and lucrative Great Lakes fur trade is described by the fictional daughter of Tecumseh. Set mostly on Mackinac Island from 1806 to 1824.

Black, 102.

MiBrF MiEmp MiKW MiT OC

516 ———.
The Gilded Torch. New York: G. P. Putnam's Sons, 1957. 343 p.

The fictionalized biography and explorations of Sieur de La Salle (1643–1687) in New France and the Great Lakes in the 1680s. Twenty-five pages are set in Michigan.

G

517 Gage, Elizabeth, pseud.
Intimate. New York: Pocket Books, 1995. 498 p.

A predatory seductress, a self-made wealthy young man, and a shrewd advertising woman become entangled in their quest for power and money. Partially set in Detroit.

518 Gail, Otto Willi 1896–1956
Hans Hardts Mondfahrt; eine Abenteuerliche Erzählung. Stuttgart: Union Deutsche Verlagsgesellschaft, 1928. 200 p.

A Detroit newspaper reporter accompanies a young German's amazing flight to the moon in a spaceship. Forty pages are set in Detroit.

In German.

Anonymous English translation published as *By Rocket to the Moon; the Story of Hans Hardt's Miraculous Flight* (New York: Sears Publishing Co., 1931).

Science fiction.

DLC

519 Galbraith, Kathryn Osebold 1945–
Something Suspicious. New York: Atheneum, 1985. 158 p.

Two young girls try to track down a bank robber and become involved in a number of mysterious adventures. Set in "Broadhead" in southern Michigan.

Juvenile.

Gale, Annie Morley, joint author *see* E.L.T. Club

520 Garbo, Norman 1919–
The Movement. New York: William Morrow, 1969. 407 p.

Members of a student protest movement clash with rigid state and university leaders. Set at "Chadwick University" probably located in the Flint area.

MiAllG MiD MiEM MiMtpT-C MiU

521 Gardner, Joan Geisel
Desires of the Heart (for Young People). Grand Rapids: Zondervan Publishing House, 1934. 218 p.

Two young people fall in love, but the fact that she is a deeply religious member of the Christian Reformed Church and he is not complicates matters. Set in Grand Rapids.

Black, 103.

Mi MiGrC

522 Gardner, Lewis J. 1836–1909
Scarred Eagle; or, Moorooine, the Sporting Fawn. A Story of Lake and Shore by Andrew Dearborn [pseud.]. New York: Beadle and Adams, 1870. 94 p.

(Beadle's Dime Novels, no. 209)

The adventures of a scout and his Miami companion as they assist a group of rangers track a traitor. Set in southeastern Michigan in 1763.

Dime novel.

Mi

Gardner, Metta, joint author *see* E.L.T. Club

523 Gariepy, Louis J.
Saw-Ge-Mah (Medicine Man). Saint Paul: Northland Press, 1950. 326 p.

The son of a lumbermill worker dreams of becoming a doctor and works hard towards that goal. Set mostly in "Blufftown" in northern Michigan.

Black, 140.

Mi MiAllG MiD MiMtpT-C MiMarqN

524 Garis, Howard Roger 1873–1962
Larry Dexter and the Stolen Boy; or, A Young Reporter on the Lakes. New York: Grosset & Dunlap, 1912. 205 p.

(Great Newspaper Series, no. 5)

A New York newspaper reporter searches for the kidnapped son of an opera diva. Partially set in Detroit, on Lake St. Clair, and in the Lake Huron town of "Marshall."

Also published as *The Young Reporter and the Stolen Boy; or, A Chase on the Great Lakes* (New York: George Sully & Co., 1912 [Young Reporter Series, no. 5]) and, under the pseudonym "Raymond Sperry," as *Larry Dexter and the Stolen Boy; or, A Chase on the Great Lakes* (Garden City, New York: Garden City Publishing Co., 1926 [Larry Dexter Series, no. 5]).

Juvenile.

MiGr-L DeU OAU

525 Garnet, A. H., pseud.
The Santa Claus Killer. New Haven and New York: Ticknor & Fields, 1981. 376 p.

A young idealistic attorney runs for mayor against a corrupt incumbent who will stop at nothing to get re-elected. Set in "Northway" (Southfield).

"A. H. Garnet" is the joint pseudonym of Alfred H. Slote and Garnet R. Garrison.

Mystery.

526 ———.
Maze. New Haven and New York: Ticknor & Fields, 1982. 311 p.

After a professor is found baked to death in the law school kitchen, a young English professor investigates. Set at "Mid-East University" (University of Michigan).

Mystery.

527 Garrigues, Adele M.
Summer Boarders. New York: The Author's Publishing Co., 1880. 188 p.

A variety of people stay at a summer boardinghouse in northern Michigan in the 1870s and make use of the mineral springs in the town of "M———."

Wright III, 2129.

Mi MiU OU ViU WU

Garrison, Garnet R. *see* Garnet, A. H.

528 Garth, David
Fire on the Wind. New York: Putnam, 1951. 378 p.

A Civil War veteran and his foster father begin to build a timber and iron ore empire from the vast resources in the Upper Peninsula from 1865 to 1870.

Black, 105.

529 Gauch, Patricia Lee 1934–
Night Talks. New York: G. P. Putnam's Sons, 1983. 156 p.

A fourteen-year-old girl from a wealthy family tries to help a troubled inner-city girl at "Camp Glenmora" amidst the ongoing activities. Set in central Michigan.

Juvenile.

530 ———.
The Year the Summer Died. New York: G. P. Putnam's Sons, 1985. 158 p.

Spending the summer with her grandparents, a fourteen-year-old Michigan girl sadly realizes that her older best friend no longer enjoys her youthful interests.

Juvenile.

531 **Gay, Margaret Cooper** 1900–1957
Hatchet in the Sky. New York: Simon and Schuster, 1954. 500 p.

The story of an exiled Scotsman whose hatred for the British leads him to side with Pontiac and his warriors at the siege of Detroit in 1763.

Black, 106.

Mi MiD MiGr MiMtpT-C MiPet

532 **Gear, Kathleen O'Neal** 1954–
People of the Lakes by Kathleen O'Neal Gear and W. Michael Gear. New York: Forge, 1994. 608 p.

Around 200 A.D., a powerful spirit mask causes discord and death among some Ohio Native-American clans. Partially set on the Michigan shores of Lakes Michigan and Huron.

Gear, W. Michael, joint author *see* Gear, Kathleen O'Neal

533 **Gent, Peter** 1942–
The Last Magic Summer: A Season with My Son. A Memoir. New York: William Morrow and Co., 1996. 227 p.

The author's slightly fictionalized reminiscences about coaching his son's baseball team through eight seasons

and his changing relationship with his son. Set in Bangor.

534 **Genung, Helen**
Valiant Dust by Helen Genung and Caryl May Hayes. New York: Lee Furman, 1936. 313 p.

The chronicle of the Dillon family, whose demanding and controlling matriarch ruins the lives of her children. Set in the Pontiac area from 1895 to 1910.

Black, 107.

MiAllG MiD MiEM MiGr MiStc

George, Jean Craighead, joint author *see* George, John Lothar

535 **George, John Lothar** 1916–
Masked Prowler; the Story of a Raccoon by John L. George and Jean George. New York: E. P. Dutton & Co., 1950. 183 p.

(American Woodland Tales)

The history and adventures of a raccoon. Set specifically in the farmland west of Ann Arbor in Superior Township.

Juvenile.

536 ———.
Bubo, the Great Horned Owl by John L. George and Jean George. New York: E. P. Dutton & Co., 1954. 184 p.

(American Woodland Tales)

The history and adventures of a horned owl. Set in a southern Michigan forest.

Juvenile.

537 **Gerber, Daniel Frank** 1940–
American Atlas by Dan Gerber. Englewood Cliffs, N.J.: Prentice-Hall, 1973. 204 p.

A young would-be poet and heir to a large pie company travels across America in search of himself. Partially set in "Brainard" (Fremont).

Mi MiAllG MiBatW MiD MiMtpT-C

538 ———.
A Voice from the River by Dan Gerber. Livingston, Mont.: Clark City Press, 1990. 196 p.

The retired chairman of a lumber and paper company reflects on his past life and what his future years hold for him. Mostly set in "Five Oaks" (Fremont).

Mi MiAllG MiAlp MiD MiMtpT-C

539 Gerland, Hazel
Samantha. New York: Pageant Press International Corp., 1969. 221 p.

A Canadian woman from a poor background leaves her restrictive environment and finds fulfillment in marriage and work. Partially set in Detroit.

MiGr-L

540 [Gerson, Noel Bertram] 1914–
Fortress Fury by Carter A. Vaughan [pseud.]. Garden City, N.Y.: Doubleday & Co., 1966. 254 p.

An American major experiences many adventures while campaigning against the British in the Old Northwest. Partially set at Fort Detroit around 1778.

541 Gessler, Dick
The 17 Mile Horror. Plymouth, Mich.: Holly Publications, 1981. 175 p.

A seemingly senseless series of murders and the singleminded vengeance of a woman's ghost are somehow connected. Set in Plymouth.

MiGr-L

542 Gessner, Robert Joseph 1907–1968
Here Is My Home. New York: Alliance Book Corp., 1941. 433 p.

The story of the rise of a Jewish immigrant who manages a dry goods store in an Upper Peninsula lumber town despite the local prejudice against him. Set in "Chippewa City" in the 1890s.

Black, 108.

Mi MiEM MiHM MiKC IEN

543 Gibbs, Philip Hamilton, Sir 1877–1962
The Reckless Lady. London: Hutchinson & Co., 1924. 312 p.

A beautiful and ambitious Englishwoman discards a husband and a lover, but eventually marries a wealthy American, and then settles in Grand Rapids.

Black, 109.

CtY DLC

544 Gideon, Nancy A. 1955–
Tempest Waters. New York: Berkley Books, 1993. 326 p.

(Stories of Love on the Great Lakes)

A young woman has inherited her father's logging company and is determined to run it despite a handsome city man's offer of assistance. Set in Copper Harbor in 1865.

Romance.

Mi MiBatW OCo ScSp UM

545 ———.
For Mercy's Sake. New York: Silhouette Books, 1995. 250 p.

(Silhouette Intimate Moments, no. 648)

A sheriff becomes suspicious when a beautiful young woman whom he rescues from a stranded car acts terribly frightened. Set in "Pine Creek" and at "Big Bear Lake."

Romance.

MiAllG IChamL OCo OXe WM

546 Gies, Joseph Cornelius 1916–
A Matter of Morals. New York: Harper
& Brothers, 1951. 245 p.

The question of academic freedom and
an unsympathetic college administra-
tion is examined in this story. Set at
"College Park" (University of Michigan) in 1938.

MiKW MiRog IC OBgU WU

547 Gilbert, Edwin 1907–1976
American Chrome. New York: G. P.
Putnam's Sons, 1965. 448 p.

A man begins work for Bellgard Motors and becomes involved in the glitz
and duplicity of the automobile industry. Set in Detroit and "Kent Hills"
(Bloomfield Hills).

548 Gildner, Gary 1938–
The Second Bridge. Chapel Hill, N.C.:
Algonquin Books of Chapel Hill, 1987.
188 p.

The story of a couple's relationship,
which is strained by the death of their
only child. Partially set in Marquette,
Muskegon, Flint, Houghton Lake, and
in the Hartwick Pines near Grayling.

549 Gilman, Julia
*William Wells and Meconaquah, White
Rose of the Miamis.* Cincinnati: Jewel
Publishing, 1985. 317 p.

The fictionalized account of the abduc-
tion of two children, William Wells
(1770?–1812) and Frances Slocum
(1773–1851) by the Miamis in 1778
and the children's subsequent lives.
Fifteen pages are set in the Detroit area
in 1795.

Mi MiKW MiMtpT-C InFw OCl

550 Gilman, Mildred Evans, 1898–
Fig Leaves. New York: Siebel Publishing Corp., 1925. 328 p.

The story of a woman's life from her
childhood, through her college days,
and finally to her marriage. Partially set
in Grand Rapids from 1906 to 1917.

Black, 110.

Mi MiAllG ICU OU UU

551 Gingrich, Arnold 1903–1976
Cast Down the Laurel. New York: Alfred A. Knopf, 1935. 341 p.

A novel within a novel, the story concerns an Austrian musician who establishes a conservatory and is embroiled
in scandal. Set in "Mill Center" (Grand
Rapids) from 1910 to the 1920s.

Black, 111.

Mi MiAllG MiEM MiGr MiU

552 Glass, Joanna McClelland 1936–
Reflections on a Mountain Summer.
New York: Alfred A. Knopf, 1974.
307 p.

A man reminisces about a 1932 Canadian vacation when he was fourteen
and how it affected the rest of his life.
Partially set in Grosse Pointe and Detroit.

553 Glassford, Eva Belle 1915–
The Giant Step. Philadelphia: Dorrance
& Co., 1953. 235 p.

An eight-year-old boy spends the summer with his grandparents and decides
he wants to become a hermit. Set in
a resort community in northern Michigan.

MiAlle MiAllG MiPh InFw NjNetS

Glenwood, Ida, pseud. *see* Gorton, Cynthia M. Roberts

554 Gochnauer, Florence Plantz
The Coveted Land. Philadelphia: Dorrance & Co., 1959. 345 p.

A French fur trader finds American rule of the Great Lakes intolerable and removes himself and his family to another location. Forty pages are set on Mackinac Island in 1811.

MiGr-L WAL WAPL WGr WSpU

555 Goff, Georgena Carter
The Black Dog. New York: Belmont Books, 1971. 156 p.

(Belmont Blue Ribbon Gothic)

A young woman falls under the influence of a mysterious psychic who is accompanied by a sinister black dog. Set in a northern Michigan town near Indian River.

Mystery.

MiAllG CU-Riv OBgU

556 Goines, Donald 1936–1974
Dopefiend. Los Angeles: Holloway House Publishing Co., 1971. 254 p.

The story of two young talented African Americans and their growing heroin addiction. Set in Detroit.

Mystery.

Mi MiAllG MiBatW MiD MiEM

557 ———.
Black Gangster. Los Angeles: Holloway House Publishing Co., 1972. 280 p.

The story of a young African American and his steady rise from a teenage ganglord to a powerful and merciless mobster. Set in Detroit.

Mystery.

MiAllG MiGr InFw OCl WMUW

558 ———.
Whoreson; the Story of a Ghetto Pimp. Los Angeles: Holloway House Publishing Co., 1972. 279 p.

The son of an African-American prostitute learns the ways of the street to become a ruthless and violent pimp. Set in Detroit.

Mystery.

Mi MiAllG MiBatW MiD MiMu

559 ———.
Street Players. Los Angeles: Holloway House Publishing Co., 1973. 190 p.

A wealthy African-American pimp tries to hold on to his successful business as others begin to have designs on his territory. Set in Detroit.

Mystery.

MiAllG MiBatW InG OXe WKen

560 ———.
White Man's Justice: Black Man's Grief. Los Angeles: Holloway House Publishing Co., 1973. 218 p.

Ghetto leader Kenyatta battles to rid his community of drug dealers with half-hearted assistance from African-American and white detectives, Benson and Ryan. Set partially in Detroit and Jackson.

Mystery.

MiAllG MiBatW MiD MiGr InG

561 [———].
Crime Partners by Al C. Clark [pseud.]. Los Angeles: Holloway House Publishing Co., 1974. 190 p.

A pair of African-American ex-convicts try to find some action but run afoul of ghetto leader Kenyatta and detectives Benson and Ryan. Set in Detroit.

Mystery.

MiAllG   MiD   InFw   InI   InLP

562 ――――.
Daddy Cool. Los Angeles: Holloway House Publishing Co., 1974. 217 p.

An African-American hit man angrily discovers that his daughter has been corrupted by a pimp and takes vengeance. Set in Detroit.

Mystery.

MiAllG   MiBatW   MiD   MiMu   InG

563 [――――].
Death List by Al C. Clark [pseud.]. Los Angeles: Holloway House Publishing Co., 1974. 183 p.

Detectives Benson and Ryan find themselves in the middle of a turf war between Kenyatta and another African-American ghetto leader. Set in Detroit.

Mystery.

MiAllG   MiBatW   MiD   MiGr   InG

564 ――――.
Eldorado Red. Los Angeles: Holloway House Publishing Co., 1974. 219 p.

An African-American numbers game racketeer is overthrown by a group of rivals and sets about a vicious plan of revenge. Set in Detroit.

Mystery.

Mi   MiAllG   MiBatW   MiD   InG

565 [――――].
Kenyatta's Escape by Al C. Clark [pseud.]. Los Angeles: Holloway House Publishing Co., 1974. 215 p.

Detectives Benson and Ryan try to arrest the dangerous Kenyatta and initiate a bloody confrontation and chase. Partially set in the Detroit area.

Mystery.

MiAllG   MiBatW   MiD   MiGr   InG

566 Gold, Herbert 1924–
The Optimist. Boston: Little, Brown, 1959. 395 p.

The story of an ambitious young man's progress through college, war, marriage, and politics. Partially set in Ann Arbor at the University of Michigan and in Detroit from 1941 to the late 1950s.

Black, 112.

567 [Goldfrap, John Henry] 1879–1917
The Bungalow Boys on the Great Lakes by Dexter J. Forrester [pseud.]. New York: Hurst & Co., 1912. 295 p.

(Bungalow Boys, no. 4)

Three boys have a series of adventures and escapes as they cross paths with a gang of wreckers and work to foil their plans. Set on Lake Huron and the Straits of Mackinac.

Juvenile.

Mi   MiAllG   MiEM   DeU   OBgU

568 [Goldsmith, David]
The Mystery of Kawbawgam's Grave by Clifford S. Cleveland [pseud.]. Marquette: Clifford S. Cleveland, 1979. 115 p.

A young couple is called to Marquette to solve a mystery involving kidnappers, ciphers, hidden treasure, and local landmarks.

Juvenile.

MiAllG   MiMarqN

569 Goodin, Peggy 1923–
Take Care of My Little Girl. New York:
E. P. Dutton & Co., 1950. 189 p.

A young woman is pressured to join the
same sorority that her mother did, but
becomes disillusioned with the system.
Set at "Midwestern University" (University of Michigan).

MiBatW   MiKW   MiMarqN   InI   OCl

570 ———.
The Lie. New York: E. P. Dutton & Co.,
1953. 191 p.

An intimate story of three women from
the same family and a devastating and
shameful secret of illegitimacy. Set in
the Detroit area.

MiU   InFw   OCl   OCU   WU

571 Gordon, David
NT GILTY. Lakewood, Colo.: Glenbridge
Publishing, 1996. 340 p.

A defense attorney with cash flow
problems murders three witnesses in
the case against his client, the son of
a wealthy real estate developer. Set in
Royal Oak.

Mystery.

Gordon, H. R., Colonel, pseud. *see* Ellis,
Edward Sylvester

572 [Gorton, Cynthia M. Roberts]
1829–1894
The Fatal Secret by Ida Glenwood,
"the Blind Bard of Michigan" [pseud.].
Philadelphia: John E. Potter and Co.,
1873. 415 p.

A young woman of Native-American
and French parentage tries to make her
way in New York and English society.
Partially set at Mackinac Island in the
1830s.

Black, 113. Wright II, 1014.

MiAllG   MiD   MiMtpT-C   OU   WU

573 Gosling, Paula 1939–
The Body in Blackwater Bay. London:
Little, Brown and Co., 1992. 282 p.

(Jack Stryker Mystery)

Sheriff Gabriel investigates a murder
on a small island and uncovers secrets
among the property owners. Set on
"Paradise Island" and in "Blackwater"
probably on Lake St. Clair.

Mystery.

Copy not located.

574 ———.
A Few Dying Words. London: Little,
Brown and Co., 1993. 332 p.

(Blackwater Bay Mystery)

The dying words of Sheriff Gabriel's
friend hint at a decades-old death
and the possible implication of the
town's most important citizenry. Set in
"Blackwater."

Mystery.

MiGr-L   OCl

575 ———.
The Dead of Winter. London: Little,
Brown and Co., 1995. 316 p.

(Blackwater Bay Mystery)

Sheriff Gabriel must deal with the
Mob, the FBI, and odd doings in Blackwater that are related to a mysterious
corpse glimpsed in the lake ice.

Mystery.

Copy not located.

Goss, Willard, pseud. *see* Davenport,
Willard Goss

576 [Graepp, L. W.]
Bleichgesicht und Rothhaut; oder,
Pontiac, der Häuptling der Ottawas.
Historische Original-Erzählung aus
der Heimath des rothen Mannes. Nach
Quellen zusammengestellt und frei
erzählt von L. W. G. Milwaukee: Ver-
lag von Geo. Brumder, n.d. 415 p.

A fictionalized narrative concerning
Pontiac's efforts to expel the British
from the Great Lakes area. Set partially
in Detroit and at Michilimackinac in
1763.

In German.

MiD MiMtpT-C IEN OYU WMUW

577 Graham, Loren R. 1933–
A Face in the Rock: The Tale of a Grand
Island Chippewa. Washington: Island
Press, 1995. 160 p.

A fictionalized history of the Grand
Island tribe of Ojibwas of Lake Superior, including the disasters of war, the
coming of the whites, and today's more
hopeful times.

Grant, Jeanne, pseud. *see* Culby, Jill

578 Graydon, William Murray 1864–
1946
From Lake to Wilderness; or, The
Cruise of the Yolande. New York:
Street & Smith, 1899. 231 p.

A group of boys on a summer boating
adventure become involved with bank
robbers. Set partially in Marquette and
on the southern shore of Lake Superior.

Juvenile.

FTS WU

579 Greathead, Sarah Estelle Ham-
mond 1855–
The Merrill Clan; Daguerreotypes
and Vignettes by S. Estelle Greathead. Boston: Christopher Publishing
House, 1937. 422 p.

An anecdotal chronicle of family and
farm life set partially in the Marshall
area from 1860 to 1870 and subsequently in California.

Mi CSjU TNJ TxDaM

580 Greeley, Andrew M. 1928–
God Game. New York: Warner Books,
1986. 308 p.

When lightning strikes a computer
while a fantasy game is in progress, the
on-screen inhabitants are convinced
that the player is God. Set partially in
Grand Beach on Lake Michigan.

Science fiction.

581 Green, Chalmers
The Scarlet Venus. New York: Fawcett
Publications, 1952. 180 p.

(Gold Medal, no. 246)

A young woman flees New York and
her notorious past and becomes involved with a boxer. Set mostly in "Pe-
wabic Point" (Iron Mountain?) on the
Menominee River.

Mystery.

MiAllG NN

582 Green, Hannah 1927?–
The Dead of the House. Garden City,
N.Y.: Doubleday & Co., 1972. 180 p.

A young woman reminisces about her
family, her forebears, and the relationship between her past and present. Partially set at Neahtawanta on Old Mission Peninsula in the 1940s.

583 Green, Phyllis 1932–
Nantucket Summer. Nashville, Tenn.:
Thomas Nelson, 1974. 122 p.

A teenage girl takes a summer job as a babysitter for a mentally disturbed mother on Nantucket Island. The first twenty-seven pages are set in Livonia.

Juvenile.

584 ———.
Walkie-Talkie. Reading, Mass.: Addison-Wesley, 1978. 96 p.

A fourteen-year-old troublemaker tries to change his behavior for the better with the help of his handicapped friend. Set in Livonia.

Juvenile.

585 Greenbaum, Leonard 1930–
Out of Shape. New York: Harper & Row, 1969. 247 p.

A graduate assistant of a murdered professor assists the police in their investigation. Set at "Milton State University" (University of Michigan).

Mystery.

Greene, Jennifer, pseud. *see* Culby, Jill

586 Greene, Merritt W. 1897–1972
The Land Lies Pretty. "Op-ja-mo-mak-ya." A Story of the Great Sauk Trail in 1832 with an Introduction to the Northwest Territory. Hillsdale, Mich.: Hillsdale School Supply, 1959. 195 p.

Bored with his teaching job in New York, Martin Langdon comes to the Michigan Territory in 1832 seeking adventure. Set in "Grannisville" (Jonesville?).

Mi MiAllG MiMtpT-C MiPh MiU

587 ———.
Curse of the White Panther; a Story of the Days of the Toledo War. Hillsdale, Mich.: Hillsdale School Supply, 1960. 191 p.

The further adventures of Martin Langdon in the Michigan Territory, including his participation in the Toledo War. Set in southern Michigan from 1833 to 1835.

Sequel to *The Land Lies Pretty.*

Mi MiAllG MiD MiMtpT-C MiPh

588 ———.
Forgotten Yesterdays; a Tale of Early Michigan. Hillsdale, Mich.: Hillsdale School Supply, 1964. 173 p.

The story of Martin Langdon continues in the early days of Michigan statehood. Set in "Grannisville" (Jonesville?) and Hillsdale County from 1838 to 1839.

Sequel to *Curse of the White Panther.*

Mi MiAllG MiGr MiMtpT-C MiPh

589 Greenfield, Jeff 1943–
The People's Choice. New York: G. P. Putnam's Sons, 1995. 309 p.

When the president-elect dies two days after the election, a renegade electoral college delegate refuses to vote for the vice president-elect. Ten pages are set in Grand Rapids and Lansing.

590
Grey Towers; a Campus Novel. Chicago: Covici-McGee Co., 1923. 287 p.

A woman returns to her Chicago alma mater as an English instructor and finds a depersonalized institution. Fifteen pages are set on Mackinac Island.

MiEM MiHolH ICU InU OBgU

591 Grice, Julia Haughey 1940–
Tender Prey. New York: Tom Doherty Associates, 1990. 410 p.

A woman is terrorized and her daughter kidnapped by a demented man. Set in the northern ski areas of "Hartwick" (Grayling) and "Ossineke Lake."

Mystery.

MiAllG MiGr MiSth InMu OCl

592 ———.
Jagged Light. New York: Tom Doherty Associates, 1991. 312 p.

A man convicted of rape is paroled and plans revenge upon his victim, who dared to testify against him in court. Partially set in Rochester.

Mystery.

MiAllG MiD MiSth MiWar OCl

593 ———.
Suspicion. New York: Tom Doherty Associates, 1992. 248 p.

A divorcée's boyfriend may be connected with the disappearances of area women. Set in "Clyattville" in the Royal Oak and Birmingham areas.

Mystery.

MiD MiJac MiLapC MiMtcM MiSth

594 ———.
The Cutting Hours. New York: Forge/ Tom Doherty Associates, 1993. 300 p.

A disturbed young man is obsessed with an older woman, and when he tries to get to her through her daughter, violence ensues. Set in a northern Detroit suburb.

Mystery.

595 ———.
Pretty Babies. New York: Tom Doherty Associates, 1994. 320 p.

A thirteen-year-old girl takes her foster parents' baby and flees home because the father is a child molester. Partially set in Detroit.

Mystery.

MiD MiFli MiJac MiMtcM MiSf

———, joint author *see* Fenton, Julia

Griffin, Jocelyn, pseud. *see* Sparrow, Laura H.

596 [Grimm, Albert Friedrich Wilhelm] 1864–1922
Das Stiefmütterchen. Eine Erzählung aus den Kupferminen am Superiorsee. Für das Christliche Volk von Alfred Ira [pseud.]. Antigo, Wis.: Antigo Publishing Co., 1898. 228 p.

A story with religious themes about the joys and hardships that a German family experience while living in the copper-mining region of the Keweenaw Peninsula.

In German.

MiMtpT-C IEN OCU OCl WLacU

Gringhuis, Dirk *see* Gringhuis, Richard H.

597 [Gringhuis, Richard H.] 1918–1974
Hope Haven; a Tale of a Dutch Boy and Girl Who Found a New Home in America by Dirk Gringhuis. Grand Rapids: Wm. B. Eerdmans Publishing Co., 1947. 132 p.

A young boy and girl travel with their family and Albertus Van Raalte (1811–1876) from the Netherlands to establish the Dutch settlement at Holland in 1847.

Juvenile.

Mi MiAllG MiBatW MiGr MiYEM

598 [———].
Tulip Time by Dirk Gringhuis. Chicago: Albert Whitman and Co., 1951. 32 p.

A fictionalized description of the planning and preparation that goes into the Tulip Festival held annually in Holland.

Juvenile picture book.

Mi MiBatW MiGr HiHolH MiYEM

599 [———].
The Young Voyageur by Dirk Gringhuis. New York: Whittlesey House, 1955. 202 p.

A fourteen-year-old boy runs away from his family in Detroit and travels with a French voyageur to Michilimackinac in 1763 where he is captured by Ojibwas.

Juvenile.

Mi MiAllG MiD MiLapC MiMtpT-C

600 [———].
The Eagle Pine by Dirk Gringhuis. New York: D. McKay Co., 1958. 181 p.

A fifteen-year-old boy works for his uncle in a logging camp and thwarts a gang of timber thieves. Set in central Michigan in the late 1800s.

Juvenile.

Mi MiBatW MiD MiFliL MiPet

601 [———].
Saddle the Storm by Dirk Gringhuis. Indianapolis: Bobbs-Merrill Co., 1962. 127 p.

A young Irish boy who lives with his parents on Beaver Island is given a horse, and the two form a close bond and have many adventures together.

Juvenile.

Mi MiAdC MiChe MiMack MiMio

602 [———].
Mystery at Skull Castle by Dirk Gringhuis. Chicago: Reilly & Lee Co., 1964. 181 p.

Two boys use a ruined castle on Lake Michigan as their secret place and run afoul of scoundrels. Set in the town of "New Volendam" in 1880.

Juvenile.

Mi MiCad MiChe MiPh MiYEM

602A **Guernsey, Clara Florida** 1836–1893
The Shawnee Prisoner: A Borderer's Story. Philadelphia: American Sunday-School Union, 1877. 329 p.

A young Virginian, captured by Shawnees near his home in 1784, is adopted into the tribe before being sent to Detroit and Frenchtown where he is reunited with his family years later.

MiFli IHi MH NRU OBgU

603 **Guest, Judith** 1936–
Second Heaven. New York: Viking Press, 1982. 320 p.

A lawyer is attracted to a divorcée who has sheltered a troubled young man, and the three become inextricably linked. Set in Birmingham and Detroit.

H

604 **Haffner, Katherine Neuhaus** 1909–

Clay in the Sand. New York: Pageant Press, 1953. 315 p.

A young woman from the city must adjust to rural life when she marries a farmer. Set in "Cherry Rapids" in the Grand Traverse area from the 1920s to the 1940s.

Mi MiAllG MiGr MiPh MiStc

605 Hager, Henry B. 1926–
Fireball. Garden City, N.Y.: Doubleday, 1963. 277 p.

An aggressive and successful advertising man designs a new promotional
campaign for Columbia Motors with
disastrous results. Set in Detroit.

Mi MiAllG MiAlp MiEM MiMtp

606 Hailey, Arthur 1920–
Wheels. Garden City, N.Y.: Doubleday,
1971. 374 p.

The entire Detroit automobile industry,
including its corporate boardrooms, as-
sembly lines, labor unions, ad agen-
cies, and retail showrooms, is described in dramatic detail.

607 Haines, Donal Hamilton 1886–
1951
Sporting Chance. New York: Farrar &
Rinehart, 1935. 295 p.

After the sudden death of his father,
a snobbish young man must make his
own way in life. Set in Detroit, northern Michigan, and at a Saginaw Bay
hunting club.

Juvenile.

Mi IC InFw OCl ScCF

608 ———.
Blaine of the Backfield. New York:
Farrar & Rinehart, 1937. 281 p.

A young college man makes the varsity
football team after some difficulties.
Set at "Western University" (University of Michigan) in "Huron" (Ann Arbor).

Juvenile.

Mi CoD InFw MB OU

609 ———.
Pro Quarterback. New York: Farrar &
Rinehart, 1940. 266 p.

A talented college football player joins
a professional team and finds the going
a bit tougher. Partially set at "Western
University" (University of Michigan)
in "Huron" (Ann Arbor) and in "Motor
City" (Detroit).

Juvenile.

Mi CL IC InFw TC

610 ———.
Shadow on the Campus. New York:
Farrar & Rinehart, 1942. 278 p.

Mysterious and sinister events, which
are caused by enemy agents, occur on
the campus of "Western University"
(University of Michigan) in "Huron"
(Ann Arbor).

Juvenile.

Mi CL InFw KyLnC TC

611 Hale, Anna W. 1909–
Mystery on Mackinac Island. Tucson:
Harbinger House, 1989. 183 p.

A thirteen-year-old Ottawa boy and
his two tourist friends investigate a
series of rental bicycle thefts. Set on
Mackinac Island.

Juvenile.

Mi MiAllG MiMack MiMtpT-C MiU

Hale, Christopher, pseud. *see* Stevens,
Frances Moyer Ross

612 Hale, Edward Everett 1822–1909
Ups and Downs. An Every-Day Novel.
Boston: Roberts Bros., 1873. 319 p.

A young Harvard graduate rescues
a carriage business from bankruptcy
and becomes a successful businessman. Mostly set in Detroit in the 1840s.

Black, 114. Wright II, 1061.

MiFli ICU InDeKN OC OCl

612A Hale, Fritz
The Detroit Connection. Los Angeles: Holloway House Publishing Co., 1982. 210 p.

A young African American couple want to start a music recording business and decide to finance it through drug pushing and armed robbery. Set in Detroit.

Mystery.

MiGr-L

613 Hall, F. H. 1926–
In the Lamb-White Days. Indianapolis: Bobbs-Merrill, 1975. 185 p.

A young man sailing alone on Lake Michigan rescues a boy from drowning and becomes involved in a murder investigation. Set in Holland and Allegan.

Mystery.

Mi MiAllG MiBatW MiStc MiWar

614 Hall, John C.
Cross Country to Danger. Grand Rapids: Baker Book House, 1983. 130 p.

While on a cross-country ski trip in the Upper Peninsula, two boys witness a freighter aground in Lake Superior and assist in the rescue of the crew.

Juvenile.

Mi MiChe MiChv MiNi MiPet

615 Hall, Lynn 1937–
Dragon Defiant. Chicago: Follett Publishing Co., 1977. 96 p.

A former champion showhorse is sold to a caring horsewoman and lives out his old age in comfort. Set in Crystal Falls in the Upper Peninsula.

Sequel to *A Horse Called Dragon* and *New Day for Dragon,* both set in Texas.

Juvenile.

616 ———.
Dragon's Delight. Chicago: Follett Publishing Co., 1981. 107 p.

The deceased showhorse Dragon's high-spiritedness and championship traits live on in his offspring. Set in Crystal Falls in the Upper Peninsula.

Sequel to *Dragon Defiant.*

Juvenile.

617 Hallet, Richard Matthews 1887–1967
Trial by Fire; a Tale of the Great Lakes. Boston: Small, Maynard and Co., 1916. 309 p.

Circumstances force a young man from a wealthy family to work as a stoker aboard a Great Lakes ore boat. Partially set on the Calumet and Hecla docks in Houghton County.

Black, 115. Streeter, 2017.

MiAllG MiU OU WLacU WM

618 ———.
Michael Beam. Boston: Houghton Mifflin Co., 1939. 451 p.

On the frontier, a woodsman falls in love with two women, one white and the other an Algonquin. Partially set on Mackinac Island and the Muskegon River around 1830.

MiRochOU MiMarqN InE OCl WU

Halliday-Antona, Annetta *see* Antona, Annetta Halliday

619 Halversen, Forest
"Scrub": The Story of a Northern Michigan White-Tailed Deer by Forest

Halvorsen [sic], Sr. Cedar Lake, Mich.: AB Publishing, 1996. 99 p.

A deer struggles for survival as he encounters coyotes, dogs, and hunters over a period of a few years are described. Set in northern Michigan.

Subtitle on spine: *Thrilling Life-Story of a Young Buck.*

MiAllG MiGr

620 Ham, Bob
Michigan Madness. New York: Bantam Books, 1991. 197 p.

(Overload, no. 10)

A pair of freelance ex-commandos in a truck track down a group of mercenaries who are about to deliver plutonium to terrorists. Set in Michigan mostly at Silver Lake.

Mystery.

MiMtcM MiWar NcR OCo

621 Hamilton, Harry 1896–
Thunder in the Wilderness. Indianapolis: Bobbs-Merrill Co., 1949. 304 p.

A young man has a number of exciting adventures in the French settlements of Kaskaskia and Vincennes in the 1760s. Fifteen pages are set in Detroit.

Black, 116.

MiD MiU IC InFw OBgU

622 [Hamilton, Jean]
Wings of Wax by Janet Hoyt [pseud.]. New York: J. H. Sears & Co., 1929. 358 p.

The new college president of "University of Woban" (University of Michigan) in "Barker" (Ann Arbor) is intent on making many reforms, which ultimately lead to his downfall.

Black, 117.

Mi MiAllG MiEM MiMtpT-C MnU

623 Hamilton, Morse 1943–
Effie's House. New York: Greenwillow Books, 1990. 208 p.

A fifteen-year-old girl tries to cope with her emotional problems related to her mother, stepfather, and father. Set in "Wahaneeka" near Clare.

Juvenile.

624 Hamilton, Violet
A Rake's Journey. New York: Zebra Books, 1995. 318 p.

(Zebra Regency)

A noblewoman visiting her sister in Detroit when the town surrenders to the British in 1812 is attracted to the handsome officer who escorts her to Montreal.

Romance.

MiAllG IC OCl OCo WM

Hamilton, W. J., pseud. *see* Clark, Charles Dunning

625 [Hanchar, Peggy S.] 1940–
Mrs. Perfect by Peggy Roberts [pseud.]. New York: Zebra Books, 1992. 480 p.

(To Love Again)

After the deaths of her husband and son, a woman raises her three grandchildren while coping with her job at an advertising agency. Set in Farmington Hills.

Romance.

MiSth MiWar IChamL InG OCl

626 [————].

Heart's Desire by Peggy Roberts [pseud.]. New York: Zebra Books, 1994. 506 p.

(To Love Again)

When a woman loses her TV talk show job in Detroit, as well as her co-host husband, she leaves the city and begins work as a news anchor in Traverse City.

Romance.

MiAllG MiD MiFli OCl WM

627 Hannibal, Edward 1936–

Blood Feud by Edward Hannibal and Robert Boris. New York: Ballantine Books, 1979. 310 p.

A documentary novel dealing with the struggles between Attorney General Robert Kennedy and Teamster President James Hoffa. Partially set in Detroit.

628 [Harbaugh, Thomas Chalmers] 1849–1924

Weptonomah, the Hunted Wolf of the Wyandots; or, The Renegade's Prisoner. A Tale of the Lake Trail by Charles Howard [pseud.]. New York: Frank Starr & Co., 1871. 97 p.

(Frank Starr's American Novels, no. 72)

A young woodsman and his German companion save a Wyandot chief and search for a woman kidnapped by a despicable Frenchman. Partially set in northern Michigan.

Also published as *The Lone Indian; or, The Renegade's Prisoner. A Tale of the Lake Trail* (New York: Beadle and Adams, 1880 [Beadle's Pocket Novels, no. 150]), and as *The Dutchman's Dread; or, Gottlieb and His Hunter Pard* (New York: Beadle and Adams,

1888 [Beadle's Boy's Library, no. 205; octavo edition]).

Dime novel.

Black, 119.

TxU

629 [————].

Silver Rifle, the Girl Trailer; or, The White Tigers of Lake Superior by Charles Howard [pseud.]. New York: Frank Starr & Co., 1873. 102 p.

(Frank Starr's American Novels, no. 126)

A pair of young men stalk Ojibwas in the forests and meet up with a mysterious young woman. Set on the Upper Peninsula shore of Lake Superior in 1763.

Also published as *The White Tigers; or, Silver Rifle, the Girl Tracker of Lake Superior* (New York: Beadle and Adams, 1884 [Beadle's Boy's Library, no. 114; quarto edition]).

Dime novel.

Black, 118.

NRU

630 Hardwick, Gary

Cold Medina. New York: E. P. Dutton, 1996. 344 p.

An African-American police detective is assigned to find the serial killer of Detroit drug dealers while a new deadly cocaine formulation hits the streets.

Mystery.

631 Hargreaves, Irene M.

McTaggart's Red Keg, 1867–1868. Logging from A–Z on the Tittabawasee in Michigan by Irene M. Hargreaves and Harold M. Foehl. Bay City: Red Keg Press, 1988. 515 p.

One logging season on the Tittabawasee River is described in great detail. Set at the lumber camp at "Red Keg" (Averill) and the Saginaw mills in 1867 and 1868.

Mi MiAllG MiDW MiLapC
MiMtpT-C

632 Harju, Irja Hokkanen 1912–
Neebish Island Memories, 1921–1927. New York Mills, Minn.: Parta Printers, n.d. 101 p.

The fictionalized reminiscences of the young son of Finnish immigrants on Neebish Island in the Upper Peninsula from 1921 to 1927.

Mi MiAllG MiHM MiMtpT-C MiSsL

Harland, Marion, pseud. *see* Terhune, Mary Virginia Hawes

633 Harley, William Nicholas
Tomahawk and Cross; a Tale of Colonial Days. Columbus, Ohio: The Book Concern, n.d. 327 p.

A story of pioneer life on the western frontier of North America from 1758 to 1781. Thirty pages are set in Detroit during Pontiac's siege in 1763.

Mi

634 Harper, Robert Story 1899–1962
Trumpet in the Wilderness. New York: M.S. Mill Co., 1940. 346 p.

A volunteer from Ohio witnesses General William Hull's surrender of Detroit to the British in the War of 1812. Partially set in Detroit and southeastern Michigan.

Black, 120.

MiD IC InG OBgU OCl

635 Harrington, Joyce 1930–
No One Knows My Name. New York: St. Martin's Press, 1980. 250 p.

As a company of actors in a summer stock theater prepare for their new season, murder strikes. Set in "Duck Creek" on the Leelanau Peninsula.

Mystery.

636 Harris, Anne L. 1964–
The Nature of Smoke. New York: Tom Doherty Associates, 1996. 284 p.

A teenage girl runs away from her lower-class family, becomes involved in a murder, and is caught up in a bioengineering scheme. Seventeen pages are set in a future Detroit.

Science fiction.

637 Harris, Wilbur S.
High School Memories: A Nostalgic Portrayal of the Small Rural High School of the 1920's. Mt. Pleasant, Mich.: Wilbur S. Harris, 1983. 156 p.

The high school career and adventures of a young man. His freshman year is spent at "Redville High School" in "Shaw County" in 1926 and 1927 before he moves to Ohio.

MiMtpT

638 Harrison, Jim 1937–
Wolf; a False Memoir. New York: Simon and Schuster, 1971. 225 p.

A young Michiganian travels around the country in the late 1960s and has a number of adventures. Partially set in the Upper Peninsula and northern Michigan.

639 ———.
Farmer. New York: Viking Press, 1976. 160 p.

A middle-aged schoolteacher and farmer faces the twin crises of love and the passage of time. Set in a farming community in northern Michigan.

640 ———.
Warlock. New York: Delacorte Press, 1981. 262 p.

A forty-two-year-old man loses his job and begins a fantasy life as a sleuth and master spy. Partially set on the Leelanau Peninsula.

641 ———.
Sundog; the Story of an American Foreman, Robert Corvus Strang, as Told to Jim Harrison. New York: E. P. Dutton, 1984. 241 p.

The fictional life of a crippled dam projects foreman is thoroughly recounted in a series of interviews. Partially set in the Upper Peninsula.

642 **Hathaway, Baxter L.** 1909–
The Stubborn Way. New York: Macmillan, 1937. 336 p.

During the Depression, a young man leaves college because of lack of funds and finds work in a dehumanizing paper mill. Set in a southern Michigan city, probably Kalamazoo.

Black, 121.

Mi MiAllG MiEM MiKC MiU

643 **[Hathway, Alan]** 1906–1977
The Devil's Playground; a Doc Savage Adventure by Kenneth Robeson [pseud.]. New York: Bantam Books, 1968. 119 p.

(Doc Savage, no. 25)

Doc Savage, possessor of superhuman strength and genius, investigates a mysterious Ojibwa cult and its evil leader. Set in the Upper Peninsula.

First published in *Doc Savage Magazine* in January 1941.

Mystery.

MiAllG AzF MWalB TxCM

644 **[Hauptman, Elaine]**
Top Marks by Gayle Corey [pseud.]. Toronto: Harlequin Books, 1988. 219 p.

(Harlequin Temptation, no. 200)

A divorced woman teaching a college course finds one of her students, a police detective, attractive. Set in Lyons and in East Lansing at Michigan State University.

Romance.

MiEM MiMtp MoK OBgU OCo

645 **[Hawkins, Nehemiah]** 1833–1928
The Mormon of Little Manitou Island. An Historical Romance by the Knight of Chillon of Switzerland and Associates [pseud.]. New York: Uplift Co., 1916. 526 p.

In the 1850s, a young woman takes refuge on Little Manitou Island to escape a nefarious plot to have her married to a Mormon elder on Beaver Island.

Black, 122.

Mi MiAllG MiEM MiMtpT-C MiU

645A **Hawley, Rose Damaris** 1889–
The Old House Remembers by Rose D. Hawley; Documented and Edited by Mary Francis Doner. Ludington, Mich.: Lakeside Printing, 1968. 35 p.

A house, built by an early settler, narrates the story of the Mason County town of Ludington and its growth through the years.

A slightly revised edition was published in 1976.

Mi MiD MiFliL MiGr MiMtpT-C

646 **Hay, Mae Pettit**
The Last Best Hope. New York: Exposition Press, 1972. 256 p.

As seen through the eyes of the fictional Thompson family, the growth of Michigan as a territory and state is traced. Set in Detroit and other Michigan locales from 1812 to 1918.

Mi MiAllG MiEM MiMtpT-C MiPh

Hayes, Caryl May, joint author *see* Genung, Helen

Hayes-Kilian, Dedie, joint author *see* E.L.T. Club

647 **Hays, Wilma Pitchford** 1909–
Pontiac: Lion in the Forest. Boston: Houghton Mifflin Co., 1965. 189 p.

(Piper Books)

A fictionalized biography of the Ottawa chief that emphasizes his political skill in organizing the campaign against the British. Partially set in and around Detroit in 1763.

Juvenile.

Hazard, Harry, pseud. *see* Badger, Joseph Edward

648 **Heise, Kenan Joseph** 1933–
Aunt Ella Stories. Chicago: Academy Chicago Publishers, 1985. 191 p.

A young boy recounts various encounters between his father and his exasperatingly clever aunt. Set in Ferndale and Detroit in the late 1930s.

Juvenile.

Heller, Robert *see* Heller, Wilhelm Robert

649 **Heller, Wilhelm Robert** 1814–1871
Eine neue Welt von Robert Heller. Altenburg: Verlag von H. A. Pierer, 1843. 2 vols.

An army officer from Louisiana and an African American have a number of adventures with two Ojibwas. Set mostly in the Kalamazoo River Valley in the early 1800s.

First published as "Die Wanderer durch Michigan" among other pieces in the annual gift book *Rosen und Vergissmeinnicht* (Leipzig: F. A. Leo, 1842?).

In German.

Mi

650 **Helms, Viola**
The Silver Dollar. Philadelphia: Dorrance & Co., 1960. 121 p.

The story of a young man and woman who fall in love, marry, and later have serious difficulties over money. Set mostly in South Haven from 1869 to the 1880s.

Mi MiGr MiPh

651 **Hemenway, Robert** 1921–
At the Border. New York: Atheneum, 1984. 240 p.

The significant parts of a man's life are told in a series of vignettes. The first forty pages are set in "Prospect" (South Haven?) in 1933.

652 **Hemingway, Ernest** 1899–1961
The Torrents of Spring, a Romantic Novel in Honor of the Passing of a Great Race. New York: Charles Scribner's Sons, 1926. 143 p.

Written as a parody of Sherwood Anderson's style, this humorous novel concerns the mundane lives of two pump factory workers. Set in Petoskey.

Black, 123.

MiD MiDW InFw OCl WU

653 **Hencey, Robert E.**
Empires. Battle Creek: The Miller Foundation, 1996. 291 p.

C. W. Post (1854–1914) begins a rivalry with John Harvey Kellogg (1852–1943) for control of the health food and cereal industry. Set in Battle Creek between 1860 and 1951.

MiAllG MiBatK IC OU

Henderson, J. Stanley, pseud. *see* Willett, Edward

654 Hendryx, James Beardsley 1880–1963
Connie Morgan with the Forest Rangers. New York: G. P. Putnam's Sons, 1925. 275 p.

A young man works with conservation officers to thwart a group of unscrupulous businessmen and to extol the virtues of proper timber management. Set in "Pine Tree" in northwestern Michigan.

Juvenile.

Mi CL FTS

Hennissart, Martha *see* Lathen, Emma, pseud.

655 Henry, Clay
Welcome Home, Lily Glow. London: T. V. Boardman & Co., 1960. 191 p.

(American Bloodhound, no. 298)

A Hollywood star returns to her hometown on a publicity tour and is murdered by someone with an old grudge. Partially set in "Somerset" in western Michigan.

Mystery.

MiAllG

656 Henry, Vera 1909?–1987
A Lucky Number. Philadelphia: J. B. Lippincott Co., 1957. 243 p.

The humorous adventures of a Canadian family living in Windsor are recounted in a series of anecdotes. Fifteen pages are set in Detroit on a shopping trip.

Mi MiBatW MiD MiOw MiStc

657 Herbst, Josephine 1892–1969
The Executioner Waits. New York: Harcourt, Brace and Co., 1934. 371 p.

A chronicle of the middle-class Trexler family between 1918 and 1929, and their growing involvement with the radical movement. Partially set in Detroit.

Sequel to *Pity Is Not Enough,* which is set in Georgia and the Dakotas.

MiD MiEM MiU InU WU

658 ———.
Rope of Gold. New York: Harcourt, Brace and Co., 1939. 429 p.

The story of the Trexler family continues as they deal with farm and union organizing as well as the auto industry from 1933 to 1937. Partially set in Detroit.

Sequel to *The Executioner Waits.*

MiU InU OCl OU WU

659 Herlihy, James Leo 1927–1993
The Season of the Witch. New York: Simon and Schuster, 1971. 384 p.

When her gay friend receives his draft notice for military service, a teenage girl runs off to New York with him. Partially set in "Belle Woods" in southeastern Michigan.

660 Herrmann, John 1900–1959
What Happens. Paris: Contact Editions, 1926. 273 p.

An irresponsible young man finds himself in a number of difficulties with women and in his work as a salesman. Set in "Benton" (Lansing), Detroit, and Ann Arbor.

Mi DeU ICU IaU ViU

661 ———.
Summer Is Ended. New York: Covici, Friede Publishers, 1932. 286 p.

For financial reasons, a young woman quits college and takes a job with a newspaper, where she meets her future husband. Set in "Benton" (Lansing) and Detroit.

Black, 124.

Mi MiAllG MiEM MiRochOU MiU

662 Hess, Norah
Winter Love. New York: Leisure Books, 1995. 393 p.

To protect her reputation, a young woman must marry her guardian when she is made pregnant by a handsome trapper. Set in "Big Pine" in the Upper Peninsula in 1887.

Romance.

MiAllG MiFli MiMtcM IChamL OCl

663 Hewitt, Sally Baker
Life with Grandma. N.p., 1954. 111 p.

A woman who lives with her husband and grandchildren on a farm reminisces about events from 1900 to the present. Partially set in an unnamed town, probably Jackson.

MiJac

664 Hildreth, Harry Dean
Wauneta. An Indian Story of Happiness as a Mental Condition. Chicago: Donohue, Henneberry & Co., 1894. 182 p.

A French-Canadian girl is adopted by a Native American and his English wife.

Partially set in the Upper Peninsula and southeastern Michigan.

Black, 125. Wright III, 2673.

Mi WHi

665 Hindman, Lita 1899–
Michigan's Irish Hills. Albion, Mich.: Elite Publishing Co., 1936. 299 p.

The story of a home economics instructor's life in Albion and at Albion College in the 1930s.

Mi MiAlbC MiGr MiMu MiU

Hirsch, Arnold S., joint author *see* Franks, Owen

666 Hirzel, Patrick S.
The Promised One. Pittsburgh: Dorrance Publishing Co., 1993. 230 p.

The story of a deal Lucifer makes with God to test the free will of a child soon to be born and how the deal affects the lives of three people. Set in Battle Creek and Detroit.

MiAllG MiBatW MiJac MiMtcM IC

667 Hivert-Carthew, Annick 1947–
Cadillac and the Dawn of Detroit. Davisburg, Mich.: Wilderness Adventure Books, 1994. 275 p.

The fictionalized account of the founding of Detroit by Antoine de la Mothe Cadillac (1656–1730) and subsequent events from 1701 to 1711.

Mi MiAllG MiD MiJac MiMtpT-C

668 Hoag, A. Eugene
The Legal Assassination of a Sheriff. New York: Vantage Press, 1985. 199 p.

The story of the political and social adventures of a county sheriff. Set in "Lunch County" (Eaton County) and "Landside" (Lansing).

Mi MiL

669 **Hoffius, Stephen**
Winners and Losers. New York: Simon & Schuster Books for Young Readers, 1993. 164 p.

Two ninth-grade boys are best friends but turn into deadly rivals when they join the same track team. Set in the Grand Rapids area.

Juvenile.

670 **Hoffman, Alice** 1952–
Second Nature. New York: G. P. Putnam's Sons, 1994. 254 p.

A young man discovered living with wolves in northern Michigan is brought to New York for assimilation and education, and experiences many difficulties.

671 **Hoffmaster, Maud Miller** 1886–1969
The Path of Gold. New York: Exposition Press, 1952. 288 p.

A talented landscape painter devotes herself to her selfish aunt and is in love with a charming cad. Mostly set in the Grand Traverse Bay area in the 1920s.

Mi MiAllG MiGr MiMtpT-C MiT

672 **Holden, Craig**
The River Sorrow. New York: Delacorte Press, 1994. 384 p.

A young doctor recovering from heroin addiction becomes unwillingly involved in a series of drug-related murders. Set in "Morgantown."

Mystery.

Holland, Petra, pseud. *see* Walters, Petra

673 **Hollands, Hulda Theodate St. Bernard** 1837–1910
Marfa; a Story of the Opium Smugglers of the St. Clair River. Detroit: n.p., 1889. 145 p.

A little girl who turns out to be a kidnapped twin becomes mixed up with a gang of smugglers on the St. Clair River until they are brought to justice.

Wright III, 2707.

DLC

674 **Holt, Alfred Hubbard** 1897–
Hubbard's Trail. Chicago: Erle Press, 1952. 319 p.

The fictionalized biography of Gurdon S. Hubbard (1802–1886), fur-trader and pioneer merchant. Partially set at Fort Mackinac and in the Muskegon River area.

MiA MiAllG MiFra MiMack InFw

675 **Holt, Isabella** 1892–1962
A Visit To Pay. Indianapolis: Bobbs-Merrill, 1939. 329 p.

This story follows two young women as they make their way in life and in the world of work. Partially set in Detroit and "Gooseford" in the 1920s and 1930s.

Black, 126.

MiD IC InFw MnM OC

676 **Holtzer, Susan**
Something To Kill For. New York: St. Martin's Press, 1994. 230 p.

Anneke Haagen, a middle-aged computer consultant, becomes involved in a series of murders concerning local antique dealers. Set in Ann Arbor.

Mystery.

677 ———.
Curly Smoke. New York: St. Martin's Press, 1995. 256 p.

Anneke Haagen investigates the connection between a series of deaths in an eclectic neighborhood and an office development. Set in Ann Arbor.

Mystery.

678 ———.
Bleeding Maize and Blue. New York: St. Martin's Press, 1996. 294 p.

When a N.C.A.A. investigator is murdered while looking into University of Michigan recruiting practices, Anneke Haagen assists the police and a campus newspaper reporter.

Mystery.

679 Hoose, Betty
Sassafras Trail. Cadillac, Mich.: n.p., 1991. 89 p.

In 1895, an Ohio couple decide to sell their farm and move, traveling through Michigan until they reach Hope in Midland County. Based on the author's family history.

Fifty copies were printed for family distribution.

Mi   MiAllG

680 Hoover, Bessie Ray 1874–
Pa Flickinger's Folks. New York: Harper & Bros., 1909. 274 p.

The story of the Flickinger family, a group of ordinary working people, and their simple way of life. Set in the Benton Harbor and St. Joseph area.

Mi   IC   MH   OCl   OU

681 ———.
Opal. New York: Harper & Bros., 1910. 330 p.

Opal Flickinger, newly graduated from the high school and aspiring to higher society, is ashamed of her ordinary family. Set in the Benton Harbor and St. Joseph area.

Sequel to *Pa Flickinger's Folks.*

Black, 127.

Mi   MH   OCl   OU   WU

682 ———.
Rolling Acres. Boston: Small, Maynard & Co., 1922. 286 p.

The story of an impractical Englishman and his daughter, the owners of a large farm, and their interactions with the local rural population. Set along the St. Joseph River.

Black, 128.

Mi   CLU   NcD   OC   OU

683 Horan, Kenneth O'Donnell 1890–
The Longest Night. Chicago: Daryl C. Doran, 1932. 231 p.

A young woman becomes an internationally acclaimed pianist and gives up the love of her life. Set mostly in "Concordia" (Jackson) between 1910 and 1930.

MiAllG   CoD   ICU   KyLoU   WGrU

684 ———.
It's Later Than You Think. New York: R. O. Ballou, 1934. 322 p.

Two people, who were formerly in love but separated twenty years earlier, meet one summer. Set in "Concordia" (Jackson).

Black, 131.

Mi   MiMarqN   IEN   OU   RPB

685 ———.
Remember the Day. Garden City, N.Y.: Doubleday, Doran & Co., 1937. 263 p.

Fictionalized reminiscences about the author's family and the many dignitaries who stayed with them around the turn of the century. Set in "Eastmeadow" (Jackson).

Black, 132.

Mi MiAllG MiD MiJac MiMtpT-C

686 ———.

Oh, Promise Me. Garden City, N.Y.: Doubleday, Doran & Co., 1938. 274 p.

More fictionalized reminiscences focusing on the author's father, who held an important position in the Republican party. Set in "Eastmeadow" (Jackson).

Sequel to *Remember the Day.*

Mi MiAllG MiEM MiJac MiStc

687 ———.

It's Not My Problem. Garden City, N.Y.: Doubleday, Doran & Co., 1938. 266 p.

A detailed look at one year in the life of a successful writer, as taken from her daily journal. Sixteen pages are set in Michigan, the remainder in Chicago.

Mi MiAllG MiD MiGr OBgU

688 ———.

Night Bell. New York: Charles Scribner's Sons, 1940. 278 p.

A surgeon's wife hospitalized for an operation observes the day-to-day comings and goings of patients and staff. Set in "Middlebury" (Jackson?).

MiAllG MiAlp MiD MiTN OBgU

689 ———.

I Give Thee Back. New York: E. P. Dutton & Co., 1942. 270 p.

A middle-aged woman looks back on her life, noting and regretting the many mistakes she has made and wishing things had been different. Set in "Middlebury" (Jackson?).

Black, 130.

Mi MiAllG MiFli MiJac MiKW

690 ———.

A Bashful Woman. Garden City, N.Y.: Doubleday, Doran & Co., 1944. 299 p.

A family saga about Welsh immigrants and their successful rise in the wagon-building business to the early automobile industry. Set in "Middlebury" (Jackson?) from 1890 to 1940.

Black, 129.

Mi MiD MiKW MiMtc MiStc

691 ———.

Papa Went to Congress. Garden City, N.Y.: Doubleday & Co., 1946. 206 p.

A fictionalized account of the author's father, who was elected the Republican representative to Congress in 1884. Partially set in "Eastmeadow" (Jackson).

Mi MiD MiGr MiMtpT-C MiStc

692 ———.

Mama Took Up Travel. Garden City, N.Y.: Doubleday & Co., 1947. 216 p.

A discouraged congressman decides to take a European trip with his family when one of the bills he sponsored fails to pass. Twenty pages are set in Michigan.

Sequel to *Papa Went to Congress.*

Mi MiD MiGr MiMu MiPh

Howard, Charles, pseud. *see* Harbaugh, Thomas Chalmers

693 Howard, Elizabeth 1907–

Sabina. New York: Lothrup, Lee & Shepard Co., 1941. 269 p.

After the death of her parents, a sixteen-year-old girl lives with her relatives and makes the best of her new life. Set in Detroit in 1846.

Juvenile.

Mi MiD MiDW MiMtpT MiYEM

694 ———.

North Winds Blow Free. New York: William Morrow & Co., 1949. 192 p.

A seventeen-year-old girl and her family journey to a Canadian settlement for escaped slaves to offer their assistance. Partially set in Michigan in the 1850s.

Juvenile.

695 ———.

Peddler's Girl. New York: William Morrow & Co., 1951. 240 p.

A young woman travels from place to place with her peddler uncle in a wagon after her mother dies. Set in Detroit and southeastern Michigan in 1840.

Juvenile.

696 ———.

Candle in the Night. New York: William Morrow & Co., 1952. 223 p.

An eighteen-year-old girl journeys to Detroit to visit her brother and is caught up in the events leading to the surrender of the fort to the British in 1812.

Juvenile.

697 ———.

A Star to Follow. New York: William Morrow & Co., 1954. 222 p.

Three daughters must adjust to living with their aunt when their father is assigned to a frontier army post. Thirteen pages are set in Detroit in 1875.

Juvenile.

MiD MiDW MiHly MiT MiWar

698 ———.

A Girl of the North Country. New York: William Morrow & Co., 1957. 222 p.

A sixteen-year-old girl lives with her parents in northern Michigan in the 1850s, and the day-to-day pioneer life of the family is described.

Juvenile.

699 ———.

Wilderness Venture. New York: William Morrow and Co., 1973. 190 p.

A sixteen-year-old girl and her brothers travel ahead of the rest of the family to set up a new home in the wilderness. Set in the St. Clair River area in 1825.

Juvenile.

700 Howard, Ellen 1943–
The Tower Room. New York: Atheneum, 1993. 137 p.

After her mother dies, a girl must live with her aunt and try to adjust to her strange new life and unfamiliar surroundings. Set in "Kirkland."

Juvenile.

701 ———.

The Log Cabin Quilt. New York: Holiday House, 1996. 32 p.

A young girl and her family move from the Carolinas to the Michigan frontier after her mother dies, and, with her grandmother's help, the girl turns their cabin into a real home.

Juvenile picture book.

702 Howard, Winston
Money Is Not Enough. Orchard Lake, Mich.: Epic Publications, 1980. 137 p.

An ambitious and ruthless insurance salesman begins a no-holds-barred struggle with his conceited manager for control of the agency. Set in Southfield.

MiGr-L CSbC GU NjWhiM

703 **Howe, Edward Everett** 1862–1913
The Chronicles of Break o' Day.
Boston: Arena Publishing Co., 1894.
342 p.

An eccentric farmer, philosopher, and
inventor is involved in foreclosure proceedings and with horse thieves. Set in
"Break o' Day" in south-central Michigan in the 1870s.

Black, 133. Streeter, 2225. Wright III,
2803.

Mi MiMtpT-C MiU AzTeS MoU

704 **Howe, Shirley Swift**
Legacy of Five Wives. Decatur, Mich.:
Heritage Valley Publishing Co., 1988.
209 p.

The fictionalized chronicle of the
Greenman family of New York, their
arrival in Michigan, and their lives in
Van Buren County from 1846 to the
1880s.

Mi MiAllG MiKW MiLap MiMtpT-C

705 **Howes, Royce Bucknam** 1901–
1973
Night of the Garter Murder. Garden
City, N.Y.: Doubleday, Doran & Co.,
1937. 274 p.

(Crime Club)

A man, who has been murdered with
a Civil War firearm, is discovered with
a pink garter on his arm. Captain Ben
Lucias of the Detroit Homicide Squad
investigates.

Mystery.

AAP CL

706 ———.
Death Dupes a Lady. Garden City,
N.Y.: Doubleday, Doran & Co., 1937.
294 p.

(Crime Club)

While on vacation, Captain Ben Lucias
becomes involved in the murder of an
automobile executive. Set in Holland
and on Lake Macatawa.

Mystery.

Mi MiAllG MiFli OU ViR

707 ———.
Murder at Maneuvers. New York:
Doubleday, Doran & Co., 1938. 272 p.

(Crime Club)

After a Russian general is murdered
while observing summer war games
at "Camp Waller" (Michigan National Guard Military Reservation at
Grayling), Captain Ben Lucias investigates.

Mystery.

Mi CLO CSt MB ViBluC

708 ———.
Death Rides a Hobby. New York: Doubleday, Doran & Co., 1939. 273 p.

(Crime Club)

A wealthy photography enthusiast is
murdered with an exploding camera,
and Captain Ben Lucias investigates a
number of suspects. Set in Detroit.

Mystery.

MiAllG CLO OBgU OU ViR

709 ———.
The Case of the Copy-Hook Killing.
New York: E. P. Dutton & Co., 1945.
223 p.

A newspaperman is murdered, and
Captain Ben Lucias must sift through
the long list of individuals who had
reasons to kill him. Set in Detroit.

Mystery.

MiAllG CL OBgU OU ViR

Hoyt, Janet, pseud. *see* Hamilton, Jean

Hudson, Meg, pseud. *see* Koehler, Margaret Hudson

710 Huggler, Thomas E. 1945–
Westwind Woods. Lansing: Michigan United Conservation Clubs, 1978. 132 p.

A group of sixth graders learn about nature and wildlife by observing the rural areas around their homes. Set in Michigan.

Juvenile.

Mi MiBatW MiGay MiLap MiMu

711 Hull, Helen Rose 1888–1971
Quest. New York: Macmillan Co., 1922. 353 p.

The disharmony between her parents shatters a young girl's childhood, but teaches her about the need to be self-reliant. Set in Lansing.

Black, 136.

Mi MiEM MWelC MnM OU

712 ———.
The Surry Family. New York: Macmillan Co., 1925. 333 p.

A story of a family in which the parents constantly argue, the son is trapped in an early marriage, and the daughter strikes out on her own. Set in "Hollister" (Lansing).

Mi MiEM MiU OU MnM

713 ———.
Islanders. New York: Macmillan Co., 1927. 312 p.

A young woman abandoned by her fiancé when he leaves for the California gold fields in 1849 becomes a drudge in service to her family. Set in south-central Michigan.

Black, 135.

Mi MiEM MiKW InTI OU

714 ———.
Morning Shows the Day. New York: Coward-McCann, 1934. 421 p.

The lives, successes, and failures of seven school chums over a thirty-year period are recounted. Set in Lansing.

Black, 137.

Mi MiAllG MiEM OU WRac

715 ———.
A Circle in the Water. New York: Coward-McCann, 1943. 408 p.

The story of an unsuccessful marriage between an obsessively ambitious man and his steadfastly sensible wife. Partially set in "Selwin" (Lansing) and Detroit.

Black, 134.

Mi MiAllG MiEM OU WRac

Hume, W. Stock, pseud. *see* Stockwell, William Hume

716 Humphreys, John Richard Adams 1918–
Vandameer's Road. New York: Charles Scribner's Sons, 1946. 297 p.

A peculiar family with a distasteful secret elicit strong suspicions and dislike from their rural neighbors. Set in the Grand Rapids area.

Black, 138.

Mi MiD MiFli MiKW MiU

717 ———.
The Dirty Shame. New York: Dell Publishing Co., 1955. 191 p.

(Dell First Edition, no. 61)

The story of an adolescent girl, her growing awareness of life around her, and her maturation. Set in "Three Falls" (Grand Rapids).

Mi CSt OBgU OKentU

718 ——.
Subway to Samarkand. Garden City, N.Y.: Doubleday, 1977. 312 p.

An ailing and weary New York college professor dreams of a way out of his predicaments. Fifteen pages are set in Grand Rapids, Traverse City, and Harbor Springs.

719 Hunt, Mabel Leigh 1892–1971
Michel's Island. New York: Frederick A. Stokes Co., 1940. 265 p.

The twelve-year-old son of a French trader has a number of adventures with his brothers and Native Americans. Set on Mackinac Island in 1801.

Juvenile.

Mi MiAllG MiD MiDW MiKW

Hunting, Gardner *see* Hunting, Henry Gardner

720 Hunting, Henry Gardner 1872–1958
Their Friendly Enemy by Gardner Hunting. New York: Macmillan Co., 1921. 209 p.

Two girls who have just graduated from high school buy the local newspaper and become editors. Set in Pentwater.

Juvenile.

Mi IDeKN InFw

721 Hyde, Dayton O. 1925–
Island of the Loons. New York: Atheneum, 1984. 155 p.

A young boy rescues an escaped convict from drowning, and is subsequently held captive on a deserted island in Lake Superior near Munising.

Juvenile.

722 ——.
Thunder down the Track. New York: Atheneum, 1986. 171 p.

A boy's father and friend buy two old steam locomotives, establish a tourist business, and are then threatened by an unscrupulous California company. Set in "Deerton" and "Onota" in Alger County.

Juvenile.

MiAllG MiChe MiDW MiFli MiMio

723 ——.
The Bells of Lake Superior. Honesdale, Pa.: Boyds Mills Press, 1995. 98 p.

A young chimney sweep with an aptitude for music brings happiness to others by tuning the town's church bells. Set in an unnamed Michigan town on Lake Superior in the 1890s.

Juvenile.

MiAllG MiBatW MiD MiMtcM MiMtpT-C

724 Hynes, James 1955–
The Wild Colonial Boy. New York: Atheneum, 1990. 356 p.

A naive young man from America is duped into delivering explosives to I.R.A. terrorists. Eleven pages are set near Ann Arbor.

Mystery.

I

725 Ingersoll, Ernest 1852–1946
The Ice Queen. New York: Harper & Bros., 1885. 256 p.

(Young People Series)

Four orphaned siblings are offered a home with their uncle in Cleveland and, to save money, decide to skate there on frozen Lake Erie. Partially set in Monroe.

Juvenile.

MiD ICarbS MB NRU OCl

726 ――――.
The Raisin Creek Exploring Club. New York: D. Appleton and Co., 1919. 290 p.

A group of boys have many adventures while they explore the country along and in the vicinity of "Raisin Creek" (Raisin River?) in southern Michigan.

Juvenile.

Mi MdBE

727 Ingram, Helen K.
Three on a Tour. Detroit: John Bornman & Son, Printers, 1895. 113 p.

A newly married couple take a lake cruise from Cleveland to Mackinac Island and are accompanied by the wife's sister. The novel is an advertisement for the Detroit & Cleveland Steam Navigation Company.

Streeter, 2300.

DLC OBgU

Ira, Alfred, pseud. *see* Grimm, Albert Friedrich Wilhelm

J

728 Jackson, Andrew Stonewall 1921–
Gentleman Pimp. Los Angeles: Holloway House Publishing Co., 1973. 190 p.

The fictionalized autobiography of an African American and his progression from theft to involvement in prostitution. Partially set in Detroit.

MiGr-L IC IChamL InFw WM

729 Jackson, Caary Paul 1902–
All-Conference Tackle by C. Paul Jackson. New York: Thomas Y. Crowell Co., 1947. 242 p.

A snobbish young man from a New England prep school looks down on some of his teammates on the University of Michigan football squad. Set partially in Ann Arbor.

Juvenile.

Mi MiD MiGr MiKW MiU

730 ――――.
Tournament Forward by C. Paul Jackson. New York: Thomas Y. Crowell Co., 1948. 179 p.

A basketball player stops being a showoff and becomes a team player in the course of a season. Set at "Northern High School" somewhere in Michigan.

Juvenile.

Mi MiGay InFw OBgU WRac

731 ――――.
Rose Bowl All-American. New York: Thomas Y. Crowell Co., 1949. 245 p.

The rivalry between two football players that began in high school continues on the University of Michigan team. Set partially in Ann Arbor.

Juvenile.

Mi MiD MiDW InFw OCo

732 ――――.
Rose Bowl Line Backer by C. Paul Jackson. New York: Thomas Y. Crowell Co., 1951. 184 p.

The captain of the University of Michigan team has difficulty accepting responsibility until the second half of the Rose Bowl game. Partially set in Ann Arbor.

Juvenile.

Mi MiGay InFw OXe IC

733 [————].
Match Point by Jack Paulson [pseud.]. Philadelphia: Westminster Press, 1956. 188 p.

A boy learns self-control and tact before winning the National Boy's Tennis Tournament at Kalamazoo College. Set partially in Kalamazoo.

Juvenile.

Mi MiAC MiDW MiKC MiMarqN

734 ————.
Rose Bowl Pro by C. Paul Jackson. New York: Hastings House, 1970. 143 p.

A Michigan State University football player with professional aspirations realizes his team needs his unselfish leadership in the Rose Bowl game. Partially set in East Lansing.

Juvenile.

Mi MiRog IC ICNE WKen

735 Jackson, Jon A. 1938–
The Diehard. New York: Random House, 1977. 190 p.

Detective Sergeant "Fang" Mulheisen of the Detroit Police investigates a series of murders, robberies, and missing assets connected with an insurance swindle.

Mystery.

736 ————.
The Blind Pig. New York: Random House, 1978. 228 p.

Sergeant Mulheisen investigates what appears to be a routine shoot-out between police and a gunman, an event which ultimately has greater significance. Set in Detroit.

Mystery.

737 ————.
Grootka: A Detective Sgt. "Fang" Mulheisen Novel. Woodstock, Vt.: Foul Play Press/Countryman Press, 1990. 337 p.

A recent murder is connected to an old unsolved case, and the retired policeman who was Sergeant Mulheisen's mentor begins his own investigation. Set in Detroit.

Mystery.

738 ————.
Hit on the House. New York: Atlantic Monthly Press, 1993. 237 p.

Sergeant Mulheisen is assigned to find out who is murdering the leading mobsters of Detroit, and his investigations lead him to a mysterious hit man.

Mystery.

739 ————.
Deadman. New York: Atlantic Monthly Press, 1994. 263 p.

The daughter of a slain mobster, who is a prime suspect in a revenge killing, has fled to Montana and is pursued by Sergeant Mulheisen. Partially set in Detroit.

Sequel to *Hit on the House.*

Mystery.

740 ————.
Dead Folk. Tucson: Dennis McMillan Publications, 1995. 235 p.

Sergeant Mulheisen travels to Utah to continue his investigation of a murdered mob boss, his missing daughter, and a hit man. Partially set in Detroit.

Limited to 326 copies.

The trade edition, with minor revisions, was published as *Dead Folks* (New York: Atlantic Monthly Press, 1996).

Sequel to *Deadman.*

Mystery.

MiGr-L

741 Jacobs, Bárbara 1947–
Las Hojas Muertes. México: Ediciones Era, 1987. 103 p.

The fictionalized reminiscences of the author's father and what his moral and idealistic principles cost him and his family. Ten pages are set in Saginaw.

In Spanish.

English translation by David Unger published as *The Dead Leaves* (Willimantic, Conn.: Curbstone Press, 1993).

MiKC InNd OCU WU WMUW

742 James, Mark
The Mound People. Traverse City: Neahtawanta Press, 1985. 77 p.

(Green Legend Series)

The story of a sand mining company that is destroying prehistoric mounds and wreaking severe ecological damage. Set in the Traverse City area.

Mi MiMtpT-C MiOC

743 Jamison, James Knox 1887–1954
By Cross and Anchor; the Story of Frederic Baraga on Lake Superior. Paterson, N.J.: St. Anthony Guild Press, 1946. 225 p.

The fictionalized biography of Father Frederic Baraga (1797–1868), mis-

sionary to the Ojibwas of the Lake Superior region. Set partially in the Upper Peninsula.

Mi MiAllG MiD MiMarqN MiMtpT-C

744 Janette, Fred E. 1870–
Captain Tiptop; a Story from the Log-Book of the Sloop-Yacht Tycoon. Akron, Ohio: Saalfield Publishing Co., 1905. 275 p.

A young man and his companions thwart a stepuncle's whiskey smuggling gang. Set on Lake St. Clair and the Detroit River, and in Detroit and Algonac.

Juvenile.

Mi MiAllG MiMack CSbC OBgU

745 Jankelson, Jacob
Myrna by Jan Kelson [pseud.]. Los Angeles: Wetzel Publishing Co., 1943. 159 p.

A young woman has adventures with low-lives and other characters in the unsavory and dangerous parts of Detroit in the 1930s.

Black, 141.

MiD

746 Jenkins, Beverly E.
Vivid. New York: Avon Books, 1995. 391 p.

(Avon Historical Romance)

Offered a practice in a Michigan town, an African-American physician finds her success and acceptance depends on winning over the mayor. Set in Niles in 1876 and 1877.

Romance.

MiAllG MiBir MiD MiFli MiSf

747 ———.
Indigo. New York: Avon Books, 1996. 359 p.

(Avon Historical Romance)

A severely injured African-American slave-stealer and conductor on the Underground Railroad is nursed back to health by a former slave. Set in Detroit in 1858.

Romance.

MiAllG MiBir MiD MiFli MiYEM

748 Jenkins, Jerry B.
The House of Tunnels. Chicago: Moody Press, 1996. 105 p.

(Toby Andrews and the Junior Deputies, book 1)

The sheriff's twelve-year-old son Toby, and his friends explore his new house and discover a secret passageway and a police operation. Set in Kalamazoo.

Juvenile.

MiAllG ICMB MoIM

749 ———.
The Man with the Terrible Secret. Chicago: Moody Press, 1996. 105 p.

(Toby Andrews and the Junior Deputies, book 2)

Toby wonders why a man who works at a youth home where his best friend lives also works at a summer camp, but pretends to be someone else. Set in Kalamazoo and Muskegon.

Juvenile.

MiAllG ICMB MoIM

750 ———.
The East Side Bullies. Chicago: Moody Press, 1996. 106 p.

(Toby Andrews and the Junior Deputies, book 3)

When Toby and his friends are harassed by a group of older boys, they eventually decide on a novel way to respond. Set in Kalamazoo.

Juvenile.

MiAllG MoIM SdB

751 ———.
The Neighborhood's Scariest Woman. Chicago: Moody Press, 1996. 105 p.

(Toby Andrews and the Junior Deputies, book 4)

An old woman living in a spooky old house is the subject of many stories and rumors, and Toby and his friends decide to find out the truth. Set in Kalamazoo.

Juvenile.

MiAllG MoIM SdB

752 Jenks, George Charles 1850–1929
Rube Rocket, the Tent Detective; or, The Treacherous Two. A Romance of the Ring. New York: Beadle and Adams, 1889. 29 p.

(Beadle's Dime Library, no. 538)

A villainous circus ringmaster and a sinister Mexican plot thievery and mayhem, but a bareback rider attempts to thwart their plans. Set in Detroit and on Belle Isle.

Dime novel.

Black, 142.

NRU

753 [Jermain, S. P.]
Wrecks and Wreckers. A Tragedy and a Mystery by Sylvanus Pierson [pseud.]. London, New York: F. Tennyson Neely, 1899. 98 p.

(Neely's Pocket Library, no. 6)

A mysterious series of shipwrecks instigated by a gang of wreckers occur on the Lake Michigan coast. Set in the northern Michigan resort town of Fairport.

Dime novel.

MiMtp InNd OBgU MH

Jerrold, Louise, pseud. *see* Clancy, Louise Marks Breitenbach

754 Jewell, Edward Alden 1888–1947
The Moth Decides. New York: Alfred A. Knopf, 1922. 282 p.

A young woman has difficulty choosing between equally acceptable suitors who vie for her hand in marriage. Set at a summer resort on Crystal Lake.

CLU MH NBuBE NcU OU

755 [Johnson, Anna] 1860–1943
To the Third Generation by Hope Daring [pseud.]. New York: American Tract Society, 1901. 298 p.

A man trades liquor to the Hurons for furs and is cursed when one of them dies from drink. Set in "Kinnard" in southern Michigan from 1855 to 1890.

MiHas ABAU INS MsCliM OU

756 [————].
Entering Into His Own by Hope Daring [pseud.]. New York: American Tract Society, 1903. 279 p.

A young orphan has many adventures and setbacks, but finally makes his way in the world with the help of his religious faith. Partially set in Harbor Springs.

MiChv MiHas MiPet IMonC OU

757 [————].
An Abundant Harvest by Hope Daring [pseud.]. Cincinnati: Jennings and Graham, 1904. 281 p.

A dean of women at a Nebraska college contracts scarlet fever and must leave her stressful job to recuperate. Set partially on Mackinac Island.

MiD IaU OU ScSuM

758 [————].
The Appointed Way. A Tale of the Seventh-Day Adventists by Hope Daring [pseud.]. Philadelphia: Griffith & Rowland Press, 1905. 336 p.

A widow and her two children are brought under the influence of a malevolent Seventh Day Adventist minister. Partially set at "Calhoun College" in "Calhoun" (Battle Creek).

MiHas NbLU

759 [————].
Madeline the Island Girl by Hope Daring [pseud.]. New York: Eaton & Mains; Cincinnati: Jennings & Graham, 1906. 282 p.

A seven-year-old orphaned girl is sent to live with her grandparents and finds a happy home with them. Set on Mackinac Island from 1883 to 1893.

Mi MiAllG OU

760 [————].
Father John; or, Ruth Webster's Quest by Hope Daring [pseud.]. New York: American Tract Society, 1907. 270 p.

A nineteen-year-old woman believes her father, long thought to be dead, is still alive and begins a search for him. Set in Detroit and on Mackinac Island in 1831.

Black, 143.

Mi MiHas MiStc MoU OU

761 Johnson, Areldene Oldt
Lonely Apartments. N.p., 1970. 476 p.

A group of career women from different backgrounds live in an old rooming house and share their life stories. Set in Ann Arbor in the 1960s.

MiGr-L

762 Johnson, Coralie Cederna 1939–
The Wishing Years. Ypsilanti: Wildwood Press, 1995. 301 p.

Fictionalized reminiscences about the author's family and her life from 1943 to 1955. Set mostly in Stambaugh in the Upper Peninsula.

Mi MiCad MiMtpT-C MiSh MiT

763 Johnson, Edith L.
Log Cabin Children. Boston: Lothrop, Lee & Shepard Co., 1942. 191 p.

A story of pioneer life and the additional dangers and excitement a family encounters during the War of 1812. Set in "Furport" on Lake Michigan.

Juvenile.

Mi MiBrF MiHly IChamL OCl

764 Johnson, Emily Rhoads
Spring and the Shadow Man. New York: Dodd, Mead & Co., 1984. 160 p.

A sixth-grade girl moves to a town with her family, and as she gets used to her new surroundings, she befriends a neighbor who has just become blind. Set in "Willoughby."

Juvenile.

765 Johnson, Enid 1892–
Nancy Runs the Bookmobile. New York: Julian Messner, 1956. 189 p.

(Career Romance for Young Moderns)

The story of a new librarian from Western Reserve University and her work with a bookmobile. Partially set in "Great Springs" in southern Michigan.

Juvenile.

MiBar MiBsA MiDW MiFli MiWalv

766 Johnson, Georgia Anna 1930–
The Baby Who Knew Too Much by Georgia A. Johnson, M.D. East Lansing, Mich.: Georgia A. Johnson Publishing Co., 1993. 233 p.

When a physician at a community hospital tries to discover reasons for her baby's seizures, it leads to a murder mystery. Set in a small Michigan town in 1960.

Mystery.

Mi MiAllG MiDW MiEM MiL

767 Johnson, Lois Walfrid 1936–
Mystery of the Missing Map. Minneapolis: Bethany House Publishers, 1994. 158 p.

(Adventures of the Northwoods, vol. 9)

Three siblings travel to the Upper Peninsula to stay with relatives, and they become involved in the search for a hidden treasure map. Set in Red Jacket (now Calumet) in 1907.

Juvenile.

MiAllG MiHM InFw OCl WM

768 Johnston, Donald
The Echoes of L'Arbre Croche. Harbor Springs, Mich.: Lord & Allerton, 1996. 325 p.

This novel, a slightly rewritten version of MacHarg and Balmer's 1917 novel *The Indian Drum* (q.v.), uses the same characters, chronology, plot, and setting as the latter.

Mi MiD MiLac MiMtpT-C MiT

Jolls, Lynda S., ed. *see* Winters, Donna M.

769 Jones, Craig 1945–
Blood Secrets. New York: Harper &
Row, 1978. 199 p.

The story of a college romance that
leads to marriage, horror, and ultimately murder. Mostly set at Michigan
State University in East Lansing.

Mystery.

770 ———.
Fatal Attraction. New York: Crown
Publishers, 1983. 280 p.

A man and his daughter try to cope with
an accidental death in the family while
a serial rapist terrorizes their unnamed
Michigan city, probably Grand Rapids.

Mystery.

771 Jones, Nettie P. 1941–
Fish Tales. New York: Random House,
1983. 175 p.

An African-American woman desperately and self-destructively searches
for love with a variety of casual sex
partners and through drug use. Partially
set in Detroit.

Mi MiAllG MiD MiDW MiSf

772 ———.
Mischief Makers. New York: Weiden-
feld & Nicolson, 1989. 163 p.

Two African-American physicians
send their light-skinned daughter north
to begin a new life as a white woman,
and she ultimately marries an Ojibwa.
Set in Detroit and on the Leelanau
Peninsula from the 1930s to the 1950s.

772A Jones, Sandie
Water Tower Mouse. N.p., 1989. 39 p.

A mouse, with the help of his friend,
finds a comfortable home inside the
Ypsilanti water tower, a historic land-
mark.

Juvenile.

MiYEM

Justice, Julius, pseud. *see* Kelly, Julius

K

773 Kakonis, Thomas E. 1930–
Michigan Roll by Tom Kakonis. New
York: St. Martin's Press, 1988. 288 p.

A professional gambler tries his luck
at a Native-American casino and runs
afoul of two brutal enforcers. Set on
the Leelanau Peninsula and in Traverse
City.

Mystery.

774 ———.
Criss Cross by Tom Kakonis. New
York: St. Martin's Press, 1990. 322 p.

A group of thieves plan to steal Christmas Eve receipts from a large retail
store in Grand Rapids, but have a violent falling-out.

Mystery.

775 [———**].**
Flawless by Adam Barrow [pseud.].
New York: Dutton, 1995. 372 p.

A young business consultant who is a
brutal serial killer lives with his convicted murderer father. Twenty pages
are set in Grand Rapids and at "Hobbes
College" (Calvin College).

Subtitle on book jacket: *A Thriller.*

Mystery.

776 [Kaler, James Otis] 1848–1912
*At the Siege of Detroit, a Story of Two
Ohio Boys in the War of 1812 as Set
Down by David Bellinger;* edited by

James Otis [pseud.]. New York: A. L. Burt Co., 1904. 353 p.

Two fifteen-year-old boys helping defend Fort Detroit witness General Hull's surrender to the British forces in the War of 1812.

A later printing was published as *The Boy Spies at the Siege of Detroit; a Story of the Ohio Boys in the War of 1812.*

Juvenile.

Black, 144. Streeter, 2462.

Mi MiD MiSsL MiYEM

777 Kantner, Rob 1952–
The Back-Door Man. New York: Bantam Books, 1986. 280 p.

Private investigator and ex-mob enforcer Ben Perkins is hired by a wealthy widow to recover money that was embezzled from her. Set in Belleville and Detroit.

Mystery.

MiAllG MiBlo MiGr MiInr MiSth

778 ———.
The Harder They Hit. New York: Bantam Books, 1987. 226 p.

Ben Perkins is hired by a psychic to find a missing woman and discovers a connection with an illicit video market. Set in Belleville, Detroit, and Ypsilanti.

Mystery.

MiAllG MiGr MiSth AzG MoK

779 ———.
Dirty Work. New York: Bantam Books, 1988. 247 p.

A popular disc jockey is suspected of a series of rape-murders and hires Ben Perkins to find evidence that will clear him. Set in Belleville and Detroit.

Mystery.

Mi MiAllG MiRoch OBgU WM

780 ———.
Hell's Only Half Full. New York: Bantam Books, 1989. 245 p.

Ben Perkins searches for a dying friend's missing son and becomes involved with a gang of white supremacists. Set in Belleville and Detroit.

Mystery.

Mi MiAllG MiGr MiRoch MiSth

781 ———.
Made in Detroit. New York: Bantam Books, 1990. 262 p.

Ben Perkins's best friend is killed when the car he starts explodes, and the police find evidence that implicates Ben. Set in Belleville and Detroit.

Mystery.

Mi MiAllG MiD MiRoch MiSth

782 ———.
The Thousand Yard Stare. New York: Bantam Books, 1991. 275 p.

The invitation to his twenty-fifth Redford High School reunion prompts Ben Perkins to recall a classmate's suicide just before graduation. Set in Belleville and Detroit.

Mystery.

MiAllG MiD MiMani MiMtcM MiSth

783 ———.
The Quick and the Dead. New York: HarperPaperbacks, 1992. 306 p.

Before the Pope arrives to beatify a local priest, Ben Perkins must find the late clergyman's missing body, buried some fifty years. Set in Belleville and Detroit.

Mystery.

Mi MiAllG MiD MiMtp OBgU

784 ———.
The Red, White, and Blues. A Ben Perkins Mystery. New York: HarperPaperbacks, 1993. 417 p.

A woman's newborn infant disappears from the hospital, and Ben Perkins takes the case when the police are baffled. Set in Detroit and Belleville.

Mystery.

Mi MiAllG MiD MiMtcM OBgU

785 ———.
Concrete Hero. A Ben Perkins Mystery. New York: HarperPaperbacks, 1994. 394 p.

The police label a computer expert's death accidental, but his widow hires Ben Perkins to find the truth behind the killing. Set in Belleville and Detroit.

Mystery.

Mi MiAllG MiD MiFli MiMtcM

Kantor, Hal, joint author *see* Levine, Morton

786 Kasischke, Laura
Suspicious River. Boston: Houghton Mifflin Co., 1996. 271 p.

A young small-town prostitute tells her grim story through a series of flashbacks that are juxtaposed with her current situation. Set mostly in "Suspicious River," probably in Allegan County.

787 [Katz, Carol] 1939–
North Country Nights by Penny Allison [pseud.]. New York: Silhouette Books, 1984. 186 p.

(Silhouette Desire, no. 143)

Pride and lack of communication bring a young couple to the brink of divorce before they work things out. Set on Manistique Lake in the Upper Peninsula.

Romance.

MiAllG MiFli MiGr MiInr OBgU

788 ———.
Then Came Laughter. Toronto: Harlequin Books, 1985. 302 p.

(Harlequin Superromance, no. 152)

A holiday romance between a psychologist and a syndicated cartoonist becomes serious despite a number of obstacles. Partially set in Ann Arbor.

Romance.

MiAllG MiGr IChamL UM WAPL

789 Kauffman, Janet 1945–
The Body in Four Parts. St. Paul, Minn.: Graywolf Press, 1993. 128 p.

The experimental, self-conscious effort of a woman to explore her "inner self" and reclaim certain aspects of her personality. Set partially in Michigan.

790 Kavanaugh, James Joseph 1929–
The Celibates. New York: Harper & Row, 1985. 326 p.

The story of two Catholic priests and their continual struggle with carnal temptations. Partially set in Flint, Lansing, and Farmington from 1954 to 1980.

791 Kay, Ross
The Go Ahead Boys on Smugglers' Island. New York: Barse & Hopkins, 1916. 247 p.

(Go Ahead Boys, no. 1)

While four boys are on a vacation cruise, they help authorities break up a diamond smuggling ring. Partially set on Lake Huron and Mackinac Island.

Juvenile.

MiGr-L FTS OAU

792 Kayle, Hilary S.
Players. New York: Berkley Books, 1991. 307 p.

A woman from an Indiana television station tries to find success as a journalist for a major network in New York. Partially set at the University of Michigan in Ann Arbor.

MiSth IaB OCl USl WLac

793 Keays, Hersilia A. Mitchell Copp
1861–1910
The Road to Damascus. Boston: Small, Maynard & Co., 1907. 447 p.

A young man struggles to overcome the stigma of his illegitimate birth and be accepted into society. Set at "Waverly University" (University of Michigan).

MiU CStclU OU PMA TU

794 Keil, Doris Parkin
The Ploughboy and the Nightingale. Toronto: Copp Clark Publishing Co., 1958. 304 p.

The fictionalized account of the visit and performances of the famed soprano Jenny Lind (1820–1887) in Chatham, Ontario, in 1851. Thirty pages are set in Detroit.

MiAllG MiD InU MH OBgU

795 Keliher, Evan C. 1931–
New Africa High: A Low Comedy. Linden, Mich.: Leader Printing & Publishing, 1976. 174 p.

A humorous narrative about the life, adventures, and experiences that students and teachers share in a Detroit inner-city high school.

Mi MiBatW MiD MiMtpT-C MiYEM

796 ——.
Detroit: Rebirth or Miscarriage? Linden, Mich.: Leader Printing; Published by the Author, 1979. 175 p.

A fictionalized examination of the social and economic problems of Detroit, as well as some suggested remedies.

Mi MiD

797 ——.
The Immoral Majority. Linden, Mich.: Leader Printing, 1982. 219 p.

The narrator saves Jesus Christ from an enraged Detroit mob and helps make preparations for the Second Coming.

MiMtpT-C

798 Kelland,   Clarence   Budington
1881–1964
Mark Tidd; His Adventures and Strategies. New York: Harper & Brothers, 1913. 316 p.

Mark Tidd, a resourceful overweight boy who stutters, recovers his father's stolen invention with the help of his three friends. Set in "Wicksville."

Juvenile.

Mi CLU InFw OBgU ViBlbV

799 ——.
Mark Tidd in the Backwoods. New York: Harper & Brothers, 1914. 282 p.

Mark Tidd and his three friends save his uncle's Upper Peninsula land from devious copper speculators. Set in "Wicksville," Baldwin, Ludington, and on the Pere Marquette River.

Juvenile.

Mi CLU NNC OSW ViBlbV

800 ———.
Mark Tidd in Business. New York: Harper & Brothers, 1915. 271 p.

Mark Tidd and his three friends run a general merchandise store when the owner must spend time in the hospital. Set in "Wicksville."

Juvenile.

Mi CSf InLP OU ViBlbV

801 ———.
The Hidden Spring. New York: Harper & Brothers, 1916. 296 p.

A young idealistic lawyer challenges a millionaire lumber magnate who has control over a lumber town and its citizens. Set in "Owasco."

Black, 145.

MiAllG MsCliM MnU OBgU OU

802 ———.
Sudden Jim. New York: Harper & Brothers, 1917. 286 p.

A young man is given the responsibility of running his father's clothespin factory. Set in the western Michigan lumber town of "Diversity."

Mi MnM NbPerS OU ViW

803 ———.
Mark Tidd, Editor. New York: Harper & Brothers, 1917. 286 p.

Mark Tidd and his family buy the bankrupt local weekly paper, and he and his three friends have adventures as newspapermen. Set in "Wicksville."

Juvenile.

Mi CLU FTS ODaWU WU

804 ———.
Mark Tidd, Manufacturer. New York: Harper & Brothers, 1918. 256 p.

Mark Tidd and his three friends try to run a lumbermill his father has been given in payment for a loan default. Set in "Wicksville."

Juvenile.

Mi MiEM CSf FTS ViBlbV

805 ———.
The Highflyers. New York: Harper & Brothers, 1919. 361 p.

The heir to an automobile factory plans to manufacture airplanes for the war effort but is beset by German spies and saboteurs. Set in Detroit.

MiStc ArStC IC MnM OU

806 ———.
Efficiency Edgar. New York: Harper & Brothers, 1920. 94 p.

A humorous story of an efficiency expert working for a Detroit company and how his predilection for order affects his marriage.

ICU MH NhU OCl OU

807 ———.
Youth Challenges. New York: Harper & Brothers, 1920. 345 p.

A disowned son finds work in an automobile factory, is promoted to a high level, and, with his new knowledge, eventually takes over his deceased father's business. Set in Detroit.

Mi FJ KAS OU VtU

808 ———.
The Steadfast Heart. New York: Harper & Brothers, 1924. 359 p.

A young man from a lowly and impoverished background advances to a position of trust and is discovered to be a lost heir. Set in "Rainbow" from the 1880s to 1900.

Mi MiAllG MiTop MiU OU

809 ———.

Mark Tidd in Italy. New York: Harper & Brothers, 1925. 264 p.

Mark Tidd, his father, and his three friends travel to Italy for a lengthy holiday and have a variety of adventures. Eleven pages are set in "Wicksville."

Juvenile.

MiEM CStoC PLhS UU ViBlbV

810 Kellogg, Elizabeth Rogers

Across the Deep Threshold. Lansing: Wellman Press, 1980. 368 p.

A fictionalized chronicle about a fourteen-year-old girl who marries a farmer and lives with his family, the Cornells. Set in the small village of "Petrieville" north of Eaton Rapids from 1859 to 1865.

Mi MiAllG MiEM MiMtpT MiSc

811 ———.

Them War the Days. Lansing: Wellman Press, 1981. 334 p.

Further details are given concerning the Cornell family, which was first introduced in *Across the Deep Threshold.* Mostly set in Eaton Rapids from 1837 to the 1880s.

Mi MiAllG MiBatW MiL MiMtpT-C

812 ———.

I Don't Cry Much. Lansing: Wellman Press, 1983. 320 p.

A fictionalized chronicle of the Cole and Place families that lived in northern Indiana from 1863 to 1898. Thirty-eight pages are set in Eaton Rapids.

Mi MiAllG MiL MiMtpT In

813 ———.

Into the Harness. Lansing: Wellman Press, 1984. 194 p.

A fictionalized speculation about the author's father, Sydney Morris Rogers, and what his life might have been like in Eaton Rapids from 1887 to 1893.

Mi MiAllG MiDW MiL MiMtpT-C

814 [Kelly, George C.] 1849–1895

The Circus Detective; or Bareback Billy's Big Round-Up by Harold Payne [pseud.]. New York: Beadle and Adams, 1895. 16 p.

(Beadle's Half-Dime Library, no. 952)

A circus performer and detective, Bareback Billy, foils a group of criminals and their plans in Big Rapids when the show arrives there on its tour.

Dime novel.

Black, 147.

Copy not located.

815 Kelly, Jack 1949–

Mad Dog. New York: Atheneum, 1992. 292 p.

A man who strongly resembles the gangster John Dillinger capitalizes on this likeness in a carnival sideshow act. Partially set in Michigan in 1934.

816 [Kelly, Julius]

The Belly of the Unknown Beast by Julius Justice [pseud.]. Detroit: Justice Publications, 1993. 162 p.

A young African-American man has plans to become the city's biggest drug dealer, but first must eliminate his potential rivals. Set in Detroit.

MiGr-L

817 Kelly, Regina Zimmerman 1898–
Beaver Trail. New York: Lothrop, Lee & Shepard, 1955. 237 p.

A young man has a number of adventures while on the wilderness trail leading to Fort Dearborn in Illinois. Partially set on Mackinac Island in 1811 and 1812.

Juvenile.

Mi MiD MiGr MiKW MiPet

Kelson, Jan, pseud. *see* Jankelson, Jacob

Kent, Fortune, pseud. *see* Toombs, John

818 Kerle, Arthur G.
Whispering Trees; a Tale of Michigamaw. St. Cloud, Minn.: North Star Press, 1971. 208 p.

The friendship between an Ojibwa boy and a white boy is tested when the latter joins a logging concern that systematically destroys the Michigan forests in the 1880s.

Juvenile.

Mi MiAC MiAlp MiD MiMuC

819 Keuning, J.
The Man in the Bearskin. A Translation of J. Keuning's "De Man Met de Berenhuid" by John H. DeGroot. Grand Rapids: Wm. B. Eerdmans Publishing Co., 1925. 191 p.

A mysterious disheveled man continually assists one pioneer family in a new settlement until his identity is finally revealed. Set in Holland in the 1840s.

The book originally appeared in 1898 as *De Man Met de Berenhuid* in the Netherlands; other publication details have not been located.

Black, 150.

Mi MiAllG MiGrC

820 Keyes, Daniel 1927–
The Touch. New York: Harcourt, Brace & World, 1968. 215 p.

An automobile designer is contaminated by a radioactive spill and fears it may have affected his unborn baby. Set in the Detroit suburb of "Elgin City."

821 Kienzle, William X. 1928–
The Rosary Murders. Kansas City: Andrews and McMeel, 1979. 257 p.

A serial murderer is at work among the Catholic community in Detroit, and Father Koesler is called on by the police to aid in their investigations.

Mystery.

822 ———.
Death Wears a Red Hat. Kansas City: Andrews and McMeel, 1980. 304 p.

Father Koesler assists the Detroit police identify a murderer who is decapitating his victims and placing the heads on church statues.

Mystery.

823 ———.
Mind Over Murder. Kansas City: Andrews and McMeel, 1981. 296 p.

Six people are prime suspects in the disappearance and apparent murder of a monsignor. Father Koesler helps the Detroit police.

Mystery.

824 ———.
Assault with Intent. Kansas City: Andrews and McMeel, 1982. 273 p.

A group of inept assassins attempt to murder a number of priests who teach in Detroit seminaries. Father Koesler aids the police investigation.

Mystery.

825 ———.
Shadow of Death. Kansas City: Andrews and McMeel, 1983. 252 p.

A murderer stalks cardinals in a plot to destroy the papacy, and Father Koesler journeys to Rome, London, and Ireland to investigate. Partially set in Detroit.

Mystery.

826 ———.
Kill and Tell. Kansas City: Andrews and McMeel, 1984. 249 p.

When a Detroit automobile executive is targeted for murder, Father Koesler identifies a number of people who would benefit from the man's death.

Mystery.

827 ———.
Sudden Death. Kansas City: Andrews, McMeel & Parker, 1985. 257 p.

When the murder of a professional football player is somehow tied to a Bible study group, Father Koesler assists the police. Set in Detroit and Pontiac.

Mystery.

828 ———.
Deathbed. Kansas City: Andrews, McMeel & Parker, 1986. 258 p.

When Father Koesler is temporarily assigned as chaplain to a Detroit hospital, he becomes involved with an outbreak of violence and murder.

Mystery.

829 ———.
Deadline for a Critic. Kansas City: Andrews, McMeel & Parker, 1987. 263 p.

A number of people have ample motives for murdering a particularly loathsome Detroit newspaper art critic. Father Koesler investigates.

Mystery.

830 ———.
Marked for Murder. Kansas City: Andrews and McMeel, 1988. 281 p.

A serial killer dressed as a priest has been systematically murdering Detroit prostitutes. Father Koesler assists in the police investigation.

Mystery.

831 ———.
Eminence. Kansas City: Andrews and McMeel, 1989. 312 p.

When miraculous cures from a mysterious religious group newly established in Detroit are reported, Father Koesler looks into the legitimacy of the claims.

Mystery.

832 ———.
Masquerade. Kansas City: Andrews and McMeel, 1990. 267 p.

The murder of a popular televangelist at a Marygrove College mystery writers' conference has Father Koesler investigating a number of suspects. Set in Detroit.

Mystery.

833 ———.
Chameleon. Kansas City: Andrews and McMeel, 1991. 289 p.

Father Koesler is involved with a murder investigation in which the victim was a prostitute dressed in a nun's habit. Set in Detroit.

Mystery.

834 ———.
Body Count. Kansas City: Andrews and McMeel, 1992. 266 p.

Father Koesler faces moral and ethical dilemmas when the seal of confession prevents him from informing the police about a murder. Set in Detroit.

Mystery.

835 ———.
Dead Wrong. Kansas City: Andrews and McMeel, 1993. 269 p.

A thirty-year-old mystery confronts Father Koesler and provides surprising revelations about his niece and a real estate magnate's son. Set in Detroit.

Mystery.

836 ———.
Bishop As Pawn. Kansas City: Andrews and McMeel, 1994. 266 p.

A new bishop is found murdered, and the negative remarks made about him the previous night at a meeting provide Father Koesler with many suspects. Set in Detroit.

Mystery.

837 ———.
Call No Man Father. Kansas City: Andrews and McMeel, 1995. 272 p.

Father Koesler assists the police and the Church prepare for the Pope's visit to Detroit and discovers a number of murder plots against the pontiff.

Mystery.

838 ———.
Requiem for Moses. Kansas City: Andrews and McMeel, 1996. 272 p.

Father Koesler reluctantly agrees to hold a service for a deceased Jewish man and is faced with a possible miracle when the man comes back to life. Set in Detroit.

Mystery.

839 [Kilchenstein, Mary I.]
Miracles by Mary Kirk [pseud.]. New York: Silhouette Books, 1990. 251 p.

(Silhouette Special Edition, no. 628)

A Navy pilot who briefly died in a plane crash but was revived finds he has the power to heal, a fact that he tries to hide from a nurse whom he helps. Set in "Bourner's Crossing" in the Upper Peninsula.

Romance.

MiGr MiMtp MiPh MiWar OBgU

840 Kilian, Michael
The Big Score. New York: St. Martin's Press, 1993. 393 p.

A Chicago artist becomes involved with a sleazy real estate developer and eventually in murder. Forty pages are set in "Grand Pier" (Union Pier?) on Lake Michigan.

Mystery.

King, Paul, pseud. *see* Kiralyhegyi, Pal

841 Kinkopf, Eric
Shooter. New York: G. P. Putnam's Sons, 1993. 270p.

A Detroit policeman finds that what looks like a routine street shooting is really a part of a conspiracy that leads to the top people in the city government.

Mystery.

842 Kintziger, Louis J.
Bay Mild. Milwaukee: Bruce Publishing Co., 1945. 220 p.

A young fisherman comes to hate his work because he believes the girl he loves is repulsed by it. Set in "Noquets Bay" (Big Bay de Noc?), "Baysette," and "Abonac" from 1930 to 1943.

Black, 151.

Mi MiAllG MiEM MiFli MiMarqN

843 [Kinzie, Juliette Augusta Magill]
1806–1870
Mark Logan, the Bourgeois by Mrs. John H. Kinzie. Philadelphia: J. B. Lippincott & Co., 1871. 678 p.

The story of a fur-trade agent, Mark Logan, who is patterned on Gurdon S. Hubbard (1802–1886). Set partially in Detroit and on Mackinac Island in the late 1820s.

Black, 152. Wright II, 1479.

CSmH

844 [Kiralyhegyi, Pal]
Greenhorn by Paul (Kiralyhegyi) King [pseud.]. New York: Macaulay Co., 1932. 308 p.

The fictionalized autobiography of a Hungarian immigrant and his struggles and adjustments to life in America. The last twenty-five pages are set in Detroit.

ArU KyRE OBgU OO

Kirk, Mary, pseud. *see* Kilchenstein, Mary I.

845 Kirk, Russell 1918–1994
Old House of Fear. New York: Fleet Publishing Corp., 1961. 256 p.

A young lawyer thwarts a group of villains attempting to prey upon an old man and his daughter. Thirteen pages are set in Michigan, the remainder in Scotland.

846 [Kirkland, Caroline Matilda Stansbury] 1801–1864
A New Home—Who'll Follow? or, Glimpses of Western Life by Mrs. Mary Clavers [pseud.]. New York: C. S.

Francis; Boston: J. H. Francis, 1839. 317 p.

The fictionalized experiences of a refined woman on the coarse Michigan frontier. Written in a satirical style and set in "Montacute" (Pinckney) in the late 1830s.

Black, 156. Streeter, 2545. Wright I, 1583.

Mi MiEM MiGr MiMtpT-C MiYEM

847 [———].
Forest Life by the Author of "A New Home." New York: C. S. Francis & Co., 1842. 2 vols.

More of the author's fictionalized experiences on the Michigan frontier are recounted. Set in Pinckney in the early 1840s.

Black, 154. Streeter, 2543. Wright I, 1580.

Mi MiEM MiHM MiMtpT-C MiSsL

848 Kjelgaard, James Arthur 1910–1959
The Explorations of Pere Marquette by Jim Kjelgaard. New York: Random House, 1951. 181 p.

A fictionalized biography of Father Jacques Marquette (1637–1675), including his explorations of the Great Lakes area of New France. Twenty-five pages are set in Michigan.

849 Klein, Norma 1938–
Give and Take. New York: Viking, 1985. 169 p.

In the summer before starting college, a naive eighteen-year-old begins dating a twenty-year-old woman with heartbreaking results. Set in "Riverview."

Juvenile.

Knight of Chillon of Switzerland and Associates, pseud. *see* Hawkins, Nehemiah

850 **Knister, Barry**
The Dating Service. New York: Jove, 1987. 331 p.

A criminal organization tries to eliminate one of its hit men, a Vietnam veteran, who takes exception to being killed. Set in Detroit and Port Sheldon.

Mystery.

MiAllG MiDW MiMtcM MiRos MiSth

851 **[Koehler, Margaret Hudson]**
Now, in September by Meg Hudson [pseud.]. Toronto: Harlequin Books, 1984. 377 p.

(Harlequin Superromance, no. 126)

A woman hired to design an effective advertising campaign for a bakery falls in love with its president and tries not to let her feelings affect her work. Set in Holland.

Romance.

MiAllG MiGr MiMtcM IGenD WOsh

Kolaczyk, Anne, joint author *see* Edwards, Andrea

Kolaczyk, Ed, joint author *see* Edwards, Andrea

852 **Korbel, Kathleen**
Hotshot. New York: Silhouette Books, 1990. 189 p.

(Silhouette Desire, no. 582)

A professional photographer must photograph a reclusive and attractive wildlife artist. Set on the shore of Lake Michigan in the Grand Haven area.

Romance.

MiAllG MiGr IChamL NRU OBgU

853 **Korfker, Dena** 1908–
Ankie Comes to America. Grand Rapids: Zondervan Publishing House, 1954. 63 p.

A little girl from the Netherlands moves to America with her parents and finds the journey full of wonders and surprises. Thirty pages are set in Grand Rapids.

Juvenile.

MiGrC

853A **Koskinen, Timo**
Bone Soup & a Lapland Wizard. Amherst, Mass.: Lynx House Press, 1984. 168 p.

Two Finns, both loggers and outdoorsmen, share ruminations on life as they hunt, fish, and sit in the local bar. Set in "Saukshead" and other places in Marquette County in the Upper Peninsula.

MiHanS MiMarqN MiMtpT-C MnU OU

854 **Kouris, John R.**
Kalamazoo Dreams. Mount Prospect, Ill.: Doppler Publishing Co., 1984. 368 p.

A young man from Indiana attends Western Michigan University from 1964 to 1968 on a football scholarship and has many social and academic adventures.

Mi MiAllG MiKW MiMani MiMtpT-C

855 **[Kroflich, Stephen A.]** 1937–
Game by Hurst Wolf [pseud.]. Fenton, Mich.: Kroflich Press, 1991. 409 p.

When the cocaine-addicted son of a wealthy industrialist is acquitted of the murder of a woman, the husband, a Vietnam veteran, plans revenge. Partially set in Flint.

Mystery.

MiAllG MiFli

856 Kruithof, Bastian

Instead of the Thorn. New York: Half Moon Press, 1941. 233 p.

The story of a family of Dutch settlers in Michigan and the hardships of pioneer life they face. Set in Holland from the 1840s to the 1860s.

Black, 158.

Mi MiAllG MiFli MiGr MiMtpT-C

L

857 Lacey, Anne

Light for Another Night. New York: Silhouette Books, 1989. 251 p.

(Silhouette Special Edition, no. 538)

A wildlife biologist studying wolves is attracted to a handsome reclusive widower. Set on "Isle Svenson" in Lake Superior near the Keweenaw Peninsula.

Romance.

MiAllG O OBgU PNo TxAu

858 [Lake, Joe Barry]

The Third Degree by Joe Barry [pseud.]. New York: Mystery House, 1943. 256 p.

A former newspaper reporter, now a U.S. Army intelligence officer, investigates a Nazi spy ring and is captured and tortured, and escapes. Forty-five pages are set in Detroit.

Mystery.

Mi MBU OU

859 Lambe, Milly

Don't Call Me Lizzie! Kalamazoo: Ihling Brothers Everard Co., 1985. 143 p.

The adolescent daughter of the high school principal grows up in a small Lake Michigan town near Muskegon. Set in "Scottstown" from 1941 to 1945.

Mi MiAllG MiGrA MiKW MiMtpT-C

860 Lang, Brad

Crockett on the Loose. New York: Leisure Books, 1975. 189 p.

A young private investigator, Fred Crockett, is hired by a man to find his missing daughter, and her trail leads to sex shops and drugs. Set in Ann Arbor.

Mystery.

MiAllG MiEM

861 ———.

Brand of Fear. New York: Leisure Books, 1976. 192 p.

Fred Crockett investigates compromising photographs of a young gay man, and the case turns violent when the blackmailer ends up murdered. Set in Ann Arbor.

Mystery.

MiAllG MiEM

862 ———.

Crockett: The Perdition Express. New York: Leisure Books, 1976. 183 p.

While at a nightclub, Fred Crockett witnesses the murder of the bass player in a popular rock band and searches for his killer. Set in Ann Arbor.

Mystery.

MiAllG MiEM

863 Langan, Ruth Ryan 1937–

Just Like Yesterday. New York: Silhouette Books, 1981. 188 p.

(Silhouette Romance, no. 121)

Years after an angry parting, a woman discovers she must negotiate a company merger with the man she once loved. Set in Harbor Springs.

Romance.

MiAllG   MiChv   IChamL   InMu   OBgU

864 ——.
The Proper Miss Porter. New York: Silhouette Books, 1987. 186 p.

(Silhouette Romance, no. 492)

A reluctant woman executive is pursued amorously and vigorously by the president of an automobile company. Set in Detroit and Torch Lake.

Romance.

Mi   MiAllG   MiGr   OBgU   PNo

865 Langdon, Kenneth 1924–
The Swede. New York: Vantage Press, 1968. 74 p.

A humorous story about a man of Swedish extraction and his adventures with his friends during hunting season. Set in the Upper Peninsula in 1950.

Mi   ABAU   InSMW

866 Lange, Dietrich 1863–1940
The Silver Island of the Chippewa. Boston: Lothrop, Lee & Shepard Co., 1913. 246 p.

To help their father's business, two boys search for a lost silver mine in the Lake Superior area in 1865 and 1866. Partially set on Isle Royale.

Juvenile.

Streeter, 2615.

Mi   MiAllG   MnHi   MnM   OCl

867 ——.
Lost in the Fur Country. Boston: Lothrop, Lee & Shepard Co., 1914. 297 p.

During a raid, a sister and brother are taken from their Kentucky home by Native Americans and after many years find their way back. Thirty-five pages are set in Michigan.

Juvenile.

FTS   MnHi   MnM   MnSP   SdSifA

868 Langille, James Hibbert 1841–1923
Snail-Shell Harbor. Boston: Henry Hoyt, 1870. 266 p.

A minister comes to an iron-smelting town and establishes a church and Sunday school. Set in Fayette at Snail-Shell Harbor in the Upper Peninsula on the northwestern coast of Lake Michigan.

Mi   MiU   NBuBE   OrU

869 Larke, Denny
There Are No Saviors. Roseville, Mich.: Green Earth Press, 1974. 239 p.

Inhabitants of a small town seem to have their lives ruled by fate rather than free will. Set in "Harmony Harbor" in northern Michigan on Lake Huron during the 1930s.

MiAllG   MiMtcM

870 Lathen, Emma, pseud.
Murder Makes the Wheels Go 'Round. New York: Macmillan, 1966. 183 p.

A Wall Street banker researching the investment potential of Michigan Motors must instead investigate the murder of one of its executives. Set in Detroit.

"Emma Lathen" is the joint pseudonym of Martha Hennissart and Mary Jane Latsis.

Mystery.

871 [Latimer, Jonathan Wyatt] 1906–1983
The Search for My Great-Uncle's Head

by Peter Coffin [pseud.]. Garden City, N.Y.: Doubleday, Doran & Co., 1937. 297 p.

(Crime Club)

A wealthy man is murdered at a country estate during a family house party, and although the motive is obvious, the suspects are many. Set at Crystal Lake.

Mystery.

MiGr CU MnU OBgU OU

Latsis, Mary Jane *see* Lathen, Emma

872 Laurie, Ann

After the Rapture. New York: Carlton Press, 1969. 193 p.

A religious tale of the apocalypse, its aftermath, and its effects on one family in particular. Set in "Port City" (Muskegon).

Mi MiCad

873 [Lauro, Shirley Shapiro Mezvinsky] 1933–

The Edge by Shirley Mezvinsky [pseud.]. Garden City, N.Y.: Doubleday & Co., 1965. 210 p.

A harrowing story of the gradual emotional breakdown of a twenty-eight-year-old Jewish housewife. Set in "Middleton."

874 Lawrence, Albert Lathrop 1865–1924

Juell Demming; a Story. Chicago: A. C. McClurg & Co., 1901. 384 p.

A young Canadian is found ill in a small town, is nursed back to health in a home, and subsequently becomes a teacher, newspaperman, and soldier. Mostly set in "Saugatauk" (Saugatuck) in the 1890s.

Black, 160.

Mi CL ICU MWC OClW

875 ———.

The Wolverine; a Romance of Early Michigan. Boston: Little, Brown, and Co., 1904. 337 p.

A young French girl is wooed by the governor of the Michigan Territory, an officer of the militia, and a land surveyor. Set in Detroit in 1835.

Black, 161. Streeter, 2694.

Mi MiD MiEM MiMtpT-C MiU

876 Lawrence, Eula M.

And Thy Mother. Boston: Bruce Humphries, 1943. 115 p.

The story of a twelve-year-old girl, her family, and how they live through the years on their forest homestead. Set in northern Michigan.

Mi OU

877 Lawrence, Mildred Elwood 1907–

Crissy at the Wheel. New York: Harcourt, Brace, 1952. 200 p.

A young girl does an admirable job of helping her father sell horseless carriages. Set in "Granite City" (Flint) in 1902.

Juvenile.

Mi MiAllG MiD MiFliL MiKW

878 ———.

Good Morning, My Heart. New York: Harcourt, Brace, 1957. 191 p.

A shy girl gradually attains self-confidence while at college and dreams of one day being the owner of a small newspaper. Set in southwestern Michigan.

Juvenile.

MiCad MiD MiDW InFw OCo

879 ———.

Reach for the Dream. New York: Harcourt, Brace & World, 1967. 192 p.

A seventeen-year-old girl hopes to become a writer and solves a mystery concerning stolen jewelry. Set in the resort town of "Bayville" near Elk Rapids.

Juvenile.

880 Lawrence, Terry 1957–
Before Dawn. New York: Silhouette Books, 1989. 187 p.

(Silhouette Desire, no. 526)

Blinded in a mining accident, a man falls in love with his therapist. Set in western and northern Michigan, Ann Arbor, and the Upper Peninsula.

Romance.

MiAllG MiGr ICRMC NRU OBgU

881 ———.
The Outsider. New York: Bantam Books, 1990. 179 p.

(Loveswept, no. 399)

A woman tries to win a contract with an Ottawa and Ojibwa gambling casino for her accounting firm. Set on the Leelanau Peninsula.

Romance.

MiAllG MiAlp MoK OBgU PNo

882 ———.
Unfinished Passion. New York: Bantam Books, 1990. 182 p.

(Loveswept, no. 441)

Former lovers are surprised to learn that they have been selected for the same jury in a court trial and must spend some time together. Set in "Derby."

Romance.

MiAllG MiGr InCo OBgU OXe

883 ———.
Passion's Flight. New York: Bantam Books, 1991. 179 p.

(Loveswept, no. 457)

A famous Soviet defector joins a dance company and falls in love with its director. Partially set at the National Music Camp at Interlochen.

Romance.

MiAllG MiGr MiT MoK OBgU

884 ———.
Fugitive Father. New York: Bantam Books, 1996. 212 p.

(Loveswept, no. 788)

Pursued by ruthless smugglers, a wounded man is nursed back to health by a young woman at an isolated lodge. Set on Bete Grise Bay on the Keweenaw Peninsula.

Romance.

MiAllG MiD MiFli OXe WM

885 Lawson, Horace Lowe 1900–
Pitch Dark and No Moon. New York: Thomas Y. Crowell Co., 1958. 214 p.

A young seaman apprentice in the Coast Guard helps detect and apprehend a smuggling ring operating in the waters of Saginaw Bay.

Juvenile.

Mi MiAllG MiAlp MiPet MiWar

886 Lea, George
Somewhere There's Music. Philadelphia: J. B. Lippincott Co., 1958. 224 p.

A young man returns from the Korean War, takes up the saxophone, and departs for the New York City jazz scene, where he becomes a drug addict. Partially set in "Ogemaw" (Saginaw?).

Black, 162.

Mi MiAllG MiD MiU OC

887 Lebedeff, Vera
The Heart Returneth. Philadelphia: J. B. Lippincott, 1943. 319 p.

The individual lives of a group of White Russians emigrés as well as their ties to Russia are recounted. Set in Detroit from the 1920s to 1941.

Black, 163.

Mi MiD MiDW MiFli OC

888 Lee, Albert 1942–
Slumlord! The True Story of the Man Who Is Beating America's Biggest Problem. New Rochelle, N.Y.: Arlington House Publishers, 1976. 155 p.

The fictionalized biographical account of Charles Costa, an inner-city landlord who apparently owns vast amounts of real estate in Detroit.

889 Lees, Richard 1948–
Out of Sync. New York: PAJ Publications, 1988. 156 p.

A young man is notified that he has been selected to be interviewed as part of a nationwide television program celebrating the U.S. Bicentennial. Partially set in Ann Arbor in 1976.

MiSf IC InHam OCl WM

889A Lemon, Richard Paul 1931–
Little Ike; a Story of My Grandfather. Sand Lake, Mich.: The Author, 1995. 201 p.

An imaginative account of the author's grandfather, a Canadian man who emigrates to Michigan and becomes a teamster. Set in southeastern Michigan from 1874 to 1885.

MiGr-L

890 Leonard, Elmore 1925–
The Big Bounce. Greenwich, Conn.: Fawcett, 1969. 192 p.

Jack Ryan is fired from a cucumber farm and makes plans with a young woman to rob its payroll. Set in "Geneva Beach" on Lake Huron in the Thumb area.

Mystery.

MiChe MiDU KyOw RPaw RWe

891 ———.
Fifty-Two Pickup. New York: Delacorte Press, 1974. 254 p.

A Detroit businessman finds himself blackmailed because of his inadvertent appearance in a pornographic movie, but plans a way out of his predicament.

Mystery.

892 ———.
Swag. New York: Delacorte Press, 1976. 229 p.

A used-car salesman and a cement truck driver team up to begin a spree of well-planned and -executed armed robberies. Set in Detroit.

Also published as *Ryan's Rules* (New York: Dell Publishing Co., 1978).

Mystery.

893 ———.
Unknown Man No. 89. New York: Delacorte Press, 1977. 264 p.

Jack Ryan, now a process server, becomes involved with a group of vicious characters and a search for a missing stockholder. Set in Detroit.

Mystery.

894 ———.

The Switch. New York: Bantam Books, 1978. 216 p.

The young wife of a millionaire real estate swindler is kidnapped, and her husband refuses to pay a ransom to the abductors. Set in Bloomfield Hills and Detroit.

Mystery.

895 ———.

City Primeval; High Noon in Detroit. New York: Arbor House, 1980. 275 p.

A killer, his defense attorney, and a policeman whose evidence has been quashed by the court are all connected in a story of retribution. Set in Detroit.

Mystery.

896 ———.

Gold Coast. New York: Bantam Books, 1980. 218 p.

The beautiful widow of a Mafia chief protects her inheritance from the Mob with the help of an ex-convict. Twelve pages are set in Detroit, the remainder in Miami.

Mystery.

897 ———.

Split Images. New York: Arbor House, 1981. 282 p.

With the help of a journalist, a homicide lieutenant investigates a series of murders that take place in Detroit and Miami and that are connected to a wealthy man.

Mystery.

898 ———.

Touch. New York: Arbor House, 1987. 245 p.

An ex-Franciscan brother working at an alcoholic rehabilitation center be-gins to exhibit the stigmata and seems to possess a gift for healing. Set in Detroit.

899 ———.

Freaky Deaky. New York: Arbor House, 1988. 341 p.

A police detective becomes involved in an extortion racket with a wealthy Detroiter and with ex-revolutionaries that have experience with explosives.

Mystery.

900 ———.

Killshot. New York: Arbor House/William Morrow, 1989. 287 p.

Two psychopaths track down a couple who witnessed and caused their bungled extortion attempt of a realtor. Partially set in Algonac.

Mystery.

901 ———.

Out of Sight. New York: Delacorte Press, 1996. 296 p.

After escaping from prison, a bank robber encounters an attractive U.S. marshal, and they begin an unlikely affair. Partially set in Detroit and Bloomfield Hills.

Mystery.

902 **Levere, William Collin** 1872–1927
Vivian of Mackinac. Chicago: Forbes & Co., 1911. 299 p.

An eighteen-year-old girl runs away to a travelling theater troupe after she and her brother are suspected of killing a counterfeiter. Partially set on Mackinac Island.

Mi MiAllG MiBeld MiKW MiStc

903 Levine, Morton
The Congregation by Rabbi Morton
Levine, with Hal Kantor. New York:
G. P. Putnam's Sons, 1985. 269 p.

The story of the rise of a rabbi from his
small-town idealism to international
fame, amidst his own personal crises.
Set in Farmington Hills.

904 [Lewis, Charles Bertrand] 1842–
1924
*Under Five Lakes: Or, The Cruise of
the "Destroyer"* by M. Quad [pseud.].
New York: George Munro, 1886.
171 p.

(Seaside Library, no. 852)

A secret underwater craft enables her
builder and crew to explore wrecks in
the Great Lakes, many of which are in
Michigan waters, and retrieve a fortune
in treasure.

Dime novel.

DLC

905 Lewis, Edwin Herbert 1866–1938
White Lightning. Chicago: Covici-
McGee, 1923. 354 p.

A young atomic scientist and the
daughter of a retired scholar argue
about issues of progress and conservation. Set partially on an small island in
the St. Mary's River.

Black, 166.

Mi MiD MiGr MiOC MiU

906 Lewis, Elizabeth Boggs Barzditis
1903?–
Granny Eloped; a Novelette. Hermosa
Beach, Calif.: The Author, 1970. 56 p.

An eighty-seven-year-old woman travels to the Keweenaw Peninsula and

reminisces about her life there as a
young girl. Set in Central Mine.

Mi MiAllG MiHM MiHanS MiStc

907 ———.
Sunset Hour. Hermosa Beach, Calif.:
The Author, 1973. 352 p.

In this highly autobiographical book, a
man meets a blind and widowed writer,
and they ultimately marry. Set on the
Keweenaw Peninsula.

MiAllG MiHM MiMtpT-C CEs CRdb

908 [Lewis, George Edward] 1870–
Nick of the Woods by Alaska Blacklock
[pseud.]. Portland, Oreg.: Jensen Publishing Co. Press, 1916. 222 p.

Two brothers work together in a variety
of Michigan logging camps. Set on the
Muskegon, Boardman, and Manistee
Rivers in the 1870s.

Subtitle on cover: *A Tale of the Manistee.*

Mi MiAllG MiGr MiMtpT-C MiYEM

909 Lewis, Janet 1899–
*The Friendly Adventures of Ollie Os-
trich.* Garden City, N.Y.: Doubleday,
Page & Co., 1923. 78 p.

A toy ostrich wanders from the little
girl who made him and has encounters with animals before finding a new
home. Set along the St. Mary's River,
probably on Neebish Island.

Juvenile.

IC OTU

910 ———.
*The Invasion; a Narrative of Events
Concerning the Johnston Family of St.
Mary's.* New York: Harcourt, Brace
and Co., 1932. 356 p.

A chronicle of the life of fur-trader John Johnston (1762–1828); his Ojibwa wife, Oshaguscodawaqua; and their family. Set in the St. Mary's River area from 1791 to 1928.

Black, 167.

Mi MiHM MiMtpT-C MiSsL MiU

911 [Lewis, Julius Warren] 1833–1920
The Flying Glim; or, The Island Lure. By Leon Lewis [pseud.]. New York: Beadle and Adams, 1887. 27 p.

(Beadle's Dime Library, no. 428)

The owner of a large island has given his poor brother a cottage, but the latter is really the leader of a gang of wreckers. Set on "Mapleton Island" near the Beaver Island group in Lake Michigan.

Dime novel.

Black, 168.

NRU

Lewis, Leon, pseud. *see* Lewis, Julius Warren

912 Lewis, Ronald J.
Murder in Mackinac. Mackinaw City: Agawa Press, 1995. 238 p.

A professor sets out to find out who murdered his neighbor and becomes involved in a fifty-year-old mystery. Partially set in Mt. Pleasant, in Mackinaw City, and on Mackinac Island.

Mystery.

Mi MiAllG MiBatW MiFli MiLapC

913 Lichtman, Wendy 1946–
Telling Secrets. New York: Harper & Row, 1986. 243 p.

A freshman at the University of Michigan is dismayed and shamed to learn that her father has been imprisoned for embezzlement. Set mostly in Ann Arbor.

Juvenile.

913A Liers, Emil Ernest 1890–1975
An Otter's Story. New York: Viking Press, 1953. 191 p.

The life history of a male otter is traced from birth through many adventures and dangers as he migrates with his family, and eventually with his mate, to Wisconsin. Partially set on the Keweenaw Peninsula.

Juvenile.

914 Lindsay, Paul
Witness to the Truth: A Novel of the FBI. New York: Random House, 1992. 318 p.

A kidnapping and the exposure of informants compel agent Mike Devlin to bypass the FBI hierarchy and assemble a small group of fellow agents. Set in Detroit.

Mystery.

915 ———.
Codename: Gentkill. A Novel of the FBI. New York: Villard, 1995. 304 p.

Rogue agent Mike Devlin searches for the serial killer of FBI agents and finds a connection to a hospital that has been threatened with bombings. Set in Detroit.

Mystery.

916 Lindsey, Howard Deroy
The Four-Leaf Clover. New York: Vantage Press, 1960. 167 p.

A group of boy scouts looking for adventure and excitement explore deserted "Death Island" in Lake Michigan and find a mystery to solve.

Juvenile.

Mi MiAlle

917 **Lippincott, David** 1925–
Unholy Mourning. New York: Dell Publishing Co., 1982. 366 p.

An unbalanced medical school student is forced to give up his studies and begins a series of horrific murders. Set in "St. Max" near the Straits of Mackinac.

Mystery.

Mi MiAllG MiMani MiMtcM MiMtpT

918 **Lippincott, Mary**
Nolaw. Lansing: Matthew Publishers, 1981. 208 p.

The fictionalized autobiography of a married woman whose obsession with an army officer threatens her sanity. Partially set in Lansing in the 1960s and 1970s.

MiEM MiLC MiSsB MdBE

919 **Lipton, James**
Mirrors. New York: St. Martin's Press, 1981. 343 p.

A talented seventeen-year-old female dancer decides to leave home and continue with more advanced studies in New York. Partially set in Detroit.

920 **Litwak, Leo E.** 1924–
Waiting for the News. Garden City, N.Y.: Doubleday, 1969. 312 p.

The story of a man's personal struggles to gain union recognition for his fellow laundry workers. Set in Detroit from 1938 to 1945.

921 **Livingston, Harold** 1924–
The Detroiters. Boston: Houghton Mifflin Co., 1958. 342 p.

The members of an advertising agency hope to win the sponsorship of a top-rated TV show for their client, Coronado Motors, but encounter a conflict of personalities. Set in Detroit.

Black, 169.

Mi MiAllG MiAlp MiD MiMtpT-C

922 **Loban, Ethel Harris** 1892–
Signed in Yellow. Garden City, N.Y.: Doubleday, Doran & Co., 1930. 308 p.

(Crime Club)

Three murder victims are found marked with yellow chalk. Set in the Lake Erie resort towns of "Lakeland" (Lakewood) and "Sylvania" (Luna Pier).

Mystery.

MiAllG

923 **Lockwood, Karen**
Lady's Choice. New York: Jove Books, 1996. 279 p.

(Homespun Romance)

A young woman newly arrived from Ireland plans to open a lace factory in a mill town but runs up against the dour lumberman owner. Set in "Bunyan" in 1889.

Romance.

MiAllG MiFli MoIM OCl ScSp

924 **Lockwood, Myna**
Delecta Ann; the Circuit Rider's Daughter. New York: E. P. Dutton and Co., 1941. 335 p.

The young daughter of a Detroit minister travels with her family to Iowa and, on the journey, meets Abraham Lincoln. Partially set between Detroit and St. Joseph in 1844.

Juvenile.

Mi ICharE InFw MnManTD ViR

925 Lockwood, Walter 1941–
Jones Unbound. Englewood Cliffs, N.J.: Prentice-Hall, 1973. 242 p.

An English professor begins living it up when his wife suddenly dies. Partially set at "College of the Pines" (Calvin College) in "Eel River" (Grand Rapids).

Mi MiAllG MiBrF MiGr MiMtpT-C

926 Logan, Tom, pseud.
Detroit P.D.: The Harder They Fall. New York: Lynx Books, 1988. 241 p.

(Detroit P.D., no. 1)

Police officers of the crime-ridden 14th Precinct track a serial rapist and discover that a faceless corpse is connected with municipal corruption. Set in Detroit.

"Tom Logan" is the joint pseudonym of Robert Marshall and Victoria Thomas.

Mystery.

Mi MiAllG MiD MiGr MiWar

927 ———.
Detroit P.D.: Run, Jack, Run. New York: Lynx Books, 1988. 249 p.

(Detroit P.D., no. 2)

The 14th Precinct is the scene for vicious gangs of youths who deal in drugs, prostitution, extortion, and murder. Set in Detroit.

Mystery.

MiAllG MiD OCo

928 ———.
Detroit P.D.: Joy Street Massacre. New York: Lynx Books, 1989. 247 p.

(Detroit P.D., no. 3)

A renegade police officer from the 14th Precinct is behind the slayings of a group of drug dealers discovered in a Detroit crack house.

Mystery.

Mi MiAllG MiGr O UM

929 ———.
Detroit P.D.: Sword of Samos. New York: Lynx Books, 1989. 243 p.

(Detroit P.D., no. 4)

A secret vigilante group takes the law into its own hands and begins murdering suspected criminals within the 14th Precinct. Set in the Greektown area of Detroit.

Mystery.

Mi MiAllG MiD O

930 Love, Edmund G. 1912–1990
A Small Bequest. Garden City, N.Y.: Doubleday & Co., 1973. 238 p.

Fictional reminiscences about a trip the author took in 1934 with a friend to view some inherited Upper Peninsula land and their subsequent adventures.

931 ———.
Set-Up. Garden City, N.Y.: Doubleday & Co., 1980. 278 p.

A retired policeman investigates an unsolved armed robbery that leads to extortion and murder. Set in an unnamed Michigan city, probably Flint.

Mystery.

932 Lowrie, Rebecca
Cambric Tea. New York: Harper & Brothers, 1928. 164 p.

In the 1890s, a young Ohio girl experiences life at home and at school, including the deaths of two siblings.

Ten pages are set at Wequetonsing near Harbor Springs.

MiEM OCl OKentU OOxM OU

933 [Lowry, Margerie Bonner] 1905–
Horse in the Sky, by Margerie Bonner. New York: Charles Scribner's Sons, 1947. 189 p.

A young woman works as a maid for a wealthy family and dreams of becoming a great lady and owning a horse. Set in Adrian in 1909.

Black, 30.

Mi MiKW IC OBgU WM

934 Ludlow, Will Cumback 1885–1907
Onawago; or, The Betrayer of Pontiac. Benton Harbor: Antiquarian Publishing Co., 1911. 311 p.

An Ojibwa medicine woman who had warned the Detroit garrison of Pontiac's attack in 1763 is a mysterious presence among the settlers of Michigan. Set mostly in "Barterville" in Berrien County from 1838 to 1858.

Black, 170. Streeter, 2778.

Mi MiAllG MiD MiMtpT-C MiSsL

935 Lundy, Ruby
Sarabeth of the Snow Country. Sault Ste. Marie: Sault Printing Co., 1995. 127 p.

A girl grows up in a small Upper Peninsula farming community before becoming a school teacher. Based on the author's life and set near Sault Ste. Marie in the 1920s and 1930s.

MiAllG MiGr

936 Lutes, Della Thompson 1869?–1942

The Country Kitchen. Boston: Little, Brown and Co., 1936. 264 p.

Fictionalized reminiscences of the author's early life with her family on a Jackson County farm in the 1870s, replete with old-fashioned recipes.

937 ———.
Home Grown. Boston: Little, Brown and Co., 1937. 272 p.

Fictionalized reminiscences of the author's life on a Jackson County farm in the 1870s and her family's move to "Millbrook" (Horton) in the early 1880s.

Sequel to *The Country Kitchen.*

938 ———.
Millbrook. Boston: Little, Brown and Co., 1938. 330 p.

Life in a small village is seen through the eyes of a young girl after her family moves there from a farm. Set in "Millbrook" (Horton) in the 1880s.

Sequel to *Home Grown.*

Black, 172.

Mi MiAllG MiD MiKW MiMtpT-C

939 ———.
Gabriel's Search. Boston: Little, Brown and Co., 1940. 351 p.

The story of a bitter young man who comes to live in Jackson County in 1833 and, through the help of his new neighbors, finds personal peace.

Black, 171.

Mi MiAllG MiMtpT-C MiPh MiYEM

940 ———.
Country Schoolma'am. Boston: Little, Brown and Co., 1941. 328 p.

The author fictionalizes her experiences as a sixteen-year-old teacher in a one-room country schoolhouse. Set in "Millbrook" (Horton), Jackson, and Jackson County in the late 1880s.

Sequel to *Millbrook.*

941 ———.
Cousin William. Boston: Little, Brown and Co, 1942. 308 p.

The author's fictionalized reminiscences concerning a ne'er-do-well cousin who comes to work on the family farm. Set in Jackson County and "Millbrook" (Horton) in the 1870s.

Mi MiAllG MiD MiJac MiMtpT-C

942 Luton, Harry Heathcote 1920–
The Log-Jam. Jackson, Mich.: Copper Orchid Publishing Co., 1994. 216 p.

The story of a special fishing spot on the "Elk River" and the effect it has on a number of people from the 1860s to the 1960s.

Mi MiJac

943 Lytle, Robert A.
Mackinac Passage: A Summer Adventure. Lansing: Thunder Bay Press, 1995. 178 p.

Pete, a teenage boy, and his friends solve a mystery involving counterfeiters and murder. Set on the Les Chenueaux Islands and on Mackinac Island in 1952.

Juvenile.

MiAllG MiMtcM MiMtpT-C MiMu MiT

944 ———.
Mackinac Passage: The Boathouse Mystery. Holt, Mich.: Thunder Bay Press, 1996. 176 p.

Pete and his three friends investigate a series of boathouse robberies and are stalked by an escaped murderer. Set on the Les Cheneaux Islands in 1952.

Sequel to *Mackinac Passage: A Summer Adventure.*

Juvenile.

MiAllG MiBlo MiGr MiMtcM MiMtpT-C

M

945 McAllister, Anne
To Tame a Wolf. London: Mills & Boon, 1987. 189 p.

A biologist and a photographer who don't see eye to eye need to cooperate on an endangered wolf project. Set at "White Birch Bay" in the Upper Peninsula.

Romance.

IArlh MW MoK USl

946 Macauley, Robie Mayhew 1919–1995
The Disguises of Love. New York: Random House, 1952. 282 p.

A psychology professor is seduced by one of his students, and his life is changed forever. Set at "Creston University" in southwestern Michigan from 1947 to 1948.

MiAllG MiEM InLP OU WU

947 McCallum, Dennis
The Summons. Colorado Springs, Colo.: NavPress Publishing Group, 1993. 351 p.

A student questions her values and finds solace with a Christian group, but they are threatened by forces of evil. Set at Michigan State University in East Lansing.

Mi InBlo MoIM OU ScCoR

948 McCallum, Mella Russell

Tents of Wickedness. New York: Century Co., 1928. 329 p.

A young farmer falls in love with a circus performer and ardently pursues her until they marry. Set in "Pressville" in Cass County in the 1870s.

Black, 174.

Mi MsCleD OrU RP TxSa

949 McCarthy, Justin 1830–1912

Dear Lady Disdain. London: Grant & Co., 1875. 3 vols.

A young lower-class Englishman proposes marriage to a woman who is above his station. Twenty-seven pages are set in "New Padua" (Ann Arbor) and at the University of Michigan.

GEU OrCS

950 McClinchey, Florence E. 1888–1946

Joe Pete. New York: Henry Holt and Co., 1929. 311 p.

An Ojibwa boy helps his mother, who was abandoned by her husband, care for his siblings and eventually advances himself through education. Set on Sugar Island in the St. Mary's River.

Black, 181.

Mi MiAllG MiD MiMarqN MiU

951 McClure, Marjorie Barkley 1882–1967

High Fires. Boston: Little, Brown and Co., 1924. 358 p.

A man and a woman from different economic and religious backgrounds fall in love and marry. Set in Detroit from 1905 to 1920.

Black, 182.

MiD MiEM MiStc IC OBgU

952 ———.

John Dean's Journey. New York: Minton, Balch & Co., 1932. 323 p.

A young man born in poverty in the Carolinas eventually finds success and happiness as an author. Partially set in Detroit in the late 1890s.

Black, 183.

Mi MiU MnM OCl OU

953 McCollom, Russell L.

A Pair of Ragged Claws by Wolf and Russell L. McCollom III. Philadelphia: Dorrance and Co, 1977. 105 p.

A peculiar story of a young man who, at the behest of a mystery woman and other characters, travels across the country in search of "Reality." Partially set in Detroit and Mt. Clemens.

Mi MiAllG

954 McCormick, Jay 1919–

November Storm. Garden City, N.Y.: Doubleday, Doran and Co., 1943. 339 p.

A young man finds a job aboard a Great Lakes freighter and works with a variety of sailors. Partially set in Detroit and Alpena in the late 1930s.

Black, 184.

Mi MiAllG MiHM MiMtpT-C MiPh

McCoy, Iola Fuller *see* Fuller, Iola

Macdonald, John Ross, pseud. *see* Millar, Kenneth

Macdonald, Ross, pseud. *see* Millar, Kenneth

955 Macfarlane, Peter Clark 1871–1924

Man's Country; the Story of a Great Love, of Which Business Was Jealous.

New York: Cosmopolitan Book Corp., 1923. 343 p.

A man loses his wife's affection because of his focus on his automobile company and then attempts to win back her love. Set in Detroit in the early 1900s.

Black, 175.

Mi MiD IC OBgU WM

956 McGaughey, William Howard Taft 1912–

Roll Out the Tanks. Philadelphia: Macrae-Smith Co., 1942. 272 p.

Whitcomb Motor Works gears up its factory and workforce to make tanks for the war effort and must contend with a gang of saboteurs. Set in Detroit.

Juvenile.

MiAlbC MiD MiFliL InGrD OCl

957 McGuane, Thomas 1939–

The Sporting Club. New York: Simon and Schuster, 1968. 220 p.

Two young members of a northern Michigan fishing and hunting club continue a rivalry with tragic results. Set in the Pere Marquette and Manistee Rivers area.

Mi MiAllG MiBrF MiSaS OBgU

958 ———.

The Bushwhacked Piano. New York: Simon and Schuster, 1971. 220 p.

A young man undertakes a motorcycle tour of America and, in his travels, comments on the absurd nature of 1970s culture. Forty pages are set along the Detroit River.

959 McGuire, Frances

Indian Drums Beat Again. New York: E. P. Dutton & Co., 1953. 123 p.

A twelve-year-old boy spends the summer on Mackinac Island and, with his close Ojibwa friend, assists in the apprehension of two career criminals.

Juvenile.

Mi MiAllG MiGr MiMtpT-C MiWar

960 MacHarg, William Briggs 1872–1951

The Indian Drum by William MacHarg and Edwin Balmer. Boston: Little, Brown and Co., 1917. 367 p.

A shipping company owner's disappearance seems to be connected with the sinking of a Great Lakes freighter in 1895. Partially set in the Harbor Springs and Petoskey area.

For a more recent telling of this tale, see Donald Johnston's *The Echoes of L'Arbre Croche* (1996).

Black, 176.

MiAlbC MiAllG MiD MiDW MiStc

961 McKenzie, Noris

Help Me Keep My Dreams; a Story of Love, Self-Sacrifice and Duty to God and Country. Belleville, Ill.: Buechler Publishing Co., 1945. 76 p.

A young nurse loses the man she loves to the priesthood but finds happiness with a doctor. Set in "Edgebrook" in southern Michigan and Detroit between 1937 and 1945.

Mi

962 McLaughlin, David

Lightning Before Dawn. Indianapolis: Bobbs-Merrill Co., 1938. 312 p.

The semidelinquent daughter of the town drunk marries a local middle-aged farmer and begins a new life in the country. Set in the Sturgis area.

Black, 185.

Mi MiEM MiFli MiKW MiPh

963 McMillan, Rosalyn
Knowing. New York: Warner Books, 1996. 405 p.

An African-American woman aspires, against her husband's wishes, to work in real estate rather than at the dull auto factory where she currently has a job. Set in Detroit.

964 McMillan, Terry 1951–
Mama. Boston: Houghton Mifflin Co., 1987. 260 p.

An African-American woman leaves her abusive husband and raises her five children on her own. Mostly set in "Point Haven" (Port Huron) in the 1960s and 1970s.

965 McNaught, Judith 1944–
Double Standards. Toronto: Harlequin Books, 1984. 220 p.

(Harlequin Temptation, no. 16)

A business executive and his attractive administrative assistant become romantically involved. Set in Detroit and Harbor Springs.

Romance.

MiFliL IArlh InG MW OBgU

966 McNeil, Everett 1862–1929
Daniel Du Luth; or, Adventuring on the Great Lakes. Being the Tale Told by Young Paul Douay of the Long Journey He Made in Indian Canoes in the Company of Daniel Greysolon Du Luth from Montreal through the Great Lakes to Lake Superior, in Quest of His Sister Stolen by the Indians When a Babe, Together with an Account of the Perilous and Thrilling Adventures that Befell Them and How the Long Quest Ended on the Island of Wanawatanda at the House of the White Medicine Girl of the Issati. As Set Down in English by Everett McNeil. New York: E. P. Dutton & Co., 1926. 389 p.

Besides the plot outlined in the subtitle, the story concerns the exploration of New France in 1678 and 1679. Partially set on the western shore of Lake Huron and at Michilimackinac.

Mi MiDW MiFli MiMtpT-C OBgU

967 McPherson, William 1939–
Testing the Current. New York: Simon and Schuster, 1984. 348 p.

The small intricate details of daily family life are seen through the eyes of an eight-year-old boy. Set in "Grande Riviere" (Sault Ste. Marie) in 1938 and 1939.

MacVeigh, Sue, pseud. *see* Nearing, Elizabeth Custer

968 Magoon, Carey, pseud.
I Smell the Devil. New York: Farrar & Rinehart, 1943. 247 p.

Two middle-aged women help a State Police investigator sift through a variety of suspects in the murder of a librarian at "Cowabet College" (University of Michigan).

"Carey Magoon" is the joint pseudonym of Elisabeth Carey and Marian Austin Waite Magoon.

Mystery.

Mi MiKW MiYEM ICU OCl

Magoon, Marian Austin Waite *see* Magoon, Carey, pseud.

Suprest Information

The Adventures of an Intellectual Hobo on the Road to Damascus

By T. A. MAJOR

K. A. HALEY

311 Sycamore Street   MANISTEE, MICH.

969 Major, Thomas Ambrose 1875–1943
Suprest Information; the Adventures of an Intellectual Hobo on the Road to Damascus by T. A. Major. Manistee: K. A. Haley, n.d. 357 p.

A humorous fictional account of student life, attitudes, and pranks at the University of Michigan and Ann Arbor in the early 1900s.

Title on cover: *Suprest in Formation.*

Mi MiAllG MiD MiMtpT-C OU

970 Malcolm-Smith, George 1901–
The Trouble with Fidelity. Garden City, N.Y.: Doubleday & Co., 1957. 191 p.

(Crime Club)

The suspicion of embezzlement in a company sends an insurance investigator travelling throughout the country. Thirteen pages are set in Detroit.

Mystery.

MiMtp MiPh InFw OCl WU

971 Maltz, Albert 1908–1985
The Underground Stream; an Historical Novel of a Moment in the American Winter. Boston: Little, Brown and Co., 1940. 348 p.

A story of the union movement in the automobile industry that mainly centers on a right-wing manager and a Communist organizer. Set in Detroit in 1936.

Black, 177.

MiAlbC MiEM MiU InU OBgU

972 [Malzberg, Barry Nathaniel] 1939–

Detroit Massacre by Mike Barry [pseud.]. New York: Berkley Publishing Corporation, 1975. 186 p.

(The Lone Wolf, no. 11)

A renegade New York cop avenging his fiancée's murder, singlehandedly battles international drug traffickers in Detroit.

Halftitle: *The Lone Wolf in Detroit: Detroit Massacre.*

Mystery.

973 Mandell, Mark
Nazi Hunter: Hell Nest. New York: Pinnacle Books, 1983. 202 p.

(Nazi Hunter, no. 5)

In his quest to bring his father to justice, the son of a war criminal finds a Rumanian Nazi masquerading as a priest in the Upper Peninsula town of "Harberstam."

Mystery.

MiGr-L OBgU

974 Mañees, Raynetta
All for Love. New York: Pinnacle Books, 1996. 283 p.

(Arabesque Romance)

An African-American woman in Atlanta on business literally runs into a famous singer, and a whirlwind romance ensues. Partially set in Lansing.

Romance.

MiAllG MiFli IChamL OXe WM

975 [Manfred, Frederick Feikema] 1912–1994
The Primitive by Feike Feikema. Garden City, N.Y.: Doubleday & Co., 1949. 460 p.

(World's Wanderer Trilogy, book 1)

A tall and awkward Iowa farm boy comes to Michigan to attend "Christian College" (Calvin College) in "Zion" (Grand Rapids) from 1930 to 1934.

A revised version was published as part of the author's trilogy *Wanderlust* (Denver: Alan Swallow) in 1962.

MiAlbC MiAllG MiGrC MiMtpT-C MiU

976 Manz, Elizabeth
Scare Tactics. New York: St. Martin's Paperbacks, 1996. 329 p.

Five years after his wife's unsolved murder, an author and his son are getting their lives back to normal when murder strikes again. Set in an unnamed Michigan town.

Mystery.

MiAllG MiBatK MiD IC OCl

977 ———.
Wasted Space. New York: St. Martin's Paperbacks, 1996. 326 p.

Instead of delivering toxic waste to the moon, a toxic-disposal firm either buries it on earth or rockets it into deep space with aliens objecting to the latter. Set in "Hartwick" in the future.

Science fiction.

MiAllG OCl ScSp WLac

March, Walter, pseud. *see* Willcox, Orlando Bolivar

978 Marlett, Melba Balmat Grimes
1909–
Death Has a Thousand Doors. Garden City, N.Y.: Doubleday, Doran and Co., 1941. 271 p.

(Crime Club)

Murder occurs at a large high school, and a member of the administrative staff assists the police detective assigned to the case. Set in Detroit.

Mystery.

Mi MiAllG CLO OOxM ViR

979 ———.
Another Day Toward Dying. Garden City, N.Y.: Doubleday, Doran and Co., 1943. 271 p.

(Crime Club)

The pregnant wife of a police detective is certain that the death of an old woman is murder and is determined to prove it. Set in Detroit.

Sequel to *Death Has a Thousand Doors.*

Mystery.

Mi CSbC MBAt MnU ViR

980 ———.
Escape While I Can. Garden City, N.Y.: Doubleday, Doran and Co., 1944. 192 p.

(Crime Club)

A young woman marries into a strange family and eventually flees for her life when her in-laws' animosity leads to murder. Set on an estate north of Harbor Springs in 1933 and 1941.

Mystery.

MiAllG MiChv MiU MnU OCl

Marshall, Robert *see* Logan, Tom, pseud.

981 Martin, C. L. G.
Day of Darkness, Night of Light (It Really Happened!). Minneapolis: Dillon Press, 1989. 46 p.

A boy helps his fellow townspeople fight to save their town from fire and, at the same time, witnesses his enemy get his comeuppance. Set in Menominee in 1871.

Juvenile.

982 Martin, Charles H.
The PK Factor by C. H. Martin. Neshkoro, Wis.: Unicorn-Star Press, 1984. 213 p.

(Psychic Mystery, no. 1)

When a college student kills another student by psychokinesis, a professor tries to solve the case. Set at Central Michigan University in Mount Pleasant.

Mystery.

MiAllG MiMtpT-C MiWalv IChamL WU

982A Martin, Emer 1968–
Breakfast in Babylon. Dublin: Wolfhound Press, 1995. 288 p.

A young Irish vagabond meets an American drug addict from Michigan in Paris, and they team up to panhandle and run various scams across Europe before ending up in New York City. Twenty pages are set in Detroit.

MiGr-L IC InNd MB OU

983 Martin, Robert Lee 1908–1976
The Echoing Shore. New York: Dodd, Mead & Co., 1955. 216 p.

(Red Badge Detective)

A man's attempt to solve a mystery brings him in close and unpleasant contact with villains and murder at Big Bear Lake in Otsego County.

Also published as *The Tough Die Hard* (New York: Bantam Books, 1957).

Mystery.

IaCfT InFw OCl ViR WRac

984 Mason, Miriam Evangeline 1900–1973
Caroline and Her Kettle Named Maud. New York: Macmillan Co., 1951. 134 p.

An eight-year-old girl moves to Michigan from New York with her family and receives a kettle instead of the gun she would rather have. Set in "Pigeon Roost" in the 1830s.

Juvenile.

985 ———.
Caroline and the Seven Little Words. New York: Macmillan Co., 1967. 184 p.

"I am going to be a doctor" are the seven words that bring Caroline ridicule from her family, which in turn serve only to increase her resolve. Set in "Pigeon County" in the 1830s.

Sequel to *Caroline and Her Kettle Named Maud.*

Juvenile.

986 Matschat, Cecile Hulse 1895?–1976
Preacher on Horseback. New York: Farrar and Rinehart, 1940. 429 p.

A circuit rider from New York who would rather have been a doctor ultimately gains religious faith. Partially set in Muskegon and the Upper Peninsula in the 1860s.

Black, 179.

Mi MiAllG MiMtp MiWar OBgU

Matsell, A. J. *see Scenes on Lake Huron*

987 Matson, Norman Häghejm 1893–1965
Day of Fortune. London: Ernest Benn, 1927. 286 p.

The chronicle of a Norwegian-American family and its individual members. Partially set in Grand Rapids.

Black, 180.

DLC

988 Mayhew, George A.
Murder at Daybreak. New York: Vantage Press, 1975. 230 p.

A sheriff searches for an alleged psychopathic killer when a number of murdered deer hunters are found. Set around "Danville" in the Houghton Lake area.

Mystery.

Mi MiFli MiGr MiRoch MiYEM

989 Mazoué, Jo Ann
Queen of the Island. Davisburg, Mich.: Wilderness Adventure Books, 1993. 231 p.

The fictionalized story of the Mormon Kingdom of James Strang (1813–1856) on Beaver Island in 1850 as seen through the eyes of his first wife, Mary.

Subtitle on cover: *The Birth of a Kingdom: Beaver Island, Michigan, 1850.*

Mi MiAllG MiD MiKW MiMtpT-C

990 Mead, Shepherd 1914–
How To Succeed at Business Spying by Trying; a Novel About Industrial Espionage. New York: Simon and Schuster, 1968. 255 p.

A humorous story concerning an industrial spy hired to find out about a chemist and cheap fuel for automobiles. Partially set in "Bass Lake," north of Holland on Lake Michigan.

Mystery.

MiAllG MiCad MiD MiEM MiLapC

990A Meadows, Lee E.
Silent Conspiracy. Ann Arbor: Proctor Publications, 1996. 273 p.

An African-American private detective is hired to investigate the strange 1955 disappearance of a popular five-man singing group. Set in Detroit.

Mystery.

MiBatW MiBlo MiKW MiMtcM MiT

991 Mears, James R.
The Iron Boys on the Ore Boats; or, Roughing It on the Great Lakes. Philadelphia: Henry Altemus Co., 1913. 255 p.

(Iron Boys Series, no. 3)

Two boys find jobs aboard a Great Lakes freighter and have a variety of adventures. Partially set in Michigan waters, in Detroit, and in Alpena.

Frank Gee Patchin (1861–1925) has been suggested as the author.

Juvenile.

CLS FTS OBgU

992 Meehan, Christopher H. 1949–
Deadly Waters. Grand Rapids: William B. Eerdmans Publishing Co., 1995. 238 p.

The president of "Redeemer Seminary" (Calvin College) asks a young Christian Reformed minister to investigate the disappearance of a teacher. Set mostly in Grand Rapids.

Mystery.

Mi MiAllG MiGrC MiLac MiMtpT-C

Meeker, Richard, pseud. *see* Brown, Forman George

993 Meier, S. B.
Mackinac Rhapsody. New York: Arete Books, 1987. 535 p.

Four women from different social backgrounds stay at the Grand Hotel on Mackinac Island in 1893 and share their life stories and personal secrets.

Mi MiAllG MiMack MiMtpT-C MiPh

994 Merlis, George 1940–
V.P. New York: William Morrow & Co., 1971. 246 p.

The vice president of the United States challenges the incumbent president for their party's nomination. Partially set in Detroit at the national convention.

Mi MiAdS MiAllG MiBatW MiMtpT-C

995 Merrill, James Milford 1847–1936
Cloudwood; or, The Daughter of the Wilderness. New York: Frank Starr & Co., 1871. 97 p.

(Frank Starr's American Novels, no. 66)

A young white woman poses as a Native American and has some exciting adventures. Set in "Wilton" on the Muskegon River in the 1840s.

Also published as *The Girl Chief; or, Dolly's Droll Disguise* (New York: Beadle and Adams, 1888 [Beadle's Boy's Library, no. 246; octavo edition]).

Dime novel.

Black, 186.

Mi

996 [———].
The Young Bear Hunters. The Haps and Mishaps of a Party of Boys in the Wilds of Northern Michigan. By Morris Redwing [pseud.]. New York: Beadle and Adams, 1882. 14 p.

(Beadle's Boy's Library, no. 34)

Three boys and a veteran hunter go on an expedition into the woods to hunt bear and deer to their hearts' content. Set in the Grand Traverse area in 1879.

Dime novel.

Copy not located.

997 [———].
Forced Apart; or, Exiled by Fate by Morris Redwing [pseud.]. Chicago: Laird & Lee Publishers, 1886. 166 p.

Jealous of his ward's marriage to a wealthy lumberman, a villain plots to discredit the man. Partially set on "Gull Lake" in western Michigan.

Wright III, 3705.

CtY FOFT FTS

998 ———.
His Mother's Letter; or, The Boy Waif's Search by J. M. Merrill. Akron: Saalfield Publishing Co., 1902. 303 p.

A young boy whose mother has died searches for his estranged father and discovers that he is a wealthy lumberman. Set in "Cliffburg" in western Michigan.

Juvenile.

OKentU

999 ———.
An American Sovereign. Boston: C. M. Clark Publishing Co., 1909. 307 p.

A fictionalized exposé of the insidious danger that threatens America from labor unions. Set in "Grandburg" (Grand Rapids) and "Lake City" (Muskegon?).

MWC MeU OU

1000 Merwin, Samuel 1874–1936
His Little World; the Story of Hunch Bardeau. New York: A. S. Barnes & Co., 1903. 201 p.

A toughened captain of a Lake Michigan lumber schooner falls in love, an emotion that is new to him. Set in "Liddington" (Ludington) and Manistee.

Mi MiAllG CL MBAt OCl

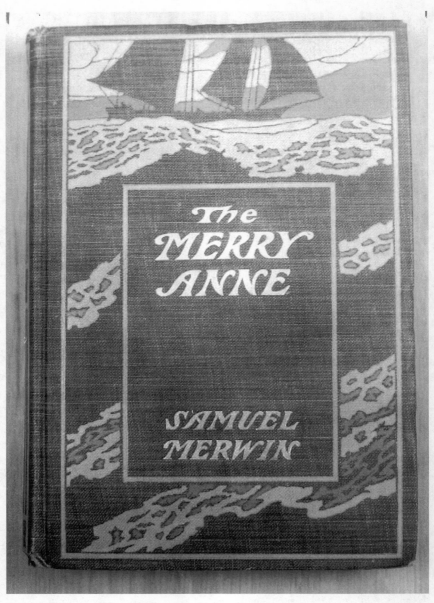

1001 ———.

The Whip Hand; a Tale of the Pine Country. New York: Doubleday, Page & Co., 1903. 299 p.

A lumberman with a struggling business battles a powerful Chicago lumbering conglomerate. Partially set in "Wauchung" on Lake Michigan in the 1890s.

Mi MiAllG MiFli MiMtpT-C MiU

1002 ———.

The Merry Anne. New York: Macmillan Co., 1904. 417 p.

The captain and crew of a lumber schooner become entangled with a whiskey smuggling ring from Chicago. Partially set in various Michigan lake ports.

Black, 187.

Mi MiAllG IC OBgU ViR

1003 **Meserve, Arthur Livermore** 1838–1896

Trapper Joe; or, The Outlaw of Lake Huron. A Story of the Northern Lake. New York: G. Munro, 1869. 100 p.

(Munro's Ten Cent Novels, no. 160)

A trapper and his young companion effect the rescue of a woman kidnapped by a gang of cutthroats. Set in the Michigan waters of Lake Huron, possibly in Saginaw Bay.

Dime novel.

Copy not located.

1004 **Messner-Loebs, William**

Tall Tales. Agoura, Calif.: Fantagraphics Books, 1987. 94 p.

(Journey Saga, book 1)

The rugged and humorous adventures of woodsman and scout Joshua

"Wolverine" MacAllistaire. Set in the Michigan Territory from 1810 to 1812.

Graphic novel.

MiAllG MiEM MiSc KKC OBgU

1005 ———.

Bad Weather. Seattle: Fantagraphics Books, 1990. 98 p.

(Journey Saga, book 2)

The further humorous adventures of woodsman and scout Joshua "Wolverine" MacAllistaire. Set in the Michigan Territory from 1810 to 1812.

Sequel to *Tall Tales.*

Graphic novel.

MiAllG MiEM MiSc KKC OCl

Mezvinsky, Shirley, pseud. *see* Lauro, Shirley Shapiro Mezvinsky

1006 **Michigan Department of Conservation**

Three Boys Go Camping. A Story of the Out-of-Doors. Prepared by the Department of Conservation in Cooperation with the Department of Public Instruction. Lansing: Franklin DeKleine Co., 1934. 57 p.

Three teenagers camp at Higgins Lake where they learn about Michigan's natural resources and conservation, and travel to other areas in northern Michigan.

Juvenile.

Mi MiAllG MiMtpT-C MH NcD

1007 **Millar, Jeff** 1942–

Private Sector. New York: Dial Press, 1979. 280 p.

During an energy crisis, two investigative reporters research a story that unveils a conspiracy among large corporations. Partially set in Detroit and Ontonagon.

Mystery.

1008 Millar, Kenneth 1915–1983
The Dark Tunnel. New York: Dodd, Mead & Co., 1944. 241 p.

(Red Badge Mystery)

An English professor becomes involved with the search for a Nazi spy ring on the campus of "Midwestern University" (University of Michigan) in "Arbana" (Ann Arbor).

Also published as *I Die Slowly* (New York: Lion Books, 1955).

Mystery.

Mi MiAllG MBAt OU WSpU

1009 ——.
Trouble Follows Me. New York: Dodd, Mead & Co., 1946. 206 p.

(Red Badge Mystery)

While searching for an A.W.O.L. sailor, a naval officer stumbles across a murder that involves Japanese spies. Partially set in Detroit.

Also published as *Night Train* (New York: Lion Books, 1955).

Mystery.

Mi MiGr MiStjo MiU OOxM

1010 Millar, Margaret Sturm 1915–1994
Vanish in an Instant. New York: Random House, 1952. 245 p.

A wealthy young woman is accused of murdering her lover, but a man without an apparent motive confesses to the crime instead. Set in "Arbana" (Ann Arbor).

Mystery.

MiAllG IC OBgU OOxM WU

1011 Millen, DeWitt Clinton 1880–1969
The College Cut-Up; or, Letters from Jack to Dad. Ann Arbor: Edwards Brothers Printers, 1927. 98 p.

An epistolary novel set from 1915 to 1917 in which a student at "Collegetown" (Ann Arbor) writes to his father about his freshman and sophomore years.

MiU DLC

1012 Miller, David C.
Blood Link [by] David C. Miller and John H. Way, M.D. New York: Charter Books, 1986. 233 p.

A Detroit physician investigates an outbreak of a lethal viral epidemic and searches for its source and a cure. Set in "Berne" (Gaylord).

CU-Riv InBer O OBgU ScSp

1013 Miller, Helen Topping 1884–1960
Born Strangers; a Chronicle of Two Families. Indianapolis: Bobbs-Merrill Co., 1949. 288 p.

The pioneer experiences of two Michigan families as based on stories told by the author's relatives. Set in Argentine from the 1820s to the 1840s.

Black, 188.

Mi MiD MiEM MiGr MiStc

Miller, Isabel *see* Routsong, Alma

1014 Miller, Nolan 1912–
A Moth of Time. New York: Harper & Brothers, 1946. 369 p.

A woman and her family must cope with financial and social problems when her husband abandons them. Set in Detroit from 1900 to 1917.

Black, 189.

Mi MiAlbC MiD MiPh MiU

1015 ———.

The Merry Innocents. New York: Harper & Brothers, 1947. 239 p.

An English professor deals with a variety of humorous and serious domestic crises in the five days preceding Christmas. Set in "Holtby" on Lake Michigan in 1945.

Mi MiDW MiStc IC OCl

1016 Milligan, Clarence P. 1889–
The Wonderland of John Devlin. Boston: Christopher Publishing House, 1945. 260 p.

The story of an ex-railroad man and his family in Ontario from the 1880s to the 1920s and their involvement in rum running. Fifteen pages are set in Detroit.

Mi CU-Riv LU OU

Mizner, Elizabeth Howard *see* Howard, Elizabeth

1017 Möllhausen, Balduin 1825–1905
Der Hochlandpfeifer. Jena: Costenoble, 1868. 1229 p.

Stemming from a clue on a torn envelope, the search for a relative involves misunderstandings and murder. Partially set on Mackinac Island and in the Straits area.

In German.

PPG

1018 ———.

Welche von Beiden? Stuttgart: Union Deutsche Verlagsgesellschaft, 1897. 2 vols. in 1.

The search for a missing daughter and heiress begins in Kentucky. Partially set in various northern Michigan locales in the mid-1800s.

In German.

MoSW NcD

1019 Monsigny, Jacqueline
Un Mariage à la Carte. Paris: Editions J.-C. Lattès, 1980, 230 p.

A man travelling via motorcycle stops at a small Michigan town (Oil City?) between Mount Pleasant and Midland where he meets a young woman who asks him to marry her.

In French.

MiU DLC IU NN

1020 Moore, Charles W.
A Brick for Mr. Jones. Detroit: Project B.A.I.T., 1975. 214 p.

The gritty story of the rise and fall of an African-American drug dealer and the role the police play in his ultimate arrest. Set in Detroit.

Mystery.

Mi NN

1021 Moore, John Eugene 1913–
Indian Paul. New York: Harcourt, Brace and Co., 1945. 159 p.

When a local Native American murders his mother, the nearby resort community is outraged, and more tragedy follows. Set in Mackinaw City.

Black, 190.

Mi MiAllG MiKW MiMtpT-C MiU

1022 Morris, Bill 1952–
Motor City. New York: Alfred A. Knopf, 1992. 337 p.

At General Motors, the Buick automobile team embarks on an ambitious advertising campaign to make their new model more popular. Set in Detroit in 1954.

1023 Morris, David D.
Red Man Red Tape Red Star in Michigan. Ann Arbor: Edwards Brothers, 1980. 198 p.

The story of the fictional Smith-Sanchez family in which the history of Michigan serves as a background. Set in "Athos" (Mason?) in south-central Michigan from 1835 to 1990.

Mi MiAlbC MiJac MiMo MiOw

1024 Morris, Hilda 1887–1947
The Long View. New York: G. P. Putnam's Sons, 1937. 366 p.

The simple life of a Quaker is contrasted with the rise of American industry from the 1860s to the 1930s. Partially set in "Dune Harbor" in southwestern Michigan and in Ann Arbor.

Black, 192.

MiD MiDW MiEM MiU OU

1025 ———.
Landmarks. New York: G. P. Putnam's Sons, 1941. 294 p.

A young artist born in Europe paints murals for a town library as he learns about American heritage. Set in "Arrowhead" on Lake Michigan.

Black, 191.

MiAllG InLP OCl OU WM

1026 Morrison, Dennis Michael
Auntie Miranda. Greenbush, Mich.: Treasure Cove Publications, n.d. 20 p.

A wealthy lumberman's embittered spinster sister causes family discord while under the influence of an evil preacher. Set in northeastern Michigan in 1881.

MiGr-L

1027 Morrison, Mary
Over the Threshold to Manhood. Elgin, Ill.: David C. Cook Publishing Co., 1911. 64 p.

Two teenage boys who live with their grandparents help them pay off the mortgage on their farm. Set in Roscommon County and Bay City.

Juvenile.

MiMtpT-C

1028 Morrison, Toni 1931–
Song of Solomon. New York: Alfred A. Knopf, 1977. 337 p.

The story of a middle-class African American from his upbringing in a subdued family to his search for himself. Partially set in an unnamed Upper Peninsula city.

1029 Muhanji, Cherry 1939–
Her. San Francisco: Aunt Lute Foundation, 1990. 179 p.

The story of a group of African-American women and their interactions and relationships with each other. Set in Detroit in the 1950s and 1960s.

1030 Mulder, Arnold 1885–1959
The Dominie of Harlem. Chicago: A. C. McClurg & Co., 1913. 385 p.

A minister of the Christian Reformed Church comes to a rural community although he really wanted to work among the poor of a large city. Set in "Harlem" in western Michigan.

Black, 194.

Mi MiAllG MiGr MiGrC MiHolH

1031 ———.
Bram of the Five Corners. Chicago: A. C. McClurg & Co., 1915. 366 p.

A young man studying for the ministry breaks his long-standing engagement with a girl and is consequently disgraced and excommunicated. Set in "Five Corners" in western Michigan.

Black, 193.

Mi MiAllG MiGr MiHolH MiMtpT-C

1032 ———.
The Outbound Road. Boston: Houghton Mifflin Co., 1919. 302 p.

Adopted by a Dutch family as a child, a young man ultimately frees himself from his narrow and strict religious upbringing. Set in "East Nassau" in western Michigan.

Black, 195.

Mi MiAllG MiGr MiHolH MiMtpT-C

1033 ———.
The Sand Doctor. Boston: Houghton Mifflin Co., 1921. 317 p.

A doctor who is unsuccessful in the business aspects of his job begins to lose his wife to another man. Set in "Sisson" on Lake Michigan.

Black, 196.

Mi MiAllG MiGr MiHolH MiMtpT-C

1034 Mullen, Joseph B.
Room 103; a Novel About Detroit's Welfare Department. Philadelphia: Dorrance, 1963. 171 p.

The stories of the various people who come to the Detroit Public Welfare Department and the reception afforded them by caseworkers.

Mi MiAlbC MiD MiDU MiRochOU

1035 Muller, Charles George Geoffrey 1897–
Puck Chasers, Incorporated. New York: Harper & Brothers, 1927. 246 p.

A group of boys form an ice hockey team and have a number of games on a small lake and a few adventures. Set at the "Fiske School for Boys" in Grand Rapids.

Juvenile.

Mi

1036 ———.
The Baseball Detective. New York: Harper & Brothers, 1928. 333 p.

A group of boys form a baseball team and during their season solve a mystery. Set at the "Fiske School for Boys" in Grand Rapids.

Sequel to *Puck Chasers, Incorporated.*

Juvenile.

Mi MiD CMerC InFw OCl

1037 Munroe, Kirk 1850–1930
At War with Pontiac: or, The Totem of the Bear; a Tale of Redcoat and Redskin. New York: Charles Scribner's Sons, 1895. 320 p.

The twelve-year-old son of a retired British major is involved in a series of adventures during Pontiac's Conspiracy in 1763. Partially set in Detroit.

Juvenile.

Streeter, 5507.

MiAlbC MiAllG MiD MiEM MiMtpT-C

1038 ———.
The Copper Princess; a Story of Lake Superior Mines. New York: Harper & Brothers, 1898. 237 p.

An Oxford graduate saves the life of the son of the mine foreman, is given a job, and discovers an immense vein of copper. Set on the Keweenaw Peninsula and in Red Jacket.

Streeter, 5506.

Mi MiAllG MiDW OClW ViU

1039 Murphy, Warren B. 1933–
The Destroyer: Blood Ties by Warren
Murphy & Richard Sapir. New York:
New American Library, 1987. 252 p.

(The Destroyer, no. 69)

An eccentric automobile tycoon and
inventor who has designed a revolutionary vehicle that will run on garbage
is the target of an assassination plot. Set
in Detroit.

Mystery.

MiGr-L IChamL IGenD InFw MoK

1040 Murray, Lloyd William 1911–
Tender Twigs. Six Lakes, Mich.: Pine
Crest Publishing, 1979. 167 p.

A fictionalized chronicle covering four
generations of one family. Set in various places in Michigan from the early
1800s to 1915.

MiAllG

1041 ———.
The Adventures of Andy Ayres. Six
Lakes, Mich.: Pine Crest Publishing,
1982. 154 p.

The story of a young boy's travels
and adventures around and through
northeastern Michigan in the 1930s.

MiBeld

1042 Muse, Helen E.
*Green Pavilions; a Novel of the French
and Indian War*. New York: Carlton
Press, 1961. 256 p.

A Virginian settles in French Detroit in
1725 and witnesses the town's growth,
its transfer to the British, and finally
Pontiac's siege in 1763.

MiD DGC GSA ISL MsHaU

N

1043 Nack, Jon
Once Upon a Time Around Detroit.
Detroit: Story-Lit Press, 1975. 150 p.

A high school principal, with her father's assistance and approval, breaks
her engagement to a lawyer for a landscape architect. Set in Detroit.

Mi

1044 Naha, Ed 1950–
RoboCop. New York: Dell Publishing
Co., 1987. 189 p.

A fatally injured police officer is transformed into a cyborg and programmed
to uphold the law. Set in a crime-ridden
Detroit of the near future.

Based on the motion picture screenplay by Edward Neumeier and Michael
Miner.

Science fiction.

MiBatW MiLud InFw O OCl

1045 ———.
RoboCop 2. New York: Jove Books,
1990. 234 p.

A policeman who was transformed into
a cyborg battles a drug ring pushing
enhanced cocaine and another cyborg
run amok. Set in a Detroit of the near
future.

Based on the motion picture screenplay
by Frank Miller and Walon Green.

Science fiction.

MiD MiFli MiGr MiStjo OCl

1046 Naylor, Gloria 1950–
Linden Hills. New York: Ticknor &
Fields, 1985.

Members of a middle-class African-
American community are examined

and shown to abandon their racial and cultural identities. Set in the Detroit suburb of "Linden Hills."

1047 [Nearing, Elizabeth Custer] 1898–
The Corpse and the Three Ex-Husbands by Sue MacVeigh [pseud.]. Boston: Houghton Mifflin Co., 1941. 229 p.

An heir to worthless cut-over land is involved in a murder at a family mansion. Set in the dying lumbertown "Moneskaw" between Cadillac and Saginaw.

Mystery.

MiGr-L MB NcGU OU

1048 Nelson, J. Raleigh 1873–1961
Lady Unafraid. Caldwell, Id.: Caxton Printers, 1951. 278 p.

The fictionalized biography of the author's mother, Rebecca Jewel Francis, a teacher of Ojibwa children in the 1860s. Set in L'Anse in the Upper Peninsula.

Mi MiD MiGr MiMarqN MiMtpT-C

1049 Nelson, Kent 1943–
All Around Me Peaceful. New York: Dell Publishing, 1989. 397 p.

A Colorado man delaying his return to his family's lumber business in Michigan looks into his grandfather's source of wealth. Eleven pages are set near Grayling.

1050 Nern, Daniel D. 1926–
Black as Night. Boston: Beacon Press, 1958. 261 p.

An African-American family leaves Atlanta, Georgia, and moves north to escape degradation, violence, and racial prejudice. Partially set in Detroit.

Black, 197.

Mi MiAllG MiCad MiSth OKentU

1051 Nieland, Dirk
'N Fonnie Bisnis. Grand Rapids, Mich.: Wm. B. Eerdmans Publishing Co., 1929. 204 p.

A humorous story of a Dutch community and a few of its colorful characters. Told in a Dutch dialect and set in Grand Rapids.

Mi MiAllG MiGrC MiMtpT-C PRA

1052 Nielsen, Helen Bernice 1918–
The Crime Is Murder. New York: William Morrow & Co., 1956. 224 p.

A young woman involved with a small town's annual music festival also becomes mixed up with murder. Set in "Bellville" on Lake Michigan, north of Muskegon.

Mystery.

MiAllG MiBatW MiMack MiPh OCl

North American, A *see Scenes on Lake Huron*

1053 Norton, Michael C.
Abomination. New York: Leisure Books, 1987. 400 p.

Three children playing in a graveyard inadvertently liberate an evil force. Set in "Greenriver" in southwesten Michigan and in "Haines City" (Ypsilanti).

Mi MiAllG MiGr MiSc CU-Riv

1054 ———.
Blizzard. New York: Leisure Books, 1988. 358 p.

A group of old friends gather for a Christmas party, become trapped by a blizzard, and are stalked by a monster with a taste for human flesh. Set in Bay View.

Mi MiAllG CU-Riv IaDa NcR

O

1055 Oates, Joyce Carol 1938–
Expensive People. New York: Vanguard Press, 1968. 308 p.

An overweight eighteen-year-old composes a memoir describing how he assassinated his mother when he was eleven. Set in "Fernwood" and "Cedar Grove" in the Birmingham area.

1056 ———.
Them. New York: Vanguard Press, 1969. 508 p.

A nightmarish story of a blue-collar family and how violence becomes a part of their everyday life. Set in Detroit from the 1930s to the 1967 riot.

1057 ———.
Wonderland. New York: Vanguard Press, 1971. 512 p.

The traumatic experience of nearly being murdered by his father affects a man throughout his life. Partially set in Ann Arbor.

1058 ———.
Do with Me What You Will. New York: Vanguard Press, 1973. 561 p.

A young woman who as a child was kidnapped by her father marries an older man and has an affair with a younger lawyer. Partially set in Detroit.

1059 ———.
Cybele. Santa Barbara, Calif.: Black Sparrow Press, 1979. 204 p.

The story of a forty-six-year-old man's affair which leads to the disintegration of his marriage and worse. Set in the Detroit suburbs of "Wainboro" and "Woodland."

1060 ———.
The Rise of Life on Earth. New York: New Directions Publishing Corp., 1991. 135 p.

Having been physically abused as a child, a woman employed as a nurse's aide in a hospital begins to show homicidal tendencies. Set in Detroit from 1961 to 1972.

1061 ———.
Zombie. New York: Dutton, 1995. 181 p.

A thirty-one-year-old psychopath convicted of sexual molestation and undergoing therapy becomes a serial murderer. Set in "Mt. Vernon" and "Dale County" in southeastern Michigan.

1062 O'Barr, James
The Crow by J. O'Barr. Northampton, Mass.: Kitchen Sink Press, 1994. 240 p.

A young man who was murdered with his girlfriend returns as a ghost to exact revenge on the gang who killed them. Set in Detroit.

Graphic novel.

MiAllG CValA INS InLap OCl

1063 Oberreich, Robert L. 1910–
The Magic Lake. Philadelphia: J. B. Lippincott Co., 1953. 184 p.

Two boys from Indianapolis spend the summer at a cottage at "Lake Tomahawk" in the Grand Traverse area and have many adventures exploring nearby places.

Juvenile.

MiAllG IC InE InFw OCl

1064 ———.
Super Summer. Philadelphia: J. B. Lippincott Co., 1954. 184 p.

Four boys spend the summer together
and become involved with stolen treasure and a haunted house. Set at "Lake
Tomahawk" in the Grand Traverse
area.

Sequel to *The Magic Lake.*

Juvenile.

MiCad MiWar MiYEM IC InE

1065 ———.
The Blood Red Belt. Garden City, N.Y.:
Doubleday & Co., 1961. 143 p.

A sixteen-year-old boy working for the
American Fur Company discovers a
British and Ojibwa plot. Set near the
Straits of Mackinac and "Fort Pleas-
ant" in the Upper Peninsula in the early
1800s.

Juvenile.

Mi MiLapC MiWar IC OKentU

1066 O'Brien, Dillon 1817–1882
Dead Broke, a Western Tale. St. Paul,
Minn.: Pioneer Co. Print, 1873. 193 p.

A widowed doctor and his son move
to Michigan and, along with the local
blacksmith and his son, witness the
town's development. Set in "P———"
between 1830 and 1860.

Wright II, 1809.

DLC MnU

1067 O'Brien, Howard Vincent 1888–
1947
The Terms of Conquest. Boston: Little,
Brown, and Co., 1923. 357 p.

A man leaves a small printing shop
to find greater opportunity in Chicago

and, after a long struggle, becomes successful. Partially set in "Cold Harbor"
(Petoskey and Harbor Springs).

MiDU IC MnMohC OCl RP

1068 O'Hara, John 1905–1970
The Ewings. New York: Random
House, 1972. 311 p.

The saga of a Cleveland family from
1912 to 1918 in which the son goes to
law school, gets married, and follows
in his father's footsteps as a lawyer.
Partially set in "Wingate" near Grand
Rapids and in Ann Arbor at the University of Michigan.

1069 Oldenburg, E. William 1936–
1974
Potawatomi Indian Summer. Grand
Rapids: William B. Eerdmans Pub.
Co., 1975. 134 p.

Six children explore a sand dune and
find a magic cave that transports them
back three hundred years to a camp of
Potawatomis. Set in the Grand Haven
area.

Juvenile.

Mi MiAllG MiHolH MiMtpT-C
MiYEM

Olney, Oliver, pseud. *see* Des Voignes,
Jules Verne

1070 Oneal, Elizabeth B. 1934–
A Formal Feeling by Zibby Oneal.
New York: Viking Press, 1982. 162 p.

A young woman tries to come to terms
with her mother's death and her father's remarriage. Set in an unnamed
university town, probably Ann Arbor.

Juvenile.

Oneal, Zibby *see* Oneal, Elizabeth B.

Optic, Oliver, pseud. *see* Adams, William Taylor

1071 Orr, Myron David 1896–1986
White Gold; a Mystery Romance of the Great Lakes. Detroit: Capper, Harman, Slocum, 1936. 179 p.

A dispute between two fishing companies deepens roots when an opium smuggling ring is uncovered. Mostly set on Saginaw Bay and in the fishing village of "Bay."

Mystery.

Black, 204.

Mi MiAllG MiAlpC MiD MiMtpT-C

1072 ———.
Cathedral of the Pines. Detroit: Capper Harman Slocum, 1938. 241 p.

A young man from a poor background becomes a brilliant but cynical and egotistical physician until a woman changes his outlook. Partially set in Newberry.

Mi MiAllG MiDW MiMtpT-C MiOw

1073 ———.
The Citadel of the Lakes. New York: Dodd, Mead & Co., 1952. 287 p.

A story of John Jacob Astor's (1763–1848) American Fur Company and Astor's efforts to corner the fur trade through unethical means. Set at Mackinac Island between 1810 and 1814.

Black, 200.

1074 ———.
Mission to Mackinac. New York: Dodd, Mead & Co., 1956. 301 p.

The conflicts among French, English, and American fur-traders reflect the tensions existing among and interests of their respective nations. Set at Mackinac Island in 1811.

Black, 201.

Mi MiAllG MiD MiHM MiMtpT

1075 ———.
The Outlander. New York: Thomas Bouregy and Co., 1959. 256 p.

A wealthy Philadelphian comes to Mackinac Island in 1819 and works with the leaders of independent fur-traders to break the monopoly of the American Fur Company.

Black, 202.

Mi MiAllG MiAlpC MiD MiMtpT-C

1076 Orton, Helen Fuller 1872–1955
The Secret of the Rosewood Box. New York: Frederick A. Stokes Co., 1937. 112 p.

A family journeys from New York to their new home, loses an heirloom bonnet box on the way, and finds it again at the end. Mostly set in northern Michigan in 1880.

Juvenile.

MiAllG MiDW MiJac MiOw MiSth

1077 Osborn, David 1923–
Open Season. New York: Dial Press, 1974. 243 p.

Each fall, three businessmen kidnap, rape, and ultimately hunt down and kill a couple selected at random. Set mostly in Schoolcraft County in the Upper Peninsula.

Mystery.

1078 Osborn, Edwin Faxon 1859–1937
Onar. Kalamazoo: Sylvan Press, 1909. 345 p.

A mysterious woman living in a miniature medieval castle in the woods deals with love and foreclosure. Partially set in northern Michigan.

Black, 199.

Mi MiAllG MiMtpT-C OU

1079 Osterman, Mark 1935–
Justifiable Homicide: A True-to-Life Work of Fiction. New Smyrna Beach, Fla.: Luthers, 1992. 282 p.

A Vietnam veteran joins the Detroit police force and, seeing the courts free criminals on legal technicalities, begins to deal out his own brand of justice.

Mystery.

MiD MiMtcM MiMtpT-C FDb OU

Otis, James, pseud. *see* Kaler, James Otis

1080 Overton, Dave
All the Way Home. New York: Carlton Press Corp., 1996. 64 p.

Unloved by his mother, a sixteen-year-old African American leaves home, finds work, and is imprisoned because of an accident. Set in Dowagiac and Battle Creek in the 1950s.

MiFli

1081 Owens, J. D.
Fancy Grosse Pointe People. Grosse Pointe: Pinque & Greene Productions, 1992. 126 p.

When the octogenarian founder of a giant Detroit advertising agency dies, a former employee reminisces about his life. Set partially in Detroit and Grosse Pointe.

MiGr-L OBgU

P

1082 Pallas, Norvin 1918–
The S.S. Shamrock Mystery. New York: Ives Washburn, 1966. 149 p.

(Ted Wilford Mystery, no. 14)

Two reporters pose as Great Lakes sailors to look into possible sabotage aboard an ore carrier. Partially set in Detroit and Sault Ste. Marie.

Juvenile.

Mi MiBar MiMtcM MiRoch MiWar

1083 Panagopoulos, Janie Lynn
Traders in Time; a Dream Quest Adventure. Spring Lake, Mich.: River Road Publications, 1993. 200 p.

Two boys from Grand Haven are transported back into time and experience adventures in the fur trade. Set on Lake Michigan and Mackinac Island in 1796.

Juvenile.

MiAllG MiCad MiFliL MiMtcM MiOw

1084 ———.
Journey Back to Lumberjack Camp; a Dream Quest Adventure. Spring Lake, Mich.: River Road Publications, 1993. 170 p.

A twelve-year-old boy travels back into time to find a logging camp and experiences the life of a lumberjack. Set in northern Michigan.

Juvenile.

MiAllG MiGr MiMtcM MiMu MiNop

1085 ———.
Erie Trail West; a Dream Quest Adventure. Spring Lake, Mich.: River Road Publications, 1995. 184 p.

An eleven-year-old girl falls asleep and dreams of the adventures her ancestors wrote about in a journal of their 1836 journey from New York to the Howell area.

Juvenile.

MiAllG MiFli MiGr MiLac MiMu

1086 ———.
North to Iron Country; a Dream Quest Adventure. Spring Lake, Mich.: River Road Publications, 1996. 216 p.

A boy's school assignment to interview an old iron miner takes him back to the 1850s as a boy from New York newly arrived in the Upper Peninsula. Set in Marquette.

Juvenile.

MiAllG MiFra MiLac MiMu MiT

1087 **Paretsky, Sara** 1947–
Deadlock: A V.I. Warshawski Mystery. Garden City, N.Y.: Dial Press, Doubleday & Co., 1984. 252 p.

A private investigator is suspicious about her cousin's allegedly accidental death, which occurred while employed on a Great Lakes freighter. Fifteen pages are set in the Soo Canal at Sault Ste. Marie.

Mystery.

1088 **Park, Nettie Wolcott**
Mehitabel: Girl Pioneer. The Story of Her Adventurous Journey West with Tod and the Triplets. Boston: L. C. Page & Co., 1946. 309 p.

In 1868, five orphans run away from a Pennsylvania farmer and have many adventures on their search for their grandparents' homestead. Partially set in Millbrook.

Juvenile.

MiD MiDW MiFra MiYEM OCl

1089 **Parker, Saul**
Inevitable. New York: Vantage Press, 1975. 259 p.

A University of Michigan law professor becomes governor of Michigan in 1988 and finds a vast difference between political theory and practice. Set in Ann Arbor and Lansing.

Mi MiKW MiSth MsJ

1090 **Parks, Cliff Bell**
Vessels of Clay. New York: Vantage Press, 1965. 181 p.

A fictionalized autobiography of a man who recounts his generally unsuccessful life and the people who meant the most to him. Set partially in a western Michigan cottage on Lake Michigan.

MiMtpT-C OBgU

1091 **Parks, L. K.** 1846–1925
With British and Braves; Story of the War of 1812. Cincinnati: Curts & Jennings, 1898. 301 p.

A fictionalized narrative describing the War of 1812 in a variety of locations as seen by a number of participants. Thirty pages are set in Detroit and Frenchtown.

Wright III, 4100.

MiAdC MiEM MnU OU ViU

1092 **Parrish, Randall** 1858–1923
A Sword of the Old Frontier, a Tale of Fort Chartres and Detroit; Being a Plain Account of Sundry Adventures Befalling Chevalier Raoul de Coubert, One Time Captain in the Hussars of Languedoc, During the Year 1763. Chicago: A. C. McClurg & Co., 1905. 407 p.

A French soldier journeys from the Illinois country in 1763 with a message to Pontiac that promises French support in his attacks against the British. Partially set in Detroit.

Black, 205. Streeter, 5655.

MiGr-L KEmU NIC NcD OKentU

1093 ———.

Beyond the Frontier; a Romance of Early Days in the Middle West. Chicago: A. C. McClurg & Co., 1915. 406 p.

A woman married against her will for political reasons travels with her husband through New France. Twenty pages are set in St. Ignace in the 1680s.

Mi IEN OCl OU ViBlbV

1093A Parrott, Michael L.

The Oakland County Child Killer. Detroit: Harlo Press, 1980. 173 p.

A mentally disturbed priest from a Birmingham parish abducts and murders three children one winter before committing suicide. Based on an actual unsolved case, the work is set in various Oakland County locales.

Mystery.

MiSf

1094 Parsons, Vivian LaJeunesse 1907–1950

Not Without Honor. New York: Dodd, Mead & Co., 1941. 342 p.

A French-Canadian leaves his farm to seek his fortune in the mines of the Upper Peninsula. Set in "Hilltown" (Iron Mountain) in the 1880s and 1890s.

Black, 206.

Mi MiAlle MiKW MiMack OU

1095 Patch, Dan E. L. 1886–1957

Past Finding Out. Chicago: Bica Press, 1939. 320 p.

A young doctor's girlfriend, the daughter of an automobile industry magnate, is kidnapped and held for ransom before being rescued. Set partially in Wayne County and Detroit.

Mystery.

Mi MiBsA MiCad MiMtpT-C ICarbS

1096 ———.

Aamon Always. Chicago: BICA Press, 1940. 314 p.

A Jewish youth who was adopted by a Christian family as a baby is framed for burglary by his stepbrother. Partially set in Wayne County.

Mi MiAllG MiD MiMtpT-C OU

1097 ———.

Ashes of Yesterday, a Historical Novel. Grand Rapids: Zondervan Publishing House, 1941. 224 p.

The history and development of Michigan is the background for the fictional life of a Margaret Thrillby and her family. Set in various Michigan locales from 1837 to 1936.

Black, 207.

Mi MiD MiGr MiMtpT-C MiWar

1098 ———.

Moon Over Willow Run. Grand Rapids: Zondervan Publishing House, 1943. 175 p.

Because of the outbreak of World War II, a young American missionary returns from India to the United States and attends college where she ultimately converts the man she loves. Set partially in southeastern Michigan.

Mi MiAllG MiBsA MiMtpT-C MiYEM

Patchin, Frank Gee *see* Mears, James R.

Paulson, Jack, pseud. *see* Jackson, Caary Paul

1099 Paylin, Jolie 1913–
Nels Oskar. Ames: Iowa State University Press, 1979. 130 p.

A Swedish farmer stricken with influenza during the epidemic of 1918 is cared for by a young woman, and they ultimately fall in love. Set in the Upper Peninsula.

Mi MiAlbC MiD MiHM MiMtpT-C

1100 ———.
The Gill Netters. Hillsdale, Mich.: Hillsdale Educational Publishers, 1979. 146 p.

A family of Danish immigrants fish for whitefish in Green Bay and move to the Menominee area when the fish migrate there in the late 1860s.

Mi MiAllG MiD MiHM MiMtpT-C

Payne, Harold, pseud. *see* Kelly, George C.

1101 Payne, Oliver
Warpath. New York: Berkley Books, 1982. 412 p.

(Northwest Territory, book 1)

A frontier trader, Owen Sutherland, falls in love with a beautiful widow new to Fort Detroit, and they are both caught up in the 1763 siege of the fort by Pontiac.

Mi MiAllG MiMtcM MiMtpT MiRoch

1102 ———.
Conquest. New York: Berkley Books, 1982. 445 p.

(Northwest Territory, book 2)

After Pontiac's defeat, Owen Sutherland marries a widow, Ellen, and together they found a frontier trading company. Partially set in Detroit from 1763 to 1764.

Sequel to *Warpath.*

MiAllG MiGr MiMio MiNhL WM

1103 ———.
Defiance. New York: Berkley Books, 1983. 430 p.

(Northwest Territory, book 3)

The Sutherlands' flourishing trading company is threatened by renegades, roving outlaw bands, and a rival company. Partially set in Detroit from 1765 to 1774.

Sequel to *Conquest.*

MiAllG MiInr MiMio MiNhL WM

1104 ———.
Rebellion. New York: Berkley Books, 1983. 415 p.

(Northwest Territory, book 4)

The Sutherlands become enmeshed in the American Revolution and give up their company to join the rebellion. Partially set in Detroit in 1774 and 1775.

Sequel to *Defiance.*

MiAllG MiNhL O WM WRac

1105 ———.
Conflict. New York: Berkley Books, 1984. 421 p.

(Northwest Territory, book 5)

The Sutherlands continue to support the Revolution even though their son has joined the British army as a physician. Partially set in Detroit from 1775 to 1777.

Sequel to *Rebellion.*

MiAdS MiAllG MiNhL O WM

1106 ———.
Triumph. New York: Berkley Books, 1985. 365 p.

(Northwest Territory, book 6)

The Sutherlands are involved in the Kaskaskia and Vincennes expeditions with George Rogers Clark (1752–1818) in 1778. Ten pages are set in Detroit.

Sequel to *Conflict.*

MiAllG MiGr MiRoch O WM

1107 ———.
Betrayal. New York: Berkley Books, 1986. 308 p.

(Northwest Territory, book 7)

The Sutherlands' daughter falls in love with a member of the rival trading company who considers her a means to his own success. Partially set in Detroit in 1779.

Sequel to *Triumph.*

MiAllG MiSsB MnManTD OXe WM

1108 ———.
Honor. New York: Berkley Books, 1987. 285 p.

(Northwest Territory, book 8)

With the American Revolution over, the Sutherlands try to put their lives and business back in order and return to their home. Fourteen pages are set in Detroit in 1782.

Sequel to *Betrayal.*

MiAllG MiMio IGenD OT WM

1109 Payne, Will 1865–1954
When Love Speaks. New York: Macmillan Co., 1906. 370 p.

Two brothers-in-law have diametrically opposed political philosophies about the manner in which their town should be run. Set in "Sauganac" on southern Lake Michigan.

AzU DeU FTaSU GEU OU

1110 Peacock, Margaret
The Story of Wafted Across; the First in a Series of Stories About an Ojibwa Family in St. Ignace, Michigan. St. Ignace: Marquette Mission Park and Museum of Ojibwa Culture, 1988. 20 p.

As a thirteen-year-old Ojibwa girl tends to her chores around the village, she thinks about a group of young men about to leave for Quebec. Set in St. Ignace in 1670.

Juvenile picture book.

MiAllG MiU

1111 ———.
Southern Feather's Story; the Second in a Series of Stories About an Ojibwa Family in St. Ignace, Michigan. St. Ignace: Marquette Mission Park and Museum of Ojibwa Culture, 1988. 27 p.

An Ojibwa woman tells her seven-year-old granddaughter how the turtle became their family's totem. Set in St. Ignace and on Michilimackinac in the late 1600s.

Juvenile picture book.

MiAllG MiU

1112 Pearson, Mary Celestia
His Own Interpreter. A Novel of Faith. New York: Exposition Press, 1956. 265 p.

The story of a young woman's life as she tries to overcome her father's scandalous behavior. Set partially in the lumber town of "Millview" from 1910 to the 1920s.

MiGr-L ABAU KyHhn KyU

1113 Peattie, Elia Wilkinson 1862–1935
The Beleaguered Forest. New York: D. Appleton and Co., 1901. 349 p.

An orphaned and impoverished young woman accepts an offer of marriage from a wealthy lumberman, but discovers he is an opium addict. Set in northern Michigan.

Black, 208. Streeter, 5688.

Mi IC NhU OU T

1114 Peckham, Howard Henry 1910–1995
Pontiac; Young Ottawa Leader. Indianapolis: Bobbs-Merrill Co., 1963. 200 p.

A fictionalized biography of the great Ottawa chief including his efforts to organize the tribes against the English. Eleven pages are set in Detroit in 1763.

Juvenile.

Peek, Junice Smyth, joint author *see* Smyth, Dan

1115 Pellowe, William Charles Smithson 1890–
The Sky Lines of Paradise. New York: Fortuny's, 1941. 271 p.

Philosophical discussions about the role of labor and capital take place after a union organizer is murdered and a young woman attempts suicide. Set in Saginaw.

Black, 209.

Mi MiAllG MiChv MiEM MiMtpT

1116 Pendleton, Don 1927–1995
The Executioner: Detroit Deathwatch. Los Angeles: Pinnacle Books, 1974. 182 p.

(Executioner, no. 19)

Mack Bolan's campaign of revenge against the Mafia members who murdered his family leads him to Detroit, where he disrupts vast organized crime operations.

Mystery.

MiAllG IChamL InU OBgU ScSp

1117 ———.
The Executioner: Shifting Target. Toronto: Worldwide Library, 1994. 221 p.

(Executioner, no. 181)

A man increases his criminal activities with stolen chemical weapons and by heading a drug ring, which attracts Mack Bolan's attention. Set in the Detroit suburb of "Talville."

Mystery.

MiAllG AzG KKc OCo USl

1118 Peple, Edward Henry 1869–1924
An Auto-Biography. A Tale of Truth—and Ruth. New York: Moffat, Yard & Co., 1915. 151 p.

An unusual story in which an automobile is the narrator. The first thirty-five pages tell of its manufacture in a Detroit automobile factory.

MiD CLU MdU OU ViRU

1119 Perkins, Stan 1913–
Arvilla and the Tattler Tree. Swartz Creek, Mich.: Broadblade Press, 1994. 702 p.

A maple tree tells the story of a Welsh woman and her rise in the fur trade.

Set on Mackinac Island and other sites along the Michigan shore from the 1790s to 1815.

Mi MiCad MiFli MiMtcM MiMtpT-C

1120 Perlman, Fredy ?–1985
The Strait: Book of Obenabi. His Songs. Detroit: Black & Red, 1988. 399 p.

A sweeping narrative history as seen and experienced by a family of Native Americans. Set in Detroit and other Michigan locales from the 1500s to the mid-1800s.

Mi MiAllG MiU NN

1121 Perry, H. L.
Hurricane of Ice. Chicago: Playboy Press, 1976. 248 p.

A monstrous blizzard destroys "Trafalgar Bridge" (Mackinac Bridge) with disastrous results for a number of people. Set in Traverse City and on the Straits of Mackinac.

Mi MiT UM

1122 Peters, Thomas R. 1929–
The Education of Tom Webber, by T. R. Peters, Sr. Hicksville, N.Y.: Exposition Press, 1977. 123 p.

A fourteen-year-old boy attends "Gull Hall Junior Military School" and has difficulty taking school and his teachers and classmates seriously. Set in Kalamazoo in 1943 and 1944.

MiDU MiSf MiStc MiSth PNo

1123 ———.
Two Weeks in the Forties by T. R. Peters, Sr. Detroit: Xpress Way Publishing, 1990. 209 p.

A teenager has trouble conforming to the ways of parochial school even though he is a star athlete. Set in Kalamazoo in 1943 and Detroit in 1946.

The first part of this book was published in 1977 as *The Education of Tom Webber.*

Mi MiAllG MiFli MiHilC

1124 Petersen, Ernest J. 1880–1964
North of Saginaw Bay by E. J. (Pete) Petersen. Sand Lake, Mich.: Tall Timber Press, 1952. 241 p.

A fourteen-year-old boy suspects that his timber-cruiser father has been murdered, rather than accidentally killed as ruled by a coroner's inquest. Set in Bay City and the Au Sable River valley in the late 1860s.

Black, 210.

Mi MiAllG MiAlpC MiD MiElk

1125 ———.
The White Squaw; a Sequel to North of Saginaw Bay by E. J. (Pete) Petersen. Sand Lake, Mich.: Tall Timber Press, 1954. 263 p.

After a young woman's father is murdered, she enlists the help of an Ojibwa boy and an old friend. Set in Antrim County, the Manistee area, and in Bay City in 1870.

Sequel to *North of Saginaw Bay.*

Black, 211.

Mi MiAllG MiDW MiMtpT MiTop

1126 Peterson, Livia Y. 1886–
Fair Wind by Livia Y. Peterson and Myrtes-Marie Plummer. Chicago: Wilcox & Follett Co., 1947. 234 p.

A teenage boy works various jobs to earn money for a sailboat. Set in "Cedarline" (Montague) on "Mirror Lake" (White Lake) and in "Loskegon" (Muskegon).

Juvenile.

MiAlle MiGr MiWar InFw OBgU

1127 Phillips, Michael James 1876–
Bunty Prescott at Englishman's Camp
by Major M. J. Phillips. Chicago:
Reilly & Britton Co., 1912. 279 p.

A sickly ten-year-old boy and his father
spend a year camping on the North
Branch of the Au Sable River near
Grayling so the boy can recuperate.

Juvenile.

Mi DLC

1128 Philo, Thomas
Judgment by Fire. New York: Bantam
Books, 1985. 279 p.

A young man's family is incinerated
in an explosion and fire, and he finds
a connection to his father's wartime
sabotage unit. Set partially in Detroit
and Benton Harbor.

Mystery.

Mi MiAllG MiBatK MiGr O

1128A Pico, Robert 1938–
Cadillac, l'Homme Qui Fonda Détroit.
Paris: Denoël, 1995. 286 p.

The fictional memoirs of the French
explorer Antoine de la Mothe Cadillac
(1658–1730), part of which describes
his establishing the settlement of Detroit in 1701.

In French.

Mi MiAllG CU MH NN

1129 Piercy, Marge 1936–
The High Cost of Living. New York:
Harper & Row, 1978. 268 p.

The story of two women and one man
from working-class backgrounds that
incorporates academic, lesbian, and
feminist themes. Set in Detroit.

1130 ———.
Braided Lives. New York: Summit
Books, 1982. 441 p.

A socially and emotionally inept young
woman finds college life disappointing
until she finds a group of kindred spirits. Set at the University of Michigan
in Ann Arbor and in Detroit from 1953
to 1957.

1131 ———.
Gone to Soldiers. New York: Summit
Books, 1987. 703 p.

A World War II saga that describes numerous characters and their adventures
in a wide variety of locales. Partially set
in Detroit.

**1132 Pierson, Clara Eleanor Dilling-
ham** 1868–1952
The Plucky Allens. New York: E. P.
Dutton & Co., 1925. 327 p.

Four children live with a kindly woman
in a large house and have a number
of adventures. Set in "Sweetwater," a
combination of Alma and Stanton.

Juvenile.

Mi InFw NAlU ViR WaU

1133 ———.
The Allens and Aunt Hannah. New
York: E. P. Dutton & Co., 1927. 290 p.

The four children introduced in *The
Plucky Allens* have more adventures—
in winter and summer—on a farm and
observe their uncle's ongoing romance.
Set in "Sweetwater."

Sequel to *The Plucky Allens.*

Juvenile.

Mi DLC InFw

Pierson, Sylvanus, pseud. *see* Jermain, S. P.

1134 Pike, Fannie Janeschek

Dark Valley Romance. Philadelphia: Dorrance & Co., 1956. 190 p.

A woman struggles to raise her family out of poverty and earn enough for an operation her father needs. Set in "Dark Valley" in northern Michigan from 1890 to the 1930s.

Mi CLU NjTS RPB TxH

1135 Pillsbury, Fred C.

The Girl from Hampton Beach; an Adventure in Unconventional Living. Boston: Meador Publishing Co., 1937. 283 p.

The spoiled son of an automobile magnate falls in love with a New Hampshire girl. Partially set in Detroit and at "Mid-Western University" (Wayne University).

Mi MiDW KyRE

1136 Pinchot, Ann Kramer 1910–

Hour Upon the Stage. New York: Dodd, Mead & Co., 1929. 288 p.

The motives of a town's leading citizen and benefactor, small-minded greed, and the Jewish community are scathingly portrayed here. Set in "Muskenaw" (Muskegon).

Black, 212.

Mi MiAllG MiDU MiGr MiKC

————, joint author *see* Pinchot, Ben

1137 Pinchot, Ben

Hear This Woman! by Ben Pinchot and Ann Pinchot. New York: Farrar, Straus and Co., 1949. 316 p.

An investigative reporter is hired to find information about a prominent woman's early life and career in her hometown. Partially set in "St. Croix" (Muskegon) from 1906.

MiSaS MiWar IC InAnd OBgU

1138 Pinkerton, Allan 1819–1884

The Spiritualists and the Detectives. New York: G. W. Carleton & Co., 1877. 354 p.

(Allan Pinkerton's Detective Stories, vol. 5)

Detective Pinkerton investigates a clever extortion scheme involving spiritualism perpetrated by a ruthless woman. Partially set in Kalamazoo and Detroit.

Mystery.

Wright III, 4269.

MiEM CLU MnU OBgU ViU

1139 Pitezel, John H. 1814–1906

The Backwoods Boy Who Became a Minister; or, The Family and Personal History of Henry Adolph by Rev. J. H. Pitezel. New York: Carlton & Porter, 1859. 163 p.

The fictionalized autobiography of a Methodist missionary minister. The final sixteen pages are set in the Upper Peninsula town of "Lake Tracy."

MiGr-L IEN KyRE NjMD OKentU

1140 Plum, Mary

Murder at the Hunting Club. New York: Harper & Brothers, 1932. 282 p.

A young woman who had just visited the men-only "Litani Hunting Club" in the Upper Peninsula is found dead, and the detective at the scene concludes that it is murder.

Mystery.

CLU IaDa MBAt NcGU NcU

Plummer, Myrtes-Marie, joint author *see* Peterson, Livia Y.

1141 **Pohlman, M. David**

The Problem of Evil. New York: St. Martin's Press, 1990. 183 p.

A man with Mob connections calls his son home to help find out who has been trying to kill his cousin. Set in "Somerville" in the Upper Peninsula on Lake Superior.

Mystery.

1142 **Pokagon, Simon** 1830–1899

O-gi-maw-kwe Mit-i-gwa-ki (Queen of the Woods). Also Brief Sketch of the Algaic Language by Chief Pokagon. Biography of the Chief by the Publisher. Hartford, Mich.: C. H. Engle, 1899. 255 p.

The fictionalized autobiography of the Potawatomi chief, which emphasizes the encroachments of white civilization and the consequent erosion of traditional Potawatomi life. Set mostly in the Hartford area in southwestern Michigan.

Black, 213. Streeter, 5756.

Mi MiD MiEM MiHM MiMtpT-C

1143 **Polacco, Patricia Ann Barber** 1944–

Meteor! New York: Dodd, Mead & Co., 1987. 30 p.

A meteor lands on a family farm yielding exciting and memorable results. Set in Union City in the 1920s.

Juvenile picture book.

1144 ———.

Boat Ride with Lillian Two Blossom. New York: Philomel Books, 1988. 27 p.

A mysterious Native-American woman takes two children on a boat ride on a Michigan pond and shares weather lore with them.

Juvenile picture book.

1145 ———.

Thunder Cake. New York: Philomel Books, 1990. 32 p.

An old woman tries to comfort her granddaughter's fear of thunderstorms by baking a special cake. Set on a Michigan farm.

Juvenile picture book.

1146 ———.

Some Birthday! New York: Simon & Schuster, 1991. 32 p.

As a special treat for a young girl's birthday, her father takes her to see a monster living in a clay-pit pond. Set in Williamston.

Juvenile picture book.

1147 ———.

Picnic at Mudsock Meadow. New York: G. P. Putnam's Sons, 1992. 32 p.

A boy hopes to impress a girl he likes by competing in various games at a Halloween picnic. Set in Union City.

Juvenile picture book.

1148 ———.

The Bee Tree. New York: Philomel Books, 1993. 32 p.

A young girl who refuses to read is shown the value of books when her grandfather takes her to find a bee tree. Set in Union City.

Juvenile picture book.

1149 ———.
My Rotten Redheaded Older Brother.
New York: Simon & Schuster, 1994.
32 p.

A young girl must contend with her
older brother's irritating and obnoxious
displays of superiority. Set in Union
City in the 1950s.

Juvenile picture book.

1150 ———.
My Ol' Man. New York: Philomel
Books, 1995. 36 p.

A fast-talking travelling salesman
spins many tales to his daughter and
son, including one about a magic rock.
Set in Williamston in the early 1950s.

Juvenile picture book.

1151 ———.
*Aunt Chip and the Great Triple Creek
Dam Affair.* New York: Philomel
Books, 1996. 38 p.

In a town where TV has totally sup-
planted reading, an old woman begins
a campaign for reading instruction and
reintroduces books into the community. Set in "Triple Creek."

Juvenile picture book.

1152 ———.
The Trees of the Dancing Goats. New
York: Simon & Schuster Books for
Young Readers, 1996. 32 p.

A Jewish farm family expands its celebration of Hanukkah by making Christmas trees for those neighbors sick with
scarlet fever. Set near Union City in the
1950s.

Juvenile picture book.

1153 **Polack, William Gustave** 1890–
1950

*Shegonaba; a Tale of Mission Work
Among the Chippewas.* Constance:
Book and Art Publishing Co., Carl
Hirsch A. G., n.d. 94 p.

The story of a Lutheran missionary
minister and his life and work among
the Ojibwas in the Saginaw area in the
1840s.

Mi CSbC MnBemS OT PSt

1154 **Pollowitz, Melinda Kilborn** 1944–
Princess Amy. New York: Bantam
Books, 1981. 168 p.
(Sweet Dreams Romance, no. 4)

A sixteen-year-old girl reluctantly
spends the summer with rich relatives
on Mackinac Island, where two boys
from different backgrounds take an interest in her.

Juvenile.

MiAllG MiGr MiInr MiMani InAnd

1155 ———.
Country Girl. New York: Bantam
Books, 1983. 182 p.
(Sweet Dreams Romance, no. 34)

After her boyfriend drops her for another girl, a teenager is fearful that her
new boyfriend will eventually do the
same. Set in Petoskey.

Juvenile.

Mi MiBatW MiRoch MiSte MiSth

1156 **Porter, Ella Blodwen Williams**
Footprints on the Sand. New York:
Macmillan Co., 1949. 163 p.

An orphan girl must struggle to be accepted at "Birch Wood Camp," where
she is the target of the resident snob.
Set at "Fairhaven" (Frankfort?).

Juvenile.

MiGay MiRochOU IC InFw OCl

Porter, Gene Stratton *see* Stratton-Porter, Geneva Grace

1157 **Porter, Monica E.**
The Mercy of the Court. New York: W. W. Norton, 1955. 252 p.

A judge chooses between furthering his own political career and giving an accused young felon another chance. Set in "Elm City" (Pontiac?) in "Clement County."

Black, 214.

Mi MiAllG MiD MiKW MiU

1158 **Pound, Arthur** 1884–1966
Once a Wilderness. New York: Reynal & Hitchcock, 1934. 399 p.

The chronicle of the Mark family, which is headed by a larger-than-life patriarch, who founds a successful cattle farm despite financial problems. Set in "Clayton County" (Oakland County) from 1865 to 1910.

The "Special Michigan Edition" contains a two-page dedication from the author addressed as follows: "To my friends in Michigan."

Black, 216.

Mi MiAllG MiD MiMtpT MiU

1159 ———.
Second Growth. New York: Reynal & Hitchcock, 1935. 347 p.

The saga of the Mark family continues, following the patriarch's sons, grandsons, and the changes that time brings to the farm. Set in "Clayton County" (Oakland County) and Pontiac from 1913 to the 1930s.

Sequel to *Once a Wilderness.*

Black, 217.

Mi MiAllG MiD MiMtpT-C MiU

1160 ———.
Hawk of Detroit. New York: Reynal & Hitchcock, 1939. 361 p.

A fictionalized historical narrative of the founding of Detroit by Antoine de la Mothe Cadillac (1658–1730) and subsequent events there from 1701 to 1711.

Black, 215.

Mi MiAllG MiD MiMtpT-C MiU

1161 **Powers, Richard** 1957–
Three Farmers on Their Way to a Dance. New York: Beech Tree Books, 1985. 352 p.

A haunting 1914 photograph of three German farmers sends a journalist on a search for its history and meaning. Nineteen pages are set in Detroit.

1162 **Pratt, Eleanor Blake Atkinson** 1899–1953?
Seedtime and Harvest by Eleanor Blake [pseud.]. New York: G. P. Putnam's Sons, 1935. 275 p.

Else, the daughter of Norwegian immigrants, hopes to escape insular farm life, but successive pregnancies prevent it. Set on the Leelanau Peninsula in the early 1900s.

Black, 218.

Mi MiAllG MiEM MiJac MiYEM

1163 ———.
Wherever I Choose by Eleanor Blake [pseud.]. New York: G. P. Putnam's Sons, 1938. 271 p.

Else's daughter, Bergit, rebellious despite her strict upbringing on the farm, leaves for Chicago and a fast life. Partially set on the Leelanau Peninsula and in Traverse City.

Sequel to *Seedtime and Harvest*.

Black, 219.

Mi MiAllG MiEM MiMtpT-C PPiU

1164 Prentis, John Harcourt 1878–1967
The Case of Doctor Horace; a Study of the Importance of Conscience in the Detection of Crime. New York: Baker and Taylor Co., 1907. 268 p.

Two men fake a murder to test a theory that a criminal can be caught through the operation of his own guilty conscience. Set in Detroit and Ann Arbor.

Mystery.

MiU CLU MWC OU ScU

1165 Prescott, Jerry J.
Deadly Sweet in Ann Arbor. Ann Arbor: Proctor Publications, 1996. 430 p.

The discovery of a murdered coed's body in an arboretum leads a pair of Ann Arbor police detectives to a sinister blackmail plot. Set at the University of Michigan.

Mystery.

Mi MiAllG MiJac MiMtpT-C MiU

1166 Price, Nancy
An Accomplished Woman. New York: Coward, McCann & Geoghegan, 1979. 288 p.

A young woman's guardian becomes her lover, and when he is reportedly killed in the war, she marries a self-made millionaire. Partially set in Detroit in the 1930s.

1167 Priestly, Lee Shore 1904–
A Teacher for Tibby. New York: William Morrow & Co., 1960. 96 p.

The story of an eight-year-old girl, her family, and their efforts to get a teacher and a schoolhouse for the area. Set on a Michigan farm in the 1860s.

Juvenile.

Mi MiCad MiD MiFli MiPet

1168 Puddefoot, William George 1842–1925
Hewers of Wood; a Story of the Michigan Pine Forests by William G. Puddefoot and Isaac Ogden Rankin. Boston: Pilgrim Press, 1903. 352 p.

A poor married couple find work in a logging camp and meet a variety of characters and ultimately tragedy. Set in northern Michigan near the town of "Woodside."

Black, 220. Streeter, 5893.

Mi MAlbC MiKW MiMtpT-C MiWar

Q

Q., John, pseud. *see* Quirk, John Edward

Quad, M., pseud. *see* Lewis, Charles Bertrand

1169 Quarrington, Paul 1953–
Home Game. Toronto: Doubleday Canada, 1983. 412 p.

A circus sideshow troupe stranded in a small Upper Peninsula town becomes involved with a fundamentalist sect and the local baseball team. Set in "Burton's Harbor" in 1938.

MiAllG MiDU MiLe MiNb MiSsB

**1170 Quiller-Couch, Sir Arthur Tho-
mas** 1863–1944
Fort Amity by A. T. Quiller-Couch.
London: John Murray, 1904. 357 p.

During the French and Indian War, a
young British officer is captured and
taken to Montreal by Ojibwas. Partially set in northern Michigan and at
Michilimackinac.

MiU IaU InU OKentU ScU

1171 Quirk, John Edward 1920–
No Red Ribbons. New York: Devin-
Adair Co., 1962. 564 p.

An ex-Navy fighter pilot returns to
civilian life and enters the business
world, which he finds rife with union
manipulation, gangsters, and politicians. Partially set in Detroit.

Mi MiAllG MiD MiMtpT-C MiStc

1172 ———.
The Hard Winners. New York: Random
House, 1965. 564 p.

When the president-elect of National
Motors suddenly dies, a successor must
be selected from a pool of ruthless
and backstabbing contenders. Set in
Detroit.

Mi MiAllG MiAlp MiD MiRochOU

1173 [———].
The Bunnies; a Peter Trees Adventure
by John Q. [pseud.]. New York: Avon
Books, 1965. 175 p.

(Avon Mystery, S176)

A mercenary aviator and secret agent
becomes involved in an investigation
of a murdered inventor of a revolutionary new automobile carburetor. Set in
Detroit.

Mystery.

MiAllG

R

1174 Ralphson, George Harvey 1879–
1940
*Boy Scouts on Old Superior; or The
Tale of the Pictured Rocks* by Scout
Master G. Harvey Ralphson. Chicago:
M. A. Donohue & Co., 1913. 162 p.

(Boy Scout Series, no. 7)

Four Chicago Boy Scouts become involved in a diamond theft that leads
them to an adventure with smugglers.
Partially set at the Pictured Rocks on
Lake Superior.

On the spine, the author is identified as
"[Archibald Lee] Fletcher."

Juvenile.

Mi MiAllG MiEM MiGr MiMtpT-C

1175 Ramin, Terese
Accompanying Alice. New York: Silhouette Books, 1991. 250 p.

(Silhouette Special Edition, no. 656)

A wounded Federal agent helped by a
divorcée planning a huge family wedding poses as her new boyfriend while
working on an investigation. Set in
Pontiac.

Romance.

MiGr MiPh MiWar OBgU WM

1176 ———.
A Certain Slant of Light. New York:
Silhouette Books, 1995. 248 p.

(Silhouette Intimate Moments, no.
634)

A U.S. marshal doing undercover
surveillance insinuates himself into an
attractive unmarried mother's home
and her life. Set in Oakland County.

Romance.

MiAllG IChamL OCo OXe WM

1177 ———.

Five Kids, One Christmas. New York: Silhouette Books, 1995. 248 p.

(Silhouette Intimate Moments, no. 680)

A blind widower and a young widowed Persian Gulf veteran with five children between them marry for convenience, but love eventually blooms. Set in Pontiac.

Romance.

MiAllG IChamL OCo OXe WM

1178 Ramm, Carl

Detroit Combat. New York: Dell Publishing Co., 1985. 173 p.

(Hawker, no. 7)

An ex-policeman and self-appointed vigilante investigates a series of kidnappings of young women and finds a deadly pornographic film ring. Set in Detroit.

Randy Wayne White has been suggested as the author.

Mystery.

Mi MiAllG IChamL TxCc UM

Rand, Addison, pseud. *see* Regli, Adolph Casper

1179 Randall, Kenneth Charles

Wild Hunter. New York: Franklin Watts, 1951. 236 p.

A eleven-year-old boy helps train a setter for pheasant season and sees the dog through a tragedy the following year. Set in the Thumb area.

Mi MiAllG MiD MiMtpT-C MiPet

1180 Rankin, Carroll Watson 1864–1945

Dandelion Cottage. New York: Henry Holt & Co., 1904. 312 p.

(Dandelion Series, no. 1)

In exchange for yardwork and general upkeep, four young girls are allowed to spend the summer together in a small cottage. Set in "Lakeville" (Marquette) on Lake Superior.

Juvenile.

Mi MiEM MiMarq OCl WEU

1181 ———.

The Girls of Gardenville. New York: Henry Holt and Co., 1906. 317 p.

Sixteen young girls establish a social club, and the story relates their individual adventures. Set in "Gardenville" (Marquette) on Lake Superior.

Juvenile.

Mi MiMarq MiMarqN InFw IChamL

1182 ———.

The Adopting of Rosa Marie (a Sequel to Dandelion Cottage). New York: Henry Holt and Co., 1908. 300 p.

(Dandelion Series, no. 2)

Four young girls "borrow" a Native-American child for a day, but she is kept indefinitely when it is learned that her parents have abandoned her. Set in "Lakeville" (Marquette) on Lake Superior.

Sequel to *Dandelion Cottage.*

Juvenile.

MiDW MiMarq IDeKN MnU WaU

1183 ———.

The Castaways of Pete's Patch. New York: Henry Holt and Co., 1911. 290 p.

(Dandelion Series, no. 3)

The automobile carrying would-be picnickers breaks down along Lake Superior, and they rescue a castaway on the beach.

Sequel to *The Adopting of Rosa Marie.*

Juvenile.

Mi MiMarq InFw KEmU WaU

1184 ———.
The Cinder Pond. New York: Henry Holt and Co., 1915. 310 p.

The father of a young girl wants her to grow up in proper surroundings, so she is sent to live with unaffectionate relatives. Partially set in "Bancroft" (Marquette) on Lake Superior.

Juvenile.

Mi MiAllG MiMarq IC KEmU

1185 ———.
Gipsy Nan. New York: Henry Holt and Co., 1926. 246 p.

After her mother dies, an eight-year-old girl is sent to visit her aunt and uncle and gets into all sorts of mischief. Set in "Craig's Corners" on Lake Superior.

Juvenile.

Mi MiMarq MiMarqN MiMtpT-C
KEmU

1186 ———.
Finders Keepers. New York: Henry Holt and Co., 1930.

A family embarks on a long vacation by automobile and meets a variety of people along the way who join them on their journey. Partially set in "Lakewood" (Marquette) on Lake Superior.

Juvenile.

Mi MiEM MiMarq KEmU WaU

1187 ———.
Wolf Rock; a Sequel to "The Cinder Pond." New York: Henry Holt and Co., 1933. 286 p.

When their boat is wrecked in a storm, two boys are marooned on a small is-land three miles off "Bancroft" (Marquette) in Lake Superior.

Sequel to *The Cinder Pond.*

Juvenile.

Mi MiMarq MiYEM TxFTC WaU

1188 ———.
Stump Village. New York: Henry Holt and Co., 1935. 248 p.

A teacher and her students have numerous adventures at their new one-room school house built on cut-over land. Set near "Bancroft" (Marquette) on Lake Superior.

Juvenile.

Mi MiMarq MiMarqN IDeKN

Rankin, Isaac Ogden, joint author *see* Puddefoot, William George

1189 Raphael, Lev
Let's Get Criminal; an Academic Mystery. New York: St. Martin's Press, 1996. 213 p.

When a university professor is murdered, the police have many suspects who disliked the man, including a gay academic couple. Set in "Michiganapolis" (Lansing).

Mystery.

1190 Rathborne, St. George H. 1854–1938
Camp Mates in Michigan; or, With Pack and Paddle in the Pine Woods. Chicago: M. A. Donohue & Co., 1913. 251 p.

(Camp and Trail Series, no. 5)

Three boys on a hunting and fishing vacation become involved in a timber dispute, a haunted house, and a kidnapping. Set in the Upper Peninsula.

Juvenile.

Black, 221.

Mi MiDW MiEM MiGr MiMtpT-C

————*see also* Carter, Herbert

1191 Rathke, Ethel Wheeler 1877–
1972
So As by Fire. New York: Vantage
Press, 1969. 226 p.

The wife of an alcoholic sets out with
him and their children to find a place
to live where there is no liquor. The
first nineteen pages are set in "Grant"
in 1906.

MiMtpT-C ArNlr

1192 Ratigan, William 1910–1984
Soo Canal! Grand Rapids: Wm. B.
Eerdmans Publishing Co., 1954. 186 p.

A fictionalized narrative of the concep-
tion and construction of the Soo Canal
despite obstacles and opposition. Set
mostly in Sault Ste. Marie in the 1850s.

Subtitle on book jacket: *A Romantic
Historical Novel.*

Black, 223.

Mi MiAllG MiD MiKW MiMtpT-C

1193 ————.
*Young Mister Big. The Story of Charles
Thompson Harvey, The Young Travel-
ing Salesman Who Built the World's
Mightiest Canal.* Grand Rapids: Wm.
B. Eerdmans Publishing Co., 1955.
152 p.

A fictionalized account of Charles T.
Harvey (b. 1829), his stay in Sault St.
Marie in the 1850s, and his idea for the
Soo Canal.

Mi MiAllG MiD MiMtpT-C MiPet

1194 ————.
The Adventures of Captain McCargo.
New York: Random House, 1956.
245 p.

A intrepid and resourceful Great Lakes
captain finds himself in a variety
messes and scrapes in the 1850s. Set
in many Great Lakes locales.

Black, 222.

Mi MiAllG MiD MiHM MiMtpT-C

1195 Rayne, Martha Louise
*Pauline; or, The Belles of Mackinac:
A Story of Love, Crime and Adven-
ture.* Detroit: Peninsular Publishing
Co., 1887. 162 p.

A young woman is forced to marry a
wealthy cad to comply with her dying
mother's wish, whereas the man who
loves her has his own troubles. Partially
set on Mackinac Island.

Mi MiD MiMtpT-C

Redwing, Morris, pseud. *see* Merrill,
James Milford

Reeder, Colonel Red *see* Reeder, Russell
Potter

1196 [Reeder, Russell Potter] 1902–
*Attack at Fort Lookout. A Story of the
Old Northwestern Frontier* by Colonel
Red Reeder. New York: Duell, Sloan
and Pierce, 1959. 184 p.

From 1811 to 1812, a young graduate
of West Point is posted at the half-
finished "Fort Lookout" (Fort Gratiot?)
located on the St. Clair River.

Juvenile.

Mi MiAllG MiDW MiOC MiYEM

1197 [Regli, Adolph Casper] 1896–
1952
Southpaw Fly Hawk by Addison Rand
[pseud.]. New York: Longmans, Green
and Co., 1952. 183 p.

By joining a minor league baseball
team, a young player learns some hard

lessons about the game as well as life. Twenty pages are set in Calumet in the Upper Peninsula.

Juvenile.

Mi MiD MiCad MiFliL IC

1198 Rencontre, Christina Irene
The Bear Walk. Marquette: Northern Michigan University, Department of English, 1995. 192 p.

A young Native American seeks to understand himself, his heritage, and his need for spirituality while coping with his aunt's alcoholism. Set in the Upper Peninsula.

Master of Arts thesis.

MiMarqN

1199 Renne, Anthony 1913–
The Pig-Tailtwister (As Related to the Author by Carl Dorski). Hicksville, N.Y.: Exposition Press, 1977. 216 p.

The story of a convicted felon, his escape from prison, and his subsequent adventures while at large. Partially set in Detroit and other Michigan locales.

MiBlo MiStc ScPT

1200 Reynolds, Jessie A.
In the Shade of the Oaks; a Story of Klinger Lake. White Pigeon: John J. Davis, n.d. 42 p.

A young Potawatomi girl long kept separated from the pioneer settlements by her father eventually marries and enters white society. Set at Klinger Lake in St. Joseph County.

Mi

1200A Richards, John 1951–
Working Stiff. Davis, Calif.: Hi Jinx Press, 1996. 224 p.

A humorous chronicle of a dysfunctional family in which the father, mother, daughter, and son take turns telling their individual stories. Set in Detroit.

MiAllG IC

1201 Richardson, Arleta 1923–
In Grandma's Attic. Elgin, Ill.: David C. Cook Publishing Co., 1974. 110 p.

(Grandma's Attic, no. 1)

When visiting her Grandma Mabel, a girl hears a series of interrelated stories about her grandmother's life and escapades as a little girl on a farm in the 1880s. Set in "West Branch."

Subtitle on cover: *Stories to Live, Love, Laugh & Learn by.*

A revised edition was published in 1994.

Juvenile.

MiBatW MiChe MiChv MiLapC OCl

1202 ———.
More Stories from Grandma's Attic. Elgin, Ill.: Chariot Books, 1979. 141 p.

(Grandma's Attic, no. 2)

More interrelated stories about farm life in the 1880s are told by Grandma Mabel to her granddaughter when she visits. Set in "West Branch."

Sequel to *In Grandma's Attic.*

A revised edition was published in 1994.

Juvenile.

MiBatW MiChe MiChv MiLapC MiSaS

1203 ———.
Still More Stories from Grandma's Attic. Elgin, Ill.: Chariot Books, 1980. 157 p.

(Grandma's Attic, no. 3)

Still more interrelated stories about Grandma Mabel's life and humorous events and adventures that took place on a farm when she was a little girl. Set in "West Branch" in the 1880s.

Sequel to *More Stories from Grandma's Attic.*

A revised edition was published in 1994.

Juvenile.

MiBatW MiChe MiLapC MiMtp OCl

1204 ———.

Treasures from Grandma. Elgin, Ill.: Chariot Books, 1984. 160 p.

(Grandma's Attic, no. 4)

Thirteen-year-old Mabel O'Dell has a number of adventures with her friend Sarah Jane at home and at school. Set in "West Branch" in 1886 and 1887.

A revised edition was published in 1994.

Juvenile.

MiChe MiChv MiLapC OCl OCo

1205 ———.

Sixteen and Away from Home. Elgin, Ill.: Chariot Books, 1985. 159 p.

(Grandma's Attic, no. 5)

Graduating from the district school, Mabel and her friend Sarah Jane attend the academy in town and have new experiences. Set in "West Branch" in 1889 and 1890.

Sequel to *Treasures from Grandma.*

Later published under the title *Away from Home.*

Juvenile.

MiChe MiChv MiEM MiLapC MiSaS

1206 ———.

Eighteen and on Her Own. Elgin, Ill.: Chariot Books, 1986. 173 p.

(Grandma's Attic, no. 6)

Eighteen-year-old Mabel O'Dell is accepted as a new teacher in another town, and her first year brings worries as well as a marriage proposal. Set in "North Branch" in 1891.

Sequel to *Sixteen and Away from Home.*

Later published under the title *A School of Her Own.*

Juvenile.

MiChe MiChv MiLapC MiSaS OCl

1207 ———.

Nineteen and Wedding Bells Ahead. Elgin, Ill.: Chariot Books, 1987. 156 p.

(Grandma's Attic, no. 7)

As Mabel begins her second year of teaching, she must board at the town busybody's house, and she becomes engaged to a young man. Set in "North Branch" in 1892 and 1893.

Sequel to *Eighteen and on Her Own.*

Later published under the title *Wedding Bells Ahead.*

Juvenile.

MiChe MiChv MiLapC MiSaS OCl

1208 ———.

At Home in North Branch. Elgin, Ill.: Chariot Books, 1988. 176 p.

(Grandma's Attic, no. 8)

Mabel settles down to married life with her minister husband, but the new shingle mill owner and his young daughter bring trouble to town. Set in "North Branch."

Sequel to *Nineteen and Wedding Bells Ahead.*

Juvenile.

MiAllG MiChe MiChv MiSaS MiLapC

1209 ———.
New Faces, New Friends. Elgin, Ill.: Chariot Books, 1989. 171 p.

(Grandma's Attic, no. 9)

Mabel must deal with hurtful town gossip when the minister of a neighboring church seems to take special interest in her. Set in "North Branch" in 1895.

Sequel to *At Home in North Branch.*

Juvenile.

MiAllG MiBatW MiChe MiChv OCl

1210 ———.
Stories from the Growing Years. Elgin, Ill.: Chariot Books, 1991. 128 p.

(Grandma's Attic, no. 10)

The early years of Mabel's marriage and the arrival of her children are detailed as is the town's development. Set in "North Branch" in the late 1890s.

Sequel to *New Faces, New Friends.*

Juvenile.

MiAllG MiBatW MiChe MiMtp MiSaS

1211 ———.
The Grandma's Attic Storybook. Elgin, Ill.: David C. Cook Publishing Co., 1993. 256 p.

(Grandma's Attic, no. 12)

Grandma Mabel continues telling her granddaughter stories of growing up on a farm with her friend Sarah Jane. Set in "West Branch" in the 1880s.

Juvenile.

MiAllG MiSaS InFw InBlo MoIM

1212 ———.
A Day at the Fair. Elgin, Ill.: Chariot Books, 1995. 32 p.

(Grandma's Attic, no. 15)

Six-year-old Mabel is annoyed when her father takes time for prayers before leaving for the fair, but learns their importance when she is lost. Set in "West Branch."

Originally published as a chapter titled "When Grandma Needed Prayer" in *More Stories from Grandma's Attic.*

Juvenile picture book.

MiAllG MiLac InFw OXe WLac

1213 [Richardson, John] 1796–1852
Wacousta; or, The Prophecy: A Tale of the Canadas by the author of "Ecarte." London: T. Cadell, 1832. 3 vols.

A renegade Englishman allied with Pontiac seeks revenge on the daughter of the woman he could not have. Set in Detroit and Michilimackinac in 1763.

A revised edition was published as *Wacousta; or, The Prophecy. An Indian Tale* (New York: DeWitt & Davenport, 1851).

Black, 226.

MiD MiU MH TxU-Hu

1214 ———.
The Canadian Brothers; or, The Prophecy Fulfilled. A Tale of the Late American War. Montreal: A. H. Armour and H. Ramsay, 1840. 2 vols.

During the War of 1812, two Canadian brothers in the British army take part in the attack on Fort Detroit and become involved with a mysterious woman and events that occurred during Pontiac's siege in 1763.

The first American edition, somewhat abridged, was published as *Matilda Mongomerie; or, The Prophecy Fulfilled. A Tale of the Late American War. Being the Sequel to "Wacousta"* (New York: Dewitt & Davenport, 1851).

Sequel to *Wacousta; or, The Prophecy: A Tale of the Canadas.*

Black, 225.

MiEM MH MWA N OKentU

1215 Riddle, Albert Gallatin 1816–1902
The Tory's Daughter; a Romance of the North-West, 1812–1813. New York: G. P. Putnam's Sons, 1888. 385 p.

A loyalist displaced during the American Revolution plans revenge by plotting with the British and Tecumseh (1768–1813) in the War of 1812. Partially set in Detroit and the Raisin River area.

Black, 227. Wright III, 4541.

MiD MiMarqN MiMtpT MnU ViU

1216 Rietveld, Jane 1913–
Great Lakes Sailor. New York: Viking Press, 1952. 188 p.

A twelve-year-old signs on as a cabin boy in a schooner and sails from Milwaukee to Buffalo in 1844. Partly set in Michigan waters, including Saginaw Bay.

Juvenile.

Mi MiD MiGr MiPet MiYEM

1217 Riley, Henry Hiram 1813–1888
Puddleford, and Its People. New York: Samuel Hueston, 1854. 269 p.

A series of connected satirical sketches about the inhabitants and environs of

a small town, "Puddleford" (Constantine), in St. Joseph County.

Wright II, 2043.

Mi MiD MiEM MiKW MiU

1218 ———.
The Puddleford Papers; or, Humors of the West. New York: Derby & Jackson; Cincinnati: H. W. Derby & Co., 1857. 353 p.

An additional five chapters are added to the author's previous book of satirical sketches about "Puddleford" (Constantine) in St. Joseph County.

Black, 228. Streeter, 2044. Wright II, 2044.

Mi MiAllG MiDU MiDW MiEM

1219 Riordan, John J. 1894–
The Dark Peninsula. AuTrain, Mich.: Avery Color Studios, 1976. 109 p.

In 1885, an eighteen-year-old travels to the lumber boomtown of Seney in the Upper Peninsula and has a number of adventures in the logging camps.

Mi MiAllG MiGay MiHM MiMtpT-C

1220 Riordan, Robert
Medicine for Wildcat. A Life Story About Samuel Charles Mazzuchelli, O.P. Milwaukee: Bruce Publishing Co., 1956. 178 p.

A fictionalized biography of the Dominican missionary Mazzuchelli (1806–1864) while in the Wisconsin Territory. Eighteen pages are set on Mackinac Island and in St. Ignace in 1830.

Juvenile.

Mi MiAdS MiMtpT-C IRivfR WPlaU

1221 **Risk, James Nicholas**
And Then There Was Me. New York: Carlton Press, 1969. 95 p.

The grim story of a young man's gradual but inexorable gravitation toward a life of crime and its results. Partially set in Detroit in the 1930s.

MiD

1222 **Risseeuw, Pieter Johannes** 1901–
Landverhuizers. Baarn, Netherlands: Bosch & Keuning N.V., 1946. 2 vols.

A chronicle of Dutch immigrants in America and of particularly significant incidents in their settlements in Michigan and Iowa.

Volume One is entitled *Vrijheid en Brood;* Volume Two is entitled *De Huilende Wildernis.*

In Dutch.

MiGrC MiHolH MiU IaOcN IaPeC

1223 ————.
Ik Worstel en Ontkom. Baarn: Bosch & Keuning N.V., 1959. 252 p.

A fictionalized narrative of Dutch settlers in the Holland area from 1852 to 1876 based on factual accounts and memoirs.

This sequel to *Landverhuizers* was reissued as the third part to *Landverhuizers* when these two titles were published as a trilogy.

In Dutch.

MiHolH

1224 **Risteen, Herbert L.**
Tomahawk Trail. New York: Cupples & Leon Co., 1948. 221 p.

(Indian Stories for Boys, no. 3)

In 1763, a sixteen-year-old boy discovers Pontiac's plan to capture Detroit and helps defend the fort after alerting the garrison.

Juvenile.

Mi MiWar DeU OKentU WEU

1225 **Ritz, David** 1943–
Family Blood. New York: Donald I. Fine, 1991. 321 p.

Two criminal and gangster families struggle to control the lucrative music entertainment business from the 1940s to the present. Twenty-two pages are set in Detroit.

1226 **Roat, Ronald Clair**
Close Softly the Doors. Brownsville, Oreg.: Story Line Press, 1991. 148 p.

(Stuart Mallory Mystery)

Private investigator Stuart Mallory helps a former girlfriend escape her mobster boyfriend and becomes involved in murder. Set in Lansing and "Hamlin" (Ludington).

Mystery.

1227 ————.
A Still and Icy Silence. Brownsville, Oreg.: Story Line Press, 1993. 325 p.

(Stuart Mallory Mystery)

Stuart Mallory investigates when an arsonist is incinerated and later discovers a connection with corrupt politicians. Set in Lansing and on Mackinac Island.

Mystery.

Mi MiAllG MiBir MiFli MiMtcM

1228 ————.
High Walk. Brownsville, Oreg.: Story Line Press, 1996. 246 p.

(Stuart Mallory Mystery)

Stuart Mallory tries to locate a missing ex-intelligence officer who is now a drug rehabilitation counselor and finds a puzzling situation. Set in Lansing and the Upper Peninsula.

Mystery.

Mi MiAllG MiD MiMtcM MiU

1229 Robbins, Harold 1916–1997
The Betsy. New York: Trident Press, 1971. 502 p.

A powerful pioneer automobile manufacturer struggles to regain control of his company from his ruthless grandson. Partially set in Detroit and Grosse Pointe.

1230 ———.
The Stallion. New York: Simon & Schuster, 1996. 364 p.

A renowned designer and racer illtreated by a powerful automobile manufacturing family vows to gain control of their company. Set in Detroit in 1972.

Sequel to *The Betsy.*

1231 Roberts, Edith Kneipple 1902–1966
Tamarack. Indianapolis: Bobbs-Merrill Co., 1940. 368 p.

A former lumber town transformed to a summer resort is inhabited by petty and desperately unhappy people. Set in "Tamarack" in the Upper Peninsula along the Wisconsin border.

Black, 229.

Mi MiAllG MiDU MiMtpT MiU

1232 Roberts, Kenneth Lewis 1885–1957
Northwest Passage. Garden City, N.Y.: Doubleday, Doran & Co., 1937. 709 p.

The fictionalized adventures of Major Robert Rogers (1731–1795) during the French and Indian War, and his subsequent governorship of Michilimackinac from 1766 to 1767.

Black, 230.

Roberts, Peggy, pseud. *see* Hanchar, Peggy S.

1233 Roberts, Willo Davis 1928–
Murder at Grand Bay. New York: Arcadia House, 1955. 220 p.

A young woman visits her widowed friend and, upon arrival, finds that an accident has occurred that is soon followed by murder. Set in "Grand Bay" on Lake Superior.

Mystery.

MiGr CS IChamL ScCoR WRac

1234 ———.
Murder Is So Easy. Fresno, Calif.: Vega Books, 1961. 157 p.

While visiting her fiancé's family, a young woman becomes dangerously involved in a mystery surrounding a little girl. Set in "Cherry Point," north of Traverse City.

Mystery.

Copy not located.

1235 ———.
The Nurses. New York: Ace Books, 1972. 288 p.

The triumphs, tragedies, and romances of six nurses are recounted following their arrival at a hospital in the northern Lake Michigan resort city of "Bay View."

Romance.

MiGr-L MnManTD NBuBE OBgU PNo

1236 ———.
Nurse Robin. New York: Lenox Hill Press, 1973. 192 p.

When his niece leaves her hospital job to take care of him, an old man expects her to marry a handsome doctor. Set in "Grand Bay" on Lake Superior.

Romance.

MiOt MiPh MiWar IP InB

1237 ———.
The Gallant Spirit. New York: Popular
Library, 1982. 511 p.

In 1852, a young girl leaves Grand
Haven with her family for Beaver Island when her father, after hearing
James Strang (1813–1856) preach, is
converted to the Mormon faith.

MiAllG MiGr MiMani MiNop IGenD

1238 ———.
Twisted Summer. New York: Atheneum
Books for Young Readers, 1996. 156 p.

A teenage girl returning to a cottage
with her family learns that a friend's
brother has been convicted of murder
and attempts to learn the truth. Set at
Crystal Lake.

Juvenile.

1239 Robertson, Keith Carlton 1914–
1991
In Search of a Sandhill Crane. New
York: Viking Press, 1973. 201 p.

A fifteen-year-old New York boy
spends two weeks at his aunt's re-
mote cabin in the Upper Peninsula and
learns to appreciate wildlife. Set near
Germfask.

Juvenile.

Robeson, Kenneth, pseud. *see* Dent, Lester
and Hathway, Alan

1240 Robinson, John Hovey 1825?–
1867
*Whitelaw; or, Nattie of the Lakeshore.
A Tale of the Ten Mile Trace* by Dr. J.
H. Robinson. New York: Frederic A.
Brady, 1861. 83 p.

A young man searches for gold and becomes involved with villainous copper
miners and the kidnapping of a beautiful young woman. Set in the Upper
Peninsula.

Wright II, 2088.

CtY ICN

1241 Rockwood, Roy, pseud.
*Dave Dashaway and His Hydroplane;
or, Daring Adventures Over the Great
Lakes.* New York: Cupples & Leon,
1913. 202 p.

(Dave Dashaway, no. 2)

A young aviator and his companion
foil a group of villains who planned to
steal a lucrative biplane contract. Set in
"Columbus" on Lake Michigan.

"Roy Rockwood" is a Stratemeyer
Syndicate pseudonym.

Juvenile.

MiAllG MiEM CtHT MWelC OAU

1242 Rodger, Esca G. 1883–1967
Year of Bitterness. N.p., 1974. 280 p.

A man realizes that he has gone into the
wrong work and perhaps married the
wrong woman. Set in "Myra" (Elmira)
in 1891.

One hundred copies were printed in
Japan for limited family distribution.

Mi MiBoy MiCenl MiEaj

1242A Rood, David A. 1926–1996
Onward and Upward in Upper Inwood,
by Dave Rood, Sr. N.p., 1995. 110 p.

A newspaper editor makes humorous
observations about his small town and
its inhabitants in a series of connected
vignettes. Set in "Upper Inwood" and
Steuben in the Upper Peninsula.

MiAllG MiU

1243 Rose, James A.

A Boy's Vacation on the Great Lakes. Providence: E. L. Freeman & Co., 1880. 216 p.

A fourteen-year-old boy and his friend take a summer trip through the Great Lakes. Set partially in Detroit, Lake Huron, Sault Ste. Marie, and Lake Superior.

Juvenile.

Mi MiD MiMtpT-C ICU OBgU

Ross, Betsey, pseud. *see* Braden, Jenness Mae

1244 Ross, Margaret Isabel

Kaga's Brother. A Story of the Chippewas. New York: Harper & Brothers, 1936. 221 p.

In 1826, a young man joins an expedition and, with his Ojibwa friend, helps defend the party from rival traders. Partially set in Sault Ste. Marie and on the Ontonagon River.

Juvenile.

Mi MiAllG MiChv MiHM MiWar

1245 ——.

Morgan's Fourth Son. New York: Harper & Brothers, 1940. 252 p.

A farmer hopes that his disinterested youngest son will develop a love for the land and become a farmer like himself. Set in the Grand Traverse area.

Juvenile.

MiAllG MiEM MiFliL ISS OCl

1246 ——.

A Farm in the Family. New York: Harper & Brothers, 1943. 261 p.

Financial setbacks send a family to a run-down farm left to them in a will, and they eventually make a go of it.

Set in "Cedar Falls" in north central Michigan.

Juvenile.

MiAllG IC IaDm OCl WM

1247 Rossi, Bruno, pseud.

Mafia Death Watch. New York: Leisure Books, 1975. 188 p.

(Sharpshooter Series)

When Johnny Rock, the "sharpshooter," is informed that the Mafia murdered a young prostitute because she wanted to leave the business, he sets out to eliminate those responsible. Set in Detroit.

Mystery.

MiGr-L.

1247A Rothstein, Margaret 1936?–

And Other Foolish Questions I Have Answered. Ann Arbor: Arbor Publications, 1979. 212 p.

The fictionalized reminiscences of a young woman's experiences teaching in Michigan public schools and her relationships with students and fellow teachers.

MiDW MiGrA MiMtpT MiU MiYEM

1248 Routsong, Alma 1924–

A Gradual Joy. Boston: Houghton Mifflin Co., 1953. 199 p.

Two unlikely people from the armed services marry and, while attending Michigan State University in East Lansing, gradually adjust to their new lives.

Black, 231.

Mi MiAllG MiCad MiD MiKW

1249 Rowe, Viola 1903–1969
A Way with Boys. New York: Longmans, Green and Co., 1957. 182 p.

A teenage girl spends the summer at her grandparent's farm as four different boys vie for her friendship. Set at "Cloverleaf Lake" in Newaygo County.

Juvenile.

MiAllG MiDW MiGr MiRog IC

Rubin, Harold *see* Robbins, Harold

1250 Rundel, Clarabelle Eberle
Sweet Liberty. Detroit: Cartwright, Mueller, Benjamin & Robison, 1944. 157 p.

A matriarch pulls her family through many difficult times and discusses the sacrifices that need to be made to defend liberty. Set in Detroit from 1941 to 1943.

Mi MiD MiGr MiKW MiMack

1251 Rupprecht, Olivia
Behind Closed Doors. New York: Bantam Books, 1991. 177 p.

(Loveswept, no. 496)

Grieving over the death of his wife, an automotive designer is shocked to learn that his sister-in-law is carrying his child via artificial insemination. Set in Detroit.

Romance.

MiAllG MoK OBgU OXe WMani

1252 Rutledge, Caleb Hobson 1855–
"Flashes from the Furnace." Mohawk, Mich.: Keweenaw Printing Co., 1912. 221 p.

A controversial preacher is assigned to a run-down town and begins a campaign against the local saloons and gambling trade. Set in "Pedukah" in the Upper Peninsula.

Black, 232.

Mi MiAllG MiD MiMtpT-C NSyU

S

Sanda, pseud. *see* Stowers, Walter H.

1253 Sandburg, Helga 1918–
Measure My Love. New York: McDowell, Obolensky, 1959. 180 p.

The strength of a young woman's love for her fruit-farmer husband is tested by adversity and by a variety of relatives. Set in southwestern Michigan.

Black, 233.

1254 ——.
The Owl's Roost. New York: Dial Press, 1962. 308 p.

The story of a family's two summers at a Lake Michigan cottage and the summer resort residents' tragedies and desires. Set in "Pokagon" (Harbert).

Black, 234.

1255 ——.
Blueberry. New York: Dial Press, 1963. 158 p.

Fourteen-year-old Kristin convinces her parents that she is capable of caring for a horse, Blueberry. Set in southwestern Michigan near Lake Michigan.

Juvenile.

1256 ——.
Gingerbread. New York: Dial Press, 1964. 192 p.

Kristin's horse has a foal named Gingerbread, and both Kristin and the new horse have growing-up troubles. Set in southwestern Michigan near Lake Michigan.

Sequel to *Blueberry*.

Juvenile.

Mi MiAdC MiCad MiStc MiWar

1257 Santalo, Lois

The Wind Dies at Sunrise. Indianapolis: Bobbs-Merrill Co., 1965. 209 p.

The story of two girls and their friendship over the period of a few years. Set at the "Windswept Dunes" resort in southwestern Michigan and "Titchipaw City" (Petoskey?).

Juvenile.

Mi IC INS InFw KyFSC

1258 Santiago, V. J.

Detroit: Dead End Delivery. New York: Pinnacle Books, 1976. 179 p.

(The Vigilante, no. 5)

A man who swore revenge when his wife was murdered is asked by a friend to look into a security leak at an automobile engine development company. Set in Detroit.

Mystery.

MiAllG

Sapir, Richard, joint author *see* Murphy, Warren B.

1259 Savage, Marc 1945–

The Light Outside. New York: Harper & Row, 1976. 202 p.

A man just released from a three-year term in prison for refusing to be inducted into the army tries to find his cousin in New York. The first twenty-six pages are set in Michigan.

MiSf MiU InAnd OCl WU

Sayler, Harry Lincoln *see* Stuart, Gordon, pseud.

1260

Scenes on Lake Huron; a Tale, Interspersed with Interesting Facts, in a Series of Letters. By a North American. Lake Mariners, Listen to This Tale. New York: Published for the Author by G. W. & A. J. Matsell, 1836. 139 p.

A fictionalized travel narrative of the anonymous author's 1822 trip by schooner from Green Bay to Detroit, including visits to Michilimackinac, Thunder Bay, and Presque Isle.

A. J. Matsell has been suggested as the author.

Black, 198 and 235. Streeter, 6151.

Mi MiAllG MiD MiMtpT-C MiU

Scharf, Marian F., joint author *see* Carroll, Marisa, pseud.

1261 Scheck, Wilson 1919–

The Boardman Valley; an Autobiographical Novel. Los Angeles: Crescent Publications, 1978. 95 p.

The fictionalized reminiscences concerning the author's boyhood on his parents' farm. Set near South Boardman in Kalkaska County from the 1920s to 1930.

MiT

1262 Schenkel, Shirley E. 1938–

In Blacker Moments; a Kate and Ray Fredrick Mystery by S. E. Schenkel. Seattle: aka/Seattle, 1994. 266 p.

A chief of detectives investigates a deliberate hit-and-run attack on his wife's friend, a nun, that leads to a forty-year-old double murder. Set in "Tanglewood."

Mystery.

SCENES

ON

LAKE HURON;

A TALE;

INTERSPERSED WITH

INTERESTING FACTS,

IN A

SERIES OF LETTERS.

———

BY

A NORTH AMERICAN.

———

LAKE MARINERS, LISTEN TO THIS TALE.

—:::✸:::—

NEW-YORK:
PUBLISHED FOR THE AUTHOR,
AND FOR SALE AT MOST OF THE BOOKSTORES,
THROUGHOUT THE UNITED STATES.
1836.

1263 Schermerhorn, James 1897–1956

On the Campus Freshman by James Schermerhorn, Jr. New York: Dodd, Mead and Co., 1925. 237 p.

A talented freshman football player is suspected of throwing a game and tries to clear himself. Set at "Dexter University" (University of Michigan) in "Dexter" (Ann Arbor).

Juvenile.

Mi MiEM CL MnU

1264 ———.

The Phantom Ship by James (Coach) Schermerhorn, Jr. New York: Cupples & Leon Co., 1936. 202 p.

A college football coach is asked by one of his former players to help with his training in Florida. Twenty pages are set at "Dexter University" (University of Michigan) in "Dexter" (Ann Arbor).

Juvenile.

MiAllG FTS OBgU ViU WEU

Schmock, Helen H. *see* Cloutier, Helen H.

1265 Schoolland, Marian Margaret 1902–1984

A Land I Will Show Thee. Grand Rapids: Wm. B. Eerdmans Publishing Co., 1949. 237 p.

A story of the 1849 founding of the pioneer Dutch settlement at Holland by Albertus Van Raalte (1811–1876) and the hardships encountered there.

Black, 236.

Mi MiAllG MiD MiKW MiMtpT

1266 Schrader, Leonard

Blue Collar. New York: Bantam Books, 1978. 149 p.

Three debt-ridden autoworkers break in to their union headquarters to steal money but find evidence of corruption instead. Set in Detroit.

Based on the motion picture screenplay by Paul and Leonard Schrader.

MiGr MiGrC CtS NbLL NBuBE

1267 ———.

Hardcore. New York: Warner Books, 1979. 174 p.

A man journeys to Los Angeles in search of his runaway daughter and is shocked to find her performing in pornographic films. Partially set in Grand Rapids.

Based on the motion picture screenplay by Paul Schrader.

MiGr MiGrC CL NBuBE PNo

1268 Schreiber, Joseph 1969–

Next of Kin. New York: G. P. Putnam's Sons, 1994. 228 p.

A fourteen-year-old boy is kidnapped by a disturbed young woman claiming to be his sister and is delivered to an old man. Set in various unnamed Michigan locales.

Mystery.

1269 Schwemm, Diane

Summer Love. New York: Bantam Books, 1995. 217 p.

(Silver Beach, no. 1)

Sixteen-year-old Elli and her brother Ethan travel to their grandparents' Lake Michigan cottage and find summer romance. Set at "Silver Beach" in northwestern Michigan.

Juvenile.

MiBlo IC MnM OCl WM

1270 ———.

Summer Lies. New York: Bantam Books, 1995. 218 p.

(Silver Beach, no. 2)

Elli and Ethan return to their grandparents' cottage a second summer and continue summer romances from the previous year. Set at "Silver Beach" in northwestern Michigan.

Sequel to *Summer Love.*

Juvenile.

MiGr-L IC MnM OCl WM

1271 ———.

Summer Promises. New York: Bantam Books, 1995. 214 p.

(Silver Beach, no. 3)

Spending their third summer at their grandparents' cottage, Elli and Ethan discover the meaning of love in their relationships. Set at "Silver Beach" in northwestern Michigan.

Sequel to *Summer Lies.*

Juvenile.

MiGr-L IC IChamL OCl WM

1272 **[Scoppettone, Sandra]** 1936–

Donato & Daughter by Jack Early [pseud.]. New York: E. P. Dutton, 1988. 341 p.

Two New York police officers, father and daughter, investigate the murders of four nuns and must also deal with personal problems. Ten pages are set in Grand Haven.

Mystery.

1273 **Scott, Mary Semple**

Crime Hound. New York: Charles Scribner's Sons, 1940. 254 p.

An assistant D.A. from St. Louis stumbles on a murder made to look accidental and assists the local sheriff. Set in "Brantford," 200 miles north of Manistee.

Mystery.

Mi AzPh CLU NhD ViBlbV

1274 **Seager, Allan** 1906–1968

The Inheritance. New York: Simon and Schuster, 1948. 337 p.

A young man tries to deal with his discovery that his late father, whom he admired, was hated by everyone in town. Set in "Athens" (Adrian).

Black, 240.

Mi MiAdC MiAllG MiD MiKW

1275 ———.

Amos Berry. New York: Simon and Schuster, 1953. 376 p.

When a son investigates his late father's life, he discovers his father, a successful executive, committed a murder that went unsolved. Set in Lenawee County.

Black, 238.

Mi MiAdC MiAllG MiD MiMtpT-C

1276 ———.

Hilda Manning. New York: Simon and Schuster, 1956. 312 p.

A young farm wife poisons her much older husband, either as a mercy-killing or because the marriage was already dead. Set in "Oakville" in Lenawee County.

Black, 239.

Mi MiAllG MiD MiKW MiMtpT-C

1277 ———.

Death of Anger. New York: McDowell, Obolensky, 1960. 213 p.

A businessman leaves his hateful wife and goes to Europe with a young nurse, and when the affair ends, he returns to his unhappy life. Set partially in southeastern Michigan.

Mi MiAdS MiAllG MiKW MiU

1278 Searight, Richard F. 1902–1975
Wild Empire. Laurium, Mich.: Iroquois Press, 1994. 238 p.

At the beginning of the copper boom in the 1840s, a middle-aged adventurer and gambler from Boston comes to the Keweenaw Peninsula. Set mostly in Copper Harbor and Houghton.

Subtitle on cover: *A Copper Rush Adventure in Michigan's Copper Country.*

MiAllG MiEM MiHM MiKW MiMtpT-C

1278A Sechrist, Berniece Sargent
Big Enough. Syracuse, Ind.: Nonpareil Press, 1955. 142 p.

A seven-year-old Detroit girl makes friends with a gypsy boy in school and, because of her violin virtuosity, is kidnapped by his mother and forced to join the caravan.

Juvenile.

MiGr-L

1279 Seemeyer, Ted 1904–
The Blond Eaglet; a Love Romance of Old Detroit. New York: Vantage Press, 1989. 60 p.

An Austrian immigrant is rescued from the Detroit River by a Native-American servant and is nursed back to health by a beautiful French girl. Set on Belle Isle in 1854.

MiBir

1280 Seese, June Akers 1935–
What Waiting Really Means. Elmwood Park, Ill.: Dalkey Archive Press, 1990. 88 p.

A middle-aged woman reflects on her life, the people whom she knows, and her desires and accomplishments. Set partially in Detroit.

MiAllG MiAlp MiEM MiSf MiU

1281 ———.
Is This What Other Women Feel Too? Elmwood Park, Ill.: Dalkey Archive Press, 1991. 151 p.

The story of a young woman and her life in the 1950s and 1960s told through dialogue, diary entries, and letters. Partially set in Detroit.

1282 [Seid, Ruth] 1913–1995
Anna Teller by Jo Sinclair [pseud.]. New York: David McKay Co., 1960. 596 p.

A son recalls the life of his seventy-four-year-old mother who is coming from Hungary to live with him. Set in Detroit and Ann Arbor.

1283 Senical, Pearl 1903–
Where the Heart Is. Philadelphia: Dorrance & Co., 1955. 277 p.

A young woman from a poor background falls in love with a handsome society man. Set in the Upper Peninsula mining town of "Irontown" from the 1920s to the 1950s.

MiMarq DLC

1284 Seno, William J.
Enemies: A Saga of the Great Lakes Wilderness. Madison, Wis.: Prairie Oak Press, 1993. 222 p.

A saga of the Great Lakes fur trade and the Canadian Alexander Henry (1739–1824). Set at Fort Michilimackinac from 1761 to 1763 where he survived the massacre of the garrison by Pontiac's warriors.

MiEmp WKen WLacU WMani WS

1285 Serbinski, Jerry
Minetown. N.p., 1992. 304 p.

The story of a group of immigrant miners at home and at work, including the labor union unrest they encounter. Set at "Coppertown" (Houghton?) in the 1920s.

MiHM   MiMtpT-C

1286 Sessions, Ellen Sue
Jennifer's True Love. New York: Avalon Books, 1996. 186 p.

(Avalon Career Romance)

Her heart broken by an egotist, a young librarian finds herself attracted to the same sort of man again. Set in "Old Pine Woods" on Lake Michigan in northwestern Michigan.

Romance.

Severance, Anne, ed. *see* Winters, Donna M.

1287 Severance, Henry Ormal 1867–1942
Michigan Trailmakers. Ann Arbor: George Wahr, 1930. 164 p.

A fictionalized account of the arrival of the author's New York and New England relatives, and their settlement of Oakland County from the 1830s to 1899.

Black, 241.

Mi   MiAllG   MiD   MiMtpT-C   MiU

1288 Seymour, Tres
The Gulls of the Edmund Fitzgerald. New York: Orchard Books, 1996. 32 p.

A young boy is dissuaded from wading into Lake Superior by a group of seagulls who tell him of shipwrecks and the sinking of the *Edmund Fitzgerald.*

Juvenile picture book.

MiAllG   MiCad   MiFra   MiHolH   MiT

1289 Shapiro, Joan Bonner
Hello, Love. New York: Zebra Books, 1993. 478 p.

(To Love Again)

A widow and widower from two different families argue about who gets custody of their granddaughter. Partially set in Grosse Pointe and Detroit.

Romance.

MiAllG   MiMtcM   OCl   OXe   WLac

1290 ———.
Daniel. Bensalem, Pa.: Meteor Publishing Corp., 1993. 219 p.

(Kismet Romance, no. 151)

A gruff Detroit surgeon meets a young divorced pharmacist in a small town and they have trouble in their relationship. Set in "Pecomish Springs" in northwestern Michigan.

Romance.

MiGr-L   MW   NjMlA   WM

1291 ———.
Sweets to the Sweet. New York: Zebra Books, 1994. 509 p.

(To Love Again)

Having difficulty adjusting to the death of her husband, a middle-aged woman takes a trip to New Hampshire and buys a bakery. Set partially in Bloomfield Hills.

Romance.

MiAllG   MiD   IChamL   OCl   WM

1292 Sheldon, Electa Maria Bronson
1817–1902

The Clevelands: Showing the Influence of a Christian Family in a New Settlement by Mrs. E. M. Sheldon. Boston: American Tract Society, 1860. 87 p.

Financial setbacks cause a family to move from New York to Michigan, and they bring with them their Christian ideals. Set in "Smithton" in the early 1800s.

MiD FTS IHi OAU RPB

1293 Sheldon, Sidney 1917–

A Stranger in the Mirror. New York: William Morrow and Co., 1976. 321 p.

The story of the rise of a comedian from his start in New York to his eventual Hollywood stardom in the 1950s. The first twenty-eight pages are set in Detroit.

1294 Sherman, Harold Morrow 1898–1987

Beyond the Dog's Nose by Harold M. Sherman ("Edward J. Morrow"). New York: D. Appleton and Co., 1927. 231 p.

Three boys visit a reclusive uncle and find a network of mysterious caves that they explore for treasure. Set near "Bean Blossom" on Lake Michigan.

Juvenile.

DLC OBgU

1295 ———.

Hit and Run! New York: Grosset & Dunlap, 1929. 248 p.

(Home Run Series)

Two gangs of boys carry on their personal rivalries by vying for positions on the local high school baseball team. Set in "Prescott" (Traverse City).

Juvenile.

Mi CLS FTS InHam PWcS

1296 ———.

Flashing Steel. New York: Grosset & Dunlap, 1929. 264 p.

(Buddy Books for Boys, no. 24)

A Michigan high school's national champion ice hockey team plays a Canadian team for the world title. The second half of the book deals with the school's basketball season. Partially set in "Yankville."

Juvenile.

MiAllG InNd KyU MH OBgU

1297 ———.

Batter Up! A Story of American Legion Junior Baseball. New York: Grosset & Dunlap, 1930. 304 p.

(Home Run Series)

The story of the formation of an American Legion baseball team in Traverse City and its progress, games against local teams, and attempt to qualify for the national championship.

Juvenile.

MiAllG MiOC GVaS OBgU PWcS

1298 [Shoemaker, Sarah Elizabeth Wolf] 1936–

Long Chain of Death by Sarah Wolf [pseud.]. New York: Walker & Co., 1987. 282 p.

Suspected of his wife's murder, a man discovers a pattern of mysterious deaths that have occurred over a period of years. Partially set in Ann Arbor and on the Leelanau Peninsula.

Mystery.

1299 Shriber, Ione Sandberg 1911–1987

Murder Well Done. New York: Farrar and Rinehart, 1941. 307 p.

The murder of an old woman, presumably for her fortune, places her three grandchildren under suspicion. Set on "Shorehaven," an island in northern Lake Michigan.

Mystery.

MiAllG CL IaAS MBU NcGU

1300 Shurtleff, Lillian Lorraine
Love and Fate Ride the Griffon II. N.p., 1979. 465 p.

On the voyage from France through the Great Lakes, a woman's husband is drowned, and she must face life alone. Set on Mackinac Island from 1833 to 1838.

Mi MiAllG MiAlp MiMtpT-C MiPetN

1301 Simonson, Ina Kokko
O Chieftain, O Pontiac. Cook, Minn.: CNH Publishing Co., 1984. 160 p.

A fictitious and fanciful version of the Ottawa chief's life. Set partially at "Fort Allouez" on Lake Huron and in Detroit from 1754 to 1769.

Mi MiAllG MnVA MnVM

Sinclair, Jo, pseud. *see* Seid, Ruth

1302 Sinclair, Upton Beall 1878–1968
The Flivver King; a Story of Ford-America. Detroit: United Automobile Workers of America, 1937. 119 p.

A fictionalized account of the beginnings and rise of the Ford Motor Company, and the effects of industrialization on one family. Set in Detroit from 1892 to the 1930s.

1303 Skillman, Trish Macdonald
Buried Secrets. New York: Dell Publishing, 1995. 407 p.

A destitute single mother is left a trust fund and a house by an unknown benefactor, and soon suspects deception. Mostly set at "Trumpeter Lake" in southwestern Michigan.

Mystery.

MiAllG IC InBlo OBgU OCl

1304 Skinner, George Wallace
The Axe-Thrower of the Tittabawassee. Weidman, Mich.: Roe Printing Co., 1935. 176 p.

A nineteen-year-old from Detroit finds a job in a lumber camp and encounters danger, murder, revenge, and a beautiful woman. Set on the Tittabawassee River in the mid-1880s.

Black, 243.

MiAllG MiCor MiD MiOw MiU

1305 Skinner, Henrietta Channing Dana 1857–1928
Heart and Soul. New York: Harper & Brothers, 1901. 307 p.

An aging man of French heritage recalls his past, including his involvement in the Underground Railroad, business concerns, and romance in Detroit society from the 1850s to 1900.

Black, 244.

Mi CU FTaSU GAuA TxArU

1306 Slobodkin, Florence Gersh 1905–
Too Many Mittens by Florence and Louis Slobodkin. New York: Vanguard Press, 1958. 28 p.

When one twin loses his red mitten, word gets around the neighborhood, and soon people are bringing single mittens to his house. Set in an unnamed Michigan town.

Juvenile picture book.

Slobodkin, Louis, joint author *see* Slobodkin, Florence Gersh

1307 **Slote, Alfred H.** 1926–
Denham Proper. New York: G. P. Putnam's Sons, 1953. 313 p.

A young man tries to rebel against his upper-class New York background and family traditions. Thirty-six pages are set in Ann Arbor at the University of Michigan in the 1920s.

MiD MiU IC InFw OCl

1308 ———.
Stranger on the Ball Club. Philadelphia: J. B. Lippincott Co., 1970. 172 p.

A new boy in town wins a place on a little league team but alienates his teammates with his temper and hostility. Set in "Arborville" (Ann Arbor).

Juvenile.

1309 ———.
Jake. Philadelphia: J. B. Lippincott Co., 1971. 155 p.

A self-confident eleven-year-old coaches his little league team, but it faces disqualification unless an adult is present. Set in "Arborville" (Ann Arbor).

Juvenile.

1310 ———.
The Biggest Victory. Philadelphia: J. B. Lippincott Co., 1972. 154 p.

Awkward and with little natural baseball ability, a boy prefers fishing but stays on his little league team to please his father. Set in "Arborville" (Ann Arbor).

Juvenile.

1311 ———.
My Father, the Coach. Philadelphia: J. B. Lippincott Co., 1972. 157 p.

A man who knows nothing about coaching agrees to be one so that his son and his friends can form a little league team. Set in "Arborville" (Ann Arbor).

Juvenile.

1312 ———.
Hang Tough, Paul Mather. Philadelphia: J. B. Lippincott Co., 1973. 156 p.

A boy stricken with leukemia cannot resist playing for his little league team, which further weakens him. Set in "Arborville" (Ann Arbor).

Juvenile.

1313 ———.
Tony and Me. Philadelphia: J. B. Lippincott Co., 1974. 156 p.

Homesick for California, a new boy in town finds a friend, who helps him improve his baseball skills. Set in "Arborville" (Ann Arbor).

Juvenile.

1314 ———.
Matt Gargan's Boy. Philadelphia: J. B. Lippincott Co., 1975. 158 p.

The star pitcher of a little league team copes with his parents' divorce and a girl who wants to join the team. Set in "Arborville" (Ann Arbor).

Juvenile.

1315 ———.
The Hotshot. New York: Franklin Watts, 1977. 87 p.

A bantam league hockey player wants to be picked for the all-city team, but he loses sight of the need for teamwork and lets his team down. Set in Ann Arbor.

Juvenile.

1316 ———.
Love and Tennis. New York: Macmillan Publishing Co., 1979. 163 p.

After defeating a nationally ranked tennis player, a fifteen-year-old boy faces the question of his own ambition. Set mostly in "Arborville" (Ann Arbor).

Juvenile.

1317 ———.
Rabbit Ears. New York: J. B. Lippincott, 1982. 110 p.

A talented fifteen-year-old pitcher loses his confidence when the other teams in the little league discover he can be rattled. Set in "Arborville" (Ann Arbor).

Juvenile.

1318 ———.
Moving In. New York: J. B. Lippincott, 1988. 167 p.

Unhappy with his family's recent move from Massachusetts, eleven-year-old Robby plans to have his father's business fail. Set in "Arborville" (Ann Arbor).

Juvenile.

1319 ———.
A Friend Like That. New York: J. B. Lippincott, 1988. 152 p.

Robby continues to miss his friends in Massachusetts, worries about his father, and finally decides to take the bus back to Boston. Set in "Arborville" (Ann Arbor).

Sequel to *Moving In*.

Juvenile.

1320 ———.
Make-Believe Ball Player. New York: J. B. Lippincott, 1989. 104 p.

A ten-year-old joins a little league team and, despite his propensity to daydream in the outfield, becomes a hero. Set in "Arborville" (Ann Arbor).

Juvenile.

1321 ———.
The Trading Game. New York: J. B. Lippincott, 1990. 200 p.

An eleven-year-old is willing to trade a 1952 Mickey Mantle baseball card from his father's collection for a card picturing his grandpa. Set in "Arborville" (Ann Arbor).

Juvenile.

1322 ———.
Finding Buck McHenry. New York: Harper Collins, 1991. 250 p.

An eleven-year-old finds a baseball card from the old Negro League and is certain that his school janitor is the man pictured on it. Set in "Arborville" (Ann Arbor).

Juvenile.

———, joint author **see** Garnet, A. H., pseud.

1323 **Smith, Alice Prescott**
Montlivet. Boston: Houghton, Mifflin and Co., 1906. 443 p.

A French trader falls in love with and rescues a beautiful Englishwoman. Set at Michilimackinac in the 1690s at the time when France and England were vying for control of North America.

Black, 246.

Mi   MiDW   MiU   MnU   OCl

1324 **Smith, Alice Ward**

Jess Edwards Rides Again. Boston: Christopher Publishing House, 1934. 145 p.

An unhappily married physician fakes his own suicide and becomes involved with the abolitionist movement. Set partially in Cassopolis in the 1850s.

Mi CLU LNX MsHaU OU

1325 **Smith, Bonnie Sours** 1942–

If You Love Me, Call Me Dorrie. Elgin, Ill.: Chariot Books, 1982. 132 p.

(Pennypincher Books)

Eleven-year-old Dorothy Whitfield is sent to live on a farm with her aunt when her widower father contracts tuberculosis. Set near Angell in Grand Traverse County.

Juvenile.

MiElk ArSsJ ICMB

1326 ———.

Dorrie and the Mystery of Angell Swamp. Elgin, Ill.: Chariot Books, 1984. 127 p.

(Pennypincher Books)

Still living with her aunt and uncle on a farm near Angell, fourteen-year-old Dorothy is curious about the new French teacher and the mysterious packages she receives.

Sequel to *If You Love Me, Call Me Dorrie.*

Juvenile.

MiGr-L AzG MnManTD ScSp

1327 ———.

A Dream for Dorrie. Elgin, Ill.: Chariot Books, 1985. 127 p.

(Pennypincher Books)

Dorothy, now a high school senior, wonders whether she should go into exciting missionary work with a handsome pilot or stay in the small town of Angell, which she has grown to love.

Sequel to *Dorrie and the Mystery of Angell Swamp.*

Juvenile.

DLC

1328 **Smith, Dinitia** 1945–

The Hard Rain. New York: Dial Press, 1980. 207 p.

A young radical from New York tries to organize auto workers and, when one of them is killed in an accident, plants a bomb. Set mostly in Detroit in the mid-1970s.

Smith, George Malcolm *see* Malcolm-Smith, George

1329 **Smith, Granville Paul** 1893–1947

Invincible Surmise. Boston: Houghton Mifflin Co., 1936. 353 p.

A man whose youth was warped by his parents' religious fanaticism seeks power and wealth, but is saved by a woman's love. Set in Detroit from the 1910s to the 1930s.

Black, 247.

Mi CLU MnM OBgU ScCleU

1330 **Smith, Hamilton**

The Forest Maid, a Tale. Written during the Spring of 1832, and Intended for Publication in the Lady's Book, But through Unavoidable Delay Never Offered to That Print. Penn-Yan, New York: H. Gilbert, 1832. 32 p.

When a young woman's betrothed is supposedly murdered while on a journey, she becomes deranged and

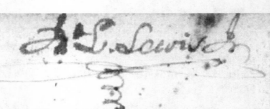

THE FOREST MAID,

A TALE.

Written during the Spring of 1832, and intended for presentation to the Lady's Book,
but through unavoidable de-
lay never offered to
that print.

BY HAMILTON SMITH.

PENN-YAN, N. Y.

RI NTED FOR THE AUTHOR, BY H. GILBERT.

1832.

goes to live alone in the woods. Set in the Raisin River area.

Wright I, 2455.

CtY MH MWA RPB ViU

1331 **Smith, John Leonard**
The Merchant of Mount Vernon. Los Angeles: The Author, 1907. 226 p.

Two sons of the founder of a lumber town vie for the same woman. Set in "Mt. Vernon" on the Chippewa River and in Ann Arbor at the University of Michigan in the late 1800s.

Mi MiKW CU OU T

1332 **Smith, Larry** 1940–
The Original. New York: Herder and Herder, 1972. 331 p.

The story of a farm couple's eldest son from his childhood to the time he takes up with a much older woman of some notoriety. Set in "Woodend" in the Grand Traverse area from 1892 to 1915.

1333 **Smith, Mark Richard** 1935–
Toyland. Boston: Little, Brown, 1965. 245 p.

Two children are taken away to be murdered by two men hired by their uncle, who will profit financially by their deaths. Set in various northern Michigan locales.

Mystery.

1334 ———.
The Middleman. Boston: Little, Brown, 1967. 312 p.

A man whose business failure and domineering wife have made him desperate and paranoid plans to murder his niece and nephew for their insurance money. Set in Charlevoix.

Prequel and sequel to *Toyland.*

Mi MiAllG MiBatK MiD MiU

1335 **Smith, Vern E.**
The Jones Men. Chicago: Henry Regnery Co., 1974. 287 p.

A grim and harrowing account of the heroin trade subculture and an African-American gang that runs a part of it. Set in Detroit.

Mystery.

1336 **Smits, Lee J.** 1887–
The Spring Flight. New York: Alfred A. Knopf, 1925. 350 p.

A young man has a series of romantic and physical experiences with a number of women before finally settling down and marrying. Set mostly in "Franklin."

Black, 249.

Mi MiAlb MiAllG MiEM OU

1337 **Smitter, Wessel** 1894–1951
F.O.B. Detroit. New York: Harper & Brothers, 1938. 340 p.

Two men find employment at Holt Motor Company, and each has his own methods for coping with the difficult and exhausting working conditions. Set in Detroit.

Black, 248.

MiAllG MiD MiEM MiMtpT-C MiU

1338 ———.
Another Morning. New York: Harper & Brothers, 1941. 355 p.

An impoverished farm family takes advantage of the government program to establish a farm colony in the Alaskan Matanuska Valley. The first twenty-four pages are set in Michigan.

MiD MiGrC MiHly IC OBgU

1339 Smucker, Barbara Claassen
1915–
White Mist. Toronto: Irwin Publishing, 1985. 159 p.

Two Native-American teenagers are summoned back in time by a chief to be made aware of humanity's destruction of the environment. Set in Saugatuck and Singapore.

Juvenile.

MiAllG MiGr CFP IaCfT KHu

1340 Smyth, Dan
No Place To Live by Dan Smyth and Junice Smyth Peek. Huntington, W. Va.: University Editions, 1994. 175 p.

A band of Potawatomis threatened by encroaching Iroquois and whites moves westward in the 1690s. Partially set in southwestern Michigan and the Upper Peninsula.

MiAllG IC

1341 Sneider, Vernon John 1916–1981
West of the North Star by Vern Sneider. New York: G. P. Putnam's Sons, 1971. 188 p.

The story of a young American drummer boy and his adventures during the War of 1812 in Ohio. Partially set in Frenchtown and Detroit.

Juvenile.

MiBatW MiBlo MiD MiLapC MiRog

1342 Snell, Roy Judson 1878–
The Phantom Violin. A Mystery Story for Girls. Chicago: Reilly & Lee Co., 1934. 273 p.

Three girls spend a summer living on the wreck of a passenger ship and become involved with gypsies and a hunt for treasure. Set on Isle Royale.

Also published as *Jane Withers and the Phantom Violin* (Racine, Wis.: Whitman Publishing Co., 1943).

Juvenile.

MiEM MiMtpT-C InFw OO WLacU

1343 Snelling, Anna L. ?–1859?
Kabaosa; or, The Warriors of the West. A Tale of the Last War. New-York: Printed for the Publisher by D. Adee, 1842. 320 p.

A Shawnee warrior and his adopted white son are involved in the War of 1812 along with militia men and their sweethearts. Partially set in Detroit and the surrounding area.

Black, 245. Wright I, 2476.

Mi MiD ICU InU OMC

1344 Snider, Paul
Edgar Henry. New York: Bernard Geis Associates, 1967. 309 p.

A saga about the Henry family whose members work in an automobile plant and also run a non-union furniture business. Set in Detroit in the 1930s and 1940s.

MiD MiOC MiRog MiRos OU

Snow, Karen, pseud. *see* Wheatley, Kathleen Musser

1345 Snyder, Guy Eugene 1951–
Testament XXI. New York: DAW Books, 1973. 144 p.

(DAW Books, no. 64)

A postnuclear war republic controlled by priests and located beneath the ruins of Detroit is at war with a democracy in the Chicago area.

Subtitle on cover: *The Book of the Twice Damned.*

Science fiction.

MiAllG CSdS MWalB OBgU OU

Sola, pseud. *see* Anderson, Olive Santa Louise

1346 Sommer, Karen J. 1947–
The New Kid, Spinner, and Me. Elgin, Ill.: Chariot Books, 1985. 127 p.

(Pennypincher Books)

Sixth grader Satch becomes friends with a Vietnamese boy from a family his church has sponsored, and difficulties with adjustment are finally overcome. Set in Owosso.

Also published as *Satch and the New Kid* (1987) and *New Kid on the Block* (1989).

Juvenile.

MiFli MiFliL OLor

1347 ———.
Satch and the Motormouth. Elgin, Ill.: Chariot Books, 1987. 130 p.

(White Horse Books, no. 2)

Eleven-year-old Satch is exasperated when he has to work with a very talkative girl on a school project and again at church. Set in Owosso.

Sequel to *The New Kid, Spinner, and Me.*

Juvenile.

MiFli MiMu MiOw IC InE

Sorin, Scota, pseud. *see* Troop, Edna Willa Sullivan

1348 Sosnowski, David
Rapture. New York: Villard Books, 1996. 295 p.

An outbreak of a new viral disease that causes its victims to sprout wings brings societal curiosity and prejudices. This satire is set in Detroit.

Science fiction.

1349 Soule, Maris Anne 1939–
Sounds Like Love. Toronto: Harlequin Books, 1986. 219 p.

(Harlequin Temptation, no. 112)

The owner of a lakeside bar hires a handsome stand-in when her musician suddenly leaves her in the lurch. Set at "Shady Lake," in Grand Rapids, and in Holland.

Romance.

MiAllG MiGr MiInr MoK OBgU

1350 ———.
The Best of Everything. Toronto: Harlequin Books, 1988. 220 p.

(Harlequin Temptation, no. 206)

A rodeo horsewoman's car breaks down on the freeway, and she falls in love with the tow truck driver. Partially set in the Kalamazoo area.

Romance.

MiAllG MiBatW MiGr OBgU WWau

1351 ———.
The Law of Nature. Toronto: Harlequin Books, 1988. 221 p.

(Harlequin Temptation, no. 225)

A young woman working at a wildlife sanctuary falls in love with the biologist and photographer who owns it. Set in the St. Ignace area in the Upper Peninsula.

Romance.

MiAllG MiBatW MiMtcM MoK OBgU

1352 ———.

Con Man. New York: Bantam Books, 1993. 226 p.

(Loveswept, no. 635)

A representative from a foundation secretly investigates a prospective grant recipient, which results in romance. Set at a riding stable in Kalamazoo.

Romance.

MiAllG MiBatW MiD IC OBgU

1353 ———.

No Promises Made. New York: Bantam Books, 1994. 226 p.

(Loveswept, no. 689)

A woman wanting to concentrate on her promising career as regional director of an Ann Arbor public relations firm tries not to fall in love with a handsome neighbor.

Romance.

MiAllG MiMtcM IC OXe WAPL

1354 ———.

Stop the Wedding! New York: Silhouette Books, 1994. 185 p.

(Silhouette Romance, no. 1038)

A wedding consultant falls in love with a man who has requested that she prevent his sister's marriage to an unsavory character. Set in Grand Rapids.

Romance.

MiAllG IChamL InMu OCo OXe

1355 ———.

Substitute Mom. New York: Silhouette Books, 1996. 184 p.

(Silhouette Romance, no. 1160)

A woman left in charge of a four-year-old while his mother is away is confronted by the boy's father and becomes involved in a custody battle. Set in Bear Lake.

Romance.

MiAllG IChamL OCo OXe WM

1356 ———.

Destiny Strikes Twice. New York: Bantam Books, 1996. 211 p.

(Loveswept, no. 804)

Returning to her late grandmother's cottage, a young woman reacquaints herself with a man who, years before, was more interested in her sister. Set at Gun Lake and in Grand Rapids.

Romance.

MiAllG OXe OCo WM

1357 **Spalding, Henry Stanislaus** 1865–1934

The Race for Copper Island by Henry S. Spalding, S. J. New York: Benziger Brothers, 1905. 206 p.

A group of French explorers searches for fabled copper mines in the Lake Superior area of the Upper Peninsula in the late 1600s.

Juvenile.

Mi MiMtpT-C LNaN OBgU OCl

1358 ———.

The Marks of the Bear Claws by Henry S. Spalding, S. J. New York: Benziger Brothers, 1908. 229 p.

The fictionalized biography of Father Jacques Marquette (1637–1675), including his Great Lakes explorations. Partially set in St. Ignace and Sault Ste. Marie.

Juvenile.

Mi DLC

1359 ———.
The Camp by Copper River by Rev. Henry S. Spalding, S. J. New York: Benziger Brothers, 1915. 192 p.

A group of boys has exciting adventures while camping on "Copper River" near Lake Superior in the Upper Peninsula.

Juvenile.

DLC

1360 [Sparrow, Laura H.]
Hostages to Fortune by Jocelyn Griffin [pseud.]. New York: Silhouette Books, 1984. 251 p.

(Silhouette Special Edition, no. 195)

Seeking refuge from a storm, a woman tries to break into a deserted lighthouse and discovers it occupied. Set in the Upper Peninsula near Grand Marais.

Romance.

MiAllG MiSth AzSaf NjMlA

1361 Spears, Raymond Smiley 1876–1950
Camping on the Great Lakes. New York: Harper & Brothers, 1913. 372 p.

(Harper's Camp-Life Series)

Two boys take a camping trip around the Great Lakes and become involved with a gang of smugglers. Partially set on the Detroit River, Lake St. Clair, and in Sault Ste. Marie.

Juvenile.

Mi MiEM MiU TxAlpS

1362 [Spenser, Avis S.]
A Tale of the West; or, Life with a Sister by Emma Carra [pseud.]. Providence: H. H. Brown, 1846. 72 p.

A young military physician prone to drinking and gambling is eventually

redeemed by the love of a woman. Mostly set at Fort Detroit from about 1810 to 1813.

Wright I, 490.

MiU CtY MWA ViU WU

1363 [———— **].**
Viroqua; or, The Flower of the Ottawas. A Tale of the West by Emma Carra [pseud.]. Boston: F. Gleason, 1848. 100 p.

The romance between an English officer and a young Ottawa woman is interrupted by Pontiac's attack, but ultimately the couple is reunited. Set at Detroit in 1763.

Wright I, 491.

MiU CSmH MWA OU ViU

Sperry, Raymond, pseud. *see* Garis, Howard Roger

1364 Spike, Paul 1947–
The Night Letter. New York: G. P. Putnam's Sons, 1979. 310 p.

Nazi agents plan to publish compromising photos of President Roosevelt to undermine his popularity. Partially set in Dearborn and Whitefish Point in 1940.

Mystery.

1365 Sprague, William Cyrus 1860–1922
Felice Constant; or, The Master Passion, a Romance. New York: F. A. Stokes Co., 1904. 322 p.

The adventures of an ex-British soldier who, with the help of a young French girl, spies on Fort Detroit for the Americans during the American Revolution in the late 1770s.

Black, 250.

MiMarqN InWinG OCoO OU

1366 Spross, Patricia McNitt 1913–
Sundogs and Sunsets. Fowlerville,
Mich.: Wilderness Adventure Books,
1990. 203 p.

A fictionalized account, told in connected dated vignettes, of the author's
childhood on a farm and later life.
Set in "Fillson" and "Hollandsville"
(Nashville?).

Mi MiL MiOw MiMtpT-C MiYEM

1367 ———.
"Linnie, Your Water's Boiling!" Davis-
burg, Mich.: Wilderness Adventure
Books, 1993. 182 p.

A continuation of the author's fictionalized reminiscences, told in connected vignettes, about her family. Set
in "Hollandsville" (Nashville?), "Ash-
ton," and "Vishton."

Sequel to *Sundogs and Sunsets.*

Mi MiAllG MiGr MiKW MiYEM

1368 Stahl, Hilda 1938–1993
Teddy Jo and the Terrible Secret.
Wheaton, Ill.: Tyndale House Publish-
ers, 1982. 128 p.

(Teddy Jo Series, no. 1)

Ten-year-old Teddy Jo is angry that
she has to spend the summer with
her strange grandfather. Set in "Middle
Lake."

Juvenile.

MiGr MiGrB InMar WaT TxWB

1369 ———.
Teddy Jo and the Yellow Room Mystery.
Wheaton, Ill.: Tyndale House Publish-
ers, 1982. 127 p.

(Teddy Jo Series, no. 2)

Teddy Jo tries to find out who has
been in her room and disturbed her
belongings. Set in "Middle Lake."

Juvenile.

MiGrB AB InMar NcR WaT

1370 ———.
Teddy Jo and the Stolen Ring.
Wheaton, Ill.: Tyndale House Publish-
ers, 1982. 121 p.

(Teddy Jo Series, no. 3)

Teddy Jo's friend has borrowed her
ring, has forgotten to return it, and now
no longer wants to be friends. Set in
"Middle Lake."

Juvenile.

MiAllG MiGrB InMar TxWB WaT

1371 ———.
*Teddy Jo and the Strangers in the Pink
House.* Wheaton, Ill.: Tyndale House
Publishers, 1982. 122 p.

(Teddy Jo Series, no. 4)

Teddy Jo overhears part of a conversa-
tion about new neighbors and is certain
something awful is happening. Set in
"Middle Lake."

Juvenile.

MiGrB WaT

1372 ———.
Teddy Jo and the Strange Medallion.
Wheaton, Ill.: Tyndale House Publishers, 1983. 127 p. (Teddy Jo Series,
no. 5)

Teddy Jo believes that a schoolmate has
taken a special necklace from an old
bag lady. Set in "Middle Lake."

Juvenile.

MiGrB AzG COc InBer OLor

1373 ———.

Teddy Jo and the Wild Dog. Wheaton, Ill.: Tyndale House Publishers, 1983. 118 p.

(Teddy Jo Series, no. 6)

Teddy Jo has seen a wild collie and her pups in the woods, but now they seem to have disappeared. Set in "Middle Lake."

Juvenile.

MiGrB NcR OLor TxWB WaT

1374 ———.

Teddy Jo and the Abandoned House. Wheaton, Ill.: Tyndale House Publishers, 1984. 128 p.

(Teddy Jo Series, no. 7)

Teddy Jo seeks shelter in an old house during a storm, finds a secret room, and loses her dog. Set in "Middle Lake."

Juvenile.

MiGrB COc NcR TxWB WaT

1375 ———.

Teddy Jo and the Ragged Beggars. Wheaton, Ill.: Tyndale House Publishers, 1984. 121 p.

(Teddy Jo Series, no. 8)

Teddy Jo is supposed to go to summer school but doesn't when she encounters two young beggars who have a secret. Set in "Middle Lake."

Juvenile.

MiGrB KWi NcR TxWB WaT

1376 ———.

Teddy Jo and the Kidnapped Heir. Wheaton, Ill.: Tyndale House Publishers, 1984. 128 p.

(Teddy Jo Series, no. 9)

Teddy Jo is kidnapped along with a

wealthy boy as they are walking along the street. Set in "Middle Lake."

Juvenile.

MiGrB TxWB

1377 ———.

Teddy Jo and the Great Dive. Wheaton, Ill.: Tyndale House Publishers, 1985. 128 p.

(Teddy Jo Series, no. 10)

Teddy Jo feels anxiety when it is her turn to use the diving board in swimming class. Set in "Middle Lake."

Juvenile.

MiGrB TxWB

1378 ———.

Teddy Jo and the Magic Quill. Wheaton, Ill.: Tyndale House Publishers, 1985. 128 p.

(Teddy Jo Series, no. 11)

Teddy Jo has a dream in which her friends are held captive on an island by an evil king. Dreamt in "Middle Lake."

Juvenile.

MiGrB TxWB

1379 ———.

The Mystery at the Wheeler Place. Denver: Accent Books, 1986. 126 p.

(Wren House Mystery, book 1)

Ten-year-old Wren and her friends solve a mystery connected with the empty house next door. Set in "Jordan."

Also published in a slightly revised form as *A Face in the Window* (Elgin, Ill.: Accent Books, 1992).

Juvenile.

InBer InMar MoIM OrRoD WaT

1380 ———.

The Disappearance of Amos Pike. Denver: Accent Books, 1986. 127 p.

(Wren House Mystery, book 2)

Wren and her friends investigate the sudden disappearance of an old man and his dog. Set in "Jordan."

Also published in a slightly revised form as *The Search for the Missing Neighbor* (Elgin, Ill.: Accent Books, 1992).

Juvenile.

MiGr InBer InGar InMit OrRoD

1381 ———.

Tim Avery's Secret. Denver: Accent Books, 1986. 127 p.

(Wren House Mystery, book 3)

Wren and her friends overhear a plot to injure a person, but no one believes their story. Set in "Jordan."

Also published in a slightly revised form as *The Secret Father* (Elgin, Ill.: Accent Books, 1992).

Juvenile.

MiGr COc InBer MoIM OrRoD

1382 ———.

The Missing Newspaper Caper. Denver: Accent Books, 1986. 125 p.

(Wren House Mystery, book 4)

When an old woman's newspapers begin disappearing, Wren sets out to find the thief. Set in "Jordan."

Also published in a slightly revised form as *The Pig Papers* (Elgin, Ill.: Accent Books, 1993).

Juvenile.

MiGr-L COc InBer MoIM OrRoD

1383 ———.

Teddy Jo and the Broken Locket Mystery. Wheaton, Ill.: Tyndale House Publishers, 1986. 122 p.

(Teddy Jo Series, no. 12)

Teddy Jo thinks that a locket found in a friend's yard and a girl hiding in her garage are connected. Set in "Middle Lake."

Juvenile.

MiAllG MiGrB InBer TxWB WaT

1384 ———.

Teddy Jo and the Missing Portrait. Wheaton, Ill.: Tyndale House Publishers, 1986. 126 p.

(Teddy Jo Series, no. 13)

When the hated portrait of an old principal disappears from the school wall, Teddy Jo investigates. Set in "Middle Lake."

Juvenile.

MiAllG MiGrB AzG InBer TxWB

1385 ———.

Teddy Jo and the Missing Family. Wheaton, Ill.: Tyndale House Publishers, 1986. 119 p.

(Teddy Jo Series, no. 14)

Teddy Jo helps a girl find her brother before they are sent to separate foster homes. Set in "Middle Lake."

Juvenile.

MiAllG MiGrB InBer InMu TxWB

1386 ———.

The Tyler Twins: Surprise at Big Key Ranch. Wheaton, Ill.: Tyndale House Publishers, 1986. 124 p.

(Tyler Twins Series, no. 1)

Ten-year-old twins journey from Detroit to near Grand Rapids to live with their divorced mother and her new husband on a ranch.

Juvenile.

MiGr CHu InL OCl TxWB

1387 ———.

The Tyler Twins: Swamp Monster. Wheaton, Ill.: Tyndale House Publishers, 1986. 105 p.

(Tyler Twins Series, no. 2)

The Tyler twins become lost in a swamp near their ranch and hear horrible cries in the approaching dark. Set near Grand Rapids.

Juvenile.

MiGr CHu OCl TxWB

1388 ———.

The Tyler Twins: Pet Show Panic. Wheaton, Ill.: Tyndale House Publishers, 1986. 126 p.

(Tyler Twins Series, no. 3)

Learning that the annual pet show will be cancelled, the Tyler twins work to find a new location. Set near Grand Rapids.

Juvenile.

MiGr InL MoIM OCl TxWB

1389 ———.

The Case of the Missing Money. Denver: Accent Books, 1987. 125 p.

(Wren House Mystery, book 5)

Wren's friend asks her help in finding the school newspaper subscription money, which is missing. Set in "Jordan."

Also published in a slightly revised form as *Double Crossed! The Case of the Missing Money* (Elgin, Ill.: Accent Books, 1993).

Juvenile.

MiGr-L InBer MoIM OrRoD WaT

1390 ———.

The Tyler Twins: Latchkey Kids. Wheaton, Ill.: Tyndale House Publishers, 1987. 128 p.

(Tyler Twins Series, no. 4)

Living with their father for the summer, the Tyler twins help a small boy and, ultimately, his mother. Set in Detroit.

Juvenile.

MiGrA InL KKc OCl TxWB

1391 ———.

The Tyler Twins: Tree House Hideaway. Wheaton, Ill.: Tyndale House Publishers, 1988. 125 p.

(Tyler Twins Series, no. 5)

About to leave their mother for the summer, the Tyler twins worry that she loves their stepsister more. Set near Grand Rapids.

Juvenile.

MiAllG OCl

1392 ———.

Mystery of the Missing Grandfather. Wheaton, Ill.: Tyndale House Publishers, 1988. 128 p.

(Tyler Twins Series, no. 6)

While staying with their father, the Tyler twins help three runaway children locate their grandfather. Set in Detroit.

Juvenile.

MiGr InL InMu OCl

1393 ———.

Deadline. Elkhart, Ind.: Bethel Publishing, 1989. 154 p.

(Amber Ainslie Detective Series, book 1)

Amber Ainslie, a private detective, is asked to investigate a threatening manuscript left for a magazine's fiction editor. Set in "Laketown."

Mystery.

MiGr InL MoIM OCo WKen

1394 ———.
Abducted. Elkhart, Ind.: Bethel Publishing, 1989. 137 p.

(Amber Ainslie Detective Series, book 2)

An eight-year-old girl is kidnapped in front of her school, and her parents and the local sheriff seek the aid of Amber Ainslie. Set in "Bradsville" and "Freburg."

Mystery.

MiGr InL MoIM OCo WMani

1395 ———.
*The Great Adventures of Super J*A*M.* Westchester, Ill.: Crossway Books, 1989. 123 p.

(Super J*A*M Adventure, no. 1)

Jonathon, a young orphan who lives at "Sugar Bush Boy's Home," is bullied at school and imagines a superhero rescuing him. Set in an unnamed Michigan city.

Juvenile.

MiGr-L AzG InL KHu MoIM

1396 ———.
The World's Greatest Hero. Westchester, Ill.: Crossway Books, 1989. 125 p.

(Super J*A*M Adventure, no. 2)

Jonathon has to choose between doing scary pranks with his friends or going to a Halloween party with a girl he likes. Set in an unnamed Michigan city.

Juvenile.

MiChe AzG ICMB InFrf MoIM

1397 ———.
Gently Touch Sheela Jenkins. Elkhart, Ind.: Bethel Publishing, 1989. 200 p.

A businessman is attracted to his efficient secretary, but she has been abused and must learn to trust before she can love again. Set in an unnamed western Michigan city.

Romance.

MiDo MiGr InFw OCo WKen

1398 ———.
Undercover. Elkhart, Ind.: Bethel Publishing, 1990. 172 p.

(Amber Ainslie Detective Series, book 3)

A woman reporter investigating the death of a businessman's brother and wife in an auto accident finds Amber Ainslie suspecting murder. Set in "Freburg."

Mystery.

MiLac AzPr InL MoIM OCo

1399 ———.
Blackmail. Elkhart, Ind.: Bethel Publishing, 1990. 174 p.

(Amber Ainslie Detective Series, book 4)

A successful woman author with an unsavory past is blackmailed, and Amber Ainslie discovers a connection with child pornography. Set in "Chambers."

Mystery.

MiLac InL OCl OCo MoIM

1400 ———.

Sendi Lee Mason and the Milk Carton Kids. Westchester, Ill.: Crossway Books, 1990. 126 p.

(A Growing Up Adventure, book 1)

Sendi has moved to a new town, and she and her new friend believe they have found missing children. Set in "Greenlea."

Juvenile.

MiAllG MiLac MiMtcM InBer OCl

1401 ———.

Sendi Lee Mason and the Stray Striped Cat. Wheaton, Ill.: Crossway Books, 1990. 128 p.

(A Growing Up Adventure, book 2)

Sendi finds a stray cat and plans to keep it, but finds out that it really belongs to an old woman. Set in "Greenlea."

Juvenile.

MiJac MiLac InBer MoIM OCl

1402 ———.

The Covenant. Nashville, Tenn.: Thomas Nelson Publishers, 1990. 286 p.

(White Pine Chronicles, book 1)

A girl is sold by her father as an indentured servant to pay off a debt, but a lumberjack bargains for her freedom. Set partially in "Prickett" and "Big Pine" in western Michigan from 1863 to 1865.

1403 ———.

Sendi Lee Mason and the Big Mistake. Wheaton, Ill.: Crossway Books, 1991. 124 p.

(A Growing Up Adventure, book 3)

To her dismay, Sendi's best friend finds out that Sendi has been cheating on her math homework. Set in "Greenlea."

Juvenile.

MiLac IGenD KKc MoIM OXe

1404 ———.

Sendi Lee Mason and the Great Crusade. Wheaton, Ill.: Crossway Books, 1991. 125 p.

(A Growing Up Adventure, book 4)

When Sendi tries to get her father to remarry her mother, the girl next door spoils her plan. Set in "Greenlea."

Juvenile.

MiLac AzPr MoIM OCl ScSp

1405 ———.

Daisy Punkin. Wheaton, Ill.: Crossway Books, 1991. 122 p.

(Daisy Punkin, no. 1)

Daisy worries that her mother won't return when she leaves to stay with her ill grandmother. Set in an unnamed Michigan town.

Juvenile.

MiGr-L IWW IaDa KKc MoIM

1406 ———.

The Inheritance. Nashville, Tenn.: Thomas Nelson Publishers, 1992. 244 p.

(White Pine Chronicles, book 2)

A young woman guards 6000 acres of virgin white pine against timber thieves, but the new owner of the land has other plans. Set near "Blue Creek" in central Michigan in 1890.

1407 ———.

Chelsea and the Outrageous Phone Bill. Wheaton, Ill.: Crossway Books, 1992. 159 p.

(Best Friends, no. 1)

Eleven-year-old Chelsea phones her best friend, who lives in Oklahoma, every day and is soon in trouble. Set in "Middle Lake."

Juvenile.

MiAllG MiChe MiHly InL OCl

1408 ——.
Big Trouble for Roxie. Wheaton, Ill.: Crossway Books, 1992. 159 p.

(Best Friends, no. 2)

Roxie has difficulty telling the truth about things but doesn't know how to change. Set in "Middle Lake."

Juvenile.

MiAllG MiChe MiFliL MiStep OCl

1409 ——.
Kathy's Baby-Sitting Hassle. Wheaton, Ill.: Crossway Books, 1992. 156 p.

(Best Friends, no. 3)

Kathy, who hates to babysit her little sister, loses her while they are playing at the park. Set in "Middle Lake."

Juvenile.

MiAllG MiChe MiHly InFw OCl

1410 ——.
Hannah and the Special 4th of July. Wheaton, Ill.: Crossway Books, 1992. 159 p.

(Best Friends, no. 4)

Hannah's great-grandmother allows her to wear a special Native-American costume, but her cousin soils it. Set in "Middle Lake."

Juvenile.

MiAllG MiChe MiHly InFw OCl

1411 ——.
The Boning Knife. Tulsa, Okla.: Victory House, 1992. 257 p.

(Carolynn Burgess Mysteries, book 1)

A woman detective investigates the murder of a man in a friend's kitchen and finds a connection with a series of deaths of elderly women. Set in "Middle Lake."

Mystery.

MiAllG MiGr InFw OCl SdAbA

1412 ——.
Roxie and the Red Rose Mystery. Wheaton, Ill.: Crossway Books, 1992. 159 p.

(Best Friends, no. 5)

Roxie helps her friend with an entry for an art contest and falls in love with her friend's older brother. Set in "Middle Lake."

Juvenile.

MiAllG MiChe MiHly IaDa OCl

1413 ——.
Daisy Punkin: The Bratty Brother. Wheaton, Ill.: Crossway Books, 1992. 127 p.

(Daisy Punkin, no. 2)

One of Daisy's brothers begins to taunt and humiliate her in front of her classmates. Set in an unnamed Michigan town.

Juvenile.

MiAllG IWW InFw MoIM OCo

1414 ——.
Kathy's New Brother. Wheaton, Ill.: Crossway Books, 1992. 159 p.

(Best Friends, no. 6)

Kathy has problems with a girl who doesn't want her on the cheerleading squad and a pest of a boy. Set in "Middle Lake."

Juvenile.

MiChe MiHly IWW IaDa MoIM

1415 ⸻.

A Made-Over Chelsea. Wheaton, Ill.: Crossway Books, 1992. 158 p.

(Best Friends, no. 7)

When Chelsea goes to a new school, she meets a confident girl who is not what she seems. Set in "Middle Lake."

Juvenile.

MiHly IWW IaDa OCl WMani

1416 ⸻.

No Friends for Hannah. Wheaton, Ill.: Crossway Books, 1992. 159 p.

(Best Friends, no. 8)

Hannah is puzzled and saddened when the other girls no longer want to be friends with her. Set in "Middle Lake."

Juvenile.

MiHly IWW IaDa OCl MoIM

1417 ⸻.

The Secret Tunnel Mystery. Wheaton, Ill.: Crossway Books, 1992. 159 p.

(Best Friends Special Edition)

Roxie, Chelsea, Hannah, and Kathy help clean out an old house in the country and find secret tunnels. Set in "Middle Lake."

Republished in 1994 as no. 16 in the Best Friends series.

Juvenile.

MiGr MiHly IWW OCl OkT

1418 ⸻.

The Dream. Nashville, Tenn.: Thomas Nelson Publishers, 1993. 239 p.

(White Pine Chronicles, book 3)

The last acres of virgin white pine in lower Michigan are threatened when the twins who have inherited the land plan to sell it. Set near "Blue Creek" in central Michigan in 1922.

Mi MiAllG MiCor MiJac MiLac

1419 ⸻.

Deadly Secrets. Tulsa, Okla.: Victory House, 1993. 284 p.

(Carolynn Burgess Mysteries, book 2)

While investigating a murder and another suspicious death, a woman detective begins to uncover a series of secrets. Set in "Middle Lake."

Mystery.

MiAllG MiCor IaDa MoIM SdAbA

1420 ⸻.

Tough Choices for Roxie. Wheaton, Ill.: Crossway Books, 1993. 158 p.

(Best Friends, no. 9)

Roxie is hurt by a girl who mocks her, as well as by Kathy, who is angry at her for liking the same boy. Set in "Middle Lake."

Juvenile.

MiHly IWW InBlo InFw OCl

1421 ⸻.

Chelsea's Special Touch. Wheaton, Ill.: Crossway Books, 1993. 157 p.

(Best Friends, no. 10)

Chelsea is forced by a sixth grader to teach her photography and tries to help a younger girl. Set in "Middle Lake."

Juvenile.

MiHly IWW IaDa MoIM OCl

1422 ⸻.

Mystery at Bellwood Estate. Wheaton, Ill.: Crossway Books, 1993. 159 p.

(Best Friends, no. 11)

Kathy has a new friend who is adopted and lives in a luxurious mansion, but always seems to be sad. Set in "Middle Lake."

Juvenile.

MiHly AzPr IWW IaDa MoIM

1423 ———.
Hannah and the Daring Escape. Wheaton, Ill.: Crossway Books, 1993. 159 p.

(Best Friends, no. 12)

Hannah's new friend begins to hide at the art academy and claims someone is following her. Set in "Middle Lake."

Juvenile.

MiHly IWW IaDa InFw MoIM

1424 ———.
Hannah and the Snowy Hideaway. Wheaton, Ill.: Crossway Books, 1993. 156 p.

(Best Friends, no. 13)

Hannah is not pleased when she finds out that a babysitting job is for a grumpy old woman. Set in "Middle Lake."

Juvenile.

MiHly IWW IaDa InFw MoIM

1425 ———.
Chelsea and the Alien Invasion. Wheaton, Ill.: Crossway Books, 1993. 157 p.

(Best Friends, no. 14)

Chelsea's new friend tells her that an invasion from outer space is coming and has proof. Set in "Middle Lake."

Juvenile.

MiHly IWW IaDa InFw OCo

1426 ———.
Roxie's Mall Madness. Wheaton, Ill.: Crossway Books, 1993. 159 p.

(Best Friends, no. 15)

Roxie's three siblings all have problems at the same time, and, to escape from them, she visits the mall. Set in "Middle Lake."

Juvenile.

MiHly IWW IaDa InFw OCo

1427 Stallman, Robert 1930–1980
The Orphan; the First Book of the Beast. New York: Pocket Books, 1980. 240 p.

A strange cat-like beast is cornered in a barn and changes shape into a six-year-old boy much to its own surprise. Set in rural southwestern Michigan in 1935.

Science fiction.

Mi MiAllG MiEM MiGr MiKW

1428 ———.
The Captive (the Second Book of the Beast). New York: Pocket Books, 1981. 207 p.

In 1936, the beast has taken the shape of an adolescent as it itself matures and begins to explore its surroundings. Partially set in "Carverville" in southwestern Michigan.

Sequel to *The Orphan.* The third and last book of the series, *The Beast,* is set entirely in the western part of the United States.

Science fiction.

MiAllG MiEM MiKW MiMani OBgU

1429 Stanger, Theophil 1875–
Mr. Pickett of Detroit. Ann Arbor: Millard Press, 1916. 143 p.

A wealthy landowner undertakes a social experiment by building a community, "Little Hague," which he rents only to immigrants. Set partially in Detroit.

Black, 251.

Mi MiAllG MiD MiEM MiMtpT-C

1430 Stchur, John W. 1947–
Down on the Farm by J. W. Stchur. New York: St. Martin's Press, 1987. 216 p.

A centipede-like monster from space lands on a Lenawee County hillside in 1809, comes to life 170 years later, and is able to control the minds of humans.

Science fiction.

Mi MiAllG MiD MiEM MiMtpT-C

1431 ———.
Paddywhack. New York: St. Martin's Press, 1989. 297 p.

A family moves from New York City to live with an elderly aunt in a quiet town, but there is some horrible secret about her dog. Set in "Granger" in southern Michigan.

Science fiction.

MiAllG CSj CU-Riv MoS O

Steele, James, pseud. *see* Cruden, Robert Lunan

1432 Steffen, Sandra
Hold Back the Night. Bensalem, Pa.: Meteor Publishing Corp., 1992. 222 p.

(Kismet Romance, no. 90)

A young woman visiting her lighthouse keeper uncle, tries to find out about her past and meets a handsome stranger. Set in "Pinesburg" on northern Lake Michigan.

Romance.

MiAllG MiMtcM MW USl

1433 ———.
Lullaby and Goodnight. New York: Silhouette Books, 1995. 186 p.

(Silhouette Romance, no. 1074)

On the run from an abusive boyfriend, a young woman and her baby are befriended by a small town police officer. Set in "Millerton."

Publisher's subseries: *Bundles of Joy.*

Romance.

MiAllG IChamL OCo OXe WM

1434 ———.
A Father for Always. New York: Silhouette Books, 1996. 187 p.

(Silhouette Romance, no. 1138)

To thwart his nasty in-laws from taking custody of his daughter, a handsome widower has a friend pose as his fiancée with unintended results. Set in "Stony Creek."

Publisher's subseries: *Fabulous Fathers.*

Romance.

MiAllG IChamL OCo OXe WM

1435 Steggerda, Orville 1909–
Tall Against the Sky. Grand Rapids: Zondervan Publishing House, 1960. 241 p.

Although he is a rugged woodsman and pioneer, a young man is no match for three women who enter his life. Set in Kent, now Grand Rapids, in the 1830s.

MiAllG MiGr MiGrC InFw TxAm

Stellini, Terry, pseud. *see* Cicala, Theresa

Sterling, Anthony, pseud. *see* Caesar, Eugene Lee

1436 [Stevens, Frances Moyer Ross]
1895–1948
Smoke Screen by Christopher Hale [pseud.]. New York: Harcourt, Brace and Co., 1935. 311 p.

When a forest fire isolates the homes of five families, murder occurs, and Lt. Bill French of the Michigan State Police investigates. Set at "Black Hawk Lake" near Lake Michigan.

Mystery.

Mi CLO GAuA MnM NNC

1437 [———].
Stormy Night by Christopher Hale [pseud.]. Garden City, N.Y.: Doubleday, Doran and Co., 1937. 296 p.

(Crime Club)

After inept local authorities bungle the inquest of a double murder, Lt. French is called in to get things back on track. Set in "Riverdale."

Mystery.

Mi MiAllG AAP OU RUn

1438 [———].
Murder on Display by Christopher Hale [pseud.]. New York: Doubleday, Doran and Co, 1939. 280 p.

(Crime Club)

Lt. French investigates a crime wave in a small town, which the inhabitants want to blame on a tramp. Set in "Serena," located thirty-eight miles northwest of Lansing.

Mystery.

Mi CFlS CLO OBgU OU

1439 [———].
Witch Wood by Christopher Hale [pseud.]. New York: Doubleday, Doran & Co., 1940. 279 p.

(Crime Club)

A paying guest at a summer estate is found an apparent suicide, but Lt. French determines it was murder. Set near "Bixby."

Mystery.

Mi MiAllG OBgU OC OU

1440 [———].
Dead of Winter by Christopher Hale [pseud.]. Garden City, N.Y.: Doubleday, Doran & Co., 1941. 270 p.

(Crime Club)

The body of a skier is found in the snow and Lt. French must find the murderer amongst the deceased's eight companions. Set in the Lake Michigan town of "Westport" (Eastport).

Mystery.

MH OOxM OU ViR

1441 [———].
Exit Screaming by Christopher Hale [pseud.]. Garden City, N.Y.: Doubleday, Doran & Co., 1942. 277 p.

(Crime Club)

Screams and gunshots awaken a small town one night, and Lt. French is called in to investigate the murder of an eccentric woman. Set in "Avondale."

Mystery.

MiAllG MnM OOxM OU TxAm

1442 [———].
Hangman's Tie by Christopher Hale [pseud.]. Garden City, N.Y.: Doubleday, Doran & Co., 1943. 209 p.

(Crime Club)

An estate manager finds the body of the city treasurer and, despite the objections of local authorities, calls in Lt. French to investigate. Set in "Oak City."

Mystery.

Mi MiAdC MiAllG OBgU InG

1443 [———].

Midsummer Nightmare by Christopher Hale [pseud.]. Garden City. N.Y.: Doubleday, Doran & Co., 1945. 224 p.

(Crime Club)

A wealthy family and its business staff are involved in a series of murders and Lt. French is called in to sort out suspects. Set on the Grand River near Grand Rapids.

Mystery.

Mi MiAllG MiGr IU OOxM

1444 [———].

Rumor Hath It by Christopher Hale [pseud.]. Garden City, N.Y.: Doubleday, Doran & Co., 1945. 224 p.

(Crime Club)

A busybody is certain that no one in his community is responsible for the murder of his best friend, but Lt. French thinks otherwise. Set in "Lawnsdale."

Mystery.

MiAllG IDec MnU OBgU OOxM

1445 [———].

Deadly Ditto by Christopher Hale [pseud.]. Garden City, N.Y.: Doubleday & Co., 1948. 222 p.

(Crime Club)

When Lt. French investigates the murder of a prominent businessman, an old uncle of one of the suspects interferes. Set in "Galt Acres" and "Oak City."

Mystery.

MiAllG MnSP OOxM OU ViR

1446 Stevens, Karen Diane

Tamarack. East Lansing: Michigan State University, Department of English, 1982. 149 p.

A woman inherits some timber holdings from her grandmother and enlists the aid of a lawyer to find a missing heir. Set in North Branch, Charlevoix, and on Mackinac Island.

Master of English thesis.

MiEM

1447 Stevenson, Louis Lacy 1879–1953

Big Game. New York: Brentano's, Publishers, 1924. 332 p.

An Ohio farm boy leaves his family and sets out, through single-minded determination and sacrifice, to amass great wealth. Fifteen pages are set in a Detroit automobile factory.

MiAdS MiAllG CLU MWC OU

1448 [Stockwell, William Hume] 1907–

Rudderless, a University Chronicle by W. Stock Hume [pseud.]. Norwood, Mass.: Norwood Press, 1930. 271 p.
The chronicle of a student's four years at "Harcourt University" (University of Michigan) in "Belham" (Ann Arbor) and his unhappiness with its educational program.

Black, 253.

Mi MiU

1449 Stone, Caroline Reidinger

Inga of Porcupine Mine. New York: Holiday House, 1942. 212 p.

The seventh-grade daughter of Finnish and Cornish parents must sacrifice the money she has earned towards art school for a greater need. Set in the Upper Peninsula.

Juvenile.

Mi MiD MiGr MiMack MiMtpT-C

1450 ———.

Clorinda of Cherry Lane Farm. New York: Liveright Publishing Corp., 1945. 214 p.

A fourteen-year-old girl in a family of migratory farmworkers attends to the educational needs of her younger sister. Set in the Saginaw area.

Juvenile.

Mi MiAdC MiAlp MiGr MiYEM

1451 Stone, Nancy Young 1925–

Whistle up the Bay. Grand Rapids: Wm. B. Eerdmans Publishing Co., 1966. 219 p.

Three boys, the sons of a Swiss immigrant, are orphaned when he dies, and they try to eke out an existence by farming. Set in Antrim on Lake Michigan in the early 1870s.

Juvenile.

1452 ———.

The Wooden River. Grand Rapids: William. B. Eerdmans Publishing Co., 1973. 192 p.

A young girl experiences life in a logging camp when she and the rest of her family join her bookkeeper father there for the winter. Set near Bay City in the 1870s.

Juvenile.

Mi MiAllG MiD MiKW MiMtpT-C

1453 ———.

Dune Shadow. Boston: Houghton Mifflin Co., 1980. 180 p.

A thirteen-year-old girl and her grandmother are the last inhabitants of a Lake Michigan town that is slowly being engulfed by a sand dune. Set in "Calash" in the 1850s.

Juvenile.

1454 Stone, Sally

Silver Fire. New York: Zebra Books, 1993. 400 p.

(Zebra Heartfire Historical Romance)

A young woman finds a badly wounded man, a British spy, in the woods and nurses him back to health. Set near Detroit during the War of 1812.

Romance.

MiAllG MiMtcM OCo ScSp SdAbA

1455

A Story of the War Entitled Missing After Winchester; a Romance of the City of the Straits. Jackson, Mich.: Daily Citizen Steam Print, 1865. 22 p.

An advertising vehicle for Wheeler and Wilson's sewing machines, the story concerns a soldier's wife who lives in abject poverty when he is listed among the missing after a Civil War battle. Set in Detroit.

Mi

1456 Stowe, Rebecca

Not the End of the World. London: Peter Owen, 1991. 130 p.

A precocious twelve-year-old girl alienated from her wealthy family and disgusted by her mundane school friends tries to "find" herself. Set in "North Bay" (Port Huron?).

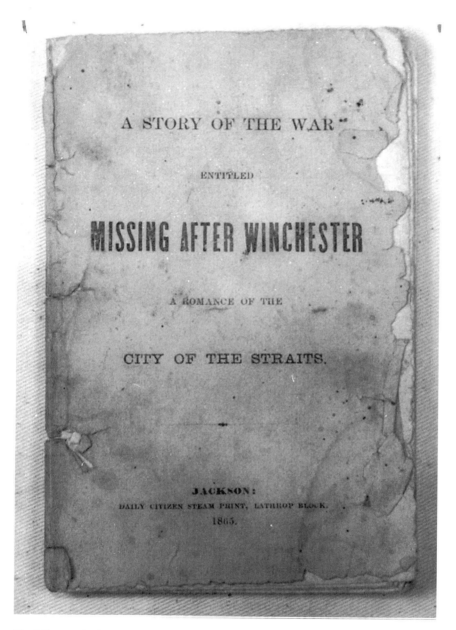

A STORY OF THE WAR

ENTITLED

MISSING AFTER WINCHESTER

A ROMANCE OF THE

CITY OF THE STRAITS.

JACKSON:
DAILY CITIZEN STEAM PRINT, LATHROP BLOCK.
1865.

Juvenile.

ICNE MoSW NjUPM

1457 ———.
The Shadow of Desire. New York: Pantheon Books, 1996. 228 p.

A woman returns home from New York to spend Christmas with her dysfunctional family and finally comes to terms with her life. Set in "Edison Woods" (Port Huron?).

1458 [Stowers, Walter H.] 1859–
Appointed: An American Novel by Sanda [pseud.]. Detroit: Detroit Law Printing Co., 1894. 371 p.

An African American who works aboard a yacht is befriended by the owner's son, and they both visit the South to investigate racial prejudice. Partially set in Detroit.

"Sanda" is the joint pseudonym of Walter H. Stowers and William H. Anderson.

Black, 254. Wright III, 5294.

Mi MiAllG MiD NcD TxHTSU

1459 [Strachey, Rachel Conn Costelloe] 1887–1940
Marching On by Ray Strachey [pseud.]. New York: Harcourt, Brace and Co., 1923. 385 p.

A girl from a religious family attends a women's college and eventually joins the abolitionist movement. Partially set in northern Michigan in the 1830s.

Black, 255.

IC KMK NhU OKentU WM

Strachey, Ray, pseud. *see* Strachey, Rachel Conn Costelloe

1460 [Stratemeyer, Edward] 1862–1930

The Rover Boys on the Great Lakes; or, the Secret of the Island Cave by Arthur M. Winfield [pseud.]. Rahway, N.J.: Mershon Co., 1901. 252 p.

(Rover Boys' Series for Young Americans, no. 5)

The three Rover brothers go on a lake cruise, and when one is kidnapped by an old enemy, pursuit ensues. Set partially on the Detroit River, Lake St. Clair, and "Needle Point Island" in Lake Huron.

Juvenile.

MH

1461 ———.
Two Young Lumbermen; or, From Maine to Oregon for Fortune. Boston: Lee and Shepard, 1903. 326 p.

(Great American Industries Series, no. 1)

Two young men become friends and find work and adventure in a variety of lumber camps from coast to coast. Forty-five pages are set in Detroit and the Saginaw area.

Also published as *The Young Lumberman; or, Out for Fortune* (New York: Street & Smith, 1920 [Alger Series, no. 111]).

Juvenile.

NAIU OKentU WaU

1462 ———.
The Fort in the Wilderness; or, The Soldier Boys of the Indian Trails. Boston: Lothrop, Lee & Shepard Co., 1905. 306 p.

(Colonial Series, no. 5)

Two young brothers, wilderness hunters and traders, become involved in Pontiac's plans to expel the British from North America. Partially set in Detroit in 1763.

Juvenile.

Mi FTS NhD OBgU OKentU

1463 Stratton-Porter, Geneva Grace
1868–1924
A Girl of the Limberlost by Gene Stratton-Porter. New York: Doubleday, Page & Co., 1909. 485 p.

The story of a young girl who desperately desires an education despite her mother's opposition. The last fifty pages are set on Mackinac Island.

Juvenile.

MiBatW MiJac MiOw MiSsB OCl

1464 [Stretton, Hesba] 1832–1911
The Children of Cloverly by the Author of "Jessica's First Prayer," "Fern's Hollow," "Bede's Charity," etc. London: Religious Tract Society, n.d. 157 p.

A soldier fighting in the Civil War sends his two motherless children from their cabin on the shores of Lake Huron to live with an uncle in England. Twelve pages are set in Michigan.

INS NcD

Strickland, Brad, joint author *see* Bellairs, John

1465 Stringer, Arthur 1874–1950
Power. Indianapolis: Bobbs-Merrill Co., 1925. 308 p.

A chronicle of a man's rise from his modest beginnings to his presidency of a national railroad. Set mostly in "Nagisaw" (Saginaw) and Detroit between 1870 and 1920.

MiU IU MnM OU ViR

1466 Stuart, Gordon, pseud.
The Boy Scouts of the Air at Eagle Camp. Chicago: Reilly & Britton Co., 1912. 247 p.

(Boy Scouts of the Air, no. 1)

Ten boy scouts search for a cache of lost money, as well as a nest of golden eagles, while battling villains. Set in Luce County near the Little Two-Hearted River.

Harry Lincoln Sayler (1863–1913) has been suggested as the author.

Juvenile.

Mi MiEM CoD DeU MH

1467 Sullivan, Alan 1868–1947
The Rapids. New York: D. Appleton and Co., 1920. 336 p.

A strong-willed engineer sees possibilities in the development of a town and its rapids into a manufacturing center. Set in Sault Ste. Marie and at the St. Mary's River.

Black, 256.

Mi MnU MoCgS ViR WvBeC

1468 Sullivan, Thomas William 1940–
Born Burning. New York: E. P. Dutton, 1989. 262 p.

An ancient teakwood chair possesses evil magic that has caused the deaths of first-born males, and a magician covets its powers. Set in "Franklin Village."

Science fiction.

MiAllG MiBir MiFli MiMack MiSf

1469 Swanson, Neil Harmon 1896–1983
The Forbidden Ground. New York: Farrar & Rinehart, 1938. 445 p.

A fur-trader and his son who have lost their licenses in a dispute with the governor undertake a campaign of revenge. Set partially in Detroit in the 1770s.

Black, 257.

Mi MiD MiMtpT MiPh MiRochOU

1470 Swanson, Walter S. J. 1917–
The Happening. South Brunswick, N.J.: A. S. Barnes, 1970. 220 p.

A man relates the story of his childhood and adolescence. Mostly set in an unnamed Michigan town, probably Adrian, in the 1930s.

Mi MiAllG MiD MiMarqN MiMtpT-C

1471 ———.
Deepwood. Boston: Little, Brown and Co., 1981. 323 p.

When a forest fire orphans a young boy, he is raised by a widow, and their relationship later becomes intimate. Set in "Au Sable City" in northern Michigan in the 1920s.

1472 Swarthout, Glendon Fred 1918–1992
Willow Run. New York: Thomas Y. Crowell Co., 1943. 237 p.

One night's wartime activity within the sprawling Willow Run B–24 bomber plant is related through the experiences of six workers. Set near Ypsilanti during World War II.

Black, 259.

Mi MiAllG MiD MiMtpT-C MiU

1473 ———.
Welcome to Thebes. New York: Random House, 1962. 372 p.

A successful author returns to his hometown to exact vengeance on the community that ruined his family. Set in "Thebes," near Grand Rapids, from 1934 to 1954.

Black, 258.

Mi MiAllG MiBrF MiEM MiMtpT-C

1474 ———.
The Ghost and the Magic Saber by Glendon Swarthout and Kathryn Swarthout. New York: Random House, 1963. 79 p.

A thirteen-year-old boy is sent to spend the summer at his grandparents' farm, where he finds an heirloom sword and a family ghost. Set near "Constantinople" in 1935.

Juvenile.

Mi MiBatW MiBlo MiOC MiPh

1475 ———.
Loveland. Garden City, N.Y.: Doubleday & Co., 1968. 283 p.

A seventeen-year-old boy finds summer employment as an accordion player in a dance-palace orchestra. Set in Charlevoix in 1934.

1476 ———.
The Melodeon. Garden City, N.Y.: Doubleday & Co., 1977. 129 p.

A thirteen-year-old boy lives with his grandparents, hears stories about his forebears, and meets a ghost on Christmas Eve. Set near Howell in the 1930s.

Also published as *A Christmas Gift* (New York: St. Martin's Paperbacks, 1992).

Juvenile.

Swarthout, Kathryn, joint author *see* Swarthout, Glendon Fred

Swayze, Fred *see* Swayze, James Frederick

1476A [Swayze, James Frederick] 1907–

Run for Your Life! The Adventures of John Rutherfurd at Pontiac's Siege of Detroit, 1763 by Fred Swayze. Toronto: Ryerson Press, 1960. 149 p.

During Pontiac's Conspiracy, a sixteen-year-old Scots boy is captured by Ojibwas, adopted into their tribe, and eventually escapes. Set in and around Fort Detroit. Based on the captivity narrative of John Rutherfurd (1746–1830).

Juvenile.

MiAllG DLC

1477 ———.
The Rowboat War on the Great Lakes, 1812–1814 by Fred Swayze. Toronto: Macmillan of Canada, 1965. 120 p.

A fictionalized story of the struggle for control of the Great Lakes during the War of 1812 between the British and Americans. Partially set at Michilimackinac.

Juvenile.

MiDW IEN KWiU NBuU OBgU

1478 Synon, Mary
Copper Country. New York: P. J. Kenedy & Sons, 1931. 243 p.

A young woman from a wealthy mining family looks for love and happiness among her upper-class peers. Set in "Ash Mountain" on the Keweenaw Peninsula.

Romance.

Black, 260.

Mi MiGr MiHM MiHanS MiIrwG

1479 Szczepańska, Nora 1914–
Sprzysię Żenie Czarnej Wydry. Poznań, Poland: Wydawn. Poznańskie, 1973. 285 p.

A story of the Ottawa chief Pontiac (d. 1769) and his attempt to drive the British out of the Great Lakes area in 1763. Partially set in Detroit and at Michilimackinac.

In Polish.

Juvenile.

MiD

T

Taylor, Allan *see* Dwight, Allan, pseud.

1480 Taylor, Benjamin Franklin 1819–1887
Theophilus Trent; Old Times in the Oak Openings. Chicago: S. C. Griggs and Co., 1887. 250 p.

A young teacher travels from New York to a frontier school where he finds lodging with local families. Set in "Bodkins" on the Raisin River in the 1830s.

Black, 261. Streeter, 6506. Wright III, 5375.

Mi MiAlbC MiAllG MiMtpT-C MiU

1481 Taylor, Lucy
Avenue of Dreams. New York: Signet Books, 1990. 454 p.

An Italian-American hopes to become important in the automobile industry as his wife begins a dressmaking business. Mostly set in Detroit from 1928 to 1963.

MiAllG MiBir MiD MiGay MiWar

1482 Taylor, Richard K.
Murder by Magic. Huntington, W. Va.:
University Editions, 1995. 119 p.

When a series of deaths occur at
the high school, a strange new boy
with connections to witches and
devil worshippers is suspected. Set in
"Huntsville" in central Michigan.

Mystery.

MiAllG IC

1483 Tebbel, John William 1912–
Touched with Fire. New York: E. P.
Dutton, 1952. 477 p.

A wealthy young Frenchman joins
Sieur de La Salle (1643–1687) on his
explorations in New France. Partially
set at Michilimackinac and Fort St.
Joseph.

MiAlbC MiCad MiDU MiKW
MiMtpT-C

1484 Tefft, Bess Hagaman 1913–1977
Ken of Centennial Farm. Chicago: Follett Publishing Co., 1959. 127 p.

Two boys are involved in a variety
of 4H projects and activities that reflect the modernization of farm management. Set in Washtenaw County.

Juvenile.

Mi MiFliL MiRos MiSf MiWar

1485 Templeman, Rebecca Cooper
Cunning Passages. Crozet, Va.: Book-
Ends Publishing Co., 1994. 208 p.

A group of teenagers set out to discover
the truth about and source of a local legend that alleges a tunnel runs beneath
their town. Set in Marshall.

Juvenile.

MiAllG InI

1486 [Terhune, Mary Virginia Hawes]
1831–1922
*With the Best Intentions; a Midsummer
Episode* by Marion Harland [pseud.].
New York: Charles Scribner's, 1890.
303 p.

Honeymooning newlyweds begin to
have a difficult time when the husband
seems to pay undue attention to another
woman. Set on Mackinac Island.

Black, 262. Wright III, 5407.

Mi CLU IaDL OU ViU

1487 Thall, Michael
Let Sleeping Afghans Lie. New York:
Walker & Co., 1990. 250 p.

An unhappily divorced toy designer
tries to prove his ex-wife's innocence
when she is charged with murder. Set
in Ann Arbor and Ypsilanti.

Mystery.

MiAllG MiSsB MiTr InE OCl

1488 Thayer, Marjorie 1908–1992
The Christmas Strangers. Chicago:
Children's Press, 1976. 46 p.

During a Christmas Eve snowstorm,
a Native-American family appears at
the door of a homestead with their sick
baby. Set in the Michigan Territory in
the 1820s.

Juvenile.

1489 Thom, James Alexander 1933–
Panther in the Sky. New York: Ballantine Books, 1989. 655 p.

A fictionalized narrative of the life of
the Shawnee chief Tecumseh (1768–
1813). Twelve pages are set at Fort
Detroit during the War of 1812 before
and after its capture.

1490 Thomas, Karen
Changing of the Guard. New York: Harper & Row, 1986. 186 p.

A sixteen-year-old girl tries to come to terms with her grandfather's death and the transformation of his orchards into a subdivision. Set in western Michigan.

Juvenile.

1491 Thomas, Newton George
The Long Winter Ends. New York: Macmillan Co., 1941. 360 p.

A young out-of-work miner from Cornwall travels to the Michigan copper mines for a job and begins a new life. Set on the Keweenaw Peninsula in 1900.

Black, 263.

Mi MiAllG MiHM MiMtpT MiU

Thomas, Victoria *see* Logan, Tom, pseud.

1492 Thompson, Ione M. 1921–
Amik! Paradise, Mich.: Cloud Nine, 1989. 218 p.

The fictionalized travels and adventures of fur-trader and pioneer John Johnston (1762–1828). Partially set on Mackinac Island and along the St. Mary's River from 1791 to 1793.

Mi MiHM MiMack MiMtpT-C MiSsL

1493 Thoorens, Léon 1921–
Pontiac, Prince de la Prairie. Bruxelles: Éditions Durendal, 1953. 106 p.

A fictionalized biography of the Ottawa chief, including his attempt to organize the various tribes against the English. Partially set in Detroit in 1763.

In French.

Juvenile.

CaOONL

1494 Thorndyke, Helen Louise, pseud.
Honey Bunch: Her First Trip on the Great Lakes. New York: Grosset & Dunlap, 1930. 184 p.

(Honey Bunch Books, no. 11)

A little girl takes a summer steamer excursion with her parents on the Great Lakes. Partially set in Detroit, on Mackinac Island, and in Sault Ste. Marie.

"Helen Louise Thorndyke" is a Stratemeyer Syndicate pseudonym.

Juvenile.

Mi MiMtpT-C MWelC NcGU OBgU

Throop, Belle, joint author *see* E.L.T. Club

1495 Thwing, Eugene 1866–1936
The Red-Keggers. New York: The Book-Lover Press, 1903. 429 p.

A college-educated ne'er-do-well embarks on illegal activities and disrupts a small farming and logging town. Set in "Red Keg" (Averill) on the Tittabawassee River from 1870 to 1871.

Black, 265.

Mi MiAllG MiD MiKW MiMtpT

1496 ———.
The Man from Red Keg. New York: Dodd, Mead and Co., 1905. 431 p.

A scurrilous newspaper editor and publisher prints scandalous stories about the residents of a small town and causes much turmoil. Set in "Red Keg" (Averill) in the 1870s.

Sequel to *The Red-Keggers.*

Black, 264.

Mi MiAllG MiD MiMtpT-C MiStc

1497 Tinker, Barbara Wilson 1909–
When the Fire Reaches Us. New York:
William Morrow, 1970. 255 p.

A young African American describes
life in a Detroit ghetto, its inhabitants,
and the destruction wrought during the
summer riot of 1967.

1498 Titus, Harold 1888–1967
"Timber." Boston: Small, Maynard &
Co., 1922. 379 p.

The pampered son of a wealthy lumberman is given a stand of hardwood to
make a start in business. Set in "Pan-
cake" and in "Blueberry County" in
northern Michigan.

Black, 269.

MiAllG MiMtpT-C MiU MiYEM OU

1499 ———.
The Beloved Pawn. Garden City, N.Y.:
Doubleday, Page & Co., 1923. 316 p.

A ruthless man establishes a fishing
settlement, which he builds into a prosperous business, while keeping his
daughter isolated from outsiders. Set
on Garden Island.

Black, 266.

Mi MiAllG OC OU

1500 ———.
Spindrift. London: Hodder and Stough-
ton, 1924. 320 p.

The captain of a yacht convicted of
murdering its owner escapes prison to
track down the killer. Set in Marquette
and other Upper Peninsula locales.

Mystery.

Black, 268.

Mi MiGr MiHM InFw OCl

1501 ———.
*Below Zero; a Romance of the North
Woods.* Philadelphia: Macrae Smith
Co., 1932. 320 p.

A young man sets out to prove himself to his father by assisting a rival
logging company. Set in "Shoestring"
and "Kampfest" in the western Upper
Peninsula.

Mi MiEM GEU TC ViR

1502 ———.
Code of the North. Philadelphia:
Macrea Smith Co., 1933. 316 p.

When the wastrel son of a lumberman
fails to show up to manage a logging
camp, a young man takes over. Set
in the western Upper Peninsula near
"Shoestring."

MiMuC OBgU OU

1503 ———.
Flame in the Forest. Philadelphia:
Macrae Smith Co., 1933. 283 p.

Witness to a theft years earlier, a
young man finds the scoundrel trying
to gain control of a woman's land. Set
in the western Upper Peninsula near
"Shoestring."

Mi MiBatW FJ OC OU

1504 ———.
The Man from Yonder. Philadelphia:
Macrae Smith Co., 1934. 272 p.

A young logger comes to town and
takes over the management of a lumber
concern and its timber, which a ruthless
villain covets. Set in "Tincup" in the
western Upper Peninsula.

MiGr-L NN TxU WaS

1505 ———.
Black Feather. Philadelphia: Macrae
Smith Co., 1936. 285 p.

A young fur-trader struggles against John Jacob Astor's (1763–1848) powerful fur company and one of its murderous agents. Set on Mackinac Island in 1818.

Black, 267.

Mi MiAllG MiChv MiMtpT-C MiT

1506 Tobin, Richard Lardner 1910–1995
The Center of the World. New York: E. P. Dutton, 1951. 286 p.

A physician tells how a banker came to his small town and set himself above and apart from its citizens. Set in "Clearwater" (Niles?) in the 1920s.

Black, 270.

Mi MiAllG MiD MiKW MiU

1507 Tolan, Stephanie S. 1942–
The Last of Eden. New York: Frederick Warne, 1980. 154 p.

While attending a prep school for girls, a fifteen-year-old's roommate questions her sexual orientation. Set near "Graylander" on Lake Huron.

Juvenile.

1508
Tom Tunnel, the Detective in Mask; or, The Chicago Crook's Deal. The Mystery of the Millionaire Miner. New York: Beadle and Adams, 1896. 29 p.

(Beadle's Dime Library, no. 924)

When a wealthy mine owner is murdered aboard a passenger steamer on Lake Superior, a detective investigates the case. Set in Marquette and Ishpeming.

Dime novel.

TxU

1509 Tomey, Ingrid 1943–
Savage Carrot. New York: Charles Scribner's Sons, 1993. 181 p.

A thirteen-year-old girl has difficulty adjusting to her father's sudden death, but does with the help of a friend and teacher. Set in "Peelee" in northern Michigan.

Juvenile.

1510 ———.
The Queen of Dreamland. New York: Atheneum Books for Young Readers, 1996. 179 p.

An invitation for a free fortune-telling brings an adopted fourteen-year-old face to face with her birth mother. Set in "Canopy" and "Potatoville" in Oakland County.

Juvenile.

MiAllG MiFli InFw InU OCo

1511 Toombs, Jane Ellen Jenke 1926–
Point of Lost Souls. New York: Avon Books, 1975. 160 p.

A woman trying to remember her lost childhood discovers clues to her identity in a pack of Tarot cards. Set on the Lake Michigan shore of the Upper Peninsula.

Mystery.

MiAllG CSbC

1512 ———.
Chippewa Daughter. Wayne, Pa.: Miles Standish Press; New York: Dell Publishing Co., 1982. 355 p.

(American Indian Series, no. 4)

A frontiersman is sent by President Jackson to investigate the selling of guns to the Ojibwas by Canadian rebels. Set in the Ontonagon area in 1836 and 1837.

Mi MiAllG MiGr MiHM MiMtpT

1513 ———.
Heart of Winter. New York: Walker and Co., 1985. 173 p.

A woman's investigation of her husband's mysterious death leads her to a sinister cryogenics laboratory. Set in and around "Ojibway" (Ontonagon?).

Mystery.

Mi MiAllG MiMtpT-C MiSsB OBgU

1514 ———.
Jewels of the Heart. New York: Pinnacle Books, 1993. 448 p.

After being rescued from a scoundrel by a Seneca in 1813, an Englishwoman marries him, and the story follows her offspring into the late 1800s. Partially set in the Upper Peninsula.

Romance.

MiD IChamL OCl OCo MoK

1515 ———.
Passion's Melody. New York: Zebra Books, 1994. 448 p.

(Zebra Lovegram)

In the 1770s, a young Ojibwa woman is rescued from her Sioux captors by an Englishman whom she vows to hate. Partially set on the St. Mary's River in the Upper Peninsula.

Romance.

Mi MiAllG MiD MiFli OCo

1516 ———.
Love's Desire. New York: Zebra Books, 1995. 383 p.

(Zebra Lovegram)

Confederate raiders capture a steamboat and take captive a young woman whose half-sister's love interest is a Union agent. Set in "Ojibway" on the Keweenaw Peninsula.

Romance.

MiAllG IChamL InE OCo WM

1517 [Toombs, John] 1927–
The Opal Legacy by Fortune Kent [pseud.]. New York: Ballantine Books, 1975. 156 p.

(Birthstone Gothic, no. 10)

A young woman marries an older man who takes her to an isolated estate where his first wife mysteriously met her death. Partially set near Marquette.

Mystery.

MiAllG DLC

1518 Townsend, M. Edna
Grandma's Chain. Middleville, Mich.: The Sun and News, 1976. 19 p.

When a woman visits her two grandchildren, she tells them stories about her school days in the schoolhouse that is now the house in which they live. Set in Barry County.

Juvenile.

MiGr MiKW MiMtpT-C

1518A Trainor, J. F.
Target for Murder. New York: Kensington Publishing Corp., 1993. 286 p.

(Angela Biwaban Mystery)

A convicted Ojibwa embezzler investigates the murder of her friend's spouse at the hands of a greedy developer. Partially set in the Upper Peninsula town of "Tilford."

Mystery.

MiD MiMtcM InE OCo WM

1519 **Trammer, Joseph**

Detroit After Dark. New York: Vantage Press, 1990. 101 p.

Two African-American police officers who are already busy investigating various crimes in an extremely violent Detroit are assigned a case involving a serial rapist.

Mystery.

Mi MiAllG

1520 **[Traver, Frances D. Guernsey]** 1815?–1855

Edward Wilton, or, Early Days in Michigan; a Tale Founded on Fact by Fanny Woodville [pseud.]. Detroit: F. B. Way & Co., 1851. 128 p.

A boy is stolen from his family by a party of Potawatomis and is adopted by the chief before returning to his family as a young man. Set along the Raisin and Kalamazoo Rivers from the late 1790s to 1813.

First published serially in the *Detroit Daily Tribune* in 1850.

Wright II, 2796.

MiK MWA

Traver, Robert, pseud. *see* Voelker, John Donaldson

1521 **[Troop, Edna Willa Sullivan]**

Blackbird, a Story of Mackinac Island by Scota Sorin [pseud.]. Detroit: Citator Publishing Co., 1907. 142 p.

An officer falls in love but declines to marry the girl when it is discovered she is half Native American. Told as a series of letters and partially set on Mackinac Island.

Black, 271. Streeter, 6585.

Mi MiAllG MiMack MiMtcM MiPet

Trotter, Hazel Barleau *see* Barleau, Hazel

1522 **Trotter, Melvin Earnest** 1870–1940

Jimmie Moore of Bucktown. Chicago: Winona Publishing Co., 1904. 231 p.

A young boy and his destitute family living in the slums are helped by the director of a Christian rescue mission. Set in an unnamed city, which is Grand Rapids.

Black, 272.

Mi MiAllG MiBrF MiEM MiKW

1523 **[Troutman, Jacqueline D.]** 1928–

Forbidden Treasure by Jackie Dalton [pseud.]. New York: Avalon Books, 1989. 184 p.

(Avalon Career Romance)

Her grandmother's gift of a gemstone leads a young geologist to discover a diamond mine and two handsome men. Set in "Leaping Water Falls" in the Upper Peninsula.

Romance.

1524 **Tucker, Norman Ralph Friedel**

The Years Ahead. London: John Long, 1948. 240 p.

The story of a young man's adventures as a soldier during the French and Indian War and subsequently as a trader who witnesses Pontiac's siege of Detroit in 1763.

Black, 273.

MiD

1525 **Tupala, Gertrude** 1922–1981

There's Gold in Them Hills! Gold! Au Train, Mich.: Avery Color Studios, 1988. 264 p.

When gold is discovered in the Upper Peninsula, a variety of people journey there to try their luck at prospecting. Set in Ishpeming in 1864 and 1865.

Mi MiAllG MiFli MiHM MiStc

1526 **Turrill, David A.** 1946–
Michilimackinac: A Tale of the Straits. Fowlerville, Mich.: Wilderness Adventure Books, 1989. 466 p.

The story of a group of French settlers and their relations with Native Americans and the British. Set on Mackinac Island from the 1720s until 1763.

Mi MiAllG MiBir MiD MiMtpT-C

U

1527 **Uhr, Elizabeth** 1929–
Partly Cloudy and Cooler. New York: Harcourt, Brace & World, 1968. 249 p.

An irresponsible young woman wants to be rid of her soon-to-be-born child and finds the means through an adulterous graduate student. Set in Ann Arbor.

MiDU MiU InFw OBgU WU

1528 **Ulseth, Clara Holton** 1862?–
Sandy Trails. New York: House of Field-Doubleday, 1947. 597 p.

The story of a girl's early years on a farm with her mother and stepfather, and of how her stepsister tries to ruin her life. Set in the Leelanau area in the early 1900s.

Mi MiAllG MiMtpT-C NOneoU

1529 **Urick, Kevin** 1952–
Nakedness. College Park, Md.: Transmutant Magazine, 1979. 68 p.

(Transmutant, no. 4)

An impressionistic story of a young man in a group of writers and dancers, and his emotional and sexual relationships with women. Set in "Larissa."

MiAllG DLC

V

Valentine, Jo, pseud. *see* Armstrong, Charlotte

1530 **Vandenberg, Frank**
Rusty. Grand Rapids: Wm. B. Eerdmans Publishing Co., 1942. 88 p.

A sixteen-year-old leaves his stepfather and is befriended by a janitor at a Christian school, where he works to earn his tuition. Set in "Long Rapids" (Grand Rapids).

Juvenile.

Mi MiEM MiGrC MiMtpT-C ArSsJ

1531 ———.
Westhaven. Grand Rapids: Wm. B. Eerdmans Publishing Co., 1943. 184 p.

A spoiled young man put out on his own by his wealthy father receives encouragement and a job from an old lumberman. Set in "Westhaven" (Grand Haven).

Mi MiGrC MoSpE OU PU

1532 ———.
He Called My Name. Grand Rapids: Wm. B. Eerdmans Publishing Co., 1944. 159 p.

A school teacher marries a no-good who later dies, and she must wait for years for the right man. Set in "White Oak" in western Michigan in the 1920s and 1930s.

MiGrC InMarC OU ViVbR

1533 ———.
As We Forgive. Grand Rapids: Wm. B. Eerdmans Publishing Co., 1946. 160 p.

A young engaged woman marries another man, and she and her first fiancé reconcile in later years. Set in "Cascade City" (Grand Rapids) from 1900 to 1944.

MiGrC InFwB OU TN ViVbR

1534 ———.
Curly. Grand Rapids: Wm. B. Eerdmans Publishing Co., 1947. 88 p.

A widow and her three children move from Chicago to Michigan, where they find friendly neighbors and a kind minister, to begin a new life. Set in "Waterford" (Grand Rapids).

Juvenile.

Mi MiGrC

1535 Van Dyke, Henry 1928–
Ladies of the Rachmaninoff Eyes. New York: Farrar, Straus and Giroux, 1965. 214 p.

Two elderly widows, one Jewish and the other African American, develop a close relationship over thirty years. Set in Allegan.

Van Til, Reinder *see* Evers, Crabbe, pseud.

Vaughan, Carter A., pseud. *see* Gerson, Noel Bertram

1536 Verdelle, A. J. 1960–
The Good Negress. Chapel Hill, N.C.: Algonquin Books of Chapel Hill, 1995. 299 p.

A twelve-year-old African-American girl raised by her grandmother in Virginia rejoins her mother and begins a new life. Set in Detroit in the early 1960s.

1537 Victor, Metta Victoria Fuller 1831–1885
Alice Wilde: The Raftsman's Daughter. A Forest Romance. New York: Irwin P. Beadle and Co., 1860. 98 p.

(Beadle's Dime Novels, no. 4)

His marriage proposal refused by his cousin, a New York man meets the beautiful daughter of a Michigan sawmill owner and falls in love. Set in "Center City" in the 1840s.

Dime novel.

Black, 274.

MiMtpT-C ICN WU

1538 ———.
The Backwoods' Bride. A Romance of Squatter Life. New York: Irwin P. Beadle and Co., 1860. 127 p.

(Beadle's Dime Novels, no. 10)

A new landowner accosts a group of squatters who have settled on his property and falls in love with one of their daughters. Set in southern Michigan in the 1840s.

Dime novel.

Black, 275.

Mi MiEM NcD PGC WaU

1539 Vis, William Ryerson 1886–1969
Saddlebag Doctor. Grand Rapids: Wm. B. Eerdmans Publishing Co., 1964. 164 p.

A newly graduated doctor journeys from New York in 1835 to set up practice in Grand Rapids and watches the settlement gradually grow into a larger town.

Mi MiAllG MiD MiGr MiMtpT-C

1540 Vlasopolos, Anca 1948–
Missing Members. Detroit: Corridors Press, 1990. 217 p.

A female police lieutenant investigates a series of brutal sex crimes and discovers to her horror that she resembles the perpetrator. Set in Detroit.

Mystery.

MiD MiDW MiPhS OBgU UM

1541 [Voelker, John Donaldson] 1903–1991
Anatomy of a Murder by Robert Traver [pseud.]. New York: St. Martin's Press, 1958. 437 p.

When a man who raped a woman is murdered by the enraged husband, a young defense attorney takes the case. Set in "Chippewa" (Marquette).

Mystery.

Black, 276.

1542 [———].
Laughing Whitefish by Robert Traver [pseud.]. New York: McGraw-Hill, 1965. 312 p.

A lawyer tries to restore to a young Ojibwa woman her share of a rich iron ore mine, which the owners have denied her. Set in Marquette and Negaunee in 1873.

Mystery.

1543 [———].
People Versus Kirk by Robert Traver [pseud.]. New York: St. Martin's Press, 1981. 279 p.

The bizarre murder of an iron-mining heiress appears to be an open-and-shut case, but an intrepid defense attorney believes otherwise. Set in "Chippewa" (Marquette).

Mystery.

1544 Vogel, Mary Park
And the Stagecoach Tipped Over. New York: Vantage Press, 1970. 227 p.

A stagecoach driver dreams of saving money and becoming a gentleman, but when persuaded to help runaway slaves, his life changes. Set in Niles from the 1850s to the 1860s.

MiAllG MiEaj MiGr MiMtpT-C MiRog

1545 Voight, Virginia Frances 1909–
Pontiac, Mighty Ottawa Chief. Champaign, Ill.: Garrard Publishing Co., 1977. 80 p.

A fictionalized biography of the Ottawa chief, including his planning of and participation in the siege of British-held Detroit in 1763.

Juvenile.

1545A Voigt, William C.
Awaken to Death. Salt Lake City: Northwest Publishing, 1995. 172 p.

An aggressive policeman suspended for killing a suspect begins to appear in people's dreams and terrorizes them until a young woman intervenes. Set in "Eagleton."

Mystery.

MiGr-L

W

1546 Wachsberger, Kenneth 1949–
Beercans on the Side of the Road: The Story of Henry the Hitchhiker. Ann Arbor: Azenphony Press, 1988. 244 p.

A young Jewish man who drops out of school and travels the country in search of himself has a number of picaresque adventures. Thirty pages are set in Lansing.

Mi MiLC MiMtpT-C MiU MiYEM

Wagner, Carol I., joint author *see* Carroll, Joellyn

———, joint author. *see* Carroll, Marisa.

1547 Waldo, Harold 1891–
Stash of the Marsh Country. New York: George H. Doran Co., 1921. 347 p.

An ambitious young man of Polish heritage attempts numerous jobs and occupations, and ultimately deems his life a failure. Set partially in Detroit in the early 1900s.

Black, 278.

Mi MiAllG MiL CLU OU

1548 ———.
The Magic Midland. New York: George H. Doran Co., 1923. 305 p.

The fourteen-year-old son of a dour preacher has many adventures with his friends, a few of which are connected with the local railroad. Set in "Sidney" (Ovid) in 1916.

Black, 277.

Mi MiAllG MiEM MiL OU

1549 [Waldron, Ethelbert Webb] 1882–1945
The Road to the World by Webb Waldron. New York: Century Co., 1922. 416 p.

A young man realizes that he has been a failure through lack of courage and decisiveness. Mostly set in "Eden" (Midland), "Huron City" (Bay City), and Ann Arbor at the University of Michigan.

Black, 279.

Mi MiAllG KyLoU OU ViU

1550 Waldron, George V. 1872?–1916
Jule Chardin; or, The Smugglers of Thunder Bay. Alpena, Mich.: n.p., 1914. 27 p.

A French-Canadian and his family live and work in a fishing settlement and smuggle whiskey for trade with the Ojibwas. Set on Thunder Bay Island from 1847 to 1851.

Mi MiMtpT-C

Waldron, Webb *see* Waldron, Ethelbert Webb

1551 Walker, Augusta 1914–
A Midwest Story. New York: Dial Press, 1959. 506 p.

The saga of a widow's four children, their experiences growing up, and their relationships with their mother. Partially set in Detroit.

MiD MiFliL MiPh MiRog MiStc

1552 Walker, George Lee
The Chronicles of Doodah. Boston: Houghton Mifflin Co., 1985. 246 p.

A nameless man endures many tests of his suitability as an executive in an unnamed automotive corporation (General Motors?). A satire on corporate executive culture set in an unnamed blighted city (Detroit).

1553 Walker, Louise Jean 1891–1976
Daisy, the Story of a Horse. Grand Rapids: William B. Eerdmans Publishing Co., 1970. 109 p.

A horse born in New Mexico is sold by her owner to a man who needs her to pull his grocery wagon. Partially set in Jackson in the 1890s.

Juvenile.

Mi MiAllG MiAlp MiPh MiWar

1554 Walker, Mildred 1905–
Fireweed. New York: Harcourt, Brace and Co., 1934. 314 p.

A seventeen-year-old girl dreams of leaving her small town, but after marriage her husband is reluctant to relocate. Set in "Flat Point" (Big Bay) on Lake Superior.

Black, 281.

Mi MiAllG MiD MiHM MiMtpT

1555 ———.
Dr. Norton's Wife. New York: Harcourt, Brace and Co., 1938. 269 p.

A doctor on the medical school faculty tries to keep his wife ignorant of the fact that she is slowly dying from multiple sclerosis. Set in "Woodstock" (Ann Arbor).

Mi MiChv MiDW MiMtpT MiU

1556 ———.
The Brewers' Big Horses. New York: Harcourt, Brace and Co., 1940. 441 p.

A woman marries into a beer-making family and, when her husband dies, carries on the business despite the temperance movement. Set in Saginaw from the 1880s to 1918.

Black, 280.

Mi MiD MiGr MiMtpT MiU

1557 [Walters, Petra]
Starlit Promise by Petra Holland [pseud.]. Toronto: Harlequin Books, 1991. 298 p.

(Harlequin Superromance, no. 462)

A widow who is about to lose her ten-year-old daughter to leukemia meets a college professor. Set mostly on the Lake Michigan shore, probably near Holland.

Romance.

MiPh MiWar AzG USl WOsh

1558 Warren, Pat 1936–
Final Verdict. New York: Silhouette Books, 1987. 252 p.

(Silhouette Special Edition, no. 410)

A prosecuting attorney who disdains emotional commitment is pursued by a beautiful lawyer who hopes to change his mind. Set in Detroit.

Romance.

MiAllG MiGr IGenD OBgU OCo

1559 ———.
Look Homeward, Love. New York: Silhouette Books, 1988. 253 p.

(Silhouette Special Edition, no. 442)

A troubled female truck driver is distressed to share a cross-country run with an arrogant but handsome man. Partially set in Detroit.

Romance.

MiAllG KyLo MoK OBgU OCo

1560 ———.
Perfect Strangers. New York: Silhouette Books, 1989. 253 p.

(Silhouette Intimate Moments, no. 288)

A woman staying alone at a cabin discovers a mysterious wounded man in the woods and hides him from pursuing gunmen. Set near "Danville" in the Upper Peninsula.

Romance.

MiAllG MiGr MiInr MiMtcM OBgU

1561 ———.
Till I Loved You. New York: Silhouette Books, 1991. 253 p.

(Silhouette Special Edition, no. 659)

An emotionally cold woman hires a contractor to renovate her country house, but finds that he is interested in her. Set in Detroit and St. Clair.

Romance.

MiAllG MiGr MiPh MiWar OBgU

1562 ———.

An Uncommon Love. New York: Silhouette Books, 1991. 252 p.

(Silhouette Special Edition, no. 678)

A clinical psychologist is hired by a construction company to combat substance abuse and meets a flirtatious employee. Set in Detroit and St. Clair.

Romance.

MiAllG MiPh IChamL OBgU WOsh

1563 ———.

Nowhere To Run. New York: Zebra Books, 1993. 319 p.

After her famous prosecutor father is found murdered, a young woman is the next target of the vengeful madman who begins a campaign of terror. Set in Detroit.

Mystery.

MiAllG MiD InMu MoK USl

1564 ———.

Shattered Vows. New York: Zebra Books, 1995. 347 p.

A serial killer is murdering nuns, and the cousin of the latest victim, while in the midst of a love affair with a detective, tries to solve the case. Set in Detroit.

Mystery.

MiAllG MiD IC OCl WM

1565 ———.

Keeping Kate. New York: Silhouette Books, 1996. 248 p.

(Silhouette Special Edition, no. 1060)

Romance ensues when a young woman takes a job as a caregiver to a widower's baby, and her mother whom she thought dead reenters her life. Set in St. Clair.

Book 3 of the author's trilogy *Reunion*. Neither book 1 (*Michael's House*) nor book 2 (*A Home for Hannah*) is set in Michigan.

Romance.

MiAllG IChamL OCo

1566 [Warriner, Edward Augustus]
1829–1908

Victor La Tourette by a Broad Churchman. Boston: Roberts Brothers, 1875. 406 p.

The seventy-year-old narrator, who was raised by Native-American foster parents, recalls his French father and his religious beliefs. Partially set in Detroit and "Bord du Lac" on the Kalamazoo River.

Wright II, 2656.

MiGr-L NBuBE NhU OU ViU

1567 Waterloo, Stanley 1846–1913

A Man and a Woman. Chicago: F. J. Schulte & Co., 1892. 250 p.

The story of a couple's unconventional romance. Partially set in the Port Huron area and in northern Michigan from the 1840s to the 1880s.

Wright III, 5817.

Mi MiDW MiMtpT-C MiPh OCl

1568 ———.

The Launching of a Man. Chicago: Rand McNally & Co., 1899. 285 p.

The story of the rise of a young man from his days at the University of Michigan in Ann Arbor to his successful career as a builder of railroads in the Upper Peninsula.

Black, 282. Wright III, 5816.

Mi MiEM MiPh MiU OCl

Watson, Elaine *see* Watson, Lois Elaine

1569 Watson, Lois Elaine 1921–
Anna's Rocking Chair by Elaine Watson. Grand Rapids: Zondervan Publishing House, 1984. 199 p.

(Serenade/Saga, no. 6)

A young Milwaukee woman marries a farmer despite her parents' disapproval and tries to adjust to her new life on a Michigan farm in the mid-1800s.

Romance.

MiAllG MiInr InL OXe ViN

1570 ――――.
To Dwell in the Land by Elaine Watson. Grand Rapids: Zondervan Publishing House, 1985. 190 p.

(Serenade/Saga, no. 24)

During the American Revolution, a group of colonial captives are forced to undertake an exhausting march from Kentucky. Eleven pages are set at Fort Detroit.

Romance.

MiChv MiGr MnManTD OXe TxAm

1571 Watson, Virginia Cruse 1872–
With La Salle the Explorer. New York: Henry Holt & Co., 1922. 366 p.

A boy and a little girl travel with Sieur de La Salle (1643–1687) to New France and have a variety of adventures in the wilderness. Twelve pages are set in Michigan.

Juvenile.

Mi MiFli MiSsL InFw OU

1572 Watt, John
"Dibs" on the Core. Los Angeles: Crescent Publications, 1975. 135 p.

The fictionalized humorous reminiscences of the author's early life in Keego Harbor and Detroit in the 1920s and 1930s.

Mi MiBatW MiFli MiMtpT-C MiWar

1573 Way, Isabel Stewart 1904–
Seed of the Land. New York: D. Appleton-Century Co., 1935. 293 p.

The story of a woman who helps her husband get started in farming, continues on after his death, and raises three children. Set in west-central Michigan from 1905 to 1930.

MiGr-L CSd KyRE MWC ViBlbV

Way, John H., joint author *see* Miller, David C.

1574 Weatherwax, Wilma M. 1914–
The Blue-Eyed Chippewa (Bayshew). Swartz Creek, Mich.: Broadblade Press, 1986. 145 p.

An Ojibwa heeding a fasting dream protects a young pioneer woman from numerous dangers. Set near Lennon in Shiawassee County from the 1830s to the 1870s.

Mi MiAllG MiDW MiMarqN MiMtpT-C

1575 Webber, Gordon 1912–1986
Years of Eden. Boston: Little, Brown, 1951. 288 p.

The story of eight years in a farm boy's life, including his mother's death and his father's remarriage. Set in the Flint area in the 1920s.

Black, 284.

Mi MiD MiGr MiRoch MiU

1576 ――――.
What End But Love. Boston: Little, Brown, 1959. 425 p.

At a Memorial Day reunion in 1934, an aging farmer recalls his early life and his family as an automobile company plans to buy his land. Set near "Basswood" and Flint.

Black, 283.

Mi MiAllG MiD MiHM MiMtpT-C

1577 Weber, Ronald 1934–
Company Spook. New York: St. Martin's Press, 1986. 134 p.

A journalist famous for exposing political corruption is contacted by a man who has details of Washington intrigue. Seventeen pages are set at Grayling and along the Au Sable River.

Mystery.

1578 Webster, Elisabeth
Red Wing's White Brother. A Real Story of a Michigan Boy and His Life with the Chippewas. Grand Rapids: Wm. B. Eerdmans Publishing Co., 1956. 64 p.

An eleven-year-old boy is captured by an Ojibwa warrior and is befriended by an Ojibwa boy his own age before being released. Set in Detroit and the Saginaw Valley in 1814.

Juvenile.

Mi MiD MiGr MiMack MiSsB

1579 Webster, Frank V., pseud.
The Boy Pilot of the Lakes; or, Nat Morton's Perils. New York: Cupples & Leon Co., 1909. 201 p.

A fifteen-year-old boy does various good deeds while tracking villains suspected of stealing his father's money. Partially set in Alpena, Detroit, and "Cove Point."

Juvenile.

MiAllG MiD MiMtpT-C OBgU ViR

1580 Weeks, Joseph
All Our Yesterdays. New York: Rinehart & Co., 1955. 374 p.

A young man ashamed of his lower middle-class background hopes to make something of himself in radio broadcasting. Set in "Boite" and Detroit from 1933 to 1935.

Black, 285.

MiA MiAllG InG OC WU

1581 Weesner, Theodore 1935–
The Car Thief. New York: Random House, 1972. 370 p.

Arrested for stealing his fourteenth car, a sixteen-year-old boy endures a stay in a detention center but continues his delinquent behavior after he is released. Set in Flint.

1582 ———.
Winning the City. New York: Summit Books, 1990. 208 p.

When a fifteen-year-old is put off the basketball team to make room for the sponsor's son, he joins a rival team and plans revenge. Probably set in Flint.

1583 Weisman, John 1942–
The Headhunters: Heroine Triple Cross by John Weisman and Brian Boyer. New York: Pinnacle Books, 1974. 187 p.

(Headhunters, no. 1)

A special internal police unit investigates an ex-officer in charge of vice and narcotics, and finds that he is connected with drug traffickers. Set in Detroit.

Mystery.

MiAllG

1584 ———.
The Headhunters: Starlight Motel Incident by John Weisman and Brian

Boyer. New York: Pinnacle Books, 1974. 179 p.

(Headhunters, no. 2)

An ex-police officer is connected with a shootout at a motel that leaves four men dead, and an internal security unit investigates. Set in Detroit.

Mystery.

MiAllG CSbC MsJ OAIM SdBro

1585 ———.
Evidence. New York: Viking Press, 1980. 268 p.

The murder of a close friend leads an investigative newspaper reporter into the various homosexual and drug subcultures of Detroit as he searches for the perpetrator.

Mystery.

1586 Welles, Patricia
Babyhip. New York: E. P. Dutton & Co., 1967. 256 p.

The story of a sixteen-year-old Jewish girl, her sexual encounters, her search for employment, and her role in the evolving hippie culture. Set in Detroit.

Mi MiD MiEM MiMarqN MiPh

1587 ———.
Angel in the Snow. New York: Pocket Books, 1980. 254 p.

A police lieutenant and his team work feverishly to identify a psychopath who has just kidnapped his fifth little girl. Set in Birmingham.

Mystery.

MiAllG MiCad MiD MiFli MiHly

1588 ———.
Members Only. New York: Arbor House, 1981. 303 p.

The deaths of three family members in quick succession while playing golf lead a medical examiner to suspect murder. Set in "Crestwood Hills" near Birmingham.

Mystery.

Mi MiAllG MiD MiFliL MiRoch

1589 Wellman, Andrew M. 1968–
S*F*W; So Fucking What by A. M. Wellman. New York: Random House, 1990. 149 p.

A young convenience store employee is held hostage by a group of terrorists and, after escaping, becomes an unwilling national celebrity. Set in Madison Heights.

1590 Welty, Joel David
Sylviron. Freeland, Mich.: Sylviron Foundation, 1987. 604 p.

A young government social worker is sent to investigate an autonomous cooperative. Set in "Charlotton" (Lansing) and "Sylviron" in northern Michigan in 2007.

Mi MiPet MiU

1591 Werry, Richard R. 1916–
Casket for a Lying Lady. New York: Dodd, Mead & Co., 1985. 212 p.

Private investigator Jane Mulroy and her assistant track down a local lawyer's sister, who has absconded to Florida with negotiable bonds. Partially set in Birmingham.

Mystery.

1592 ———.
A Delicately Personal Matter; a J. D. Mulroy Mystery Novel. New York: Dodd, Mead & Co., 1986. 202 p.

(Red Badge Novel of Suspense)

Private investigator Jane Mulroy and her assistant are hired to find the cause of a man's sudden change in behavior, which leads to murder. Set in Birmingham.

Mystery.

MiAllG MiFli MiInr MiLapC MiPet

1593 Weston, Susan Brown 1943–
Children of the Light. New York: St. Martin's Press, 1985. 262 p.

A young man in Illinois finds himself transported into the future where he meets survivors of a nuclear war. Sixteen pages are set in western Michigan along Lake Michigan.

Science fiction.

1594 Wexstaff, Bernice C. 1898–1987
The Black Panther of the Great Lakes. Grand Rapids: Wm. B. Eerdmans Publishing Co., 1957. 83 p.

The story of thirteen-year-old Benjy, his love of boats, and his friendship with an old sailor who teaches him about self-reliance. Set in "Indian Village" (Charlevoix).

Juvenile.

Mi MiAllG MiD MiMtpT-C MiPet

1595 ———.
Haunt of High Island. Grand Rapids: Wm. B. Eerdmans Publishing Co., 1958. 103 p.

Benjy and his friend ignore an old sailor's warning about lake spirits and begin to search for treasure. Set on High Island and in "Indian Village" (Charlevoix).

Sequel to *The Black Panther of the Great Lakes.*

Juvenile.

Mi MiAllG MiAlp MiChv MiPh

1596 [Wheatley, Kathleen Musser] 1923–
Willo by Karen Snow [pseud.]. Ann Arbor: Street Fiction Press, 1976. 284 p.

A feminist telling of a woman's life from her early years, including her role as a mother, up to her husband's retirement. Partially set in Bronson and at the University of Michigan from 1928 to the 1940s.

MiAllG MiDW IU OU WMani

1597 Wheeler, Edward Lytton 1854?–1885
Deadwood Dick, Jr. in Detroit; or, Turning the Tables on Satan. New York: Beadle and Adams, 1889. 13 p.

(Beadle's Half-Dime Library, no. 612)

A wealthy and villainous grain industry magnate plans to steal his ward's fortune but is thwarted by Deadwood Dick. Set in Detroit.

Dime novel.

Black, 286.

Mi TxU

1598 Wheeler, Harriet Martha 1858–1924
The Woman in Stone. New York: Broadway Publishing Co., 1903. 168 p.

An Ojibwa woman falls in love with a white man and becomes deranged when he is killed. Twenty-eight pages are set at Michilimackinac, in Sault Ste. Marie, and in Detroit in the 1760s.

MiGr WBB WU

Wheeler, Myron "Bud," pseud. *see* Bean, Wiley E.

1599 Whelan, Gloria Ann 1923–
A Clearing in the Forest. New York: G. P. Putnam's Sons, 1978. 126 p.

An elderly widow and a young neighbor become friends, and together they battle a company that wants oil drilling rights on her land. Set near "Oclair" in northern Michigan.

Juvenile.

1600 ———.

A Time To Keep Silent. New York: G. P. Putnam's Sons, 1979. 127 p.

When his wife dies, a pastor and his daughter move from a large and affluent church and establish a mission in a small northern Michigan town.

Juvenile.

1601 ———.

The Pathless Woods. New York: J. B. Lippincott, 1981. 181 p.

A fictionalized account of Ernest Hemingway's (1899–1961) sixteenth summer when he was beginning to assert his independence. Set in Horton Bay and Walloon Lake in 1915.

Juvenile.

1602 ———.

Next Spring an Oriole. New York: Random House, 1987. 60 p.

(Stepping Stone Book)

In 1837, ten-year-old Libbie Mitchell moves from Virginia with her parents and has encounters with friendly Potawatomis and French neighbors. Set near Saginaw.

Juvenile.

1603 ———.

The Secret Keeper. New York: Alfred A. Knopf, 1990. 186 p.

The babysitter of a ten-year-old boy at a posh resort community is warned not to allow the boy's father near him. Set

at "Blue Harbor" and "Lakeville" in the Leelanau area.

Juvenile.

1604 ———.

Hannah. New York: Alfred A. Knopf, 1991. 63 p.

A new teacher in the district convinces a blind nine-year-old girl's parents that she could go to school and learn braille. Set in northern Michigan in 1887.

Juvenile.

1605 ———.

Night of the Full Moon. New York: Alfred A. Knopf, 1993. 63 p.

(Stepping Stone Book)

Thirteen-year-old Libbie Mitchell visiting friends at a Potawatomi village is taken along with them when soldiers force them to relocate. Set in the Saginaw area in 1840.

Sequel to *Next Spring an Oriole.*

Juvenile.

1606 ———.

That Wild Berries Should Grow: The Story of a Summer. Grand Rapids: William B. Eerdmans Publishing Co., 1994. 125 p.

Made to recuperate at her grandparents' farm, a fifth-grade girl from Detroit eventually finds excitement in the country. Set in Greenbush on Lake Huron in 1933.

Juvenile.

1607 ———.

Once on This Island. New York: HarperCollins, 1995. 186 p.

On Mackinac Island in 1812, a twelve-year-old girl observes with dismay the many changes in her family after the British capture the fort and island.

Juvenile.

1608 ———.
The Indian School. New York: Harper-Collins, 1996. 89 p.

An orphan is sent to live with her stern aunt and uncle at a mission school, and she befriends a Native-American girl. Set in "Coldriver" in northern Michigan in 1839.

Juvenile.

1609 White, Edmund Valentine 1940–
A Boy's Own Story. New York: E. P. Dutton, 1982. 218 p.

The story, probably autobiographical, of a boy's childhood and his emerging awareness that he is gay. Partially set at "Eton" (Cranbrook) in the 1950s.

1610 ———.
The Beautiful Room Is Empty. New York: Alfred A. Knopf, 1988. 228 p.

A gay young man passes through adolescence and early adulthood having a variety of experiences. Set at "Eton" (Cranbrook) and the University of Michigan.

Sequel to *A Boy's Own Story.*

1610A White, Franklin
Fed up with the Fanny. Decatur, Ga.: Blue/Black Press, 1996. 324 p.

A harried African-American advertising executive tries to deal with his troubled nephew, his fiancée, and her best friend. He also finds financial support for the community organization he sponsors. Set in Detroit.

DLC

1611 [White, Georgia Atwood]
Free as the Wind by Dascomb Atwood [pseud.]. New York: Liveright Publishing Corp., 1942. 331 p.

The saga of a prosperous Dutch family whose younger members long to leave their farm. Set in "Zuppanville" in southwestern Michigan from 1848 to 1941.

Mi MiBatW MiHolH MiMtpT OU

1612 White, Leslie Turner 1903–
Log Jam. Garden City, N.Y.: Doubleday, 1959. 284 p.

A young man attempts to thwart ruthless rival logging companies and deliver his timber more quickly by using a railroad. Set in northern Michigan in the 1870s.

Mi MiBrF MiEM MiHly MiWar

White, Randy Wayne *see* Ramm, Carl

1613 White, Stewart Edward 1873–1946
The Blazed Trail. New York: McClure, Phillips & Co., 1902. 413 p.

An honest young lumberman fights the tricks and attacks of an aggressive and sneaky logging company. Set in the Saginaw area and the Upper Peninsula in the 1880s.

Black, 288.

Mi MiAdC MiBrF MiDW MiMtpT-C

1614 ———.
The Riverman. New York: McClure Co., 1908. 368 p.

A skillful river boss is convinced to go into timber business with a New York lawyer who later turns treacherous. Partially set in "Redding" in western Michigan in the 1870s.

Black, 289.

Mi MiD MiFliL MiKW MiMtpT-C

1615 ———.

The Adventures of Bobby Orde. New York: Doubleday, Page & Co., 1910. 340 p.

The nine-year-old son of a river boss has a number of outdoor adventures and helps clear a neighbor of a murder charge. Set in the lumbermill town of "Monrovia."

Juvenile.

Black, 287.

MiAllG MiGr ICU MnM OU

1616 ———.

The Rules of the Game. New York: Doubleday, Page & Co., 1910. 644 p.

After a poor initial showing, college graduate Bob Orde joins his father in the logging industry in California. Partially set in northern Michigan from 1898 to 1902.

Sequel to *The Adventures of Bobby Orde.*

1616A ———.

The Glory Hole. Garden City, N.Y.: Doubleday, Page & Co., 1924. 495 p.

A man and his wife receive a large bequest from an expatriate uncle and the sudden wealth changes their lives and brings tragic consequences. Set in "Little Falls" (Grand Rapids) around 1900.

Mi MiAllG MiEM MiMtpT-C MiU

1617 Whitlock, Brand 1869–1934

The Stranger on the Island. New York: D. Appleton and Co., 1933. 267 p.

A French-Canadian fugitive from justice flees to a religious colony ruled by a polygamous "King Gorel" (James Strang). Set on Beaver Island in the 1850s.

Black, 291.

Mi MiD MiGr MiMtpT-C MiU

1618 Whitney, Phyllis Ayame 1903–

The Mystery of the Gulls. Philadelphia: Westminster Press, 1949. 202 p.

A woman has inherited a hotel and must prove it a success before she can keep it, but mysterious happenings are driving guests away. Set on Mackinac Island.

Juvenile.

1619 Whittier, Charles Albert

In the Michigan Lumber Camps. New York: F. Tennyson Neely Co., 1900. 137 p.

(Boy's Vacation Series, no. 1)

Three boys spend their summer vacation in a lumber camp, learn about logging, and have adventures hunting and fishing. Set on the Au Sable River and at Gladwin.

Juvenile.

Streeter, 6915.

Mi MiStc MB

Wickenden, Dan *see* Wickenden, Leonard Daniel

1620 Wickenden, Leonard Daniel 1913–1989

The Wayfarers by Dan Wickenden. New York: William Morrow and Co., 1945. 371 p.

A newspaperman grieving for his late wife finds himself isolated from his four children and hopes for a change.

Set in "Broadfield" (Grand Rapids) in the 1930s.

Mi MiAllG MiHly MiKW OC

1621 Widdemer, Margaret 1884–1978
The Great Pine's Son; a Story of the Pontiac War. Philadelphia: John C. Winston Co., 1954. 182 p.

With the help of a French girl, the sixteen-year-old son of the Indian Commissioner warns the British about Pontiac. Set partially at Fort Detroit in 1763.

Juvenile.

Mi MiD MiFliL MiGr MiStc

1622 Willard, Nancy 1936–
Things Invisible To See. New York: Alfred A. Knopf, 1985. 263 p.

A baseball hits a seventeen-year-old girl and brings guilt and love to the young man who caused the injury. Set in Ann Arbor and the world of spirits in 1941 and 1942.

MiAllG MiHolH MiLivS ICL NbU

1623 ———.
Sister Water. New York: Alfred A. Knopf, 1993. 255 p.

The mystical story of a family connected by love and death, and of strange unseen powers that control events around them. Set in Ann Arbor.

1624 [Willcox, Orlando Bolivar] 1823–1907
Shoepac Recollections: A Way-Side Glimpse of American Life by Walter March [pseud.]. New York: Bunce & Brother, 1856. 360 p.

Fictionalized reminiscences of the author's boyhood in 1820s Detroit, when his family had to eke out an existence after his father' death.

Also published as *Walter March; or, Shoepac Recollections* by Major March (Boston: J. French and Co.; Detroit: Raymond & Selleck, 1857).

Black, 292. Streeter, 6934. Wright II, 2737.

Mi MiAllG MiD MiMtpT-C MiU

1625 [Willett, Edward] 1830–1889
The Trader Spy; or, The Victim of the Fire Raft by J. Stanley Henderson [pseud.]. New York: Beadle and Adams, 1869. 100 p.

(Beadle's Dime Novels, no. 176)

In 1763, a sailor finds himself in the midst of the attack on Fort Detroit by Pontiac and his warriors, and worries about a young woman who has been kidnapped by the Ottawas.

Also published as *The Trader Traitor; or; Old Bark, the Marksman* (New York: Beadle and Adams, 1887 [Beadle's Boy's Library, no. 165; octavo edition]).

Dime novel.

Black, 293.

Mi

1626 Willey, Margaret 1950–
The Bigger Book of Lydia. New York: Harper & Row, 1983. 215 p.

The death of her father still affects a shy fifteen-year-old girl, but she begins to cope when an anorexic girl comes to live with her. Set in southwestern Michigan.

Juvenile.

1627 ———.
Finding David Dolores. New York: Harper & Row, 1986. 150 p.

An aloof and alienated thirteen-year-old girl keeps a dossier on an older boy and shares her obsession with a new friend. Set in "St. Martins" (St. Joseph).

Juvenile.

1628 ———.
If Not for You. New York: Harper & Row, 1988. 154 p.

A high school freshman girl witnesses the slow disintegration of two adolescents' marriage when she babysits for the couple. Set in "St. Martins" (St. Joseph).

Juvenile.

1629 ———.
Saving Lenny. New York: Bantam Books, 1990. 151 p.

Unable to distinguish among friendship, infatuation, and love, two young and immature adolescents become inseparable. Set in "St. Martins" (St. Joseph).

Juvenile.

1630 ———.
The Melinda Zone. New York: Bantam Books, 1993. 135 p.

A fifteen-year-old girl whose parents are divorced sees how family life should be when she spends the summer with her aunt, uncle, and cousin. Set in St. Joseph.

Juvenile.

1631 ———.
Facing the Music. New York: Delacorte Press, 1996. 183 p.

A fifteen-year-old girl mourning the recent death of her mother becomes a singer in a high school rock band, which causes unforeseen consequences. Set in Grand Haven.

Juvenile.

1632 **Williams, Arthur J.**
A Fast Ride to Hell. New York: Vantage Press, 1989. 51 p.

A twelve-year-old girl is killed when she is thrown onto a freeway by a mentally disturbed man, but she returns to life and seeks revenge. Set in Detroit.

MiGr-L

Williams, Bob *see* Williams, Robert K.

1633 **[Williams, Robert K.]**
The Island House: A Tale of Mackinac Island by Bob Williams. Minneapolis: James D. Thueson, Publisher, 1989. 210 p.

While a Minnesota family is on vacation, the sixteen-year-old son has a summer romance that causes his mother to reexamine her own marriage. Set on Mackinac Island in 1938.

MiAllG MiChe MiFli MiGr MnU

Willis, Nancye, ed. *see* Winters, Donna M.

1633A **Wilson, Donald C.**
The Winds of Tomorrow. Southfield, Mich.: DCW Publishing Co., 1995. 402 p.

An African-American publisher of an ethnic weekly buys a large, failing Detroit daily newspaper and attempts to make it a success despite racial tensions among the staff and outside agitators.

Title on book jacket: *The Winds of Tomorrow . . . Are the Winds of Change.*

MiSf NcU

1634 **Wilson, Helen Ann Finnegan**
1907–1980
The King Pin. New York: Macmillan Co., 1939. 340 p.

The humorous story of a lumberman and patriarch who is constantly seeking business ventures that will make him and his family wealthy. Set in "Lakewood" (Marquette).

Black, 294.

Mi MiD MiKC MiMarqN MiU

1635 [———].
Deborah Todd by Holly Wilson [pseud.]. New York: Julian Messner, 1955. 192 p.

The story of a girl's fifth-grade year and the various scrapes and escapades in which she is involved with her friends. Set in "Henry's Bend" (Marquette).

Juvenile.

Mi MiBrF MiDW MiFliL MiYEM

1636 [———].
Caroline the Unconquered by Holly Wilson [pseud.]. New York: Julian Messner, 1956. 189 p.

A sixteen-year-old girl runs away from her uncle in Detroit to be with her prospector father and falls in love with a cad. Set in "Henry's Bend" (Marquette) in 1853.

Juvenile.

Mi MiAllG MiBrF MiDW MiFliL

1637 [———].
Snowbound in Hidden Valley by Holly Wilson [pseud.]. New York: Julian Messner, 1957. 186 p.

A young girl and her Ojibwa classmate become close friends, but the latter's family is suspected of arson by the community. Set in "Henry's Bend" (Marquette).

Juvenile.

Mi MiBrF MiD MiFli MiGr

1638 [———].
Always Anne by Holly Wilson [pseud.]. New York: Julian Messner, 1957. 188 p.

A fifteen-year-old girl eventually learns that she need not emulate the popular girl in class to win friends and be a success. Set in "Henry's Bend" (Marquette).

Juvenile.

Mi MiAllG MiDW MiRoch MiYEM

1639 [———].
The Hundred Steps by Holly Wilson [pseud.]. New York: Julian Messner, 1958. 190 p.

The sixteen-year-old daughter of an ore freighter captain longs to be accepted into a snooty clique at school. Set in "Clifton" (Marquette).

Juvenile.

Mi MiAllG MiBar MiD MiRoch

1640 [———].
Stranger in Singamon by Holly Wilson [pseud.]. New York: Julian Messner, 1959. 192 p.

An eleven-year-old spends a year living with her cousins and subsequently changes for the better. Set in the lumbering town of "Singamon" in the Upper Peninsula.

Juvenile.

Mi MiAllG MiBrF MiD MiDW

1641 [———].
Double Heritage by Holly Wilson [pseud.]. Philadelphia: Westminster Press, 1971. 173 p.

During the Detroit cholera epidemic of 1832, a young girl of Native American and white parents experiences prejudice and decides which culture to follow in her life.

Juvenile.

MiBrF MiD MiFliL MiOw MiStc

Wilson, Holly, pseud. *see* Wilson, Helen Ann Finnegan

1642 Wilson, Robert Charles 1951–
Crooked Tree. New York: G. P. Putnam's Sons, 1980. 350 p.

A lawyer and his Ottawa wife become entangled in the legend of an evil spirit returning and inciting bear attacks. Set in "Wabanakisi" (Cross Village?).

1643 ——.
Icefire. New York: G. P. Putnam's Sons, 1984. 379 p.

Rioting inmates in a high-security prison for the criminally insane escape and terrorize the guards and doctors. Set on "Scale Island," north of Grand Marais.

1644 ——.
Second Fire. New York: Jove Books, 1993. 372 p.

When archaelogists come to dig at an ancient Ojibwa site, they are opposed in the courts, and a shaman summons the Ancient Ones. Set in "Watersdrop" in the Upper Peninsula.

Mi MiAllG MiBir MiD MiFli

1645 Wilson, Robert Charles 1953–
Mysterium. New York: Bantam Books, 1994. 276 p.

One morning, a town suddenly vanishes and its inhabitants find themselves in an odd world that has some connection with UFOs and the federal goverment. Set in "Two Rivers."

Science fiction.

Winfield, Arthur M., pseud. *see* Stratemeyer, Edward

1646 Winter, Jeanette
The Christmas Tree Ship. New York: Philomel Books, 1994. 32 p.

When a schooner captain and his annual cargo of Christmas trees bound for Chicago is lost on Lake Michigan, his family carries on the tradition. Set in Manistique around 1910.

Juvenile picture book.

1647 Winters, Donna M. 1949–
Elizabeth of Saginaw Bay. Grand Rapids: Zondervan Publishing House, 1986. 196 p.

(Serenade/Saga, no. 34)

A twenty-year-old newlywed travels into the Michigan wilderness with her banker husband and endures many troubles. Set at Saginaw Bay in 1837.

Romance.

Mi MiAllG MiChv MiGr MiMu

1648 ——.
Jenny of L'Anse Bay. Grand Rapids: Zondervan Publishing House, 1988. 224 p.

(Serenade/Saga, no. T13)

Travelling to a mission school, a seventeen-year-old woman becomes a teacher to the Ojibwas and falls in love with the chief's son. Set in L'Anse in the late 1860s.

Romance.

Mi MiAllG MiChe MiStjo MnManTD

1649 ——.
Mackinac. Edited by Nancye Willis. Caledonia, Mich.: Bigwater Publishing, 1989. 169 p.

(Great Lakes Romances, no. 1)

In 1895, the daughter of a Grand Rapids cabinetmaker journeys to Mackinac Island's Grand Hotel to collect a large overdue bill, and falls in love with the manager.

Romance.

Mi MiAllG MiHM MiMtpT-C MiPh

1650 ———.

The Captain and the Widow. Edited by Anne Severance. Caledonia, Mich.: Bigwater Publishing, 1990. 186 p.

(Great Lakes Romances, no. 2)

When an accident aboard a ship kills her husband, a twenty-year-old woman takes over as manager of their fledgling steamship line. Set in South Haven in 1897.

Romance.

Mi MiAllG MiKW MiMtpT-C MiPh

1651 ———.

Sweethearts of Sleeping Bear Bay. Edited by Anne Severance. Caledonia, Mich.: Bigwater Publishing, 1991. 194 p.

(Great Lakes Romances, no. 3)

While on a Great Lakes cruise with her father, a licensed river pilot becomes involved with the second mate. Set in Glen Haven and other Lake Michigan locales.

Sequel to *The Captain and the Widow.*

Romance.

Mi MiAllG MiAlp MiMtpT-C MiYEM

1652 ———.

Charlotte of South Manitou Island. Edited by Anne Severence. Caledonia, Mich.: Bigwater Publishing, 1992. 248 p.

(Great Lakes Romances, no. 4)

In 1892, when an eleven-year-old girl's father dies in a Lake Michigan storm, the son of the South Manitou Island lighthouse keeper teaches her perseverance.

Romance.

Mi MiAllG MiGr MiMtpT-C MiYEM

1653 ———.

Aurora of North Manitou Island. Edited by Ann Severence. Caledonia, Mich.: Bigwater Publishing, 1993. 296 p.

(Great Lakes Romances, no. 5)

A newlywed's sailor husband is injured in a storm, and a former lady friend comes to nurse him back to health. Set on North Manitou Island in 1898 and 1899.

Romance.

Mi MiAllG MiGr MiMtpT-C MiYEM

1654 ———.

Bridget of Cat's Head Point. Edited by Pamela Quint Chambers and Lynda S. Jolls. Caledonia, Mich.: Bigwater Publishing, 1994. 241 p.

(Great Lakes Romances, no. 6)

A young woman leaves South Manitou Island for the mainland to seek employment and is courted by three men. Set in the Leelanau and Traverse City areas in 1899.

Romance.

Mi MiAllG MiGr MiMtpT-C MiYEM

1655 ———.

Rosalie of Grand Traverse Bay. Edited by Pamela Quint Chambers. Caledonia, Mich.: Bigwater Publishing, 1996. 327 p.

(Great Lakes Romances, no. 7)

A young woman is falsely accused of misusing the mortgage payment on her aunt and uncle's home and store, but she meets a lawyer who assists her. Set in Traverse City in 1900.

Romance.

MiAllG MiGr MiT OCl

Wirt, Ann, pseud. *see* Benson, Mildred Augstine Wirt

1656 **Wise, Winifred Esther** 1906–
Swift Walker; a True Story of the American Fur Trade. New York: Harcourt, Brace and Co., 1937. 288 p.

The fictionalized biography and adventures of fur trader Gurdon S. Hubbard (1802–1886). Partially set at Michilimackinac, on the Grand River, and on the Muskegon River from 1816 to 1830.

Juvenile.

Mi MiD MiFliL MiMtpT-C MiU

1657 **Witheridge, Elizabeth Plumb** 1907–
Never Younger, Jeannie. New York: Atheneum, 1963. 150 p.

An eleven-year-old girl spends 1914 on her grandparent's farm while her parents are in Europe, and she begins to worry as war threatens. Set in northern Michigan.

Juvenile.

MiGay MiLapC MiSf MiStc MiWar

1658 **Woiwode, Larry** 1941–
What I'm Going To Do, I Think. New York: Farrar, Straus and Giroux, 1969. 309 p.

Recently married and expecting a child, Chris and Ellen honeymoon at their grandfather's cabin and try to come to terms with their new life. Set on the Leelanau Peninsula.

1659 ———.
Indian Affairs. New York: Atheneum, 1992. 290 p.

Seven years after their marriage and her miscarriage, Ellen and Chris return to the lodge so he can finish his dissertation, but events test their love. Set on the Leelanau Peninsula.

Sequel to *What I'm Going To Do, I Think.*

Wolf, pseud. *see* McCollom, Russell L.

Wolf, Hurst, pseud. *see* Kroflich, Stephen A.

Wolf, Sarah, pseud. *see* Shoemaker, Sarah Elizabeth Wolf

1660 **Wolff, Maritta Martin** 1918–
Whistle Stop. New York: Random House, 1941. 449 p.

The story of a dull-witted and mean-spirited family of eight and their squalid life and social interactions. Set in the outskirts of the southern Michigan town of "Ashbury."

Black, 298.

1661 ———.
Night Shift. New York: Random House, 1942. 662 p.

A waitress struggles to support her family while her husband is in a mental hospital, but her well-meaning sister complicates matters. Set in southern Michigan.

Black, 297.

MiAlbC MiAllG MiD MiEM MiHM

1662 ———.
Back of Town. New York: Random House, 1952. 436 p.

A man returns to his hometown from California with his dying wife and begins affairs with his former sweetheart and a young girl. Set in southern Michigan.

Mi MiAllG MiEM MiMtpT-C MiU

1663 ———.
Buttonwood. New York: Random House, 1962. 343 p.

A factory worker and ex-war hero supports his demanding mother and dreadful aunt, but keeps his private life secret from them. Set in southern Michigan.

Black, 296.

1664 Wolfschlager, Irene Hollands
Moccasined Feet. Boston: Ginn and Co., 1929. 138 p.

The adventures and experiences of two boys in a pioneer settlement and its wild surroundings. Set near Lake St. Clair and the St. Clair River in the 1790s.

Juvenile.

Mi MiAlbC MiAllG MiD MiWar

1665 Wolk, George
400 Brattle Street. New York: Wyden Books, 1978. 265 p.

A CIA-funded experiment using hypnotized agents is subverted by a terrorist organization that plans to take over the United States. Partially set in Detroit.

Mystery.

1666 Wood, Jerome James 1846–1903
The Wilderness and the Rose; a Story of Michigan. Hudson, Mich.: Wood Book Co., 1890. 133 p.

The rise and decline of "Keene Corners," a settlement in Lenawee County, is the background for the actions of a variety of local denizens in the 1840s.

Black, 299. Wright III, 6065.

Mi MiAllG MiD MiK MiMtpT-C

Woodville, Fanny, pseud. *see* Traver, Frances D. Guernsey

1667 Woodward, Martha Cornell
The Hon. Geoffrey Wiley: A Philosophical Novel. Chicago: G. P. Brown and Co., 1889. 190 p.

A man with extensive social connections and a questionable reputation is observed by a young woman. Twenty pages are set in Sault Ste. Marie.

OBgU

1668 Woodward, Sigrid E.
Kathleen. Philadelphia: Dorrance and Co., 1929. 287 p.

A beautiful young girl seems destined to love and marry the boy next door until her dying mother tells her she was adopted. Set partially in "Irondale" (Ironwood).

Mi DLC

1669 Woodworth, Samuel 1785–1842
The Champions of Freedom; or, The Mysterious Chief. A Romance of the Nineteenth Century, Founded on the War Between the United States and Great Britain. New-York: Charles L. Baldwin, 1816. 2 vols.

A fictionalized narrative of the War of 1812 that stresses its military aspects and in which the young hero is assisted by the spirit of a Miami chief. Fourteen pages are set at Detroit.

Wright I, 2760.

MiD CtW ICU RPB ViU

THE

CHAMPIONS OF FREEDOM,

OR

THE MYSTERIOUS CHIEF,

A Romance of the Nineteenth Century,

FOUNDED ON THE

EVENTS OF THE WAR,

BETWEEN THE

UNITED STATES AND GREAT BRITAIN,

WHICH TERMINATED IN MARCH, 1815.

IN TWO VOLUMES.

BY SAMUEL WOODWORTH.

Miracles our Champions wrought,
Who their daring deeds shall tell?
O how gloriously they fought!
How triumphantly they fell!
Montgomery.

VOL. I.

NEW-YORK:
Printed and Published by Charles N. Baldwin, Bookseller,
No. 49 Division-street.

1816.

1670 Woolson, Constance Fenimore
1840–1894
Anne. New York: Harper & Brothers, 1882. 540 p.

A young woman living with her impoverished family is sent to school for a year by a rich aunt so she may earn her living as a teacher. Partially set on Mackinac Island.

Black, 300. Streeter, 7036. Wright III, 6100.

Mi MiEM MiGrC MiOC IEN

1671 ———.
Jupiter Lights. New York: Harper & Brothers, 1889. 347 p.

On a visit to her dead brother's remarried wife, a young woman requests to raise their son herself. Partially set at "Port aux Pins" on the southern shore of Lake Superior.

Wright III, 6106.

MiDU MiEM ICU InLP OBgU

1672 Wray, Kent W.
Boy from Shacktown, by George. Kalamazoo: RBM Ministries, 1992. 156 p.

(By George Series, no. 1)

George, an eighth-grader, tries to solve the mystery of his father's missing boots and their connection to the robbery of a local store. Set in "Westville" (Plainwell).

Juvenile.

Mi MiAllG

1673 ———.
Misguided Missiles, by George. Kalamazoo: RBM Ministries, 1993. 156 p.

(By George Series, no. 2)

George and his friends doubt that another boy's homemade rocket will work and solve mysteries about break-ins and blackmail. Set in "Westville" (Plainwell).

Juvenile.

MiAllG

1674 ———.
Devil in Wilsons' Woods, by George. Kalamazoo: RBM Ministries, 1993. 166 p.

(By George Series, no. 3)

While camping at Gun River, George and his friends investigate a hidden building in the woods, which involves them in a marijuana distribution ring.

Juvenile.

MiAllG

1675 ———.
Dinosaur Detectives, by George. Kalamazoo: RBM Ministries, 1993. 155 p.

(By George Series, no. 4)

When an old man finds a dinosaur bone in a gravel pit, George and his friends agree to help him dig for the rest, but a theft occurs. Set near "Westville" (Plainwell).

Juvenile.

MiAllG

1676 ———.
Secret of Brigham Mansion, by George. Kalamazoo: RBM Ministries, 1994. 163p.

(By George Series, no. 5)

A flickering light seen in an old mansion leads George and his friends to a mystery about a coded message and the Underground Railroad. Set in "Westville" (Plainwell).

Juvenile.

MiAllG

1677 ———.
Midnight Merry-Go-Round, by George. Kalamazoo: RBM Ministries, 1995. 171 p.

(By George Series, no. 6)

George and his friends become involved with a grave-robbing, an antique carousel horse, and a Chicago lawyer and his partner. Set in "Westville" (Plainwell).

Juvenile.

MiAllG

1678 Wright, Betty Ren 1927–
Ghosts Beneath Our Feet. New York: Holiday House, 1984. 137 p.

A girl, her mother, and her stepbrother spend the summer with an old uncle to help him and also encounter a ghost. Set in the Upper Peninsula town of "Newquay."

Juvenile.

1679 ———.
A Ghost in the Window. New York: Holiday House, 1987. 152 p.

While visiting her divorced father, a fourteen-year-old girl discovers she has a psychic gift and helps solve an old mystery. Set in "Trevor" in the Upper Peninsula.

Sequel to *A Secret Window,* which is set entirely in Milwaukee.

Juvenile.

1680 Wright, James North 1838–1910
Where Copper Was King; a Tale of the Early Mining Days on Lake Superior. Boston: Small, Maynard, & Co., 1905. 352 p.

A story of the copper mining industry on the Keweenaw Peninsula in the 1860s, with much detail given about the techniques, dangers, and working conditions associated with mining.

Black, 302. Streeter, 7045.

Mi MiD MiGr MiHM MiMtpT-C

1681 Wright, John Couchis 1874–
Ella; a Story of the White Slave Traffic. Harbor Springs, Mich.: Published Privately by John C. Wright, 1911. 132 p.

A seventeen-year-old girl thinking she has a job lead from a Chicago employment agency finds herself trapped in a house of prostitution. Twenty-four pages are set in Harbor Springs.

Streeter, 7046.

Mi MiAllG OU

1682 Wright, Zita L.
Danger on the Ski Trails. New York: Lothrup, Lee & Shepard Co., 1965. 188 p.

A group of young people in a ski club are puzzled by and investigate a series of accidents on their ski run. Set in "Chipamung," an Upper Peninsula mining town.

Juvenile.

Mi MiAllG MiFliL MiPet MiPh

1683 Wunsch, Josephine McLean 1914–
Flying Skis. New York: David McKay Co., 1962. 212 p.

A fifteen-year-old girl's desire to make her high school ski team is rewarded through hard work and practice. Set in "Kingsley Harbor" (Houghton?).

Juvenile.

Mi MiD MiFliL MiLapC MiOC

1684 ———.
Passport to Russia. New York: David McKay Co., 1965. 209 p.

As seen through the eyes of one of its members, a university orchestra tours the Soviet Union giving concerts in a variety of locations. Fifteen pages are set at the University of Michigan.

Juvenile.

Mi MiBar MiBlo MiD InFw

1685 ———.
Summer of Decision. New York: David McKay Co., 1968. 184 p.

A sixteen-year-old girl spends the summer at a resort with her family and likes the wrong sort of boy. Set at "Crescent Cove" (Bowers Harbor?) on Old Mission Peninsula.

Juvenile.

Mi MiBatW MiD MiDU MiPh

1686 ———.
Girl in the Rough. New York: Silhouette Books, 1981. 188 p.

(First Love from Silhouette, no. 2)

A studious girl is hurt when her younger sister begins dating a boy she likes and subsequently begins taking golf lessons to improve her self-esteem. Set in Detroit.

Juvenile.

MiAllG MiGr MiL MiTr OBgU

1687 ———.
Class Ring. New York: Scholastic Book Services, 1983. 172 p.

(Wildfire Book, no. 44)

A seventeen-year-old girl is flattered when an outgoing girl becomes her friend, but experiences heartache when her boyfriend is stolen. Set in "Pine Ridge" and Petoskey.

Juvenile.

MiBir MiEM MiMtcM MiMu MiTr

1688 ———.
Free As a Bird. New York: Silhouette Books, 1984. 188 p.

(First Love from Silhouette, no. 77)

A city girl takes a job as junior hostess at a rustic summer inn and begins to regret the work until she meets a boy. Set in "Bayport" on Lake Michigan.

Juvenile.

MiAllG MiGr MiMtcM MiTr
IChamL

1689 ———.
Breaking Away. New York: Silhouette Books, 1985. 154 p.

(First Love from Silhouette, no. 139)

A teenage girl must transfer from a private school and move to a smaller house when her father is indicted for embezzlement. Set in "Springwell," a Detroit suburb.

Juvenile.

MiGr MiRic MiRoch IArlh ScSp

1690 ———.
The Perfect 10. New York: Silhouette Books, 1986. 156 p.

(First Love from Silhouette, no. 182)

An intrigued sixteen-year-old girl is determined to find out about a handsome but aloof boy in her school. Set in a small eastern Michigan town.

Juvenile.

MiAllG MiGr MiTr MiWar IGenD

1691 ———.
Lucky in Love. New York: Crosswinds, 1987. 155 p.

(Keepsake, no. 5)

A young girl becomes suspicious when her best friend tells her why she and the boy she likes would never be compatible. Set in "Stony Creek."

Juvenile.

MiChe MiFliL IChamL InE OCo

1692 ———.
Between Us. New York: Crosswinds, 1989. 156 p.

(Keepsake, no. 42)

A tenth-grade girl who has a poor self-image because she thinks she's homely and overweight learns to accept herself. Set in "Glen Oaks."

Juvenile.

MiGr IChamL OCo OXe UM

1693 **Wydra, Frank Thomas** 1939–
The Cure. New York: Dell Publishing Co., 1992. 441 p.

When the head of an AIDS research project for a drug company is murdered, his replacement finds all the records and data missing. Set in Detroit.

Mystery.

Mi MiAllG MiBir MiD MiMtcM

Wylie, Philip, joint author *see* Balmer, Edwin

Y

1694 **Yorty, Jeane**
Far Wilderness. Grand Rapids: William B. Eerdmans Publishing Co., 1966. 224 p.

A sixteen-year-old boy travels with his parents and sister from Albany to a new Michigan homestead in 1835. Set in the Flint River area.

Juvenile.

Mi MiAllG MiAlp MiD MiMtpT-C

Young, Al *see* Young, Albert James

1695 **Young, Albert James** 1939–
Snakes by Al Young. New York: Holt, Rinehart and Winston, 1970. 149 p.

When his parents are killed in an automobile accident, a young African American is reared by his kind grandmother and discovers he has an aptitude for blues music. Set in Detroit.

1696 ———.
Who Is Angelina? by Al Young. New York: Holt, Rinehart and Winston, 1975. 280 p.

A young African-American woman embarks on a voyage of self-discovery while traveling from California to Mexico. Partially set in Detroit where the protagonist visits her father.

Z

1697 **Zanger, Molleen** 1948–
Gardenias Where There Are None. Tallahassee: Naiad Press, 1994. 168 p.

A young lesbian graduate student ignores her studies when she rents an old house and is contacted by a ghost through her computer. Set in Adrian.

Romance.

Mi COPL InE OCl WU

1698 **Zara, Louis** 1910–
This Land Is Ours. Boston: Houghton Mifflin Co., 1940. 778 p.

The saga of a pioneer and adventurer who participates in important events in the Old Northwest from 1755 to 1835. Ninety pages are set in Detroit during Pontiac's siege of 1763.

Black, 303.

Mi MiAllG MiD MiMtpT-C MiU

1699 Zeigen, Frederic 1874–1942
"Therold Archer Knowlton," Poet. A Love Story of Violet and Violets. Chicago: W. B. Conkey Co., 1910. 339 p.

The progress, obstacles, and heartbreaks of a young English poet during his pursuit of true love. Partially set in Detroit and the Saginaw area in the 1820s.

Limited to three hundred copies.

Mi MiAllG MiD MiYEM

1700 Zenowich, Christopher 1954–
The Cost of Living. New York: Harper & Row, 1989. 267 p.

A recent college graduate abandons his career plans to earn easy money as a discount store manager. Set in "Sterne" in southeastern Michigan and in Ann Arbor.

1701 Zerler, Kathryn Schultz 1950–
A Slip in Time; an Historic Adventure at the Benton Harbor Ship Canal. St. Joseph, Mich.: Sleeping Cat Press, 1994. 148 p.

A psychic and her friend travel back to 1895 where they help two women thwart a man's embezzlement scheme. Set in St. Joseph and Benton Harbor.

Mi MiBsA MiKW MiMtpT-C InFw

1702 Zimmerman, Robert Dingwell 1952–
Death Trance; a Novel of Hypnotic Detection by R. D. Zimmerman. New York: William Morrow and Co., 1992. 254 p.

Maddy Phillips, a blind paraplegic psychologist, hypnotizes her brother Alex to probe for clues to the murder of his former lover. Set on a Lake Michi-gan island southwest of the Mackinac Bridge.

Mystery.

1703 ———.
Blood Trance by R. D. Zimmerman. New York: William Morrow and Co., 1993. 236 p.

(Maddy and Alex Phillips Mystery of Hypnotic Detection)

When Alex finds one of his sister's former patients, knife in hand, standing over the dead body of her stepmother, the brother-sister duo investigate. Set on a Lake Michigan island.

Mystery.

1704 ———.
Red Trance by R. D. Zimmerman. New York: William Morrow and Co., 1994. 237 p.

(Maddy and Alex Phillips Mystery of Hypnotic Detection)

Psychologist Maddy Phillips hypnotizes her brother, Alex, in an attempt to solve a series of murders he witnessed during a recent trip to Moscow. Partially set on a Lake Michigan island.

Mystery.

Title Index

Titles and subtitles, as well as titles under which a book was subsequently published, are included here. Titles are given in italics; subtitles in roman. In addition, for those books originally published in a foreign language, the English title is entered if the book has been translated.

Initial articles are omitted. Numbers refer to the items. An "n" following a number indicates that the title in question will be found in the notes section of that item.

When there are duplicate titles, the surnames of the authors are given in parentheses.

B

G

H

I

N

O

T

Y

Series Index

Titles of publishers' series are included here. Also included are quasi- or unofficial series, such as the names of detectives who appear on a regular basis in mystery novels and who are not represented in the title index.

Initial articles are omitted. Numbers refer to the items. An "n" following a number indicates that the title in question will be found in the notes section of that item.

When there are duplicate series titles, the surnames of the authors are given in parentheses.

A

Adventures in the Northwoods, 767
Alger Series, 1461n
Allan Pinkerton Detective Stories, 1138
Amber Ainslie Detective Series, 1393, 1394, 1398, 1399
American Bloodhound, 655
American Girls Series, 94n
American Heritage Series, 478
American Indian Series, 1512
American Woodland Tales, 535, 536
Amos Walker Mysteries, 421, 422, 423, 424, 426, 428, 430, 431, 432, 434
Angela Biwabam Mystery, 1518A
Anneke Haagen Mysteries, 676, 677, 678
Arabesque Romance, 486, 487, 974
Avalon Career Romance, 1286, 1523
Avon Flare, 316
Avon Historical Romance, 746, 747

B

Bachelors and Babies, 391
Beadle's Boy's Library, 42n, 628n, 629n, 995n, 996, 1625n
Beadle's Dime Library, 246, 247, 248, 752, 911, 1508
Beadle's Dime Novels, 43, 44, 228, 522, 1537, 1538, 1625
Beadle's Half-Dime Library, 814, 1597
Beadle's Pocket Novels, 228n, 628n
Belmont Blue Ribbon Gothic, 555
Best Friends, 1407, 1408, 1409, 1410, 1412, 1414, 1415, 1416, 1417n, 1420, 1421, 1422, 1423, 1424, 1425, 1426
Best Friends Special Edition, 1417
Birthstone Gothic, 1517
Blackwater Bay Mystery, 574, 575
Book of the Beast, 1427, 1428
Boy Scout Series (Carter), 200
Boy Scout Series (Ralphson), 1174

Subject and Genre Index

Subjects and genres are listed below. Genres are given in bold typeface, e.g., **Juvenile literature, Mystery novels.** Numbers refer to the items.

Chronological Index

Brief author-title entries are given under the year of publication. Subtitles of the novels are omitted in this index. Novels that have been published in different years with alternate titles also appear under the date of the subsequent printing. Initial articles are omitted.

No Date
(estimated or supposed date given in parentheses)

Carmichael, Jack B. *New Slain Knight* (1990).

Cauffman, Joseph G. *Half a Day's Journey* (1976).

Dalm, P. A. *Immigrant* (1920s).

Graepp, L. W. *Bleichgesicht und Rothhaut* (1890s).

Harju, Irja. *Neebish Island Memories, 1921–1927* (1984).

Harley, William N. *Tomahawk and Cross* (1900s).

Major, Thomas A. *Suprest Information* (1910).

Morrison, Dennis M. *Auntie Miranda* (1980s).

Polack, William G. *Shegonaba* (1920s).

Reynolds, Jessie A. *In the Shade of the Oaks* (1890s).

Stretton, Hesba. *Children of Cloverly* (1870s).

1816

Woodworth, Samuel. *Champions of Freedom.*

1832

Richardson, John. *Wacousta.*

Smith, Hamilton. *Forest Maid.*

1835

Beaumont de la Bonninière, Gustave. *Marie.*

1836

Scenes on Lake Huron.

1839

Kirkland, Caroline M. *New Home—Who'll Follow?*

1840

Richardson, John. *Canadian Brothers.*

1842

Kirkland, Caroline M. *Forest Life.*

Warriner, Edward A. *Victor La Tourette.*

1877

Adams, William T. *Out West.*
Guernsey, Clara F. *Shawnee Prisoner.*
Pinkerton, Allan. *Spiritualists and the Detectives.*

1878

Adams, William T. *Lake Breezes.*
Anderson, Olive. *American Girl and Her Four Years in a Boy's* College.

1879

Adams, William T. *Going South.*

1880

Coomes, Oliver. *Giant Rifleman.*
Garrigues, Adele M. *Summer Boarders.*
Rose, James A. *Boy's Vacation on the Great Lakes.*

1881

Cadwell, Clara. *De Barr's Friends.*
Coomes, Oliver. *Long Beard, the Giant Spy.*
————. *One-Armed Alf, the Giant Hunter of the Great Lakes.*

1882

Merrill, James M. *Young Bear Hunters.*
Woolson, Constance F. *Anne.*

1885

Ingersoll, Ernest. *Ice Queen.*

1886

Lewis, Charles B. *Under Five Lakes.*
Merrill, James M. *Forced Apart.*

1887

Crofoot, Frederic S. *Detroit Unveiled.*
Lewis, Leon. *Flying Glim.*
Rayne, Martha L. *Pauline.*

Taylor, Benjamin F. *Theophilus Trent.*
Willett, Edward. *Trader Traitor.*

1888

Cragin, Isabella S. *Saint Peter and Tom.*
Riddle, Albert G. *Tory's Daughter.*

1889

Badger, Joseph E. *Crafty Crazy Slack.*
Chipman, William P. *Roy Gilbert's Search.*
Dean, Frederic A. *Heroines of Petosega.*
Hollands, Hulda T. *Marfa.*
Jenks, George Charles. *Rube Rocket, the Tent Detective.*
Lewis, Charles B. *Miser's Lost Ward.*
Wheeler, Edward L. *Deadwood Dick, Jr. in Detroit.*
Woodward, Martha C. *Hon. Geoffrey Wiley.*
Woolson, Constance F. *Jupiter Lights.*

1890

Terhune, Mary V. *With the Best Intentions.*
Wood, Jerome J. *Wilderness and the Rose.*

1891

Allen, Emory A. *Jolly Trip.*

1892

Waterloo, Stanley. *Man and a Woman.*

1893

Catherwood, Mary H. *White Islander.*

1894

Clark, A. Arnold. *Beneath the Dome.*
Hildreth, Harry D. *Wauneta.*
Howe, Edward E. *Chronicles of Break o' Day.*
Stowers, Walter H. *Appointed.*

1895

Ingram, Helen K. *Three on a Tour.*
Kelly, George C. *Circus Detective.*

Sullivan, Alan. *Rapids.*

Gail, Otto W. *Hans Hardts Mondfahrt.*
Lowrie, Rebecca. *Cambric Tea.*
McCallum, Mella R. *Tents of Wickedness.*
Muller, Charles G. *Baseball Detective.*

1929

Detzer, Karl W. *Pirate of the Pine Lands.*
Dixon, Franklin W. *Lone Eagle of the Border.*
Douglas, Lloyd C. *Magnificent Obsession.*
Ford, Richard C. *Sandy MacDonald's Man.*
Fox, Frances M. *Nannette.*
Hamilton, Jean. *Wings of Wax.*
McClinchey, Florence E. *Joe Pete.*
Nieland, Dirk. *'N Fonnie Bisnis.*
Pinchot, Ann. *Hour Upon the Stage.*
Sherman, Harold M. *Hit and Run!*
————. *Flashing Steel.*
Wolfschlager, Irene H. *Moccasined Feet.*
Woodward, Sigrid E. *Kathleen.*

1930

Bodenheim, Maxwell. *Virtuous Girl.*
Curwood, James O. *Green Timber.*
Doner, Mary F. *Dancer in the Shadow.*
————. *Lonely Heart.*
Dos Passos, John R. *42nd Parallel.*
Dreyer, Myrta M. *Beckoning Hands.*
Fox, Frances M. *Magic Canoe.*
Loban, Ethel H. *Signed in Yellow.*
Rankin, Carroll W. *Finders Keepers.*
Severance, Henry O. *Michigan Trailmakers.*
Sherman, Harold M. *Batter Up!*
Stockwell, William H. *Rudderless.*
Thorndyke, Helen L. *Honey Bunch: Her First Trip on the Great Lakes.*

1931

Gail, Otto W. *By Rocket to the Moon.*
Synon, Mary. *Copper Country.*

1932

Benson, Mildred A. *Secret of the Sundial.*

Brill, Ethel C. *White Brother.*
Brody, Catherine. *Nobody Starves.*
Céline, Louis-Ferdinand. *Voyage au Bout de la Nuit.*
Clancy, Louise M. *Love Isn't Important.*
Doner, Mary F. *Fool's Heaven.*
Herrmann, John. *Summer Is Ended.*
Horan, Kenneth. *Longest Night.*
Kiralyhegyi, Pal. *Greenhorn.*
Lewis, Janet. *Invasion.*
McClure, Marjorie B. *John Dean's Journey.*
Plum, Mary. *Murder at the Hunting Club.*
Titus, Harold. *Below Zero.*

1933

Balmer, Edwin. *When Worlds Collide.*
Brody, Catherine. *Cash Item.*
Brown, Forman. *Better Angel.*
Conroy, Jack. *Disinherited.*
Cuthrell, Faith Baldwin. *Love's a Puzzle.*
Rankin, Carroll W. *Wolf Rock.*
Titus, Harold. *Code of the North.*
————. *Flame in the Forest.*
Whitlock, Brand. *Stranger on the Island.*

1934

Brown, Vera. *Tarnished Fame.*
————. *Wings of Love.*
Céline, Louis-Ferdinand. *Journey to the End of the Night.*
De Jong, David C. *Belly Fulla Straw.*
Doner, Mary F. *Forever More.*
Gardner, Joan G. *Desires of the Heart.*
Herbst, Josephine. *Executioner Waits.*
Horan, Kenneth. *It's Later Than You Think.*
Hull, Helen R. *Morning Shows the Day.*
Michigan Department of Conservation. *Three Boys Go Camping.*
Pound, Arthur. *Once a Wilderness.*
Smith, Alice W. *Jess Edwards Rides Again.*
Snell, Roy J. *Phantom Violin.*
Titus, Harold. *Man from Yonder.*
Walker, Mildred. *Fireweed.*

Widdemer, Margaret. *Great Pine's Son.*

1955

Arnold, Elliott. *White Falcon.*
Babcock, Elinor G. *Absalom.*
Carr, Harriett H. *Where the Turnpike Starts.*
Catton, Bruce. *Banners at Shenandoah.*
Cooper, Sylvia. *Thunder Stone.*
Derleth, August W. *Land of Sky-Blue Waters.*
Ellison, James W. *I'm Owen Harrison Harding.*
Erno, Richard B. *My Old Man.*
Fisher, Aileen. *Timber!*
Gringhuis, Richard H. *Young Voyageur.*
Humphreys, John R. *Dirty Shame.*
Kelly, Regina Z. *Beaver Trail.*
Martin, Robert Lee. *Echoing Shore.*
Porter, Monica E. *Mercy of the Court.*
Ratigan, William. *Young Mister Big.*
Roberts, Willo D. *Murder at Grand Bay.*
Sechrist, Berniece S. *Big Enough.*
Senical, Pearl. *Where The Heart Is.*
Weeks, Joseph. *All Our Yesterdays.*
Wilson, Helen F. *Deborah Todd.*

1956

Brucker, Margaretta. *Big, Brave and Handsome.*
Daly, Edwin. *Some Must Watch.*
Dempsey, Vincent. *Cabin Boy.*
Frazier, Neta O. *Secret Friend.*
Jackson, Caary P. *Match Point.*
Johnson, Enid. *Nancy Runs the Bookmobile.*
Nielsen, Helen B. *Crime Is Murder.*
Orr, Myron D. *Mission to Mackinac.*
Pearson, Mary C. *His Own Interpreter.*
Pike, Fannie J. *Dark Valley Romance.*
Ratigan, William. *Adventures of Captain McCargo.*
Riordan, Robert. *Medicine for Wildcat.*
Seager, Allan. *Hilda Manning.*
Webster, Elisabeth. *Red Wing's White Brother.*

Wilson, Helen F. *Caroline the Unconquered.*

1957

Brucker, Margaretta. *Three Boys and a Girl.*
Butler, Beverly. *Lion and the Otter.*
Cloutier, Helen H. *Isle Royale Calling.*
Fuller, Iola. *Gilded Torch.*
Henry, Vera. *Lucky Number.*
Howard, Elizabeth. *Girl of the North Country.*
Lawrence, Mildred E. *Good Morning, My Heart.*
Malcolm-Smith, George. *Trouble with Fidelity.*
Martin, Robert Lee. *Tough Die Hard.*
Rowe, Viola. *Way with Boys.*
Wexstaff, Bernice C. *Black Panther of the Great Lakes.*
Wilson, Helen F. *Snowbound in Hidden Valley.*
———. *Always Anne.*

1958

Blish, James. *VOR.*
Chase, Leah M. *Song of the Maples.*
Daly, Edwin. *Legacy of Love.*
Gringhuis, Richard H. *Eagle Pine.*
Keil, Doris P. *Ploughboy and the Nightingale.*
Lawson, Horace L. *Pitch Dark and No Moon.*
Lea, George. *Somewhere There's Music.*
Livingston, Harold. *Detroiters.*
Nern, Daniel D. *Black As Night.*
Slobodkin, Florence. *Too Many Mittens.*
Voelker, John D. *Anatomy of a Murder.*
Wexstaff, Bernice C. *Haunt of High Island.*
Wilson, Helen F. *Hundred Steps.*

1959

Dickinson, Lulu J. *Table in the Wilderness.*
Erno, Richard B. *Hunt.*

Arnow, Harriette. *Weedkiller's Daughter.*
Boatman, Alan. *Summer's Lie.*
Brennan, Alice. *Fear No Evil.*
Doner, Mary F. *Return a Stranger.*
Eckert, Allan W. *Conquerors.*
Jackson, Caary P. *Rose Bowl Pro.*
Johnson, Areldene O. *Lonely Apartments.*
Lewis, Elizabeth B. *Granny Eloped.*
Slote, Alfred H. *Stranger on the Ball Club.*
Swanson, Walter. *Happening.*
Tinker, Barbara W. *When the Fire Reaches Us.*
Vogel, Mary P. *And the Stagecoach Tipped Over.*
Walker, Louise J. *Daisy, the Story of a Horse.*
Young, Albert J. *Snakes.*

1971

Brennan, Alice. *Never to Die.*
Coughlin, William J. *Destruction Committee.*
Curzon, Daniel. *Something You Do in the Dark.*
Farley, Carol. *Bunch on McKellahan Street.*
Goff, Georgena. *Black Dog.*
Goines, Donald. *Dopefiend.*
Hailey, Arthur. *Wheels.*
Harrison, Jim. *Wolf.*
Kerle, Arthur G. *Whispering Trees.*
McGuane, Thomas. *Bushwhacked Piano.*
Merlis, George. *V.P.*
Oates, Joyce Carol. *Wonderland.*
Robbins, Harold. *Betsy.*
Slote, Alfred H. *Jake.*
Sneider, Vernon J. *West of the North Star.*
Wilson, Helen F. *Double Heritage.*

1972

Brown, Elizabeth L. *Candle of the Wicked.*
Childs, Walter C. *Crisis Corporation.*
Doner, Mary F. *Thine Is the Power.*
———. *Not by Appointment.*
Goines, Donald. *Black Gangster.*
———. *Whoreson.*

Green, Hannah. *Dead of the House.*
Hay, Mae P. *Last Best Hope.*
O'Hara, John. *Ewings.*
Roberts, Willo D. *Nurses.*
Slote, Alfred H. *Biggest Victory.*
———. *My Father, the Coach.*
Smith, Larry. *Original.*
Weesner, Theodore. *Car Thief.*

1973

Augustine, Robertson. *Kau-Bau-Gwas-Shee.*
Bellairs, John. *House with a Clock in Its Walls.*
Gerber, Daniel. *American Atlas.*
Goines, Donald. *Street Players.*
———. *White Man's Justice: Black Man's Grief.*
Howard, Elizabeth. *Wilderness Adventure.*
Jackson, Andrew S. *Gentleman Pimp.*
Lewis, Elizabeth B. *Sunset Hour.*
Lockwood, Walter. *Jones Unbound.*
Love, Edmund G. *Small Bequest.*
Oates, Joyce Carol. *Do with Me What You Will.*
Roberts, Willo D. *Nurse Robin.*
Robertson, Keith C. *In Search of a Sandhill Crane.*
Slote, Alfred H. *Hang Tough, Paul Mather.*
Snyder, Guy. *Testament XXI.*
Stone, Nancy Y. *Wooden River.*
Szczepańska, Nora. *Sprzysię Żenie Czarnej Wydry.*

1974

Ambers, Henry J. *Unfinished Building.*
Doner, Mary F. *Darker Star.*
East, Ben. *Last Eagle.*
Farley, Carol. *Most Important Thing in the World.*
Franks, Owen. *Gotcha, Gipper!*
Glass, Joanna M. *Reflections on a Mountain Summer.*
Goines, Donald. *Crime Partners.*
———. *Daddy Cool.*
———. *Death List.*

1985

1986

Settings Index

The novels selected for this bibliography usually have a strong sense of Michigan places interwoven into their plots and provide a recognizable background in, through, and across which the characters operate. This index provides access to the novels by actual locality and includes names of cities and towns, as well as counties, rivers, schools, and other geographic and topographic entities.

Authors of Michigan novels often use imaginary place-names for a variety of reasons. Sometimes it is merely to invent a locale in which to set their characters and action. Other times, in those novels that expose civic small-mindedness or general bad behavior, it is to disguise an actual town or city in order to protect the real inhabitants from scorn or ridicule. It is not unthinkable that the reason also may be to protect the author from litigation arising from libel laws.

Imaginary place-names include cities, towns, counties, rivers, schools, colleges, summer camps, etc. Imaginary place-names used by more than one author have separate entries with the authors' surnames given in parentheses.

Actual place-names and imaginary place-names are listed together alphabetically, the differentiation being that the latter appear in quotation marks. Occasionally, actual Michigan place-names have been used by authors to denote a totally different locale, and such names also appear in quotation marks. Numbers refer to the items.

M

T

Michigan Imprints Index

Listed here are the novels that have been published or printed in Michigan towns and cities. The arrangement is alphabetical by location, with the publishers or printers listed alphabetically underneath.

Numbers refer to the items. An "n" following a number indicates that the publisher in question will be found in the notes section of that item.

Cities or publishers enclosed in square brackets with a question mark indicate that these are either unverifiable from internal evidence in the books themselves and represent best guesses, or are inferred from other sources.

[?]

[Areldene Johnson?], 761
Living Arts Publishing, 204
[Sally B. Hewitt?], 663
[?], 415A, 1242A

Albion

[E.L.T. Club?], 389
Elite Publishing Co., 665

Alpena

[George V. Waldron?], 1550

Ann Arbor

Arbor Publications, 1247A
Azenphony Press, 1546
Edwards Brothers Printers, 1011, 1023
George Wahr, 1287
Millard Press, 1429

Proctor Publications, 475A, 990A, 1165
Sarah Jennings Press, 237A
Street Fiction Press, 1596

AuTrain

Avery Color Studios, 1219, 1525

Bath

Enterprise Press, 166A, 167

Battle Creek

Miller Foundation, 653

Bay City

Red Keg Press, 631

Benton Harbor

Antiquarian Publishing Co., 934

Titles in the Great Lakes Books Series

Freshwater Fury: Yarns and Reminiscences of the Greatest Storm in Inland Navigation,
    by Frank Barcus, 1986 (reprint)

Call It North Country: The Story of Upper Michigan,
    by John Bartlow Martin, 1986 (reprint)

The Land of the Crooked Tree,
    by U. P. Hedrick, 1986 (reprint)

Michigan Place Names,
    by Walter Romig, 1986 (reprint)

Luke Karamazov,
    by Conrad Hilberry, 1987

The Late, Great Lakes: An Environmental History,
    by William Ashworth, 1987 (reprint)

Great Pages of Michigan History from the Detroit Free Press, 1987

Waiting for the Morning Train: An American Boyhood,
    by Bruce Catton, 1987 (reprint)

Michigan Voices: Our State's History in the Words of the People Who Lived It,
    compiled and edited by Joe Grimm, 1987

Danny and the Boys, Being Some Legends of Hungry Hollow,
    by Robert Traver, 1987 (reprint)

Hanging On, or How to Get through a Depression and Enjoy Life,
    by Edmund G. Love, 1987 (reprint)

The Situation in Flushing,
    by Edmund G. Love, 1987 (reprint)

A Small Bequest,
    by Edmund G. Love, 1987 (reprint)

The Saginaw Paul Bunyan,
    by James Stevens, 1987 (reprint)

The Ambassador Bridge: A Monument to Progress,
    by Philip P. Mason, 1988

Let the Drum Beat: A History of the Detroit Light Guard,
    by Stanley D. Solvick, 1988

An Afternoon in Waterloo Park,
    by Gerald Dumas, 1988 (reprint)

Contemporary Michigan Poetry: Poems from the Third Coast,
    edited by Michael Delp, Conrad Hilberry and Herbert Scott, 1988

Over the Graves of Horses,
    by Michael Delp, 1988

Wolf in Sheep's Clothing: The Search for a Child Killer,
    by Tommy McIntyre, 1988

Survival and Regeneration: Detroit's American Indian Community,
    by Edmund J. Danziger, Jr., 1991

Steamboats and Sailors of the Great Lakes,
    by Mark L. Thompson, 1991

Cobb Would Have Caught It: The Golden Age of Baseball in Detroit,
    by Richard Bak, 1991

Michigan in Literature,
    by Clarence Andrews, 1992

Under the Influence of Water: Poems, Essays, and Stories,
    by Michael Delp, 1992

The Country Kitchen,
    by Della T. Lutes, 1992 (reprint)

The Making of a Mining District: Keweenaw Native Copper 1500–1870,
    by David J. Krause, 1992

Kids Catalog of Michigan Adventures,
    by Ellyce Field, 1993

Henry's Lieutenants,
    by Ford R. Bryan, 1993

Historic Highway Bridges of Michigan,
    by Charles K. Hyde, 1993

Lake Erie and Lake St. Clair Handbook,
    by Stanley J. Bolsenga and Charles E. Herndendorf, 1993

Queen of the Lakes,
    by Mark Thompson, 1994

Iron Fleet: The Great Lakes in World War II,
    by George J. Joachim, 1994

Turkey Stearnes and the Detroit Stars: The Negro Leagues in Detroit, 1919–1933,
    by Richard Bak, 1994

Pontiac and the Indian Uprising,
    by Howard H. Peckham, 1994 (reprint)

Charting the Inland Seas: A History of the U.S. Lake Survey,
    by Arthur M. Woodford, 1994 (reprint)

*Ojibwa Narratives of Charles and Charlotte Kawbawgam and Jacques LePique, 1893–
    1895. Recorded with Notes by Homer H. Kidder,*
    edited by Arthur P. Bourgeois, 1994, co-published with the Marquette County
    Historical Society

Strangers and Sojourners: A History of Michigan's Keweenaw Peninsula,
    by Arthur W. Thurner, 1994

Win Some, Lose Some: G. Mennen Williams and the New Democrats,
    by Helen Washburn Berthelot, 1995

Sarkis,
    by Gordon and Elizabeth Orear, 1995

The Northern Lights: Lighthouses of the Upper Great Lakes,
    by Charles K. Hyde, 1995 (reprint)

Kids Catalog of Michigan Adventures, second edition,
    by Ellyce Field, 1995

Rumrunning and the Roaring Twenties: Prohibition on the Michigan-Ontario Waterway,
    by Philip P. Mason, 1995

In the Wilderness with the Red Indians,
    by E. R. Baierlein, translated by Anita Z. Boldt, edited by Harold W. Moll, 1996

Elmwood Endures: History of a Detroit Cemetery,
    by Michael Franck, 1996

Master of Precision: Henry M. Leland,
    by Mrs. Wilfred C. Leland with Minnie Dubbs Millbrook, 1996 (reprint)

Haul-Out: New and Selected Poems,
    by Stephen Tudor, 1996

Kids Catalog of Michigan Adventures, third edition,
    by Ellyce Field, 1997

Beyond the Model T: The Other Ventures of Henry Ford, revised edition,
    by Ford R. Bryan, 1997

Young Henry Ford: A Picture History of the First Forty Years,
    by Sidney Olson, 1997 (reprint)

The Coast of Nowhere: Meditations on Rivers, Lakes and Streams,
    by Michael Delp, 1997

From Saginaw Valley to Tin Pan Alley: Saginaw's Contribution to American Popular Music, 1890–1955,
    by R. Grant Smith, 1997

The Long Winter Ends,
    by Newton G. Thomas, 1997 (reprint)

Bridging the River of Hatred: The Pioneering Efforts of Detroit Police Commissioner George Edwards, 1962–1963,
    by Mary M. Stolberg, 1998

Toast of the Town: The Life and Times of Sunnie Wilson,
    by Sunnie Wilson with John Cohassey, 1998

These Men Have Seen Hard Service: The First Michigan Sharpshooters in the Civil War,
    by Raymond J. Herek, 1998

A Place for Summer: One Hundred Years at Michigan and Trumbull,
    by Richard Bak, 1998

All-American Anarchist: Joseph A. Labadie and the Labor Movement,
    by Carlotta R. Anderson, 1998

Michigan in the Novel, 1816–1996: An Annotated Bibliography,
    by Robert Beasecker, 1998